CHRISTIAN ETHICS AND MORAL PHILOSOPHY

"Work out your own salvation with fear and trembling; for God is at work in you, both to will and to work for his good pleasure."

PHILIPPIANS 2:12-13

"Daily to discourse about virtue, and of those other things about which you hear me examining myself and others, is the greatest good of man, and the unexamined life is not worth living."

PLATO, *Apology,* 38

Christian Ethics and
Moral Philosophy

by GEORGE F. THOMAS

——— 1955 ———

Charles Scribner's Sons New York

TO MY STUDENTS

IN

CHRISTIAN ETHICS AND MORAL PHILOSOPHY

1927-1955

CONTENTS

Part III. Christian Ethics and Society

Part IV. Faith and Reason in Ethics

CONTENTS

PREFACE

One of the problems which confronts any Christian who is also a philosopher is the relation of Christian ethics to moral philosophy. I have been forced to face this problem as a teacher of both philosophical and Christian ethics and have become convinced that the tension between the "Hellenic" and the "Hebraic" elements in the Western ethical tradition should not be dealt with by ignoring one or the other of them. Hence, the neglect of the long and honorable tradition of moral philosophy by Christian moralists and of Christian ethics by moral philosophers seems to me a great mistake.

For thirteen years I taught philosophy at several different institutions and had the responsibility of teaching both introductory and advanced courses in ethics. The reading of the classical moralists from Plato to Nicolai Hartmann awakened in me a deep interest in the perennial problems of ethics. But I was perplexed, on the one hand, by the indifference of most recent moral philosophers to the long tradition of Christian ethical thinking which has had such a profound influence upon Western thought and life, and, on the other, by the sterility of much of the meticulous analysis of ethical categories in our time. Was it possible that the assumption of recent moral philosophers that ethics should divorce itself completely from religion was a mistake? Might this divorce be responsible for the impoverishment of ethics by the substitution of minute analysis for profound wisdom?

Like most men who had studied theology a generation ago, I had paid little attention to Christian ethics during my seminary years. Most of the books on the subject seemed to be written without any recognition of either the radicalism of the Christian ethic of love or the difficulty of sinful men living by the law of love in a sinful world. However, the situation changed with the publication of the books of Brunner, Berdyaev, Nygren, Reinhold Niebuhr, Temple, and others in the period between the two world wars. During the same period, the revival of interest in Biblical and systematic theology, especially in the doctrines of revelation, man, and history, led to a better understanding of the theological presuppositions of Christian ethics. This stimulated me to re-examine the New Testament foundations of Christian ethics and the further development of ethical thinking by Christian thinkers like Augustine, Aquinas, Luther, and Calvin.

The purpose of this book is first to present an interpretation of Christian ethics and then to make an analysis of the relation of Christian ethics to moral philosophy. The book is divided into four parts: I. The Development of Christian Ethics; II. The Christian Doctrine of Man; III. Christian Ethics and Society; and IV. Faith and Reason in Ethics. The first part deals in some detail with the New Testament foundations of Christian ethics (chapters I-V) and the problem of law and liberty in Christian thought (chapter VI). Although I am well aware of the limitations of my knowledge of the Bible, the ethical teachings of Jesus and Paul are of decisive importance for Christian ethics and a knowledge of them by all of my readers cannot be taken for granted. In the second part, some theological beliefs which are essential for an understanding of Christian ethics are set forth. The emphasis is on the doctrine of man, and other doctrines are treated only insofar as they are required for an understanding of man's moral situation, responsibility, and possibilities when confronted by the demands of the Christian ethic.

In the third part, some of the social implications of the Christian ethic are considered. Christians must be more realistic and less Utopian in their hopes for society than they were before the First World War. But Christian faith and love have profound implications for social justice and peace, especially for Christians whose destiny it is to live in a period of social revolution. The Christian moralist cannot speak with authority on social, political, and economic issues, but he has the responsibility of pointing out ethical problems even when he does not have the technical knowledge to solve them. Throughout this part, I have been influenced by a number of social and political philosophers and have made free use of their insights.

In the last part, the relation of Christian ethics to moral philosophy is considered, first in general terms (chapter XVII) and then in terms of some specific problems (chapters XVIII-XXII). The thesis is advanced that moral philosophy can best make its contribution to the good life when its true insights are adopted but transformed under the influence of Christian faith and love. I attempt to analyze and evaluate some theories of moral philosophers about happiness, duty, value, virtue and character, and to show what is distinctive about the Christian conception of each of these. Obviously, my analysis of the moral philosophers is too brief, but lack of space prevented a more adequate treatment. In any case, it is the approach and method which is most important.

I am indebted to too many people to mention more than a few. To Canon B. H. Streeter of Oxford University, my former tutor in theology, I owe my introduction to both the New Testament and philosophy, as well as my conviction that faith and reason belong together. To my teachers in philosophy at Yale and Harvard and my colleagues and pupils in the departments of philosophy at Swarthmore, Dartmouth, and the University of North Carolina, I owe much of my understanding of philosophy. To my colleagues and pupils in the Department of Religion at Princeton, I owe a deeper appreciation of Christian theology and ethics. I wish to thank especially those who read one or more chapters of the book and made valuable criticisms and suggestions: Professors Brand Blanshard and John Smith of Yale; John Knox and John Bennett of Union Theological Seminary; Burton Throckmorton of Bangor Theological Seminary; V. E. Devadutt of Ohio Wesleyan University; and Philip H. Ashby, Anthony Chadwick, Richard Van Wagenen, and Dean Douglas Brown of Princeton. To my colleague Professor Paul Ramsey and my former colleague Professor Leland Jamison of Macalester College I am especially indebted for many stimulating discussions and helpful criticisms.

Quotations from the Bible, unless otherwise marked, are from the Revised Standard Version of the Bible, copyrighted 1946 and 1952.

I am also grateful to Princeton University for two leaves of absence which provided the necessary leisure for the writing of considerable portions of the book; to Paul Braisted and Charles Russell of the Edward W. Hazen Foundation who kindly put at my disposal for several months a room in New Haven where several chapters were written; to the Dartmouth College Library and Yale Divinity School Library for the loan of books and other courtesies; and to Mrs. Joel Nystrom who typed the whole manuscript and worked carefully and patiently on it during the tedious process of revision. I am indebted above all to my wife who was unfailingly sympathetic and helpful from beginning to end.

GEORGE F. THOMAS

Princeton, New Jersey

Part I

THE DEVELOPMENT OF CHRISTIAN ETHICS

CHAPTER 1

The Old Testament Background

COVENANT AND LAW

SINCE both the Christian ethic and the religious beliefs upon which it depends can be understood only against the background of the Old Testament, we must begin by considering briefly the fundamental religious beliefs and ethical ideals of the ancient Hebrews. The primary ethical principle of the Old Testament is that of *obedience to God's will.* This sets the ethics of the Old Testament sharply apart from all forms of the humanistic ethics which has so deeply influenced Western moral philosophy. The Hebrews believed profoundly that men should seek for the meaning of their existence not merely in their own happiness and achievement, but in their service of the divine will and purpose.

This conviction did not arise as a result of scientific observation of human nature or philosophical reflection on ultimate reality. It came to the Hebrews through a process of *revelation.* The beginning of this revelation to the Hebrews was in a series of historical events. Their God became known to them through their *deliverance from bondage* in Egypt. The Hebrews believed that they owed their escape from Egypt, their preservation during the years of nomadic existence that followed, and their success in establishing themselves in a new home in Palestine to the gracious intervention of God, whom they called by the name of Yahweh. At the spring feast of the Passover they celebrated annually their deliverance from Egypt. In the midst of the sufferings of later times, they remembered that

3

voluntary and undeserved act of divine mercy and found in it a source of new hope. If He had delivered them from their enemies once, could He not do so again? If He had redeemed them from slavery, would He not redeem them also from exile or oppression?

The Hebrews believed that the exodus from Egypt had been followed by the ratification at Mt. Sinai of a solemn *covenant* or agreement between God and themselves. He had promised to continue His protection and favor to them; He had taken them to be "His people," chosen from among all the peoples of the earth. On their side, they had pledged themselves to be faithful to Him. The significance of this interpretation of Israel's early history for her ethical thinking was great. It is sometimes said that the ethics of the Old Testament consists of an arbitrarily imposed code of laws handed down by the God of the Hebrews and enforced by fear of punishment. This view overlooks the fact that the God who revealed His will to them was the gracious and merciful God who had delivered them from Egypt and had promised to continue His favor towards them. Therefore, His will seemed to them anything but arbitrary, and He was to be obeyed, not primarily from fear of punishment, but from gratitude for His kindness. Indeed, it is hardly too much to say that the covenant relationship of the Hebrews with Yahweh was the basis of their national life.

Some time after the Hebrews had settled in Palestine the "code of the covenant" in the Book of Exodus[1] came to be accepted by them as binding and was believed to have been revealed by God to Moses on Mt. Sinai. The level of the morality required in most of these early laws of Israel may not seem, by later standards, very high. However, they demanded not only strict *justice* but also *kindness* between Hebrew and Hebrew. "The impoverished, the widow, and the orphan are to receive ungrudging aid, not as a charity, but as justice to them. Succour is theirs by rights."[2] It is probable that these demands rested in large part upon the *sense of solidarity* of the family and tribe which was part of Israel's heritage from her nomadic past. However, the limitations of this early code are ob-

[1] Ex. 20:22-23:33.
[2] Elmslie, W. A. L., in *Record and Revelation*, H. Wheeler Robinson (ed.), Oxford, The Clarendon Press, 1938, p. 280.

vious. On the one hand, it subordinates the individual too much to the group; on the other, it has little to say about his obligations to the members of other groups. Nevertheless, it provided the foundation of social responsibility and concern for the weak and poor upon which the higher ethical ideals of later periods could be erected.

THE PROPHETIC REVOLUTION

The eighth-century prophets preserved all that was best in the ethics of the early Hebrews but raised it to a higher level. Their first contribution was their clear and strong insistence that God demands *righteousness* rather than *sacrifice* or *ritual*. In primitive religions, the demands of the gods were concerned with ritual tabus and ceremonies as much as, if not more than, moral conduct. As a result, primitive man tended to think that if he faithfully kept the festivals, respected the tabus, and performed the sacrifices, he had done all his god required of him. The eighth-century prophets protested vigorously against such an external and unethical conception of religion. They insisted passionately that the religious observances of Israel were futile because of the immoral lives of the people, above all, their cruelty and callous disregard of the welfare of others.

Yahweh requires *justice* in men's relations with one another, says Amos. They must cease to defraud the poor of their rights, reducing them to slavery while they themselves drink and eat in their fine houses. Of what avail is it for greedy and unjust men to crowd into the sanctuaries for feasts and sacrifices?

> I hate, I despise your feasts,
>   and I take no delight in your solemn assemblies.
> Even though you offer me your burnt offerings and cereal offerings,
>   I will not accept them, . . .
> But let justice roll down like waters,
>   and righteousness like an ever-flowing stream.[1]

Because of those who "trample upon the needy, and bring the poor of the land to an end,"[2] who "buy the poor for silver and the

[1] Amos 5:21, 22, 24.
[2] Amos 8:4.

needy for a pair for sandals,"[3] God has set a "plumb line" in the midst of Israel, and "will never again pass by them."[4] Similarly, Hosea draws a dark picture of Israel:

> For the Lord has a controversy with the inhabitants of the land.
> There is no faithfulness or kindness,
>   and no knowledge of God in the land;
> There is swearing, lying, killing, stealing, and committing adultery;
>   they break all bounds and murder follows murder.[5]

God wants *kindness, compassion* and *faithfulness,* not idols of silver and gold, or sacrifices and offerings. "For I desire steadfast love and not sacrifice, the knowledge of God, rather than burnt offerings."[6] Micah sums up the ethical conception of religion of these eighth-century prophets in an unforgettable question: "What does the Lord require of you but to do justice, and to love kindness, and to walk humbly with your God?"[7]

A second ethical advance of the eighth-century prophets was their insight into the *universality* and *impartiality* of the moral law. As we pointed out, the early Hebrews had felt a sense of solidarity with one another but had had little conception of a universal moral law. But Amos insists that God makes the same demands upon all peoples and that He will judge all of them alike by their obedience or disobedience to these demands. The fact that the Israelites are His chosen people, set apart from all others by His favor, does not entitle them to receive special privileges but entails special responsibility:

> You only have I known of all the families of the earth;
> therefore I will punish you for all your iniquities.[8]

Yahweh cares for other peoples as well as for Israel:

> Are you not like the Ethiopians to me,
>   O people of Israel? says the Lord.

---

[3] Amos 8:6.
[4] Amos 7:8.
[5] Hosea 4:1, 2.

[6] Hosea 6:6.
[7] Mic. 6:8.
[8] Amos 3:2.

> Did I not bring up Israel from the land of Egypt,
>   and the Philistines from Caphtor and the Syrians from Kir?[9]

Therefore, Israel need not think that she can escape punishment; she will be condemned for her transgression against the moral law in exactly the same way as the neighboring peoples.

What was the source of this lofty conception of religion as demanding justice, mercy, and kindness to all and of God as judging all peoples by the same moral standards? There can be no doubt that it was the experience of God as *transcendent, righteous Will.* In a vision in the Temple at the beginning of his prophetic career, Isaiah saw Yahweh "high and lifted up" in His holiness and felt himself in the presence of that holiness to be unclean and unworthy:

> Woe is me! For I am lost; for I am a man of unclean lips,
>   and I dwell in the midst of a people of unclean lips;
>   for my eyes have seen the King, the Lord of hosts![10]

The experience of "the holy," Otto has shown, is that of a transcendent, mysterious, majestic Being in whose presence man feels his creatureliness and abases himself in awe.[11] The holiness of God to the prophets meant not only His mysterious otherness but also His perfect purity and righteousness. The will of a God of perfect righteousness, therefore, was the source of high moral demands upon man. His righteousness was not a static quality belonging to His will apart from the world; it was a dynamic, active force seeking to foster righteousness in His children. He made it felt in the form of moral imperatives; and He judged all by their attitude towards those imperatives. He rewarded those who obeyed with prosperity and happiness; He blazed forth in wrath and destruction against those who set their wills against His purposes. This was the source of the sternness and the sense of moral urgency of the prophets. Because they had had a vision of the holiness of God, they knew that His demands were far more exacting than those of the traditional morality of their people.

[9] Amos 9:7.
[10] Is. 6:5.
[11] Otto, Rudolf, *The Idea of the Holy,* London and New York, Oxford University Press, 1931.

God's demand for righteousness and justice is also the source
of the *deepened sense of sin* and of the need for *divine forgiveness*
which is so characteristic of the great prophets. Isaiah regards sin
as a *rebellion* against God. To Jeremiah, it is more than particular
external acts of transgression; it is a settled disposition of the will
and heart at the very center of the personality. It is a corruption
of the whole self, a *sickness* which affects the body of society from
head to foot and perverts the moral sense until good seems evil
and evil, good. Indeed, it is so deeply rooted as to be ineradicable:

"Can the Ethiopian change his skin or the leopard his spots?
Then also you can do good who are accustomed to do evil."[12]

Because of the sin of Israel and her stubborn refusal to repent
and amend her ways, prophets like Isaiah see her immediate
future in dark terms. If God is righteous, He is bound to visit
judgment upon Israel for her religious infidelity and her social
injustice. Isaiah warns Judah that she is to be invaded by Assyria
and her sons and daughters are to be carried away into captivity.
A century later, when Judah was tottering towards her fall, Jeremiah
prophesied that Jerusalem would be destroyed and her independence
completely lost. But this was not the last word of the prophets
about the future. Hosea pictured Yahweh's attitude towards Israel
as that of a loving husband to a faithless wife. Yahweh longed to
restore her to favor and would take the initiative in seeking her
out despite her unworthiness.

How can I give you up, O Ephraim!
How can I hand you over, O Israel!
My heart recoils within me, my compassion grows warm and tender.
I will not execute my fierce anger,
   I will not again destroy Ephraim;
for I am God and not man, the Holy One in your midst,
and I will not come to destroy.[13]

For the prophetic conception of history was ultimately *optimistic*.
The prophets were convinced that God had a purpose for man
and that the meaning of historical events was to be found in their

[12] Jere. 13:23.
[13] Hos. 11:8, 9.

relation to that purpose. God was not an unmoved and passionless spectator, indifferent to the fate of His children in time. He would put forth His mighty power to restore His people to righteousness and prosperity. He was the lord of history, and His purposes would ultimately prevail.

How do the prophets conceive of Israel's future? According to Isaiah, God raises up great empires like Assyria and uses them to punish those who disobey Him. But when they wax fat with pride and boast that they have conquered other peoples by their own strength and prowess, He casts them down. He has not forgotten Israel and His purpose to bless her. After she has been punished for her sins by the scourge of war, famine and captivity, a "righteous remnant" will be restored to their native land. God will raise up a *Messiah*, an ideal king of the line of David, to rule over her. A *new age* will dawn for Israel, blessed by justice, prosperity and peace.[14] In the later development of this "messianic hope" for a better earthly future for Israel, a Messianic king is often not mentioned and God is expected to redeem Israel and rule her directly Himself.

One of the noblest visions of the future was seen by Jeremiah in the darkest days of Judah's history. God is to establish a "new covenant" with Israel, writing His law not upon tables of stone but upon the heart of every individual. "I will put my law within them, and I will write it upon their hearts; and I will be their God, and they shall be my people. And no longer shall each man teach his neighbor and each his brother, saying, 'Know the Lord,' for they shall all know me, from the least of them to the greatest, says the Lord; for I will forgive their iniquity, and I will remember their sin no more."[15]

The anonymous prophet of the Babylonian Exile, whom we call the "Second Isaiah" because his prophecies are found in the latter part of the book of Isaiah,[16] sees an even greater vision of the future. He comforts the Hebrew captives in Babylon by the promise that Yahweh will liberate them and lead them back in safety to

[14] Is. 9:6, 7.
[15] Jere. 31:33-34.
[16] Is. 40-55.

Israel. He is the Lord of all nations, holding them in His hand and disposing of them according to His will. His purpose embraces not only the happiness of Israel but the *salvation of all peoples*. His purpose is that Israel shall be a missionary people, a "light to lighten the Gentiles." Her sufferings, hitherto regarded as punishment for her own sins, are really vicarious. She is a "servant of the Lord" whose sufferings, borne with patience, will effect the redemption of the nations which have persecuted her. The unknown prophet bases this universalistic outlook for the future upon a pure monotheism. He pours scorn upon those who believe that there are other gods besides Yahweh. The "gods" of Babylon are only idols, fashioned by men's hands out of wood or metal and are powerless to prevent Yahweh from accomplishing His purpose.

Thus, prophetic religion culminates, on the one hand, in Jeremiah's profound experience and description of *personal religion,* and, on the other hand, in the "Second Isaiah's" *pure monotheism* and *universalism*. It cannot be maintained that all, or even most, of the Jews after the Exile followed these great prophets of spiritual religion. Indeed, it is probable that they were understood only by a minority. The "Second Isaiah's" universalistic vision of Israel as a "light to lighten the Gentiles" was largely frustrated by the attempt of her leaders after the Exile in Babylon to isolate her from any contact with the surrounding peoples who might corrupt her religion. Jeremiah's personal religion was partially frustrated by the formalism that developed after the Exile. Nevertheless, universalism lived on, as the beautiful little book of Jonah shows; and personal religion found its finest expression in the Psalms.

The prophets assumed that man can discern right from wrong and choose the right. They were well aware of the corruption of man's will by sin and of the way in which sin deadens his conscience. "Woe to those," cries Isaiah, "who call evil good and good evil, who put darkness for light and light for darkness, who put bitter for sweet and sweet for bitter!"[17] But the prophets would have denied the deterministic theory that men's thoughts and actions are governed by factors wholly beyond their control. Man,

[17] Is. 5:20.

they believed, possesses a measure of *freedom* and consequently a capacity for moral change. Though he may be hardened by sin, he can repent. The Psalmist prays, "Create in me a clean heart, O God, and put a new and right spirit within me."[18] Nor are man's freedom of will and capacity for moral renewal negated by the strong assertion of the *divine sovereignty* over human life. The Hebrews assumed both human freedom and divine control. It cannot be maintained that the Old Testament found any logical solution of the apparent contradiction involved in this. But it makes a contribution towards a "practical reconciliation," as Wheeler Robinson says, in the prophetic insight that true moral freedom is to be found in "the willing surrender of human personality to the divine."[19]

The prevailing attitude of the Old Testament towards the relation of human freedom to the *divine grace* is rather different from that of traditional Christian theology. The theology of St. Paul, St. Augustine, Luther, and Calvin emphasizes the need of special grace to save men who are enslaved to sin. On the whole, the prophets, psalmists, and the later rabbis insist upon the moral ability of the sinner because they do not believe him to be in bondage to sin. Though there is an impulse to evil in him, there is also an impulse to good. If he will only repent of his sin, he will be forgiven. They do not often seem to doubt his ability to repent and then to amend his life, if he will honestly try. Indeed, they seem sometimes to believe that God will take the initiative in man's repentance.[20] Now and then, they come closer to moral despair. The author of Psalm 51 cries out, "Behold, I was brought forth in iniquity, and in sin did my mother conceive me. . . . Create in me a clean heart, O God, and put a new and right spirit within me. Cast me not away from thy presence, and take not thy holy Spirit from me."[21] In such passages as these, the need is recognized for God to bring about a radical change in the sinner, to give him a new heart and spirit. The famous description in Jeremiah of the "new covenant" and Ezekiel's vision of the "dry bones" of Israel

---

[18] Ps. 51:10.
[19] Robinson, op. cit., p. 320.

[20] Ps. 85:4-6.
[21] Ps. 51:5, 10, 11.

brought to life again by the Spirit of God also point to the *need for redemption* by a special act of God.[22]

THE DEVELOPMENT OF THE LAW

We have analyzed the religion and ethics of the prophets from the eighth to the sixth centuries before Christ. But the Hebrews believed that God mediated His moral demands to them not only through the prophet's inspiration but also through the proclamation of His commandments by the lawgiver. It is essential, therefore, for us to glance briefly at the later development of the Law.

Old Testament scholars have shown that the Law of Moses in the Pentateuch was the product of centuries of social and moral experience. The decisions of elders, kings, and judges, as well as of priests, contributed to the process. A custom might in time become law and thus receive divine sanction. From time to time, the process of legal development resulted in the formation of *codes of laws*. Three of the most important of these codes are found in the books of Exodus, Deuteronomy, and Leviticus. Of these the "Code of the Covenant" in Exodus is the earliest, as we have seen. The code in Deuteronomy was compiled later, the code in Leviticus last of all.

There is much that is of ethical value in the Law. It is well for Christians to remember that Jesus quotes his two-fold commandment of love from Deuteronomy[1] and Leviticus.[2] The code of laws in Deuteronomy seems to have been influenced by the eighth-century prophets and was probably part of an attempt in the seventh century to enforce by law the prophetic principles of justice, mercy and fidelity to Yahweh. Although there are a number of purely ceremonial laws in the book, there are also many moral laws at a comparatively high level. For example, every seventh year, debtors are to be released from their debts[3] and Hebrew slaves from their slavery.[4] One is to lend to the needy

---

[22] Jere. 31:33, 34; Ezek. Ch. 7.
[1] Deut. 6:5.
[2] Lev. 19:18.
[3] Deut. 15:1.
[4] Ibid., 15:12.

enough for their need.[5] He is not to lend to his brother for interest, though to a foreigner he may do so.[6] He is not to oppress a poor and needy hired servant but is to pay him his wages on the same day.[7] No one is to be put to death for the sin of a member of his family but only for his own.[8] Special care is to be given to the needs of the stranger, the fatherless, and the widow.[9] Of course, there is also much that is at a lower level, such as the terrible injunction to the Hebrews to destroy every living thing when they capture a city of the Canaanites.[10]

On the whole, the book of Leviticus has less ethical value than the book of Deuteronomy, since it is made up mainly of ceremonial laws. But Chapter 19 has been called by Montefiore an "oasis" because it consists largely of ethical laws. "You shall do no injustice in judgment; you shall not be partial to the poor or defer to the great."[11] "You shall not take vengeance or bear any grudge against the sons of your own people, but you shall love your neighbor as yourself."[12] "The stranger who sojourns with you shall be to you as the native among you, and you shall love him as yourself; for you were strangers in the land of Egypt."[13]

An elaborate *oral tradition* was developed by the rabbis in the centuries before Christ in order to apply the written law to concrete situations and adapt it to new problems and needs. This oral tradition made it possible to enrich the written Law with the ethical insights of later religious thinkers, though Jesus' references to those who followed the "traditions of the elders" but neglected "weightier matters of the law," who "tithe mint and rue and every herb, and neglect justice and the love of God"[14] indicate that it had serious dangers.

It has often been said that since the Law covered the whole range of conduct, it imposed a *burden* upon the Jew which was intolerable. It is evident from the Gospels that there were many Jews of Jesus' time, the "people of the land," who did not even

---

[5] Deut. 15:7, 8
[6] Ibid., 23:20.
[7] Ibid., 24:14, 15.
[8] Ibid., 24:16.
[9] Ibid., 24:17-22.
[10] Ibid., 20:16.
[11] Lev. 19:15.
[12] Ibid., 19:18.
[13] Ibid., 19:34.
[14] Lk. 11:42.

attempt to keep all of the ceremonial laws, especially those contained in the oral tradition. But this is only one side of the truth. "These commandments," says Elmslie, "were not arbitrary impositions, but the statutes and judgments of Yahweh, the precious revelation, therefore, of a way of living in which a man will find true blessedness, the health of his life, and to which, as he understands its wisdom, he can and will freely give his assent."[15] Certainly, no one can read Psalm 1, which speaks of the "blessed" man whose "delight is in the law of the Lord,"[16] or Psalm 19, which affirms that "the law of the lord is perfect" and "more to be desired than gold,"[17] without realizing that, at least for many pious Jews, the Law was also a great source of *joy*.

THE APOCALYPTIC HOPE

During the period between the Old and the New Testaments, there was a further development of Israel's *hope for the future*. As we saw, the prophets believed that God was the Lord of history, and that He would bring into existence a new age in the future. This new age was to be realized on the earth and within the limits of history; there was to be nothing other-worldly about it. In the period before the coming of Christ this prophetic hope was transformed by a group of Jews whose writings have come to be known as the "Apocalyptic Literature." The book of Daniel and other Apocalyptic writings such as the book of Enoch form a bridge between the Old and New Testaments with respect to the hope for the future. Their importance for Christianity is shown by the fact that there are apocalyptic visions in the Gospels, e.g., the thirteenth chapter of Mark, and that the book of Revelation is an Apocalyptic book. What is the nature of this Apocalyptic Literature?

If we are to understand it, we must remember that since the eighth century before Christ the Hebrews had suffered oppression at the hands of the great empires that surrounded them. Finally, Israel was engulfed in the Roman Empire and after 63 B.C. she never

[15] Elmslie, op. cit., p. 294.
[16] Ps. 1:2.
[17] Ibid., 19:7, 10.

recovered her freedom. During these long centuries of oppression she was upheld by the hope of deliverance by her God. But as one oppressor succeeded another, the earlier "Messianic" hope of the prophets for a restoration of Israel and a renewal of her national life in an earthly kingdom began to appear inadequate. To the Apocalyptists the world seemed to be under the dominion of demonic powers of darkness and evil. Deliverance could come only through its destruction by the almighty hand of God. This catastrophic intervention of God would be followed by a new age. The dead would be resurrected and would appear along with the living at a last judgment, after which the righteous would receive their eternal reward in the new age and the wicked would be destroyed or punished. The Apocalyptic writers conceived God sometimes as acting directly to bring about these spectacular changes. In the book of Enoch, however, He was pictured as acting indirectly through a mysterious heavenly being called the "Son of Man."

It is easy to see what lay behind these "apocalypses" or "revelations" of the future. Many dismiss them contemptuously as a creation of mythological fancy to provide an escape from the hard realities of an evil world. Undoubtedly, they are bizarre in their imagery and symbolism. But it would be a great mistake to overlook the profound faith which gave rise to them. Like the prophets, the Apocalyptic writers assume not only that God is righteous Himself but also that He has a moral purpose for history. They believe that He is the sovereign Lord of history and that in His good time He will overthrow the power of arrogant kings and empires. Righteousness, however much and long it may have to suffer at the hands of evil men and nations, will ultimately be vindicated. Righteous men cannot cast down the wicked from their seats of power. Human strength is too weak. But God, who unites in Himself perfect goodness and supreme power, will destroy both the great heathen empires and the demonic powers of darkness. Moreover, the earth as it is cannot become the sphere in which the new age is to be realized; it must be radically transformed or completely destroyed. Consequently, the blessings of the new age are conceived in terms more appropriate to another world than to this one and are depicted in brighter and more glorious colors than those suitable to any earthly Messianic kingdom.

To the modern mind this combination of pessimism and otherworldliness seems fantastic and one can find very little in the Apocalyptic writings to supplement the ethical insights of the prophets. Nevertheless, they deserve a place, though not one of the highest places, in the world's religious literature. Their solution of the problem of evil in history may seem to us crude and unconvincing; but they give expression to an imperishable hope that springs from a profound and unconquerable faith.

CHAPTER 2

The Kingdom of God and the Law

SINCE the end of the nineteenth century, many New Testament scholars have interpreted Jesus as one who was completely dominated by the Apocalyptic faith that the end of the present age was at hand and a New Age was about to break in. In reaction against this tendency, others have minimized the importance of the Apocalyptic influence. Anyone who wishes to understand the ethics of the Gospels must, on the one hand, do justice to the Apocalyptic framework, and, on the other hand, realize the limits of its influence upon the nature and content of Jesus' teaching.

The Gospel of Mark tells us that after John the Baptist was arrested by Herod, "Jesus came into Galilee, preaching the Gospel of God, and saying, 'The time is fulfilled, and the kingdom of God is at hand; repent and believe in the gospel.'"[1] This indicates that Jesus' teaching, like that of the Apocalyptic writers of his time, announced the coming of a New Age which he called "the Kingdom of God." Indeed, his whole career was devoted to the attempt, directly and through his disciples, to prepare his fellow-Jews for the coming of this New Age. Therefore, he is not to be regarded primarily as a moral teacher. His words, as well as his deeds, had the intensely practical purpose of arousing his hearers to the imminence of the Kingdom and urging them to prepare themselves for its coming.

[1] Mk. 1:14, 15.

17

THE NATURE OF THE KINGDOM

What did he mean by the "Kingdom of God"? Whereas John the Baptist seems to have dreaded the coming event as primarily a judgment upon sin, Jesus regarded it as a "Gospel" or "good news." Though the Kingdom is to be inaugurated after a last judgment and though many are to be excluded from it, it is to bring joy to those who are gathered into it. Entrance into it, indeed, brings one into possession of the *highest good* and the *purest blessedness*. It is so much greater in worth than any other good that one should be willing to give all he has to gain it. "The kingdom of heaven is like treasure hidden in a field, which a man found and covered up; then in his joy he goes and sells all that he has and buys that field. Again, the kingdom of heaven is like a merchant in search of fine pearls, who, on finding one pearl of great value, went and sold all he had and bought it."[1] Who would not willingly part with everything to win that whose worth is incommensurable with all other values?

For the Kingdom of God will bring *eternal life*. Eternal life is more than mere endless survival of life; it is a qualitatively superior life, life on a higher plane than that of this age. Sometimes, Jesus seems to use "eternal life" as virtually synonymous with the "Kingdom of God." He tells his disciples that those who have left possessions, friends, and loved ones will receive a "hundred-fold now in this time" and "in the age to come eternal life"[2] At other times, he speaks of heavenly treasures that are imperishable.[3] Doubtless, it is eternal life with its imperishable good which he has in mind when he says, "For whoever would save his life will lose it; but whoever loses his life for my sake, he will save it."[4]

The most fundamental thing about the Kingdom is that it is the *Reign of God* in the lives of men and rests upon *obedience to God* as the Lord of all life. Those persons belong to the Kingdom who acknowledge God's sovereignty in their lives. Of course, as the

[1] Mtt. 13:44-46.
[2] Mk. 10:29-30.
[3] Mtt. 6:19-21.
[4] Lk. 9:24.

Lord of all nature and history, God is already in control of the lives of men and nations, in the sense that, even when they think they are free to disregard Him and follow their own purposes, they serve His will. But He wants men to serve Him willingly rather than unwillingly so that He may bless rather than punish them. For He is not only their King; He is also their compassionate and merciful Father. Therefore, God seeks to restore His disobedient children to Him. He takes the initiative to save them from their sins and forgive them. He seeks them out in His love as a man seeks out his lost sheep and rejoices when they are recovered.[5] When they repent and turn back to Him, He welcomes them back as a father welcomes his prodigal son.[6] Thus the Gospel or good news of the Kingdom of God is that God offers His love and forgiveness even to those who by their sin have rebelled against His will. Those who will accept His offer while there is yet time will be forgiven and restored to their proper relationship to God.

But each person must *decide* for himself whether he will accept or reject God's offer of forgiveness and become a member of the Kingdom. No one can take the responsibility of deciding for another. Even members of the same family may be divided from one another by their decisions, one accepting and another rejecting. Like John the Baptist, Jesus does not believe that one will enter the Kingdom automatically merely because he is a Jew. God calls men individually, and each must respond by a free act of his own will. In this sense, one can speak of the "religious individualism" of Jesus.

Those who accept the Reign of God individually are gathered together into the family of His children, and they become brothers of one another. They constitute a *community* of those who serve God. Thus, the Kingdom of God is not only the Reign, it is also the Realm, of God. Like the Hebrew prophets, Jesus was no individualist in the modern sense of the term. He directed his preaching not only to individual Jews but also to Israel as a whole. As his public ministry drew to a close, he went up to Jerusalem to make an

[5] Lk. 15:3-7.
[6] Lk. 15:11-32.

appeal to the whole nation in its Holy City. But he seemed to put his faith increasingly, as Isaiah had done, in a righteous "remnant" of Israel who would remain faithful despite all persecutions. It is significant that he associated twelve disciples with him in a close fellowship. According to Matthew and Luke, he said to them at the Last Supper, "You are those who have continued with me in my trials; as my Father appointed a kingdom for me, so do I appoint for you that you may eat and drink at my table in my kingdom, and sit on thrones judging the twelve tribes of Israel."[7] This seems to envisage the Kingdom as a new Israel, made up of those who have accepted the Gospel.

This new Israel was to be more *inclusive* than the old Israel. It is true that Jesus confined his efforts to his own people and stated on one occasion that he was sent only "to the lost sheep of the house of Israel."[8] But he taught that some Jews were to be "thrust out" and that Gentiles "will come from east and west, and from north and south, and sit at table in the kingdom of God."[9] We do not know how these two statements are related to one another. But we know that the disciples after his resurrection believed that they had been commissioned to preach repentance and forgiveness of sins in his name "to all nations, beginning from Jerusalem."[10] Thus, he seems to have taught that the Kingdom of God was not national or racial; it was, potentially, universal.

The blessings of the Kingdom of God are primarily *spiritual* rather than physical. In distinguishing between the spiritual and the physical, however, we must be careful not to read into the Gospel a dualism that is foreign to it. Jesus was not an ascetic in his attitude towards the body and its values. Because he ate and drank like other men, he was actually accused by some of being "a glutton and a drunkard."[11] He does not require his disciples to fast. He accepts marriage as part of the divine order established at the beginning of Creation. He heals men's bodies as well as their souls. He makes the test of true discipleship simple acts of

---

[7] Lk. 22:28-30; Mtt. 19:28.
[8] Mtt. 15:24.
[9] Lk. 13:29.

[10] Ibid., 24:47; cf., Mtt. 28:19.
[11] Lk. 7:34.

kindness that relieve physical needs. Thus, he accepts the Hebraic view of the unity of the personality and is concerned about man's physical as well as his spiritual welfare. What is meant in speaking of the Kingdom of God as spiritual is not that natural goods and joys are to be excluded from man's earthly existence, but that one must not neglect the deeper needs of the soul because of one's pre-occupation with material possessions and worldly pleasures. One must not be anxious about food and raiment but realize that God will provide for one's bodily needs. "But seek first his kingdom and his righteousness, and all these things shall be yours as well."[12] One must lay up treasures in heaven rather than on earth. One must seek values that endure rather than those that pass away. Moreover, one must be prepared to part with earthly possessions, with part of the body, or with life itself rather than risk the loss of the Kingdom.

This is one aspect of the *strangeness* of the Kingdom to men's ordinary ways of living and thinking in the world. The Kingdom of God is not like the kingdoms of this world. It seems to break into the life of the world as from another world. This does not mean "other-worldliness," as medieval Christianity thought. It does not mean that men are to despise the values and joys of this world and long only for the rewards of the life to come. It is rather that, where the power of the Kingdom is felt, a *new life* manifests itself and the aims and standards of that new life seem utterly differ-ent from those of the men of this age. This "otherness" of the Kingdom is illustrated most strikingly by the transvaluation of values in the Beatitudes, but it is found in the whole of Jesus' teachings as well as his life.

THE COMING OF THE KINGDOM

When is the Kingdom of God coming? Christian orthodoxy has tended to think of it in exclusively future and other-worldly terms, regarding earthly existence as a weary and sad pilgrimage towards the "Heavenly City." Many recent New Testament scholars, under the influence of the Apocalyptic interpretation of Jesus' career and

[12] Mtt. 6:33.

teaching, have also stressed the future coming of the Kingdom. In reaction against this futuristic view, others have insisted that the Kingdom was realized with the coming of Jesus and the redemptive processes set in motion by him.

Both of these extremes are to be avoided because each of them leads to a distortion of many of Jesus' sayings. On the one hand, the *future consummation* of the Kingdom is an ineradicable aspect of his teaching. There is much evidence that the early Christians, who were anticipating his second coming in glory to establish the Kingdom, exaggerated the extent of the Apocalyptic element in his teaching. But it is impossible to understand his career or his teaching about the Kingdom unless we accept the fact that he believed the Kingdom to be imminent but still to come. "Truly, I say to you, this generation will not pass away before all these things take place," he says. . . . "But of that day or that hour no one knows, not even the angels in heaven, nor the Son, but only the Father. Take heed, watch; for you do not know when the time will come."[1] It is possible that some or all of these words may show the influence of the early Church. But Jesus' whole career seems to be based upon an assumption that the Kingdom will come in the future, that no one knows the exact time except God, and that men should be ready and prepared for it at any time.

However, Jesus seems to act not merely as the "herald" but also as the "bringer" of the Kingdom,[2] manifesting its power by the authority of his teaching, his healings and exorcisms, and his transforming effect upon the lives of others. In and through him the divine powers of the Kingdom seem to be *already* working, destroying the demonic powers that are the source of human evils and bringing liberation and joy to the lives of men. Luke records a saying of Jesus which expresses his exultation at these present manifestations of the power of the Kingdom. When some of his followers whom he had sent out to proclaim the Kingdom returned saying, "Lord, even the demons are subject to us in your name," he said to them, "I saw Satan fall like lightning from heaven."[3]

[1] Mk. 13:30, 32, 33.
[2] C. J. Cadoux, *The Historic Mission of Jesus,* London, Lutterworth Press, 1941, p. 51.
[3] Lk. 10:17-18.

Thus, the Kingdom is already present, but only in its *beginnings*. From the first proclamation of the Gospel, many have been gladly embracing and preparing themselves for the Kingdom. Others still have an opportunity to do so, though the time is running short. But many are not responding to the call and the forces of evil are still at work. Only in God's good time will a final separation be made and the harvest be gathered. This implies that the remainder of the present age will be a time of tension. The sons of the Kingdom must watch and pray lest they enter into temptation; like the wise virgins, they must have their lamps ready for the coming of the bridegroom. Moreover, though they may even now enjoy by anticipation the blessings of the coming age, they must also expect to suffer persecution at the hands of the children of this world.

CONDITIONS OF MEMBERSHIP

But there are *conditions* that must be met by anyone who would enter into the Kingdom. According to Jesus, the Kingdom is only for those who repent of their sins, believe in the Gospel, and do the will of God. In insisting upon *repentance*, Jesus is only repeating what all the prophets from the eighth century to John the Baptist had said. Repentance, as the Greek word "metanoia" indicates, means a change of mind, an about-face of the self. It is not mere sorrow over one's sins and one's worldly way of life; it is a resolute turning away from them that is at the same time a turning towards a new life. It is an indispensable condition of God's forgiveness; even God cannot forgive a person who does not know that there is anything wrong with his life and does not ask forgiveness for it. It is also necessary as the first step towards that new life of obedience to God which is the basis of fellowship with Him. It is a test of the sincerity of one who seeks membership in the Kingdom. If he does not repudiate the old life, how can he really desire the new? If he does not turn away from the service of Mammon, how can he really serve God?

In insisting upon *belief* in the Gospel, Jesus is also reaffirming one of the fundamental insights of the Old Testament. One must not only believe that God exists; one must also put one's trust in Him.

Only if one does so can one have confidence that God will forgive him for his sins and restore him to favor. He must believe that God is his heavenly Father, willing to show compassion upon him as a human father pities his children. Thus, belief in the Gospel implies more than a *belief that* God is Lord and King; it implies *faith in* Him as one's Father whose love will be given to one even if he is undeserving. To Jesus, faith in God is also a recognition of one's dependence upon Him for everything. One must "receive" the Kingdom of God as a gift from God, his heavenly Father, as one receives one's "daily bread," the forgiveness of one's sins, and deliverance from evil. If one has a childlike faith, he will ask God for all that he needs. "Ask, and it will be given you; seek, and you will find; knock, and it will be opened to you," says Jesus. . . . "If you then, who are evil, know how to give good gifts to your children, how much more will your Father who is in heaven give good things to those who ask him?"[1]

Along with repentance and faith *obedience* is a necessary condition of entrance into the Kingdom. Jesus warned his hearers that, as trees are known by their fruits, men are known by their deeds. "Not every one who says to me, 'Lord, Lord,' shall enter the kingdom of heaven, but he who does the will of my Father who is in heaven."[2] The importance of this for the ethics of Jesus is great. Though the establishment of the Kingdom is to be effected by divine action and is thus a divine gift rather than a human achievement, the moral response of men to the offer of it is of decisive importance. As we saw, they are free to accept or reject the divine invitation to the Kingdom; but if they accept, their lives and deeds must be radically changed. It must not be supposed that obedience to God's will in their deeds is to be accomplished by their own unaided efforts. They are to pray to him not only to forgive their sins but also to give them deliverance from evil. Nevertheless, Jesus clearly insists that the *divine initiative* in offering the Kingdom must be met by a *human response* that includes not only repentance and faith but also amendment of life. This is the answer to those who say that, since the Kingdom of God is to come by

[1] Mtt. 7:7, 11.
[2] Mtt. 7:21.

divine intervention and cannot be "built" by men, it can have no
implications for moral and social action. The Hebrew mind attrib-
utes everything to God, but it also assumes the freedom and
responsibility of men. God will establish the Kingdom in His own
good time; but men must decide for themselves here and now
whether, with God's help, they will meet its conditions and therefore will reap its fruits.

That is why the preaching of the Gospel is also a *warning of
judgment*. It is why Jesus speaks with such a strong sense of
urgency. He invites his hearers to accept the gift of the Kingdom;
but he also presents them with the necessity of making a decision
for or against it. They must choose either to accept it or to reject
it. They cannot refuse to choose; and they cannot delay their choice
indefinitely. Indefinite postponement may mean rejection, for no
man knows the day or the hour when the Kingdom will come. It
will come like a thief in the night. Therefore, the proclamation of
the Kingdom creates a crisis for every person. He must decide,
and he must decide before it is too late. Moreover, his decision does
not affect his earthly future alone; it determines his eternal destiny.
His eternal life or death, happiness or misery, is at stake.

JESUS' RELATION TO THE KINGDOM

We have spoken of the nature of the Kingdom, the time of its
coming, and the conditions of membership in it. We must now
ask, What was Jesus' conception of *his own relation* to the Kingdom? We shall probably never know with certainty. The first
three Gospels—Matthew, Mark, and Luke—represent Jesus as
centering his teaching on the Kingdom of God rather than himself;
the Fourth Gospel, John, pictures him as making exalted claims for
himself as Son of God. Almost all modern New Testament scholars
agree that the first three Gospels are earlier and more authentic
than the fourth. But this does not settle the problem because the
testimony of the first three Gospels themselves is not consistent,
and the interpretation of each of them is very difficult.

Did Jesus claim to be the *Messiah* or "anointed one" who was
to be God's agent in establishing and ruling the Kingdom? Many

New Testament scholars believe that, from the time of his baptism by John, he was conscious of a divine call to be the Messiah but that he was reticent about making claims for himself because of his fear that he would be regarded as a political Messiah of the line of David. When he was acknowledged by Peter at Caesarea Philippi as the Messiah, they say, he tacitly accepted the title. But he realized that he was to be a very different kind of Messiah than most Jews expected—not a triumphant king who would overthrow the enemies of his people at the head of an army and reign in an earthly kingdom, but a humble "Son of Man" who would have to suffer persecution and death at the hands of the religious and political leaders of the people. He was convinced that his suffering, like that of the "Suffering Servant" of the Second Isaiah, was in some mysterious way necessary for the forgiveness of his people. After his death, God would intervene to destroy the present age and send the heavenly "Son of Man" in the clouds with great power and glory to "gather his elect" into the Kingdom. Those who hold this view believe that Jesus identified himself with this apocalyptic heavenly being, but interpreted his earthly life and death in the light of the "Suffering Servant" passages in the Second Isaiah. It may seem strange and incredible to us that he could both have regarded himself as a humble human servant during his earthly life and also have believed that he would be exalted to the status of a heavenly being after his death, they say, but we must accept the evidence of the records.

On the other hand, some New Testament scholars are impressed by the fact that there is only one definite claim of Jesus to Messiahship in the earliest Gospel of Mark. Only at his hearing before the high priest the night before his crucifixion, according to Mark, did Jesus seem explicitly to claim Messiahship.[1] Moreover, may not Jesus have cherished apocalyptic hopes for the future without dreaming that he himself was to be the heavenly "Son of Man" who was to fulfill them? How *could* he have identified himself with such a supernatural being? Would not such an exalted claim have been completely inconsistent with his humility and reticence

[1] Mk. 14:62.

about himself and with his concentration upon the preaching of the Kingdom?

Whether Jesus claimed to be the Apocalyptic heavenly "Son of Man," we shall probably never know. In view of the conviction of his disciples after his death that he was the Messiah, it is probable that he himself claimed to be the Messiah in some sense. But the most essential question for Christians is not whether he himself *claimed* to be the Messiah, but whether he *was* the Messiah. The strongest argument for Jesus' Messiahship is not what he said about himself but what he was and did. The first acknowledgment of his Messiahship seems not to have been based on any claims of Jesus about himself; it sprang out of the total impression he had made upon Peter. It has always been so. Those who have acknowledged Jesus as the Christ have done so primarily because of the redemptive power and the new life they have found in him.

However, the most important question about Jesus is not whether he was the Messiah expected by the Jews but whether he was the *Redeemer* of all men. Christians have always believed not only that God revealed Himself in Jesus uniquely but also that in Jesus He was "reconciling the world to Himself." Did Jesus' conduct provide any ground for this belief? There can be little doubt of the answer. From the beginning of his public career, Jesus *spoke with authority* to those who heard him. After he had called his disciples to him, he was always Master to them. He kept them with him wherever he went and instructed them privately. He sent them out to proclaim the Kingdom and cast out demons. At the end, he took them with him to Jerusalem for his final appeal to the nation. At their last supper together the night before his crucifixion he bound them to himself in a solemn rite.

Moreover, he required *loyalty to himself* as a sign of loyalty to the Kingdom. After Caesarea Philippi, he said to his disciples, "If any man would come after me, let him deny himself and take up his cross and follow me. For whoever would save his life will lose it; and whoever loses his life for my sake and the gospel's will save it."[2] Again, he told them, "Whoever receives one such child

[2] Mk. 8:34, 35.

in my name receives me; and whoever receives me, receives not me but him who sent me."[3] His cleansing of the Temple,[4] his challenge to the religious leaders in the parable of the vineyard,[5] and his sharp criticism of the scribes[6] confirm by deeds the impression left by these words: he was convinced that he was entitled to speak and act with authority on behalf of God and His Kingdom.

He did not hesitate, therefore, to ask men to render acts of service in his name and even to sacrifice their lives for his sake and the Gospel's. To serve in his name was to serve the Kingdom; to sacrifice one's life for his sake was to sacrifice it for the sake of the Gospel he proclaimed. Thus, he claimed men's absolute loyalty to himself as well as to God and the Kingdom. It is possible that some of the sayings demanding loyalty to himself were heightened by the early Christians because persecution and death were a grim reality in their lives. But it is difficult to avoid the conclusion that, despite his reticence about making claims with respect to his own person, he was conscious of speaking and acting with divine authority.

In any case, Christians have never separated their loyalty to the Kingdom from their loyalty to Christ. From the time of St. Paul, union with Christ as Redeemer has always been a primary source of moral guidance and power to Christians who would live as members of the Kingdom. It will always be an integral part of the Christian life.

EFFECT OF THE APOCALYPTIC HOPE

The hope of Jesus and his disciples for the consummation of the Kingdom of God in the near future was not fulfilled. As time passed and Christ did not come again, a visible future consummation of the Kingdom began to seem less important to many. Men could be born again into the new life here and now through conversion, and eternal life would simply be a continuation of this new life beyond the grave. This seems to be the primary view of

[3] Ibid., 9:37.
[4] Ibid., 11:15-18.

[5] Ibid., 12:1-12.
[6] Ibid., 12:38-40.

the author of the Fourth Gospel. In that Gospel Jesus says, "Truly, truly, I say to you, unless one is born anew, he cannot see the kingdom of God."[1] He says at a feast in Jerusalem, "Truly, truly, I say to you, he who hears my word and believes him who sent me, has eternal life; he does not come into judgment, but has passed from death to life."[2] In sayings like these, the fact is emphasized that through rebirth by the Spirit the Christian passes into a new life in the present age. Thus, in the Fourth Gospel, the Apocalyptic element in Jesus' teaching is subordinate. Though there are references now and then to a future last judgment, they are secondary.

There was loss as well as gain in this development. The substitution of a present experience of eternal life for faith in a future consummation tended to destroy the tension between the actual and the ideal and to weaken hope for the triumph of the ideal in time. Medieval other-worldliness carried this tendency still further. Hope for the rewards of heaven virtually took the place of hope for the realization of the Kingdom within history. Many forgot altogether that Christ had taught his disciples to pray, "Thy kingdom come, thy will be done, on earth as it is in heaven." Thus, mystical and other-worldly conceptions united to destroy the sense of urgency of the early Christians. Most Christians no longer felt that the Kingdom might break in upon them at any time, and that they must be ready for its coming.

During the early, medieval, and Reformation periods, however, it was believed that, however long the delay might be, the second coming of Christ was sure to occur. Therefore, the teaching of Jesus about a catastrophic intervention of God to bring the present age to an end and establish a new age did not appear to be mistaken. But since the latter part of the nineteenth century, many thoughtful Christians have come to believe that the hope of such a supernatural intervention in history is vain. This has been due in part to evolutionary conceptions of continuous development in nature and optimistic ideas of progress in history. But it has been due also to the growing realization by New Testament scholars

[1] Jo. 3:3.
[2] Jo. 5:24.

that Jesus derived his scientific and cosmological views from his own times. This implies that by virtue of his human nature Jesus was limited in his knowledge. It is in his Apocalyptic beliefs that this limitation is most obvious.

The question arises for modern Christians whether this discredits his teaching as a whole. The answer to this question depends upon the relation of Jesus' Apocalyptic beliefs to the rest of his teachings. Now, there is wide agreement among New Testament scholars that the fundamental teachings of Jesus about God, man, and the good were not derived from and are not dependent upon his Apocalyptic beliefs. They were derived primarily from the Old Testament, the Rabbis, and his own religious consciousness. Moreover, it is not true that Jesus' ethical teaching was merely what Schweitzer called an "interimsethik." Jesus did not regard his ethical principles as binding only for the brief interim before the Kingdom was to come; they were to have permanent validity for human life. There is not a shred of evidence that he would have wanted to change any of his fundamental ethical principles if he had anticipated that after nineteen hundred years the Kingdom would still not have come. Of course, his ethic holds for human life only under conditions of earthly existence. Obviously, some of his sayings such as those that demand forgiveness and love of enemies presuppose those conditions and would be irrelevant after evil was destroyed. But they are affected in no way by the duration of earthly existence, whether short or indefinitely long.

However, there is one important qualification to this statement that has to do with something Jesus did *not* say rather than with something he said. As we shall see later, he had very little to say about social justice and gave no counsel for dealing with evildoers except that of not resisting them. This presents realistic Christians, who have a sense of social responsibility, with a problem. Once they accept the fact that the Kingdom of God will probably not come in the near future and that they must expect to live for an indefinite time as members of an earthly society, what should they do about evildoers? They cannot refuse to take responsibility in the matter without bringing down great evils upon the heads of others as well as themselves. Considerations like these forced

Christians, after responsibility for society had begun to fall into their hands in the fourth century, to develop a theory of social justice. For example, they justified the necessity for the state to defend its members from violence by means of laws enforced by the police and army. Most Christians of our time do the same. This does not require the rejection of any of Jesus' ethical principles. But it does require realism in the application of them to social relationships.

Did the Apocalyptic hopes of Jesus affect his ethical teaching in more *positive* ways? The answer is that they provided him with a different perspective upon moral problems. In the first place, Jesus' belief in the imminence of the Kingdom accounts for the *sense of urgency* in his appeals to his people for repentance and amendment. By foreshortening the time between present acts and the final judgment upon them, it brought home more vividly the fateful importance of men's moral decisions. One of the most tragic limitations of man's imagination is that he sees the immediate consequences of his acts more clearly than the more remote ones. As a result he tends to choose transitory values instead of enduring ones. But the anticipation of imminent final judgment brings distant consequences very near. Without it one is likely to fall into folly like the rich man who said to himself, "Soul, you have ample goods laid up for many years; take your ease, eat, drink and be merry," and did not know that God was about to say to him, "Fool! This night your soul is required of you; and the things you have prepared, whose will they be?"[3]

In the second place, the Apocalyptic point of view stresses the fact that there is an *absolute difference* between faith and unfaith, right and wrong, and that the choice between them will determine not merely one's temporal but also one's eternal destiny. The Apocalyptic thinkers insist that the issue between good and evil cannot be escaped by plausible arguments about the relativity of moral judgments and the mixture of good and evil in the motives of men. Moral decisions are freighted with infinite significance for good or evil.

Neither the deepening of the sense of urgency nor the illumina-

[3] Lk. 12:19, 20.

tion of the eternal issues involved in moral decisions, however, affects the *criterion* of moral judgments as to what is right and wrong. But in one important respect the Apocalyptic perspective does affect the moral criterion itself. The demands of "group morality" reflect the experience of the group as to the kinds of actions that maintain its own unity and strength. But when one asks, not "What does my society demand of me?" but "What does God demand of me?," one's criterion of moral goodness changes. One ceases to be content with the *relative goodness of men* and begins to be concerned about the *absolute goodness of God*. The Apocalyptic point of view on morality brings about precisely this change. It raises one above prudential considerations of advantage to oneself. It does not permit one to consider only the relative values of his own group. It asserts that what matters supremely is obedience to the absolute will of God. Since God is a holy Being, this means that perfect righteousness like His is required. In this way, Jesus' vision of final judgment and eternal life enabled him to cut away as with a sharp knife all considerations of personal and social advantage and to see with piercing clarity the demands of God's absolute and perfect will.

To summarize, although the Apocalyptic element in Jesus' thinking provides the framework rather than the content of his ethical teaching, it gives his ethical teaching a strong sense of urgency, it throws into relief the eternal significance of moral decisions, and it stimulates men to conceive and practice an absolute goodness like that of God. Thus, his Apocalyptic hope is the source of much of the moral intensity and idealism which give his ethical principles their power.

AN ETHIC OF PERFECTION

Jesus' ethical absolutism helps to explain the fact that his ethic is an *ethic of perfection*. This may be illustrated in several ways. First, the *motives* of members of the Kingdom in their conduct must be free from desire for human approval. Otherwise, they will do good deeds not because these are demanded by God, but because they will be rewarded by men. We are reminded of a famous passage in Plato's *Republic* where Glaucon insists that most men act virtuously not for the sake of virtue, but because of the rewards society bestows upon those who conform to its requirements. Glaucon argues that the only way to determine whether a man is virtuous, in reality as well as in appearance, would be to see what he would do if he had a ring which would render him invisible to human eyes and enable him to perpetrate the most evil deeds without being punished for them.[1] Jesus' test of moral sincerity is simpler. When men pray, fast or give alms, they should not seek to be "seen" or "heard" by other men, but should act in secret so that only God will see or hear them. For those who do these good deeds to be approved and praised by men "have their reward" here and now, but those who do them for the approval of God alone will be rewarded later.[2] The implication is that the desire to please man usually excludes the desire to please God. Those who seek the approval of men are content to conform to the imperfect standards of social morality and do not feel the higher demands of the absolute will of God upon their conscience. Jesus appeals to a similar perfectionistic motive when he speaks of the desire to "be" or "be called" by the name of "sons of your Father who is in heaven."[3] It is because the disciples profess this desire that Jesus calls them "the salt of the earth" and "the light of the world."[4]

The ethical perfectionism of Jesus is manifested also in the *norm* or standard of goodness to which he appeals. Aristotle bases his conception of morality upon the moral judgments and practices of the wise and good men of Greece, since morality is conceived by him in exclusively human terms. It is discovered by empirical observation, without reference to any transcendent Good as a standard.[5] As we saw, Jesus raises men's minds above the morality of even the best men to the perfect goodness of God. The most striking passage in which this is illustrated is, "You, therefore, must be per-

[1] Plato, *The Republic*, II, p. 359.
[2] Mtt. 6:1-18.
[3] Ibid., 5:45.
[4] Ibid., 5:13, 14.
[5] Cf. Aristotle's criticism of Plato's "Idea of the Good" in the *Nicomachean Ethics*, Book 1.

fect, as your heavenly Father is perfect."[6] Jesus is here contrasting God's perfect love with the imperfect love of "taxgatherers" and "Gentiles."[7] But there is also another passage in which he contrasts the perfect goodness required by God with the goodness of the best men of his time. "For I tell you," he says, "unless your righteousness exceeds that of the scribes and Pharisees, you will never enter the Kingdom of Heaven."[8] Since the scribes and Pharisees were religious and moral perfectionists themselves, zealously seeking to follow every precept of the written and oral Law, this must have seemed shocking to those who heard it. It throws in high relief, as nothing else could do, the fact that Jesus demanded moral perfection as measured by divine rather than human standards.

The perfectionism of Jesus is shown, in the third place, by the *inwardness* of his ethical teaching. Not only acts but also *desires* and *passions* which do not express themselves in acts must be right. Perhaps the most striking examples of this are found in the Sermon on the Mount, in the form reported by Matthew, where Jesus quotes certain sayings from the Law of Moses and sets over against them higher and harder demands. The Law said, "You shall not kill;" "But I say to you that everyone who is angry with his brother shall be liable to judgment,"[9] etc. The Law said, "You shall not commit adultery"; "But I say to you that everyone who looks at a woman lustfully has already committed adultery with her in his heart."[10] Abstention from overt deeds that are manifestly harmful to others is not enough. It is necessary to master the passions and desires of the heart as well. It is not merely that these may lead to harmful deeds if they are not checked. Anger and lust sometimes lead to murder and adultery, but often they do not. The point is that such desires are evil in themselves. Rage and lust are opposed to love, which affirms the worth of other persons and treats them as ends in themselves.

Similarly, *dispositions of will* and *personal qualities* have moral significance. The dispositions to make peace, to forgive, to receive

---

[6] Mtt. 5:48.
[7] Ibid., 5:46, 7.
[8] Ibid., 5:20.

[9] Ibid., 5:22.
[10] Ibid., 5:27, 28.

like a child are essential to perfect goodness. Qualities such as those described in the Beatitudes, e.g., meekness, purity of heart, and mercifulness, are also indispensable. This indicates that Jesus was as concerned with the hidden springs of character in a person as with his conduct, with his being as well as with his doing. "What comes out of a man is what defiles a man."[11] Character, in the broadest sense of the term, determines conduct. "A sound tree cannot bear evil fruit, nor can a bad tree bear good fruit."[12] Jesus would have regarded as strange those modern ethical theories such as Utilitarianism which are interested only in the consequences of an act and neglect its origin in character.

However, it would be a mistake to suppose that "inwardness" is all that counts with Jesus. In the passage we have just quoted on the importance of character he also says, "Every tree that does not bear good fruit is cut down and thrown into the fire. Thus you will know them by their fruits."[13] It is the man who not only "hears" Jesus' words but "does" them whose house is built securely upon the rock.[14] Thus, Jesus stresses the *wholeness* of morality. Goodness is to be manifested in every phase of morality from the motives, dispositions, and character within to the deeds in which these are expressed outwardly. All of these phases form an organic unity in the truly good man.

There is also a fourth respect in which the ethics of Jesus is perfectionistic: its *uncompromising opposition to egoism* in every form. "The absolutism and perfectionism of Jesus' love ethic," says Reinhold Niebuhr, "sets itself uncompromisingly not only against the natural self-regarding impulses, but against the necessary prudent defenses of the self, required because of the egoism of others."[15] Thus anxiety over food and clothing, concern for material possessions, pride in all its forms, and resistance of the enemy are prohibited.[16] Similarly, love is to be universal, and family loyalty is to

---

[11] Mk. 7:20.
[12] Mtt. 7:18.
[13] Ibid., 7:19, 20.
[14] Ibid., 7:24-27.
[15] Niebuhr, R., *An Interpretation of Christian Ethics,* New York, Harpers, 1935, p. 39.
[16] Ibid., pp. 41-45.

be subordinated to a higher loyalty.[17] The reason given by Jesus for this absolute rejection of every form of egoism is significant. "The justification of these demands is put in purely religious and not in socio-moral terms," says Niebuhr. "We are to forgive because God forgives; we are to love our enemies because God is impartial in his love. The points of reference are vertical and not horizontal. Neither natural impulses nor social consequences are taken into consideration. To do good to an enemy may prompt him to overcome his enmity; and forgiveness of evil may be a method of redemption which commends itself to the most prudent. It must be observed, however, that no appeal to social consequences could ever fully justify these demands of Jesus. Non-resistance may shame an aggressor into goodness, but it may also prompt him to further aggression."[18]

It may be doubted whether Jesus was as indifferent to "natural impulses" and "social consequences" as this suggests. It is difficult, if not impossible, to deny that there is a "prudential" element in some of his teachings. But his emphasis obviously falls upon the absolute will of God. The reason will be clear from what we have already said. It is due not only to the Apocalyptic point of view of Jesus which dwarfs into insignificance all considerations of relative value in the presence of the absolute good of the Kingdom, but also to his pure and clear prophetic consciousness of the perfect goodness of God and of His moral requirements upon men. It obviously presents us with the problem of adapting the demands of his perfectionistic ethics to the imperfections of human nature and the necessities of society. This is what Niebuhr calls "the problem of compromise, the problem of creating and maintaining tentative harmonies of life in the world in terms of the possibilities of the human situation,"[19] and at the same time setting these tentative achievements "under the criticism of the ultimate ideal."[20] This is, of course, the difficult problem of the practicality of the Christian ethical ideal in a sinful world.

[17] Ibid., pp. 50, 51.
[18] Ibid., p. 46.

[19] Ibid., p. 59.
[20] Ibid., p. 61.

JESUS AND THE LAW

What was Jesus' attitude towards the *ethic of law* which was dominant in his time? It is difficult for modern orthodox Christians, both Catholic and Protestant, to realize that Jesus' ethic is not an ethic of law. The majority of Christians in our day, like the Jews in Jesus' day, tend to identify morality with conformity to a code of rules or laws, written and unwritten, which define their duties in the various situations of life. Yet Jesus' attitude towards the Jewish Law as well as the whole spirit of his teaching are definitely opposed to ethical legalism. His attitude towards the Law was more like that of the prophets than that of the scribes of his day. He was not content with a meticulous analysis of the Law; he sought to apprehend the will of God in its purity by an act of direct insight. This accounts for the fact that "he taught them as one who had authority, and not as the scribes."[1]

His independence in interpreting the Law does not imply that he was indifferent to it. He had been nourished on the Law as well as the Prophets. He was influenced deeply by the humanitarian feeling of the laws in the book of Deuteronomy. On more than one occasion he quotes from the Law or shows his approval when others quote from it.[2] His two-fold law of love is quoted directly from Deuteronomy and Leviticus.[3] According to Matthew, Jesus said, "Think not that I have come to abolish the law and the prophets; I have come not to abolish (A.V., destroy) them but to fulfil them."[4]

In fulfilling the Law, however, he *reinterpreted* it; and the changes he introduced were often radical. As we have seen, he *deepened* the meaning of certain laws by insisting upon their application to desire and passion as well as action, e.g., lust and anger as well as adultery and murder. Equally striking is the way he *broadened* the application of other laws. The best example of this is his treatment of "Thou shalt love thy neighbor." It is generally agreed that this law from the book of Leviticus originally meant to require

---

[1] Mk. 1:22.
[2] Ibid., 10:19.
[3] Dt. 6:4-5; Lev. 19:18.
[4] Mtt. 5:17.

love of neighbor only in relation to one's fellow-Jews, though a later law in the same chapter required love for resident aliens also.[5] But Jesus says, "Love your enemies," thus extending the application of the law to those one would be least likely to love. Moreover, on more than one occasion Jesus reinterpreted a law in such a way as to *transform* it. For example, the law of Moses permitting divorce, he held, was not an expression of the absolute will of God for man and woman but a concession to human sin.[6]

In addition to this reinterpretation of the Law of Moses, Jesus effected a *simplification* by stressing the dependence of all the other laws upon the two-fold law of love. Matthew represents him as saying, "On these two laws depend (A.V., hang) all the law and the prophets."[7] This seems to mean that all the other teachings of the legal and prophetic writings are specifications of the law of love when it is applied to the various situations of human life, or at least that they can be shown to imply the law of love. This proves that, though Jesus in his own teaching did not explicitly make the distinction between general principles and specific rules, he discriminated between primary and secondary elements in the Law. Thus, while it is probably too much to say that he reduced all the law to the two-fold law of love, he clearly subordinated all the other laws to it.

When the higher law of love is involved, moreover, he does not hesitate to set aside oral traditions of the scribes concerning the application of a law. He allows his disciples to pluck and eat grain on the sabbath to satisfy their hunger. "The sabbath was made for man, not man for the sabbath; so the Son of man is Lord even of the sabbath."[8] He heals a man with a withered arm on the sabbath. "Is it lawful on the sabbath to do good or to do harm, to save life or to kill?"[9] In both cases his reason is that the service of human needs takes precedence over the scribal interpretation of the sabbath law. He does not require his disciples to wash their hands in the way prescribed by the scribes, on the ground that this would be to

[5] Lev. 19:13.
[6] Mk. 10:5-12.
[7] Mtt. 22:40.
[8] Mk. 2:27, 28.
[9] Ibid., 3:4.

"leave the commandment of God, and hold fast the tradition of men,"[10] and that "there is nothing outside a man which by going into him can defile him."[11] He does not insist that his disciples fast. "As long as they have the bridegroom with them, they cannot fast."[12] Thus, Jesus not only reinterprets, transforms and simplifies the written Law, he also does not hesitate on occasion to *abandon the oral tradition* of the scribes which interprets and applies the Law to all the details of life.

What are we to say about *his own* ethical teaching? Is it possible to regard it as a "New Law" supplementing or supplanting the "Old Law" of Moses? To this question we must definitely give a negative answer. It is true that his primary ethical principle takes the form of a commandment: "Thou shalt love thy neighbor as thyself." But this saying does not command a specific kind of act for a specific kind of situation. It commands a practical disposition or attitude which is to manifest itself in many different kinds of acts according to the needs of particular situations. It is also true that more specific kinds of acts are sometimes commanded or prohibited. But these are usually illustrations of kinds of acts that may be required by the practical disposition of love. As we shall see, when we attempt to apply them as rules in a literal fashion, we may easily reduce them to absurdity. For example, what would be the effect on personal character if we made into a general rule the injunction "Give to everyone who begs from you"?

Of course, when we maintain that Jesus' teaching consists, not of specific laws or rules, but of a general commandment of love illustrated in various ways, we are making a distinction which Jesus does not employ himself. He uses only the distinction, common among the Rabbis, between the "first" or the "great" commandment and the other commandments of the Law. But Jesus was a prophetic religious teacher rather than a moral philosopher. Furthermore, he was a religious teacher who was heir to the ethical tradition of the lawgivers, prophets, and wise men of Israel. It is not surprising, therefore, that he used all the forms of teaching known to that

---

[10] Ibid., 7:8.
[11] Ibid., 7:15.
[12] Ibid., 2:19.

tradition. Prophets as well as lawgivers had used the form of the moral law or precept. The wise men frequently employed it, along with the maxim or aphorism. It would have been strange if Jesus had not made extensive use of it, since he was proclaiming the absolute will of God which must be obeyed by those who would enter the Kingdom.

That Jesus' teachings are not to be regarded as a New Law is borne out by the fact that he makes no attempt to be comprehensive. His teachings are occasional and cove. only a small proportion of the many kinds of situations in which men must act. In many cases, moreover, we do not know how general Jesus meant the application of a saying to be. Was his counsel to the rich man, "Go, sell what you have, and give to the poor, and you will have treasure in heaven; and come, follow me,"[13] meant to apply only to the rich man himself, or to the "religious" who renounce the world in order to become perfect Christians, or to all Christians?

But the denial that Jesus' "precepts" constitute a "New Law" does not imply that they are not to be taken very seriously. As C. H. Dodd has pointed out, they indicate the "quality" and "direction" our actions must take under all circumstances.[14] For example, the precepts "turn the other cheek" and "give to him who asks" cannot be literally applied as laws in every situation without leading to much harm; but they indicate the patient, forbearing, and generous attitude we should maintain and illustrate the kinds of actions in which that attitude will seek to manifest itself.

Thus, Jesus' ethic is not an ethic of law. He is not attempting to supersede or supplement the "Old Law" of Moses by a "New Law" of his own. His purpose is not to lay down a comprehensive code of rules for society. Rather, he is seeking to state the general character of God's absolute and perfect will for men, setting forth the way men must follow if they are to live as members of the Kingdom of God. He lays down precepts to illustrate the kinds of things they must and must not do, but these are incidental to his main purpose. He is not, be it noted, denying the need of laws or rules as the basis

[13] Mk. 10:21.
[14] Dodd, C. H., *Gospel and Law*, New York, Columbia University Press, 1951.

of order in society. But he is not attempting to provide such laws or rules himself. He is setting forth the principles of life in the Kingdom and describing the blessings of that life. He is pointing out in general terms the way men must follow as members of the Kingdom and seeking to make it concrete by means of precept, parable, and personal example.

CHAPTER 3

The Law of Love

THE fundamental principle of the Christian ethic is love of God and love of neighbor. If we are to understand the full meaning of this principle, we must consider the embodiment of love in Jesus' life and death as well as its expression in his teachings. For example, he shows forth the meaning of love by his generous attitude towards sinners. By identifying himself with their lives, he manifests love for all men, even the unworthy, and he shows that man's love of neighbor should be, like God's love, redemptive, a love which takes the initiative and seeks out the sinner where he is. Again, Jesus heals the troubled souls and diseased bodies of men out of love and compassion. Early in his public ministry he touched a leper and healed him from pity. This simple act of touching a person who was afflicted with a loathsome disease and required to live as an outcast says much about the quality and depth of his love for all men. His supreme demonstration of the costliness of love is his voluntary acceptance of death on the Cross. Indeed, his death illuminates the meaning of his whole life, revealing in a sudden flash of light the depth of love that was behind all his deeds of kindness and mercy.

LOVE OF GOD

The first commandment, says Jesus, is: "Thou shalt love the Lord thy God with all thy heart, and with all thy soul, and with all thy mind, and with all thy strength." This commandment was quoted by Jesus from the book of Deuteronomy.[1] Nygren has attempted to show that Jesus' real meaning is that man shall have faith in God rather than that he should love Him. Defining "agape" or "love" in the Christian sense as "spontaneous" and "uncaused" love, he argues that man cannot manifest such a love for God since his love is caused by the antecedent love of God for him. Love for God, therefore, must mean faith in Him, "the acknowledgement of God's absolute sovereignty."[2]

This argument is not convincing. It denies the plain meaning of Jesus' words. After all, the meaning of the words "Thou shalt love the Lord thy God" had become fixed in Judaism, since they were repeated daily by every loyal Jew. Moreover, to argue that the word "agape" cannot refer to a love that is "caused" as well as to a love that is "uncaused" is to overlook the flexibility of words. The same word is frequently used to express two or more meanings that are similar in essence but not identical in all respects. This is the case with "agape" in the New Testament. There are, of course, differences between God's love for man and man's love for God. God, from whom no secrets are hid, knows man to the depths of his being; man can know only as much of the infinite and transcendent God as it is given a mortal to know. Moreover, since God is invisible, man cannot love Him as he loves visible creatures like his neighbors. According to the First Epistle of John, "If any one says, 'I love God,' and hates his brother, he is a liar; for he who does not love his brother whom he has seen, cannot love God, whom he has not seen."[3] Finally, man's love for God must always differ from his love of his neighbor, since man is not the equal of God. This means that man must love God with awe as the Creator upon whom he depends for his whole existence and value.

That which characterizes man's love of God, according to the Bible, is *fellowship* with Him and *grateful obedience* to His will. "This is the love of God," writes the author of the First Epistle of John, "that we keep his commandments."[4] When man serves God's

---

[1] Deut. 6:5.
[2] From *Agape and Eros* by Anders Nygren, 1953, The Westminster Press, used by permission. I, p. 93.
[3] I Jo. 4:20.
[4] I Jo. 5:3.

will with his whole self he enters into a relation with God in which
the barriers between the creature and the Creator are down and he
loves God as he is loved by God. This is the testimony of plain men
and mystics alike. It was certainly the conviction of Jesus and his
whole life was based upon it. Without it, his references to God as
Father and his insistence that men obey Him and trust Him and
ask Him for the things they need would have no meaning.

LOVE OF NEIGHBOR

The second commandment is, "Thou shalt love thy neighbor as
thyself." What is it to love one's neighbor? In the first place, it is
to love a *person,* not mankind or humanity. This is evident from
the fact that in the examples Jesus gives the objects of neighbor
love are always persons, e.g., the wounded man in the parable of
the Good Samaritan. Most of our relations with others are largely
impersonal. When we hand our railway ticket to the conductor, we
hardly think of him as a person at all; we see only an official whose
relation to us is confined to the function of collecting our ticket.
When we employ a carpenter to repair the roof, we are interested
in him only as a skilled worker who can perform a function useful
to us. We do not deal with him as a whole, concrete person, but
with one aspect of him: his function and his relation to our purposes.
We do not really come into contact with him as a three-dimensional
person; we touch him only on the surface which is turned towards
us.

In contrast, when we treat a man as a person, we are interested
in him as a whole; he becomes a being with a life and interests
independent of our own. If the railway conductor or carpenter is
not in a hurry and we are not preoccupied with our own concerns, he
may begin to talk with us about his children or the state of the
nation and we may be surprised to discover how much more he is
than a functionary. What has brought about this transformation?
A person has *revealed* himself to us, and we now see something
of him as he is *in himself.* We do not usually take the time or
trouble to gaze intently at our neighbor and look deeply into his
life. As a result, we see only a part of him. One reason is that we

are unwilling to pay the price in time and effort required for full and complete knowledge of a person. More important, we know that if we came to have that kind of knowledge, it might cost us suffering. For the only way in which a person can be really known is through identification with his life in all its interests, hopes, fears, joys, and sorrows. That is why a man may have innumerable acquaintances but few friends or none at all. An acquaintance costs little in time and energy and nothing in suffering; a friend may cost much in all of these. That is also why marriage, which fully involves a man and a woman in each other's lives, may be the source of both the greatest happiness and the greatest suffering of all social relationships. Yet the tragic fact is that even married people often fail to achieve a genuine personal relationship to each other, because one or both are unable or unwilling to pay the cost.

Clearly, it is *self-centeredness* which prevents us from passing from impersonal to personal relationships with others. We are too enclosed in the narrow circle of our own interests, ambitions, and activities to enter deeply into the lives of others. The result is that we are unable to achieve community with others, knowing and being known by them, sharing a common life with them. In our isolation from them we cannot even become aware of their needs. Even if by some chance their needs are thrust upon us, we do not feel them as we feel our own. If we sense them at times, we have no desire to relieve them because they are the needs of people from whose lives we are separated as by a high wall. The result is that we develop a shell of indifference to the lives and needs of others which effectively prevents us from hearing their silent cries for recognition, comradeship, and help. There are some whose ambition and will to power alienates them still further from their fellows. They are the active oppressors of the weak, the exploiters of the poor, the tyrants of whole peoples. But it is safe to say that great egoists who are moved only by the lust for power and domination over others are a small minority of men. The egoism of most of us is on a smaller scale, but it, too, is a source of evil and suffering to our neighbors.

At any rate, while Jesus says little about the great sinners, those who actively oppress and tyrannize over the lives of large numbers of men, he says much about those who ignore other persons and fail to serve their needs. Their sins are sins of omission rather than commission. Thus, in the parable of the Good Samaritan the sin of the Priest and Levite was simply that they "passed by on the other side" and did nothing to help the wounded man.[1] Again, in the description of the last judgment[2] those who are cast out into the eternal fire of punishment are those who did not give food to the hungry or drink to the thirsty, did not clothe the naked or visit the sick or the prisoner. Perhaps the most striking example is that found in the parable of the rich man and a poor man named Lazarus.[3] In the two sentences that describe the earthly lives of these men, we are not told of any positive wrong done by the rich man to Lazarus. It is merely implied that he did nothing to relieve the suffering of Lazarus but passed him by with complete indifference. He is cast into Hades to suffer torment, while Lazarus is carried by angels to Abraham's bosom.

Egoistic preoccupation with one's own affairs and indifference to those of others is not the only cause of the refusal to treat others as persons. Another cause is moral and spiritual *pride*. Jesus shocked the Pharisees by his sympathetic treatment of a "woman of the city." One of the things that enraged them most was that he ate with "publicans and sinners"; instead of keeping himself aloof from them, he invited ritual defilement by letting down the bars to social intercourse between the "righteous" observers and the "wicked" non-observers of the Law.[4] The laws of ritual cleanness were scrupulously respected by the Pharisees and scribes, ostensibly to preserve themselves from defilement. But their actions, Jesus charged, were motivated primarily by spiritual pride. "They do all their deeds to be seen by men; for they make their phylacteries broad and their fringes long, and they love the place of honor at feasts and the best seats in the synagogues, and salutations in the market places, and being called rabbi by men."[5]

Modern scholarship, Jewish and Christian alike, has made it

---

[1] Lk. 10:31-32.
[2] Mtt. 25:31-46.
[3] Lk. 16:19-31.

[4] Lk. 15:1, 2.
[5] Mtt. 23:5-7.

clear that there was another and brighter side of the Pharisees than that which appears in the indictments of them in the Gospels. Nevertheless, if our Gospels are to be trusted at all, there were many scribes and Pharisees whose earnest effort to obey the whole of the written Law and of the oral traditions produced in them a kind of self-righteousness and complacency and separated them from normal fellowship with those who did not observe all of the ethical or ceremonial laws. One does not need to suppose that the scribes and Pharisees were guilty of conscious hypocrisy, for most hypocrisy is unconscious, the hypocrisy of those who have deceived themselves into thinking that they are good. They probably did not even know that they were neglecting justice and mercy and faith in their preoccupation with the rules of tithing and washing. A legalistic morality inevitably tends to neglect "weightier matters" which cannot be as easily covered by rules as less important matters can. But, consciously or not, the result was a moral self-righteousness and blindness that isolated them from the common people and prevented them from serving the needs of those who needed their help most, sinners. Perhaps this was what Jesus meant when he said to them, "you shut the kingdom of heaven against men; for you neither enter yourselves nor allow those who would enter to go in."[6]

In contrast to this tendency of men to isolate themselves from their fellows because of indifference or a sense of their own moral superiority, neighbor love treats each individual as a person and seeks *community* with him. This shows itself most simply by refusing to be separated from one's neighbor by artificial barriers of wealth, class, and nation. "When you give a dinner or a banquet, do not invite your friends or your brothers or your kinsmen or rich neighbors, lest they also invite you in return, and you be repaid. But when you give a feast, invite the poor, the maimed, the lame, the blind, and you will be blessed, because they cannot repay you."[7] Needless to say, this saying has always been honored by Christians

[6] Mtt. 23:13.
[7] Lk. 14:12-14.

more in the breach than in the observance, even in democratic countries like our own, and is a good illustration of the revolutionary
character of Jesus' teaching.

The best example of love of neighbor, of course, is found in the
parable of the Good Samaritan, which was told by Jesus in reply
to the question, "Who is my neighbor?"[8] It is the story of a Samaritan who out of compassion went to the help of a man who had
been stripped and beaten by robbers. As if to contrast his act more
sharply with the heartlessness of the Priest and Levite who had
"passed by on the other side" of the road, Jesus shows how much
trouble he took with the wounded stranger: he "went to him and
bound up his wounds, pouring on oil and wine; then he set him
on his own beast and brought him to an inn, and took care of him.
And the next day he took out two denarii and gave them to the
innkeeper, saying 'take care of him; and whatever more you spend,
I will repay you when I come back.' " The story revolutionizes the
ordinary conception of a neighbor. The test of a neighbor is his
willingness, at some cost of time, money, and trouble, to give practical assistance to one in need.

From what has been said, it is obvious that love of neighbor means
far more than is usually understood by the Golden Rule, "As you
wish that men should do to you, do so to them."[9] This saying is
sometimes thought to require nothing more than ordinary justice
or fair play: we should regard others as having a right to the same
treatment we desire and claim for ourselves. Interpreted in this
way, it would be only a plea for the just treatment of others as
our equals, or mere prudential counsel that we must be good to
others if we want them to be good to us. If it is read apart from
Jesus' other sayings, and in the light of our ordinary ideas about
the way decent men should treat their neighbors, it is easily taken
to mean little more than ordinary "justice" or what is sometimes
called "mutuality."

But love of neighbor, as Jesus uses the term, goes far beyond this.
In the first place, while ordinary love is restricted, Christian love
is *universal* in its range. As the story of the Good Samaritan indi-

[8] Lk. 10:29-37.
[9] Lk. 6:31.

cates, one's neighbor is defined as anyone who may happen to cross one's path, whatever his nation or race or kind. We easily forget how radically this departed from the practice and standards of the ancient world. Modern nationalism and racism remind us that we should never have taken it for granted. That Jesus fully realized the radical implications of universal love is apparent from his injunction "love your enemies." We are not merely to love our enemies in the negative sense of not hating them, but also in the more positive and active sense of seeking to make peace with them, forgiving them without limit. This universal love which is not satisfied to "resist evil" but seeks to "overcome evil with good," has little in common with modern humanitarian "benevolence" or the "sentiment of humanity."

In the second place, Christian love is not based upon the expectation, much less the promise, of a *return* of love. The uncalculating, unselfish quality of Christian love is vividly expressed in Jesus' words contrasting it with the kind of love shown by sinners. "If you love those who love you, what credit is that to you? For even sinners love those who love them. And if you do good to those who do good to you, what credit is that to you? For even sinners do the same. And if you lend to those from whom you hope to receive, what credit is that to you? Even sinners lend to sinners, to receive as much again. But love your enemies, and do good, and lend, expecting nothing in return; and your reward will be great. . . ."[10] The love that is suitable to the members of the Kingdom, Jesus is saying, must surpass that of ordinary men. It must not, like their prudential love, depend upon return or reciprocation. It must be bestowed freely and generously. It does not give to receive; it gives because giving is its very nature.

In the third place, Christian love is independent of the *merit* or *worth* of those upon whom it is bestowed. Ordinary love is evoked by admirable or lovable qualities in the person loved: beauty, goodness, friendliness, cheerfulness, personal charm. But the love Jesus describes is given irrespective of merit of any kind. This is best illustrated by his own acts of kindness and helpfulness to those who were

[10] Lk. 6:32-35.

physically or mentally sick, and his friendly fellowship with outcasts and sinners. When the scribes and Pharisees asked Jesus why
he ate with publicans and sinners, he replied, "They that are whole
have no need of a physician, but those that are sick."[11] Even more
instructive are the parables of the Prodigal Son, the Laborers in the
Vineyard, and the man who invited to his feast "the poor, the
maimed, the blind, and the lame."[12] God "is kind to the ungrateful
and the selfish,"[13] and "makes his sun rise on the evil and on the
good, and sends rain on the just and on the unjust."[14] His sons must
not measure out their love carefully in proportion to the merit of the
person loved but must give generously to all.

In the fourth place, the love Jesus describes is not patterned on
the imperfect love of men for each other, but upon the *perfect love
of God* for His children. This is implied in the saying reported by
Luke, "Be merciful even as your Father is merciful,"[15] and stated
explicitly in the form of the saying found in Matthew, "You therefore must be perfect, as your heavenly Father is perfect."[16] Men are
to imitate the divine love, not the prudential love of men. This is
one of the clearest examples of the direct influence of religious presuppositions on Jesus' ethic. Both the generous love of God as Father
towards all men and their capacity as His children to mirror that
love in their relations with their fellows are assumed in the saying.
Men are to act as spiritual beings made in the divine image, not as
animals competing with one another in the struggle for existence
nor even as gregarious beings bound together by social needs and
feelings of a purely natural kind. Only if they are motivated in all
their acts by a love like God's will they be able to "excel the goodness of the scribes and Pharisees," i.e., attain the goodness that comes
from spontaneous, generous, self-giving love.

Nygren has done more than anyone else, perhaps, to make clear
the *radical* nature of love of neighbor in the New Testament. Beginning with Jesus' saying, "I came not to call the righteous, but
sinners,"[17] he has pointed out that these words constitute an assault

---

[11] Mk. 2:17.   [15] Lk. 6:36.
[12] Lk. 14:21-23.   [16] Mtt. 5:48.
[13] Lk. 6:35.   [17] Mk. 2:17.
[14] Mtt. 5:45.

on the traditional Jewish conception that "between the righteous and the sinners stands a sharp line of division in the sight of God and man."[18] Jesus sets aside the idea that God's attitude towards men is an attitude of retributive justice based on their relation to the Law. It is His nature to manifest freely and generously His love to the sinful as well as to the righteous. The best expression of this new idea is to be found in the parable of the Laborers in the Vineyard.[19] A householder hired laborers to work in his vineyard, some starting early, some at the third hour, some at the sixth, some at the ninth, and some as late as the eleventh. When he came to pay them their wages, the first-comers naturally expected to be paid proportionately more than the later ones. When the householder paid all the same wage, the first-comers said, "These last worked only one hour, and you have made them equal to us who have borne the burden of the day and the scorching heat." But he replied to one of them, "Am I not allowed to do what I choose with what belongs to me? Or do you begrudge my generosity?"[20]

As Nygren points out, one cannot "save" the householder in the parable from the charge of injustice, according to any reasonable *human* standard of justice. Of course, he paid the first-comers what he had agreed to pay them, and the fact that he paid more proportionately to the late-comers for their work violated no law or promise. But human justice surely requires higher pay for more work. It is clear, therefore, that the whole point of the parable is that God is not bound by human standards of justice in his dealings with men. "In spontaneous, 'uncaused' love," Nygren says, "the Householder gives the late-comers a reward far exceeding what they can claim. Those who have worked longest, bound as they are by the idea of justice and merit, reckon that they ought to have more. . . . Their claim is dismissed; spontaneous Agape stands on a higher level than mere distributive justice and supersedes it."[21] The same point is made in the parable of the Prodigal Son. The older brother represents the principle of merit and justice and quite properly com-

[18] Nygren, A., op. cit., I, p. 47.
[19] Mtt. 20:11-16.
[20] Mtt. 20:12-15.
[21] Nygren, op. cit., I, pp. 63, 64.

plains that his younger brother's reckless conduct has not deserved
the love shown him by the father.[22] Thus, God's love is not measured
out according to the value of the person loved, as human love is;
rather, God is the Creator and His love is *creative of worth*. Even
the sinner has some worth as a creature made in the image of God;
and God's love is "creative," not in the sense that it gives value to
a being that is wholly without value, but that it brings to fulfillment
possibilities of value that were present but frustrated.

Though God's love is given us irrespective of our actual worth,
it is effective in our lives only when we *respond* to it in the right
way. For example, Jesus makes it clear that the forgiveness of our
sins is conditional upon our willingness to forgive others. Moreover,
we are commanded in the Gospels to love our neighbor and are
told in the First Epistle of John that the test of our love of God is
our love of our neighbor. In other words, God's love is given to us
whether we deserve it or not; but it is given with the purpose of
awakening in us the desire and capacity to love Him and our
neighbor. Hence, we must regard ourselves not as passive recipients
of God's love but as active and responsible beings called by God to
cooperate with Him in the achievement of His purpose of love in
our own lives and in the lives of others.

Thus, God does not love us *from the need* of anything we can
give Him in return; but He loves us *with the purpose* that we should
return His love and thus enter into communion with Him by giving
ourselves to Him. His agape-love moves downward to us, but it
seeks to start in us a reciprocal movement upwards towards Him.
Similarly, we are to love our neighbor without regard to his worth
or his return of our love; but we are to strive through our love to
awaken in him the capacity to give as well as receive love and thus
to help him realize his potential worth. The result may be that our
giving to him will be met by his giving to us, and a fellowship of
mutual giving and receiving will be established between us.

Love of neighbor like this is wholly different from "erotic" love.
In love of the latter kind, the self is relatively passive; it reacts to an
external stimulus, as shown by phrases such as "falling in love,"
"being swept off one's feet," and "smitten with love." Love of neigh-

[22] Ibid., p. 64.

bor is also different from the love we call "friendship," which depends upon the presence of certain qualities in the friend. "Friendship" differs from "erotic" love, of course, in that the sexual urge is absent from it and it is usually less intense. But friendship, like erotic love, is not normally given irrespective of the worth or lack of worth of the friend; it does not endure unless it is reciprocated in some measure by him; and it is confined to a few persons who are regarded as one's equals. Aristotle thought that friendship must be between persons who were equals and that in its purest form it must be between persons who were both virtuous. In contrast, "love of neighbor" in the Christian sense is given to all, inferiors as well as equals; indeed, it pays no attention to differences of age, rank, wealth, and birth. In its purest form it delights in transcending these differences and cares for those who are not virtuous and are in special need of help.

"Love of neighbor" also differs from "love of country." Here, love is devoted to a particular group, its ideals and values and the achievements of its members. What is characteristic of love in this sense is that it arises from the common life and interests shared with others of the group. It is partly based upon a consciousness that the group is "my" group and that I participate in its worth and glory. Of course, I am conscious that it is more than "my" group, it is "our" group, and that I must be prepared to subordinate my interest and even to sacrifice my life for its welfare and greatness. Thus, it combines egoistic and altruistic elements. But, though not wholly egoistic, it differs from "love of neighbor" at the crucial points: it is based upon the worth of the group; and it is exclusive of other groups and often hostile to them.

It is only when we realize these contrasts between "love of neighbor," on the one hand, and "erotic love," "friendship," or "love of country," on the other, that we can fully appreciate its *revolutionary* character. Its radical difference from all of these forms of "natural" love is due to the fact that it is based, not upon natural impulse, feeling, or interest of any kind, but upon imitation of the perfect love of God. No one can hope to love his neighbor in this way—or even approximate it—by his own natural will alone. He needs the aid of the divine grace which can bestow upon him the capacity to love. Only by imitating the love of God and by receiving the aid of God's grace can man achieve a kind of love which is qualitatively different from and on a higher level than every kind of natural love.

But this does not mean that love of neighbor is really not the love of a *man* for his neighbor but the love of *God* in and through a man for his neighbor. One of the most dangerous errors in Nygren's treatment of the New Testament idea of "agape" love is to be found at this point. "It is not really man, but God," he says, "who is the subject of this love. . . . It is not that God's love for man and man's love for his neighbor are two different things; they are one thing. Agape is used to denote God's love, not human love; God's love present in the Christian heart."[23]

Statements like these may, of course, be regarded merely as descriptions of a mystical union of the Christian with Christ in which he seems to be possessed completely by the Spirit of Christ and his will seems to be identified with that of Christ as if it were no longer his own. The classic expression of this "Christ mysticism" is St. Paul's expression "in Christ" and his statement, "It is no longer I who live but Christ who lives in me."[24] But there is a difference between such statements as these and Nygren's statement that "the real agent is no longer the ego, but God, or Christ, or God's Agape, or Christ's Spirit."[25] The latter statement seems to imply that the Christian is no longer the agent at all, that his will has been replaced by that of God or Christ or the Spirit. It would rob man of the moral responsibility and freedom that are of the essence of personality and make the commandment to love his neighbor meaningless. Any assertion of the power of the divine grace which does this is based upon a subpersonal or impersonal rather than a personal conception of God's dealings with man and is as dangerous for religion as for ethics. Instead of conceiving of neighbor love as God's love for man "poured out" through him upon his neighbor, we should think of it as man's voluntary and free response, in gratitude and joy, to God's love in Christ.

[23] Ibid., I, pp. 95, 96.
[24] Gal. 2:20.
[25] Nygren, op. cit., I, p. 98.

LOVE OF SELF?

We have spoken of love of God and love of neighbor. We come now to a very controversial question. When Jesus says, "Thou shalt love thy neighbor as thyself," does he imply a third commandment, "Thou shalt love thyself"? The Golden Rule, "As you wish that men would do to you, do so to them,"[1] might seem to favor this view, as it assumes that each person wishes others to be benevolent towards him as he is towards himself. On the other hand, Jesus does not speak explicitly of such a third commandment, and no writer of the New Testament does so. Moreover, the common understanding of Jesus' teaching has been that it is opposed to love of self.

Love of self was accepted as part of the Christian ethic by some early and medieval Christian thinkers. St. Augustine takes it for granted that every man seeks enduring happiness as his highest good. Man's quest for happiness is not successful, Augustine thinks, until he seeks it above himself, until he turns away from the transitory things of time to the eternal Good that is God. Once he has come to know love of God, "amor Dei," he learns that true love of self requires love of God as the Highest Good of the self and that he should love himself "for the sake of God."[2] This way of thinking had a powerful influence on medieval Christian thought. St. Bernard of Clairvaux held that man must begin with love of self but that he can by degrees pass through love of God for the sake of the self to love of God for His own sake and of the self only in Him and for His sake.[3] Now and then the most daring mystics have advocated the complete negation of the self until its individual existence is lost in God. Fenelon believed in a perfect love of God which was wholly disinterested and without regard for the good of the self.[4]

In our own day Nygren maintains that the idea of self-love is alien to the New Testament and must be rejected. "Self-love is man's

[1] Lk. 6:31; Mtt. 7:12.
[2] Augustine, *On Christian Doctrine*, I, Chs. 22, 23, 26.
[3] Bernard, St., *On the Love of God*, New York, Morehouse-Gorham Co., 1950.
[4] Fenelon, *Christian Perfection*, New York, Harpers, 1947.

natural condition," he says; "it is also the basis of the perversion of
his will to evil. Every man knows how by nature he loves himself.
So, runs the commandment, thou shalt love thy neighbor as much
as by nature thou lovest thyself. Thus, so far from love to one's
neighbor presupposing and including self-love, it excludes it and
overcomes it."[5] Nygren is surely right in this contention that the
second commandment simply recognizes the existence of self-love as
a natural fact and commands each man to love his neighbor as by
nature he loves himself. If so, a commandment of self-love, even the
highest and most spiritual, is incompatible with the Christian ethic.

However, the Christian rejection of self-love has sometimes been
misunderstood. Self-contempt is not a requirement of the Christian
ethic. As Brunner points out, the Christian who is conscious that his
sins have been forgiven and that he is "justified" in the sight of God
can and should "accept himself."[6] He should gratefully acknowledge
the worth God has bestowed upon him in creating him and in redeeming him through Christ. His "self-acceptance" should also
bring with it a "self-respect" based upon recognition that one is
an object of God's love and mercy, redeemed from slavery to sin
and death and adopted into sonship. This is why their humility
has never prevented Christians from standing firmly for their convictions and their way of life despite criticism. Indeed, it has not
prevented them from turning the world upside down in order
to bring it into harmony with their ideal of the Kingdom of God.
However, Christian "self-acceptance" and "self-respect" must never
be confused with "self-assertion," the basis of which is self-centeredness or pride in the self rather than faith in God.

What are we to say about the *concern* of the self for its physical
needs and spiritual condition? The Lord's Prayer contains petitions
for "our daily bread" and for forgiveness and deliverance from
temptation. Moreover, sayings like "seek ye first the kingdom of
God and his righteousness" imply that the self is to seek the highest
good above everything else. The question "What doth it profit a
man if he gain the whole world but lose his own life?" assumes a
concern of each man for this highest good.

[5] Nygren, op. cit., I, p. 72.
[6] Brunner, E., *The Divine Imperative,* copyright 1947, by W. L. Jenkins, The
Westminster Press, p. 171.

But if *love of self* is a source of evil which is to be overcome, how can *concern of the self* for the realization of eternal life in the Kingdom of God be legitimate? The clue to this paradox is to be found in Jesus' reply to the request of James and John—or, as Matthew reports it, of their mother—that he would grant them to sit at his right hand and at his left in his glory. "Whoever would be first among you must be your servant, and whoever would be first among you must be slave of all. For the Son of man also came not to be served but to serve, and to give his life a ransom for many."[7] The same paradox is stated in the saying, "Whoever would save his life will lose it, and whoever loses his life for my sake will find it."[8] If we are to understand these words of Jesus, we must distinguish between *love of self* and *love of the good*. In the former, the interest of the self is centered upon itself; its desire is to have its wants satisfied and to cling to its individual life as long as possible. In the latter, the self seeks to transcend itself by devoting itself to the Kingdom of God as the highest good and is prepared to give up anything, even its life, to that end.

This explains how it is possible for a person to be concerned for the Kingdom of God without loving himself. For the object of his desire is not satisfaction of himself but participation in the highest good, eternal life. And the eternal life of the Kingdom is not a "reward" in the sense of something external to this life which compensates one for its difficulties and evils. It is simply a continuation of this life in the form of a fulfillment of its possibilities as they have already begun to show themselves. It is the consummation of the life of love that has already begun. Moreover, the Kingdom is not sought as a private possession of the self; it is a relationship with God and one's neighbors into which one enters, a fellowship in which one forgets his preoccupation with his private interests. Therefore, the aspiration for its life demands the rejection of all self-love. The principle of life "in the flesh" is love of self, aiming at the *satisfaction* of its own desires; the principle of life "in the Spirit" is love of God and love of neighbor leading to the *transcendence* of the self. Every person must choose which of these two opposing

7 Mk. 10:43-45.
8 Mtt. 16:25.

principles he will follow. If he chooses life "in the Spirit," he will do so from love of the Kingdom for its own sake, not from love of his own self. Thus, man's concern for eternal life in the Kingdom is not refined egoism in which love of a higher self replaces love of a lower one; it is his aspiration as a spiritual being to transcend himself by giving himself fully to God and his neighbors.

CHAPTER 4

The Life of Love

THE full meaning of love in the Christian sense reveals itself only when we consider some of its illustrations and applications. It was one of the greatest errors of the legalistic interpretation of Christian ethics that sayings of Jesus which were meant as *illustrations* of the central principle of love were taken as *absolute rules* constituting a "New Law" which supplemented or supplanted the "Old Law" of Moses. These sayings, even when they have the form of commandments, are to be taken as examples of God's will for men in concrete situations rather than as laws to be followed literally. They are, as Brunner says, "paradigms of love."[1] However, the fact that they are illustrations of the principle of love rather than laws does not mean that they are not to be taken seriously; it means only that they are to be taken not as rules prescribing definite acts but as *indications* of the way love will lead one to act in certain kinds of situations.

FORGIVENESS AND RECONCILIATION

It will be remembered that one of the examples we gave of the inwardness of Jesus' conception of morality was his *condemnation of anger*.[2] This condemnation throws a flood of light upon the relation of love to one of the strongest of human passions and to the

[1] Brunner, E., *The Divine Imperative,* copyright 1947, by W. L. Jenkins, The Westminster Press, p. 135.
[2] Mtt. 5:22-24.

strained relations between persons often caused by it. It implies that uncontrolled anger leads to bitter or slighting words which wound another deeply because they violate his sense of dignity, and that the breach of good feeling anger produces between two persons should be overcome as quickly as possible. Thus, it tells us that uncontrolled anger is one of the worst enemies of brotherhood between men. It also suggests that love must restore the harmony that has been broken by anger, because it is only love that can provide the incentive to restore normal relations by reconciliation. A wrong done to another person creates a condition of enmity which is so evil that the removal of it takes precedence even over an act of worship.

There is obviously an inner connection between these sayings about anger and reconciliation and the strong emphasis of Jesus upon *forgiveness*. In the Lord's Prayer, we are told to pray, "And forgive us our debts as we also have forgiven our debtors,"[3] and at the end of the prayer it is explained that "if you forgive men their trespasses, your heavenly Father also will forgive you; but if you do not forgive men their trespasses, neither will your Father forgive your trespasses."[4] The importance of readiness to forgive is stressed again in Jesus' reply to Peter's question, "Lord, how often shall my brother sin against me, and I forgive him? As many as seven times?" Jesus said to him, "I do not say to you seven times, but seventy times seven,"[5] i.e., an unlimited number of times. Following this passage he told a parable about a servant who was released by his lord from a debt of ten thousand talents and promptly proceeded to imprison a fellow servant for a very small debt to himself. Berating him as a wicked servant who should have had mercy on his fellow servant, the lord imprisoned him until he should pay all his debt. "So also my heavenly Father will do to every one of you," Jesus concluded, "if you do not forgive your brother from your heart."[6]

That these injunctions to forgive are closely connected with the commandment to love one's neighbor is clear. Forgiveness is the natural response of one who knows he has been forgiven by God

[3] Mtt. 6:12.
[4] Mtt. 6:14, 15.

[5] Mtt. 18:21, 22.
[6] Mtt. 18:23-35.

from mercy and knows that he should be moved by the same mercy in dealing with others. Jesus makes it clear that the continuation of the divine mercy and forgiveness to a man is conditional upon his showing forgiveness himself. An unforgiving person is not humble enough to be forgiven, however ready God is to forgive him. But this is only one side of forgiveness. If its *ground* is to be sought in the mercy that springs from love, its *aim* is found in the restoration of that fellowship between man and God and between man and man which has been broken by sin. Both persons need to forgive and be forgiven, for both are in some measure to blame. All men are sinful and, bound to one another by the visible and invisible ties of their common life, they are all guilty of hurting one another. Without mutual forgiveness, repeated again and again, the common life of families, communities, and even nations could not be maintained. The wounds its members receive from one another would become too deep to be healed. Forgiveness aims at the restoration of harmony through reconciliation.

Needless to say, *peace* cannot be made between men without reconciliation between those who have wronged one another. "Blessed are the peacemakers," said Jesus, "for they shall be called sons of God."[7] Since the highest condition of men is to be called "sons of God," this beatitude indicates the high worth of those who undertake to restore peace by reconciling men to one another. Though Jesus had in mind primarily those who make peace between individuals, St. Paul interpreted the work of Jesus himself as that of reconciling all humanity to God, and saw in that work an act of God Himself. "God was in Christ reconciling the world to himself." His forgiveness of men's sins was the means of reconciliation, "not counting their trespasses against them, and entrusting to us the message of reconciliation."[8] In the Epistle to the Ephesians, the thought is carried further and this divine act of reconciliation through the forgiveness of sins becomes the basis of reconciliation between two peoples, the Jews and the Gentiles, hitherto estranged from one another.[9]

[7] Mtt. 5:9.
[8] II Cor. 5:19.
[9] Eph. 2:14-16.

Thus, forgiveness is an act of mercy springing from love, and its aim is to restore harmony between men. Men should show forgiveness to one another, and become reconciled to one another in brotherhood. They should also make peace between other men, bringing them to mutual forgiveness and reconciliation. If they do so, they will show themselves sons of God, who reconciled all men to Himself and brought them into peace with one another through the love and forgiveness He manifested on the Cross. Therefore, forgiveness is not only one of the choicest *fruits* of love, it is also one of the most effective *weapons* of love in maintaining, restoring, and extending peace and brotherhood among men.

NON-RESISTANCE AND LOVE OF ENEMIES

One of the most illuminating passages in the Gospels and one of the most difficult for legalists and literalists is that in which Jesus urges his disciples not to resist evildoers. "You have heard that it was said, 'An eye for an eye and a tooth for a tooth.' But I say to you, Do not resist one who is evil. But if any one strikes you on the right cheek, turn to him the other also; and if any one would sue you and take your coat, let him have your cloak as well; and if any one forces you to go one mile, go with him two miles. Give to him who begs from you, and do not refuse him who would borrow from you."[1] This passage in Matthew is followed by the equally famous and provocative one about love of one's enemy. "You have heard that it was said, 'You shall love your neighbor and hate your enemy.' But I say to you, Love your enemies and pray for those who persecute you, . . ."[2]

There are passages with a similar meaning in other books of the New Testament and some of them may be echoes of Jesus' sayings. For example, St. Paul writes to the Corinthians, "To have lawsuits at all with one another is defeat for you. Why not rather suffer wrong? Why not rather be defrauded?"[3] He writes to the Romans, "Repay no one evil for evil, but take thought for what is noble in

[1] Mtt. 5:38.
[2] Mtt. 5:43-44; cf. Lk. 6:27-30.
[3] I Cor. 6:7.

the sight of all. . . . Do not be overcome by evil, but overcome evil with good."[4] The author of the First Epistle of Peter writes, "Do not return evil for evil or reviling for reviling; but on the contrary bless, for to this you have been called, that you may obtain a blessing."[5]

The first thing we should notice about the saying, "Do not resist one who is evil," is that it is opposed to the Old Testament law permitting retaliation for an injury but limiting it to the equivalent of the injury, "An eye for an eye, and a tooth for a tooth."[6] The fact that Luke does not represent Jesus as referring to the Law of Moses casts some doubt upon the authenticity of this and other contrasts to the Law found in Matthew 5. Nevertheless, the contrast gives us an insight into Jesus' meaning. Moreover, when the saying is read in the light of the examples that follow, it takes on a wider meaning. All three of the examples describe ways one should respond to an evil done to him by another. If one is struck on the right cheek, sued for his coat, or forced to go one mile, he should retaliate not "in kind" but "in reverse," i.e., he should not resist the evil but voluntarily take upon himself a greater one. The absurdity of a literalistic interpretation of Jesus' teaching is well illustrated by these examples. What is one to do if the aggressor is not content to strike both cheeks but insists also upon kicking one or knocking one down? What should one do if, having taken one's coat and one's cloak, a person enters one's house and takes all of one's clothes? What ought one to do if, after he has gone the second mile, an attempt is made to force him into permanent servitude?

On the other hand, if these sayings are taken as illustrations of the way one should react to an injury inflicted upon him, they are very illuminating. As we have seen, love does not depend upon the worth of the neighbor or upon his return of one's love. Since it is an expression of an unchanging disposition of the self, it should not vary according to differences of attitude or conduct among those who are to be loved. Like God's love, it is to be given to the evil as well as to the good. When Jesus says, "Do not resist one who is

[4] Rom. 12:17, 21.
[5] I Pet. 3:9.
[6] Ex. 21:24; Lev. 24:20; Deut. 19:21.

evil," therefore, he means that we are to continue to love a person even when he does us harm and that we are to show our love not merely by enduring the injury silently but also by actively seeking to fulfill his needs. When he says, "Love your enemies," he is only giving an extreme example of the inclusiveness of this love. Love of one's enemies provides the acid test of whether one's love is a perfect love like God's or is restricted to those whom it is easy to love.

Of course, Jesus is aware that to ask men to abstain from avenging themselves for injuries and to love their enemies is to ask of them something that is not "natural." He makes it clear that he is not asking his disciples to do only what most men are already able and willing to do. Even taxgatherers, he says, are willing to love those who love them and even Gentiles salute their brethren. What he is asking is that we should do "more than others," that we should be "perfect" in our love.

The practical difficulties involved in these passages must not blind us to the profound psychological insight and practical wisdom in them. St. Paul seems to have seen this when he wrote, "Do not be overcome by evil, but overcome evil with good." It is well known that in personal relationships the natural tendency to return evil for evil both aggravates the original evil and adds another evil to it. On the other hand, a refusal to retaliate for an insult or injury often prevents the fire of rage from spreading and may even put it out. If the refusal to return evil for evil is accompanied by a positive and active effort to demonstrate one's good will to the evildoer, it is likely to be still more effective. The person who tries to *get* what he wants at the expense of others may be shamed by one who is willing to *give* as much as he can. This may be what St. Paul has in mind when he says that by giving food or drink to our enemy we "will heap burning coals upon his head."

What is the explanation of this? Insults and injuries are often due to an aggressiveness which springs from insecurity and fear. Modern psychoanalysis has shown how the sense of inferiority that haunts men often arises from causes forgotten long ago and may lead to compensatory acts of self-assertion. Moreover, competition with one's fellows for success and approval begins in early youth and encourages self-assertion. Thus, personal and social causes combine to produce anxiety or insecurity and the aggressiveness in which it expresses itself. Society defends its own unity and the welfare of its members against this aggressiveness by a complex system of rights enforced by sanctions of various kinds. We are all taught to defend the rights guaranteed to us by this system against the encroachments of others. In this way, egoism is kept within bounds by justice.

But the mere defense of our rights against the encroachments of others does little or nothing to root out the aggressive impulses in them or in ourselves. Indeed, the defense of our rights is likely to appear to those who encroach upon them as an act of self-assertiveness on our part. Aggressive egoism is then pitted against defensive egoism. Moreover, we are likely to pass from a defense of our rights to an exaggerated assertion of them. Since self-assertiveness of others is then matched by our own, they can justify their injustice to us by our injustice to them. For the assertion of one's "rights" is likely to lead one to go beyond his rights and wrong or defraud others of theirs. Is it not better to break out of this vicious circle of "claims" and "counterclaims," self-assertion and self-defense? The only way to do so is to rise above the level of ordinary justice, at which one asserts his rights and defends himself against wrongs, to the level of love. Only in this way does one have a chance to change the inner attitude of the evildoer rather than merely check the external expressions of that attitude, to remove his sense of insecurity and bitterness by good will rather than oppose and perhaps deepen it by striking back.

There are three different kinds of persons: those who seek to get as much and give as little as possible; those who are prepared to give as much as but no more than they get; and those who are willing to give as much as they can without concern for what they get. The evildoers about whom Jesus is speaking belong, of course, to the first group. What he is saying is that they will continue to be evildoers and to provoke others to evildoing so long as they are dealt with only by those of the second group whose defense of their rights has an element of egoism in it. Only if they have the good fortune to encounter persons of the third kind who will give them more than their rights and will continue to show them good will despite their wrongdoing is there any likelihood of transforming them from enemies into friends of others.

The emphasis of Jesus is obviously upon active, generous treatment of evildoers rather than passive, dogged endurance of the injuries inflicted by them. This is shown not only by the three examples he gives of the way to deal with evildoers, but also by the saying that follows, "Give to him who begs from you, and do not refuse him who would borrow from you."[7] A literalistic interpretation here, too, would lead to absurdity. To give to every beggar and lend to every borrower would encourage idleness in others and land oneself in bankruptcy. But if we do not interpret the saying as a law or rule, it is a fine expression of the spirit of kindness and generosity generated by love. When Jesus sent forth his disciples to preach, heal, and exorcise demons, he said to them, "Freely ye have received, freely give."[8] To the rich man who asked him the way to eternal life, he said, "Go, sell what you have, and give to the poor, and you will have treasure in heaven; and come, follow me."[9] These sayings show that love requires of us a kind of *giving* that is rare. It is giving that is based upon such a deep sensitiveness to the needs of others that one will wish to give as much rather than as little as he can. It is giving that is made possible by a complete absence of anxiety about our own needs. The kind of person who is capable of not returning evil for evil is the kind of person who has learned to give with abandon both of his possessions and of himself.

We have attempted to show that non-resistance to evildoers and love of enemies point the way to a transformation of them. However, the ground on which Jesus justifies such conduct is not good consequences of this sort but the will of God that His children should manifest a perfect love like His own. It would seem to follow that non-resistance is demanded of us whether or not it succeeds in converting the evildoer and that love of the enemy is required whether or not it disarms him. Experience shows that the good consequences we have described do not always follow non-resistance

[7] Mtt. 5:42.
[8] Mtt. 10:8 (A.V.).
[9] Mk. 10:21.

and love of enemies. The evildoer or enemy may not respond to love by abandoning his aggressiveness; he may even be encouraged to become more aggressive. This raises an important question: Is Jesus, after all, a literalist with respect to these injunctions, holding that we must obey them to the letter whatever the consequences for the self or for society? Such a literal interpretation of the sayings under discussion would imply a legalistic view of Jesus' teachings as a whole. But Jesus is not laying down laws; he is declaring the *absolute will* of God for men, describing the life that would manifest perfect love to all men. He disregards the *limitations* imposed by the necessities of society or the imperfections of individuals. This does not mean that his teaching as such is impractical. It does mean, however, that we must apply it in such a way as to take into account the limitations of our social situation and human nature. This will make painful decisions, compromises, and partial failures inevitable under the imperfect conditions of human life.

But one thing is certain: Jesus is not describing the way men *will* live at some future time when the Kingdom has fully come and goodness has triumphed over evil; he is indicating the way they must try to live *now*. He is talking about a time when evil is powerful and aggressive against the good. It may be necessary in applying his absolutistic and perfectionistic principles to "compromise" with the necessities imposed by our human situation. But Christians cannot accept the view that these principles are "irrevelant" to the conditions of human existence here and now. They must, each in his own situation, seek to apply them as best they can.

"JUDGE NOT . . ."

We have been considering the attitude of love towards those with whom we are angry, from whom we have been estranged, who have insulted or injured us, or who are our enemies. Another illustration of the attitude of love towards those we consider evil in some way is presented in the well-known words of Jesus about *judging* others. "Judge not, that you be not judged," he says. "For with the judgment you pronounce you will be judged, and the measure you give will be the measure you get."[1] Jesus probably had in mind the kind of judging that results from censoriousness.

The habit of sitting in judgment upon others is due, on the one hand, to this censoriousness which is an expression of a merciless and unforgiving attitude, and, on the other hand, to the blind complacency which overlooks one's own sins.[2] The fact that it leads one to arrogate to himself the function of judging which belongs to God alone indicates that its deepest root is *pride*. It is an expression of the egoism that exalts the self at the cost of depreciating others.

What are the *consequences* of judging others? The most obvious is the *exclusion* of those we judge from fellowship with us. As we have seen, the Pharisees differed from Jesus most sharply at this point, withdrawing themselves from intercourse with sinners because of their contempt for them and their fear of being defiled by them. The fundamental principle of their religion was that God would reward the righteous and punish the wicked; the fundamental assumption of their morality was that every man should preserve and increase his own righteousness. Thus, their treatment of those who did not keep the letter of the Law was dictated by strict justice rather than mercy, and they made virtual outcasts out of them.

Another effect of judging others is that men do little or nothing to *help* those they judge to be wicked or worthless. In condemning others, one absolves oneself from all responsibility for them. One applies a law or standard to their conduct, finds them wanting when measured by it, and does not notice good qualities and possibilities they may possess because one is not looking for them. Consequently, one regards them as hopeless and worthy of help from no one.

After excluding from fellowship and denying help to those he judges, the "righteous" man begins to *insult* and *persecute* them. At the best, he treats them with contempt as members of an inferior group; at the worst, he uses any kind of power at his disposal to force them to do and say what they should.

"Judging" is one of the great dangers of legalistic religion and morality. Legalism encourages the illusion that men can be divided into two classes, the "good" and the "bad," the "clean" and the "un-

[1] Mtt. 7:1, 2.
[2] Mtt. 7:3-5; Lk. 6:41-42.

clean," on the basis of their obedience or disobedience to a code of laws. As a result, it makes almost inevitable a self-righteous, though often unconscious, hypocrisy on the part of the "good"; and it dooms the "bad," the "sinners" to the despair of the despised and rejected. Such a classification of men is not only too simple; it is also unjust because it judges by human standards of good and evil. Above all, it is merciless because it builds up barriers that prevent men from loving many of their neighbors. Christ came not to condemn the world but to save it.[3] Those who seek to follow him must do likewise, leaving the judgment of others to God from whom no secrets are hidden and whose standards of judgment alone are truly just.

It is to be noted that the judgment against which Jesus warns is personal judgment and has nothing to do with the judgment rendered in a court of law. A literal interpretation of the words "judge not" led Tolstoy to condemn every attempt of judges and juries to pass judgment upon their fellows in courts of law. But legal judgment of this kind need not and should not imply any claim to moral superiority of the judge over the judged, since the judge is only applying the law of the state. The judge does not—or should not—claim to be passing a final or ultimate judgment, even in the case of the most hardened criminal. He is simply an instrument of society for the protection of its citizens, and may be well aware that others bear a large share of responsibility for the evil done by the criminal. However, a problem is raised by the fact that the judge in a court of law is supposedly motivated by justice rather than love, and we shall have to consider later the relation of justice to love.

SERVICE AND GREATNESS

We have seen that love of neighbor is not a sentimental but a practical thing. "Let your light so shine before men," said Jesus, "that they may see your good works and give glory to your Father who is in heaven."[4] What is the nature of these "good works"? Obviously, they consist of deeds of *service* to others. But we must under-

[3] Jo. 3:17.
[4] Mtt. 5:16.

stand the term "service" in a broad sense. It has sometimes been held
that neighbor love meant for Jesus merely the service of men's immediate, physical needs. Consequently, it has been said, Christian
love enables the weak to survive by bringing relief to their physical
needs; it brings to all a measure of simple happiness by satisfying
their basic desires; but it does little or nothing for the development
of the spiritual capacities and the attainment of a higher type of
man. This criticism is associated especially with the name of
Nietzsche, but it is made in a somewhat different form by as careful a thinker as Nicolai Hartmann in his analysis of "brotherly
love." In effect, Hartmann says that Christian love serves indiscrimi-
nately the immediate needs of all men alike and thus merely maintains the necessary conditions of life in the present.[5] It is essential,
he thinks, to supplement it by what Nietzsche called "love of the
remote," which is willing to look beyond the needs of the many
in the present to the possibilities of a higher kind of life in the
future.

Doubtless this criticism is based upon the fact that the service of
elementary, physical needs is often used by Jesus to illustrate the
practical character of neighbor love. In the parable of the Good
Samaritan and in the description of the separation of the sheep
from the goats at the Last Judgment, the test of goodness is whether
one satisfied the needs of wounded, sick, hungry, or thirsty people.
Moreover, Jesus spent much of his own time in healing men's bodies.
Consequently, no Christian can afford to depreciate the importance
of fulfilling elementary human needs. Indeed, the teaching and example of Jesus have been the inspiration for the building of hospitals
for the sick, the reform of prisons, the provision of food for the
poor, the sending of medical and agricultural missionaries to distant
lands, and the gigantic efforts of relief and rehabilitation for war-
torn peoples. Furthermore, modern Christians have discovered that
spiritual life and growth are in a measure dependent upon physical
health, decent housing, and other external conditions. The importance of this for economic and social reform is obvious. Thus, it is

[5] Hartmann, N., *Ethics,* New York, Macmillan, 1932, Vol. 2, Ch. XXX, sec. (e).

no accident that the service of *physical needs,* upon which life and all its values depend, has played such a large part in Christian history.

But it would be a great mistake to suppose that this is the only form of service required by love of neighbor. After all, the primary aim of Jesus was not the healing of men's bodies or the improvement of their economic condition, but their liberation from sin and suffering into a fuller life. That he expected his disciples to follow his example in this respect is shown by one of his most beautiful sayings. "When he saw the crowds, he had compassion for them," says Matthew, "because they were harassed and helpless, like sheep without a shepherd. Then he said to his disciples, 'The harvest is plentiful, but the laborers are few; pray therefore the Lord of the harvest to send out laborers into his harvest.' "[6] Following this he sent out the twelve to preach the coming of the Kingdom, as well as to heal the sick and cast out demons.[7] In the parable of the sower, the preaching of the word of the Kingdom is compared to the sowing of seed, some of which "fell into good soil and brought forth grain, growing up and increasing and yielding thirtyfold and sixtyfold and a hundredfold."[8]

The proclamation of the Good News of the Kingdom is not the only kind of service to the higher *spiritual needs* of men in the New Testament. In the Gospels, a number of occasions are described in which Jesus sought to help individuals by counsel, warning, or otherwise. He counselled the rich man to sell all he had and give to the poor and follow him.[9] He stayed with the tax collector Zacchaeus, inspired him to give half of his goods to the poor and restore fourfold to those he had defrauded, and thus brought salvation to his house.[10] Moreover, he obviously conceived his mission as including the salvation of the nation as well as the individual. He openly challenged the Scribes and Pharisees, the religious leaders of the people; he rode into Jerusalem at the time of the Passover and drove out the moneychangers from the Temple; and in the parable of the vineyard he warned the religious leaders that because of their

[6] Mtt. 9:36-38.
[7] Mtt. 10:5-8.
[8] Mk. 4:2-8.

[9] Mk. 10:17-22.
[10] Lk. 19:1-10.

abuse of their authority God would take it away from them and give it to others. Thus, like the prophets before him, Jesus sought a reformation of the religious and moral foundations of the whole national life.

By his teaching and even more by his example, therefore, Jesus demonstrates that we are not only to satisfy the physical and immediate needs of men but also to further their spiritual and ultimate welfare. The importance of service of every kind as an expression of love is best indicated by the fact that Jesus makes willingness to serve others and to suffer in their behalf the criterion of *greatness* and *leadership*. This is the meaning of his question to James and John when they asked for positions of pre-eminence in the coming Kingdom: "Are you able to drink the cup that I drink, or to be baptized with the baptism with which I am baptized?"[11] He is referring, of course, to the "cup" and the "baptism" of his coming suffering for men. He says to the disciples afterwards: "You know that those who are supposed to rule over the Gentiles lord it over them, and their great men exercise authority over them. But it shall not be so among you; but whoever would be great among you must be your servant, and whoever would be first among you must be slave of all. For the Son of man also came not to be served but to serve, and to give his life as a ransom for many."[12] On another occasion, when the disciples were discussing with one another which was the greatest, he said to them, "If any one would be first, he must be last of all and servant of all."[13] For the true greatness which is based upon service is impossible without humility.

It is not too much to say that this interpretation of leadership and greatness in terms of service and suffering rather than of domination wrought a revolution in men's thinking which has been the basis of much that is best in Western political and social life. It has deflated the pretensions of the ruthless militarist, the political dictator, the ecclesiastical prince, and, on a smaller scale, the petty local tyrant. On the other hand, it has given dignity to the quiet, undramatic service of the mother, the teacher, the nurse, the doctor,

[11] Mk. 10:38.
[12] Mk. 10:42-45.
[13] Mk. 9:35.

the minister, the missionary, and the public servant. It has inspired reformation of the Church and revolution in the state when a system has developed that has permitted men to lord it over their brothers rather than serve them. It has provided democracy with its conception of the ideal leader as one who serves the will of the people rather than imposes his own will upon them. Above all, it has brought about a genuine transvaluation of values in the Western world as a result of which the humility of the will to serve has supplanted the egoism of the will to power as the highest ideal of character.

THE BEATITUDES

It is obvious that only a person who possesses certain *qualities* and *dispositions* is capable of following the life of love as we have described it. In the Beatitudes these qualities and dispositions are indicated by Jesus. They are intelligible only as manifestations of the transvaluation of values we have just mentioned.

The form of the Beatitudes in Luke differs considerably from that in Matthew, and many New Testament scholars believe that it is closer to the original words of Jesus. Luke lists only four Beatitudes and follows these with a list of four corresponding woes. In the opinion of most men, poverty, hunger, weeping, and being hated, excluded, and reviled by others bring sorrow; but those who experience them are declared by Jesus to be blessed. In the opinion of the world, riches, satiety, laughter, and the good opinion of men bring happiness; but those who experience them have already received their happiness and will have to hunger, mourn, and weep in the future. This "reversal of fortunes," this "turning of the tables" is in the tradition of the Hebrew prophets. The prophets predicted that rich, powerful, and wicked men and nations would meet retribution, while the poor, weak, and righteous would be exalted. New Testament scholars have pointed out that the "people of the land" with whom Jesus associated regarded poverty, hunger, suffering, and persecution at the hands of the wicked and mighty as the usual lot of the righteous. This suggests that the reason "the poor" are blessed is not merely that they are poor in this world's goods, but that they are also "poor in spirit" or humble, while the rich are miserable because they are proud and deluded by their temporary prosperity. Those who "hunger" are blessed, not because of their lack of food, but because they also "hunger and thirst after righteousness," while those who eat and drink their fill are foolishly satisfied with their moral condition.[1] Those whom men "hate," "exclude," and "revile" (Luke) are the same as those who are "persecuted for righteousness' sake" and "on my account" (Matthew), i.e., they suffer for their religious and moral faithfulness.

Matthew also lists among the blessed the "meek," the "merciful," the "pure in heart," and the "peacemakers," describing further the moral and spiritual qualities that are necessary for members of the Kingdom. With the exception of purity of heart, these are primarily qualities and attitudes of the blessed man in relation to other men. We have already discussed the significance of *peacemaking* in Jesus' teaching. The *meek* man is the humble and gentle man. One who compares himself with the holiness of God loses the pride and aggressiveness that may easily be generated by comparing himself with his fellows. The radical character of Jesus' teaching is nowhere more evident than here. "Now, to the ordinary mind," Robinson says, "it is the aggressive, the self-confident, the self-asserting, the self-advertising who win their way in the world and gain the earth for themselves. The 'humble' man is in all respects the exact opposite of this, and it is he who, as Jesus sees, will ultimately 'inherit the earth.' The capacity for submissive endurance will in the long run prevail over dominant aggressiveness."[2] *Mercy* is closely associated with humility. Only the humble are able to abstain from judging others and to forgive injuries done to themselves. Only the humble have

---

[1] T. W. Manson, *The Mission and Message of Jesus*, New York, Dutton, 1938. "In the Judaism of the last two centuries B.C.," he says, "the term (poor) was practically a synonym for Hasid, i.e. 'saintly' or 'pious' in the best sense. . . . The use of the word 'poor' in this way goes back to the days of the Seleucid rule in Palestine. Then it was the poor above all who remained faithful to their religion and the Law. The well-to-do upperclasses in Jerusalem allowed themselves to be tainted with heathenism. Hence 'rich' tends to mean 'worldly' and 'irreligious,' and 'poor' the opposite. . . . In Matthew the paraphrase 'poor in spirit' is an attempt to make this fact clear."
[2] Robinson, T. H., *The Moffatt New Testament Commentary: The Gospel of Matthew*, New York, Harpers, p. 29.

overcome egoism enough to manifest in a practical way compassion for all human need. Jesus means by "mercy" far more than the sentiment of pity; he means the natural expression of pity in practical action. It is a costly virtue, not a sporadic feeling that costs nothing. Finally, "purity in heart" is a necessary condition of fellowship with God. It means "a concentration of the whole personality on God, the exclusion of everything else. It is only as the spiritual window is kept clean that a distinct vision of God can be won."[3]

SEX, MARRIAGE, AND THE FAMILY

Jesus' teaching concerning the relations between man and woman illustrates the transforming effect of neighbor love upon natural love. "You have heard that it was said, 'You shall not commit adultery.' But I say to you that every one who looks at a woman lustfully has already committed adultery with her in his heart."[1] This saying is a good example of the "inwardness" of Jesus' conception of goodness. Many regard sexual desire as a natural force beyond the power of the will to control. Does Jesus really mean that it is possible to suppress all sexual desire outside of marriage? Or is he referring, not to an occasional involuntary and transitory sexual impulse, but to the deliberate and prolonged sexual desire which keeps one in a state of excitement? In any case, he condemns lust as evil in itself, even when it does not lead to actual adultery. Why is he so severe on this point?

His condemnation of divorce gives us a clue to the answer. "It was also said, 'Whoever divorces his wife, let him give her a certificate of divorce.' But I say to you that every one who divorces his wife, except on the ground of unchastity, makes her an adulteress; and whoever marries a divorced woman commits adultery."[2] According to Mark[3] and Luke[4] the exception of unchastity allowed in this passage in Matthew is not made. Most New Testament scholars agree that the stricter form of the saying in Mark and Luke is probably the authentic one. Jesus does not normally qualify the hard

[3] Ibid., p. 31.   [3] Mk. 10:11.
[1] Mtt. 5:27-28.   [4] Lk. 16:18.
[2] Mtt. 5:31-32.

demands of his perfectionistic ethic to make them practical for our weak human nature.

Divorce was easy for the husband in Jesus' time. Some of the rabbis went far in justifying it, e.g., Hillel, though others were more strict, e.g., Shammai. But while Moses "permitted" divorce, Jesus says, he did so because of "your hardness of heart." "But from the beginning of creation, 'God made them male and female.' 'For this reason a man shall leave his father and mother and be joined to his wife, and the two shall become one' (or 'one flesh'). So they are no longer two but one. What therefore God has joined together, let not man put asunder."[5] Why does Jesus interpret the passages he quotes from Genesis as requiring permanent monogamous marriage without the possibility of divorce? Perhaps the reason is that divorce brings an evil into the life of a woman which is as grievous as adultery, since it constitutes a betrayal of trust and destroys a vital relationship that has become an integral part of her being. It is a violation of her right to be treated as a person, as an end rather than as a mere means to the end of another. As such, it is wholly incompatible with love of neighbor.

Jesus' saying about lust should be read in the light of this high ideal of marriage. Sexual desire is an aspect of the love between a man and a woman which normally gives rise to marriage with its sharing of the whole of life. When it is separated from love, it loses its spiritual and personal meaning. It treats a member of the other sex, not as a person to be respected as an end, but as an animal to be used as a means to one's own satisfaction.

Jesus' strong defense of permanent monogamous marriage and his condemnation of divorce indicate how far he was from the ascetic Christianity which has treated marriage as a state inferior to celibacy and permitted it only as a remedy for sin. At the same time, there is not a trace in Jesus' teaching of the family egoism which centers the interest of a family in itself, and shuts it off from the community as a whole. More than that, Jesus makes it very clear, by personal example and by teaching, that a man must never allow his family to become the supreme object of his loyalty and devotion. There are several incidents and sayings in the Gospels

[5] Mk. 10:6-9; cf. Mtt. 19:3-9.

which stress the necessity of breaking family ties when they interfere with the wider and higher requirements of the Kingdom. Mark
has recorded what may have been a tragic break of Jesus with
his own family for this reason. When his mother and his brothers
came to him and called him, "A crowd was sitting about him; and
they said to him, 'Your mother and your brothers are outside, asking
for you.' And he replied 'Who are my mother and my brothers?'
And looking around on those who sat about him, he said, 'Here are
my mother and my brothers. Whoever does the will of God is my
brother, and sister, and mother.' "[6]

In any case, his teaching is explicit in recognizing the inevitability
of division within a family over the ultimate issues of life. "Do not
think," he said, "that I have come to bring peace on earth; I have
not come to bring peace, but a sword. For I have come to set a man
against his father, and a daughter against her mother, and a daugh-
ter-in-law against her mother-in-law; and a man's foes will be those
of his own household."[7] Despite his anticipation of these tragic
results of family division and treachery following the preaching of
the Kingdom, Jesus does not hesitate to demand loyalty to himself
above loyalty to family. "He who loves father or mother more than
me is not worthy of me; and he who loves son or daughter more
than me is not worthy of me; and he who does not take his cross
and follow me is not worthy of me. He who finds his life will lose
it, and he who loses his life for my sake will find it."[8]

He was well aware of the separation, suffering, and sacrifice these
demands would cause. But the claims of the Kingdom were supreme. It was the pearl of great price to buy which one must be
ready to sell all he had. One must "seek *first* His Kingdom and His
righteousness." The suffering and sacrifice in the family, he implies,
will be justified by the result: an extension of the personal love and
relationships of the family to the larger fellowship which consists of
all the members of the Kingdom. All sons of the Heavenly Father
will become brothers of one another. This is doubtless the meaning
of the saying already mentioned: "Here are my mother and my

---

[6] Mk. 3:31-35; cf. Mtt. 12:46-50; Lk. 8:19-21.
[7] Mtt. 10:34.
[8] Mtt. 10:37-39.

brothers! Whoever does the will of God is my brother, and sister, and mother."[9]

The ethic of Jesus has sometimes been called a "family ethic." Love of neighbor which is all-inclusive and whole-hearted requires an extension to all men of the kind of love normally found only between the members of a family. Neighbor love means brotherly love for every man. The egoism of the family is to be broken down and the unselfish love that is normally confined within its limits is to flow forth to the family of all mankind. That Jesus saw the broader implications of this principle is clear from the parable of the Good Samaritan. The implication of the principle that the circle of the family and the neighborhood is to be extended without limit is that love can and should transcend all barriers, including those between races and nations. "There is neither Jew nor Greek," Paul says, "there is neither slave nor free, there is neither male nor female; for you are all one in Christ Jesus."[10] Love of neighbor must break down every obstacle to fellowship set up by the limited and "closed" societies of men; its goal is to create a universal and "open" community in which all will be brothers.

There is a final implication of Jesus' teaching about marriage and the family: love of neighbor does not negate, it preserves and transforms, natural love. Nygren shows a tendency to exalt "agape" over "eros" by treating it as supernatural and divorcing it from natural love. This antithesis between love of neighbor and natural love is actually based, not upon the teaching of the New Testament, but upon Nygren's sharp separation of grace and nature. Divine grace seems to come into human nature as into something wholly worthless and separated from the divine. Therefore, "agape" is regarded as something wholly divine poured from above into the human self and through it as through a channel upon the neighbor. "Eros," natural love, is completely opposed to it; it is "egocentric" while "agape" is "self-giving." It would seem to follow from this that "agape" must destroy or exclude natural love in all its forms.

In the Gospels, on the other hand, erotic love becomes the basis of permanent monogamous marriage when it is the physical expres-

9 Mk. 3:34.
10 Gal. 3:28.

sion of a genuinely personal love between man and woman. As a result, marital love is not only compatible with, it can become a powerful ally of, love of neighbor. Similarly, as we have seen, the parental, filial, and brotherly love of the family is purified of egoistic elements when it is extended to those outside the family and is transformed into one of the strongest forces for the creation of a wider community. Thus, sexual love and family love, both forms of natural love, are not negated but fulfilled when they are taken up into the life of Christian love. Love of neighbor is not an unnatural thing for man, at war with all of his natural affections. The spiritual life consisting of love of God and love of neighbor is not something that can grow only by renouncing all the natural joys of ordinary human existence. It transforms rather than destroys the affections of our animal and social existence.

EARTHLY OR HEAVENLY TREASURE

It has always been recognized that the Christian ethic is a *spiritual* ethic. It is based upon the profound conviction of the primacy of spiritual over material and worldly interests. This conviction does not spring from a dualistic view of the relation of soul and body such as that of Plato's *Phaedo* or Plotinus. Jesus shared the Hebraic view that the material world and its resources, including the human body and its desires, are the creation of God and as such are good. Therefore, the spiritual life is developed, not by detachment from the world and subjugation of the body, but by the proper use of the world and the body for the higher ends of the Kingdom. While material things are not evil, however, they are definitely to be subordinated to the welfare of the soul, and the life of the body in time may have to be sacrificed for eternal life. Therefore, one must choose, once and for all, between God and Mammon. "No one can serve two masters; for either he will hate the one and love the other, or he will be devoted to the one and despise the other. You cannot serve God and Mammon."[1]

All of Jesus' sayings about *possessions* must be read in the light of this principle of the primacy of the spiritual. Probably the most

[1] Mtt. 6:24.

famous of them is the saying to his disciples after the refusal of a
rich man to take his counsel to give all he had to the poor and to
follow him. "How hard it will be," said Jesus, "for those who have
riches to enter the kingdom of God! . . . It is easier for a camel
to go through the eye of a needle than for a rich man to enter the
kingdom of God."[2] Moreover, sayings like "Woe to you that are
rich" are unequivocal warnings against wealth. The most impressive
passages, however, are those in which Jesus reveals the nature of
the danger. The warning against anxiety over food and clothing is
one of these. "Do not lay up for yourselves treasures on earth. . . ,"
says Jesus; "but lay up for yourselves treasures in heaven . . . for
where your treasure is, there will your heart be also."[3] This passage
indicates that Jesus saw in anxiety about physical needs a temptation to become completely absorbed in material things and to forget
spiritual values altogether. Such anxiety is unnecessary, since God
can be trusted to provide for the body and its needs. It is also futile,
since earthly treasure may be lost or destroyed and can never bring
security. Thus anxiety about possessions *distracts* one from a single-
minded concern for the Kingdom and its righteousness and sacrifices spiritual values that endure to material values that pass away.

But that is not all. Riches tempt men into a life of luxury and
pleasure which makes them *callous* to the need of those near them.
Thus, the rich man who was clothed in purple and fine linen and
who feasted sumptuously every day was indifferent to the misery
and need of the poor man at his gate.[4] His luxury insulated him
from contact with the suffering of others. Moreover, wealth makes
men *covetous* and produces strife among them. Thus, when a man
said to Jesus, "Teacher, bid my brother divide the inheritance with
me," he replied, "Man, who made me a judge or divider over you?"
and added, "Take heed, and beware of all covetousness; for a man's
life does not consist in the abundance of his possessions."[5] The
parable of the Rich Fool which follows this incident drives home a
further point: the utter *folly* of complacency over material things
coupled with disregard of the soul, since death may at any time
separate us from the former and leave us with the latter alone.

[2] Mk. 10:23-25.
[3] Mtt. 6:19-21.

[4] Lk. 16:19 ff.
[5] Lk. 12:13-15.

"But God said to him, 'Fool! This night your soul is required of you; and the things you have prepared, whose will they be?' So is he who lays up treasure for himself, and is not rich toward God."[6]

Thus, Jesus teaches that anxiety or insecurity which leads to the feverish pursuit of wealth is unnecessary and useless; that preoccupation with transitory material values excludes concern for heavenly or spiritual ones that endure; that riches are the source of callousness to the need of others; that covetousness for riches brings about disunity and strife between those who should love one another; and that it is supreme folly to lavish all one's care on that which is wholly external to the self and may be taken away from it at any moment. This is the *negative* side of his teaching about possessions.

The *positive* side is best expressed in the saying, "Seek first his kingdom and his righteousness, and all these things shall be yours as well." This is simply a way of saying that men should put first things first; if they do, they will find that whatever they need to meet their physical wants will be provided. It does not mean, as has sometimes been said, that they are to do nothing to provide for those wants themselves but are to wait passively for God to do everything for them. The birds of the air "neither sow nor reap nor gather into barns";[7] but, as Robinson says, "few men have to work as hard for their living as the average sparrow."[8] But they are not to make their primary aim in life the satisfaction of physical needs.

In addition, Jesus teaches that men are to regard material things as a trust and are to be faithful in the use of them. "He who is faithful in a very little is faithful also in much," he says; "and he who is dishonest in a very little is dishonest also in much. If then you have not been faithful in the unrighteous mammon, who will entrust to you the true riches? And if you have not been faithful in that which is another's, who will give you that which is your own?"[9] By "the unrighteous mammon" Jesus seems to mean simply "worldly goods." His point is that these are to be used in the service of God and that men are tested by the use they make of them. The parable of the talents,[10] which describes the way in which one of

---

[6] Lk. 12:20, 21.
[7] Mtt. 6:26.
[8] Robinson, op. cit., p. 59.

[9] Lk. 16:10-12.
[10] Mtt. 25:14-30.

the servants of a master added nothing to the money entrusted to him, also warns that neglect of opportunity will be punished by the deprivation of it. Thus, Jesus recognizes not only that material things are necessary, but also that through their proper use an opportunity is provided for spiritual development.

However, this should not be taken as a justification for the opinion that "Jesus sees no danger in wealth but only in the wrong use of it." This opinion is a dangerous half truth, which has furnished an excuse to many worldly Christians to disregard Jesus' plain and severe warnings against the *dangers* of wealth. Of course, there is no evil in material things as such; the evil lies in the inversion of values by which material things are made primary rather than secondary. But there is a strong tendency for material values to become primary and even to crowd out spiritual values altogether, and it was this side of the truth which was stressed most by Jesus. There are far more sayings about the dangers of wealth than about the opportunities it offers. Modern Christians try to forget that their Master said, "Woe to you that are rich." In the light of our earlier interpretation of the saying, "Blessed are the poor," it is unlikely that Jesus meant to idealize poverty as such. But when one considers the tendency of sense-bound and proud man to be dazzled by near and tangible goods and to be blind to remote and intangible ones, one must conclude that his warnings against the dangers of wealth are among the most valuable of his teachings.

CHAPTER 5

The Ethics of St. Paul

AT THE turn of the century many Biblical scholars and Liberal theologians sharply contrasted the teachings of St. Paul with those of Jesus. Biblical scholars had tried to rid themselves of all dogmas about Jesus derived from traditional creeds and theologies and to rediscover his humanity. In the letters of Paul, on the other hand, the human Jesus of history seemed to be supplanted by Christ the Risen Lord. He was no longer the herald of the Kingdom; he was the Lord sent by God to save men from their sins. Christians were urged not so much to follow his teaching as to unite themselves with him and his Spirit. Paul seemed to have substituted the Christ of faith for the Jesus of history; the Church for the Kingdom; and life in the Spirit for moral effort in the world.

Few reputable Biblical scholars or theologians today would draw such a sharp contrast between Jesus and Paul. The tendency now is to emphasize the fundamental unity rather than the differences between them. Indeed, in some circles it is declared that the religion *about* Christ rather than the religion *of* Jesus is the essence of Christianity. This remarkable change of attitude towards Paul makes it imperative for us to come to grips with his ethical teaching. Upon our decision with respect to the validity of his general position will depend our whole interpretation of the nature of Christian ethics.

THE NEW LIFE

When we study Paul's religious experience and thought, we are struck by the identity of his basic religious presuppositions with

83

those of Jesus. His whole teaching is based upon a profound conviction of the sovereignty of God and the necessity of obedience to His will. God is the Creator and the Judge of men. He is also the Redeemer and Father of men. Their salvation is a gift of His mercy. These principles of Jewish ethical monotheism are at the heart of his religion and ethics.

But when Paul thinks of God as Father, it is always as Father of the Lord Jesus Christ; and when he thinks of Him as Redeemer, it is always in relation to the redemption He wrought through Christ. It is at this point that the primary difference between him and Jesus begins to appear. For Jesus, men's consciousness of sonship to God is immediate, depending upon their faith in Him, and their redemption is given directly by Him. For Paul, man becomes confident of his sonship to God and is redeemed through the mediation of Christ. By an act of adoption or redemption he must pass from the status of a slave who fears his Master to that of a son who loves his Father.[1] God in Christ has taken the initiative in redeeming man and adopting him into sonship. As Paul puts it, "God was in Christ reconciling the world to himself."[2] The Cross was the certain proof of the redemptive love and mercy of God.

Why was it necessary that God should reconcile men to Himself through the suffering of Christ upon the Cross? Why would it not have sufficed for men to repent of their sins and amend their lives? Questions like these must have suggested themselves to him as a Jew before his conversion. His answers to them are clear. Men by themselves *could* not repent of their sins and win the righteousness necessary for their salvation. Their wills were perverted by and enslaved to *sin*. With the higher, spiritual side of their nature, the "mind," they longed to do what was good; but with the lower side, the "flesh," they rebelled against it. Through the Law revealed to Moses they knew what was right and wrong. But the Law gave them no power to embrace the right and shun the wrong. This was not a mere matter of speculation to Paul. As a young Pharisee, he had found it impossible to attain perfect righteousness by ful-

[1] Gal. 4:1-7.
[2] II Cor. 5:19.

filling *all* the commandments of the Law. Moreover, he observed the same moral failure in the lives of Jews and Gentiles alike in the Mediterranean world.[3] The trouble was that sin dominated the whole being of men; it was radical in the sense of corrupting the self to its very roots. If so, it could not be overcome by even the most strenuous effort of the will, since the will itself was under its power. If it was to be overcome at all, it must be by a power above the self capable of effecting a complete reorientation of the whole personality. "Wretched man that I am! Who will deliver me from this body of death?"[4]

After his conversion Paul was convinced that through Christ, God had redeemed man from this slavery to sin and death. All that was necessary on his part was to put aside all his pride, acknowledge that he could not save himself by his good works, and accept humbly the grace God had offered him. This is the meaning of Paul's doctrine of *justification by faith.* Man cannot win acquittal at the bar of God's judgment by his own righteousness attained through strict obedience to the Law; he must acknowledge his moral powerlessness and throw himself upon the mercy of God, trusting that he will be forgiven. He can venture this trust in God's mercy because God through the suffering of His Son on the Cross has shown His mercy. Faith is essential to the reception of God's grace in his life. However, it is not by virtue of man's faith but by virtue of God's grace that he is "justified." It is more accurate, therefore, to say that "by grace we are saved through faith."

If we stop at this point, however, we will misunderstand Paul's conception of salvation. For man through his faith is united with Christ and is given the strength to "work out" his own salvation. He is not only *forgiven* his sins, in the sense of being pardoned for them; he is also given power through the Spirit of Christ to *overcome* sin in his life. The Spirit of Christ takes possession of his spirit, and he is now able to live "in the Spirit" rather than "in the flesh." Christ is in him and he is "in Christ." Thus, the righteousness for which he strove in vain is now bestowed upon him as a gift. But he must also by his own effort make it his own.

[3] Rom. 1:18-3:18.
[4] Rom. 7:24.

Paul expresses the close relationship between divine grace and human effort in a striking verse: "Work out *your own* salvation with fear and trembling; for *God* is at work in you, both to will and to work for his good pleasure."[5]

The result of this transformation is a completely *new life*. "Therefore, if anyone is in Christ," Paul says, "he is a new creation; the old is passed away, behold, the new is come."[6] He has entered into a "new covenant" with God, not a covenant whose terms are written down in a code but a covenant in the Spirit, "for the written code kills, but the Spirit gives life."[7] Sometimes the process of change is pictured as a sudden one: one is united with Christ in his crucifixion, dying to sin, and rises with him in his resurrection into newness of life. This expresses the radical change in orientation brought about by the conversion Paul had experienced. But sometimes the progressive growth of the new life into which one enters at conversion is stressed. Even at the end of his strenuous and heroic career as a missionary Paul does not claim to be "already perfect." "But one thing I do," he says, "forgetting what lies behind and straining forward to what lies ahead, I press on towards the goal for the prize of the upward call of God in Christ Jesus."[8] Thus, the Christian already enjoys "newness of life," but he is also eagerly striving to be "perfect," to realize the possibilities of his new life.

This tension between the new life already being enjoyed and the perfection yet to be realized provides Paul with one of his chief arguments for moral effort on the part of his converts. For example, in warning the Corinthians against sexual immorality, he appeals to the fact that they have been joined to Christ so that their bodies are parts of his body and asks them to treat their bodies in a way consistent with this fact. "Shall I therefore take the members of Christ and make them members of a prostitute? Never! Do you not know that he who joins himself to a prostitute becomes one body with her?"[9]

Paul is not naive in this appeal to Christians to be consistent with the principle of the new life in them. He knows well enough

[5] Phil. 2:12, 13 (italics mine).
[6] II Cor. 5:17.
[7] II. Cor. 3:6.

[8] Phil. 3:13-14.
[9] I Cor. 6:15-16.

that the profession of many a Christian is better than his practice. Nor is he merely using the psychological device of suggesting to his converts that they are better than they actually are. He means that Christians truly are a "new creation," are members of the "body of Christ," are "in the Spirit." Because they are different from what they were, they should manifest it by conduct different from that of the "old nature." The conduct of a person springs from the substance of his being: what Christians *ought to do* depends upon what they *are*. He does not attempt to persuade his converts of the validity of Christian *ideals*; he describes the *reality* of the new life into which they have entered and shows them what it implies for their conduct. His ethic is an *ethic of redemption,* an ethic for the regenerate.

AN ETHIC FOR THE CHURCH

It is also an *ethic for the Church*. As Jesus describes the life of members of the Kingdom of God who imitate the perfect love of God, Paul describes the life suitable to members of Christ's body, the Church. At the outset we saw that Paul says little about the Kingdom of God as such. But he is no less *eschatological* in his outlook than Jesus. This may be more obvious in his earlier letters such as I Thessalonians, but it is also apparent in his later letters such as that to the Philippians.[1] Therefore, his counsel to his churches is rooted in the conviction that their "commonwealth is in heaven."[2] He thinks of the Church as constituting the first fruits of the Kingdom and of its members as living in anticipation of the blessings of the Kingdom.

But there is certainly a difference of emphasis between him and Jesus at this point. The Church had come into existence since the death of Jesus, and had gathered a community of men and women around the faith that the Messiah of the Kingdom had already come in the person of Jesus. Moreover, this community was in-

---

[1] For example, Phil. 3:20, 4:5.
[2] Phil. 3:20.

spired by his presence, felt his power as its Risen Lord, and was guided by his Spirit as its invisible Head. Thus, the ethic of the Kingdom inevitably became also an ethic of the Church.

As the coming of the Kingdom was deferred year after year, many moral problems arose in the Church which required attention. These problems had to do with the relation of members of the Church to one another, to the pagan world around them, and to the situations that confronted Christians in the period of waiting for the "new age" to dawn. What should be the attitude of the Church to those of its members who succumbed to the sexual temptations of the pagan world? Should Christians make use of pagan law courts to settle their quarrels? Should Christians have slaves? Much of the moral counsel of Paul consists of answers to questions like these which had arisen in his mission churches. In dealing with them it was necessary for him to apply the perfectionistic principles of Jesus to the actual situations confronting imperfect Christians in a pagan world.

The interest of this moral counsel lies precisely in the fact that it does not consist of abstract ethical principles but is *practical* through and through. As a result, it often illuminates the concrete meaning of a Christian ethical principle. Of course, some of the practical problems with which Paul dealt were problems of his own time and have little more than historical interest for us today, for example, his discussion of whether Christians should eat meat offered to idols. But it will usually be found that there are ethical principles implied in his treatment of such problems, principles that are as valid for us as for the early Christians. The greatest danger in the practical part of Paul's ethical teaching, as the history of the Church has shown, is that later Christians will regard it as authoritative in detail for their own quite different situations. Thus, his counsel that slaves should obey their masters or that citizens should subject themselves to the existing political authorities may have been wise under the social conditions of his time. But it can hardly be regarded as unconditionally valid for all later Christians. Therefore, the fact that Paul tried to deal with the practical problems of his day makes it essential to distinguish between the permanent and the transitory, the spirit and the letter, of his ethical teachings.

AN ETHIC OF LIBERTY

We have spoken of the general character of Paul's ethic as an ethic for regenerate men required by their new life and as an ethic for members of the Church who are waiting for the Kingdom but meanwhile must deal with the practical problems of their life together in a pagan world. What are the distinctive principles of this ethic?

First, the Christian ethic is an *ethic of liberty*. We saw that Jesus was independent in his treatment of the Jewish Law and that there is implicit in his teaching the subordination of law to love as the fundamental principle of morality. Paul rejects the Law as the way to salvation and makes the primacy of love over law more explicit. As the "Apostle to the Gentiles," he insists again and again that Christians are free from the necessity of obeying the ceremonial laws regarding circumcision, unclean meats, and holy days. "Before faith came," he asserts, "we were confined under the law, kept under restraint until faith should be revealed. So that the law was our custodian until Christ came, that we might be justified by faith."[1] But now Christians are free from subjection to it, and Paul resists every attempt of Jewish Christians to bring the Galatians or other Gentile Christians into bondage to it again.

But Christian liberty to Paul means something more than freedom from the Law. The freedom that springs from the presence and power of the Lord within is also freedom from sin. Since Christians now live "in the Spirit" rather than "in the flesh," they are no longer in bondage to sin. If so, their freedom cannot be lawless and irresponsible; it is freedom under the control of the Spirit of Christ.

There are three ways in which Paul shows the nature of this *responsible freedom*: (a) After agreeing with the Corinthians that those who know the unreality of idols are free to eat food offered

[1] Gal. 3:23, 24.

to them, he warns that they should not be so proud of this knowledge as to hurt others who do not have it. "Only take care," he
says, "lest this liberty of yours somehow become a stumbling-block
to the weak."[2] In other words, one's own freedom from scruples
founded upon ignorance and superstition must never make one
indifferent to the effects of his emancipated conduct upon those
who have such scruples. (b) Freedom is to be used, not as a source
of privilege for oneself, but as an opportunity for service to others.
For example, Paul reminds the Corinthians that as an apostle he
has a right to receive food and drink from them and "the right
to be accompanied by a wife,"[3] but that he has not made use of
these rights because he has wanted to "make the gospel free of
charge."[4] "For though I am free from all men," he continues, "I
have made myself a slave to all, that I might win the more."[5] How
could anyone who sought to imitate Christ think of his freedom in
any other way? (c) Freedom is not to be used as "an opportunity
for the flesh."[6] "For the desires of the flesh are against the Spirit,"
says Paul, "and the desires of the Spirit are against the flesh."[7]
This is a striking example of Paul's appeal to the principle of consistency with the new life. It means that the freedom of a Christian
must be limited by the fact that his life is under the control of
Christ. As Paul puts it, "If we *live* by the Spirit, let us also *walk*
by the Spirit."[8] The Christian is not free to do as he pleases.

Thus, Paul's insistence upon freedom from the Law is in no
sense antinomian. Freedom from the Law does not mean freedom
from good works; it means only freedom from the necessity of
winning salvation by good works. How far he is from depreciating
the importance of moral restraint is indicated by a striking passage.
After listing certain vices as "works of the flesh," he says bluntly,
"I warn you, as I warned you before, that those who do such things
shall not inherit the kingdom of God."[9] That moral conditions must
be met if one is to enter the Kingdom is also indicated by another
passage: "For he who sows to his own flesh will from the flesh

[2] I Cor. 8:9.
[3] I Cor. 9:4, 5.
[4] I Cor. 9:18.
[5] I Cor. 9:19-22.

[6] Gal. 5:13.
[7] Gal. 5:17.
[8] Gal. 5:25 (italics mine).
[9] Gal. 5:19, 21.

reap corruption; but he who sows to the Spirit will from the Spirit reap eternal life."[10]

In short, while Paul rejects the Law as a way to salvation, he never dreams of freeing Christians from the moral requirements of the Law. "Though the Christian in a certain sense is no longer 'under Law,'" says Bultmann, "that does not mean that the demands of the Law are no longer valid for him; for the agape demanded of him is nothing else than the fulfilment of the Law."[11] Although "Christianity is the end of the Law so far as it claimed to be the way to salvation," "so far as it contains God's demand, it retains its validity."[12] On the other hand, Paul recognized clearly the necessity of a higher goodness than that of mere obedience to law. "There are two kinds of goodness," writes John Knox, "the goodness of the law and the goodness of the Spirit. The only goodness we can make is of the first kind. We make it by adding obedience to obedience, as a mason places bricks end to end and one on top of another. Such is legal goodness, and it is just as much alive as is a brick wall. Such goodness, like a brick wall, is not without its important uses; it may well serve to protect one from certain evils to which the undisciplined person may succumb. But such goodness is sterile and therefore in the final reckoning spurious. True goodness is living and fruitful, and man cannot make it, no matter how hard he tries. . . . True goodness is God's goodness, not our own; it is God's gift, not our achievement."[13]

AN ETHIC OF LOVE

Second, the Christian ethic is an *ethic of love*. Here Paul follows the teaching of Jesus, of course, but he points out its deeper meaning and makes further applications of it. We have noticed in an earlier chapter an example of the way he reveals Jesus' deeper meaning.

[10] Gal. 6:8.
[11] Bultmann, Rudolf, *Theology of the New Testament,* New York, Scribners, 1951, I, p. 261.
[12] Ibid., I, p. 341.
[13] Knox, John, *Chapters in a Life of Paul,* New York, Abingdon-Cokesbury, 1950, p. 157.

"Repay no one evil for evil. . . . No, if your enemy is hungry, feed him; if he is thirsty, give him drink; for by so doing you will heap burning coals upon his head. Do not be overcome by evil, but overcome evil with good."[1] It is a plain fact of experience that a patient and generous love often does effect a change in aggressive people, and Paul has made this explicit in an unforgettable way.

Paul also makes more explicit the power of love as a moral principle which *generates virtues* that constitute the highest character. For example, he stresses the *humility* produced by love; the willingness of love to stoop to the needs of others. "Do nothing from selfishness or conceit," he writes to the Philippians, "but in humility count others better than yourselves. . . . Have this mind among yourselves, which you have in Christ Jesus, who, though he was in the form of God, did not count equality with God a thing to be grasped, but emptied himself, taking the form of a servant, being born in the likeness of men. And being found in human form he humbled himself and became obedient unto death, even death on a cross."[2]

Another important manifestation of love for Paul is *forbearance*. The meaning of this attitude is best illustrated, perhaps, by his counsel to the Corinthians concerning the strife between those who felt that it was proper to eat meat offered to idols and those who did not. He warns the former that they are not to treat with contempt those who have scruples about eating idol meats. He also warns the latter not to be censorious of those who exercise their Christian liberty in the matter. Thus, forbearance or self-restraint for the sake of others is necessary on both sides. Those who feel their solidarity with the Christian community will willingly show forbearance because of their love for one another. Without this attitude, the peace and harmony of the whole community will be endangered.

With humility and forbearance Paul associates *patience* or "long-suffering." Patience is shown especially in slowness to anger. As Enslin points out, "anger was not for Paul, as for the Stoic, an unqualified vice."[3] He himself had known times of anger and some-

[1] Rom. 12:17, 20-21.   [2] Phil. 2:3-8.
[3] Enslin, M. S., *The Ethics of St. Paul*, New York, Harpers, 1930, p. 268.

times writes with indignation to his converts, though his anger is
not aroused "at a personal grievance" but "at the action of men
whom he believed were hostile to the Lord."[4] But he sees the
danger that anger when cherished will lead to sinful acts. Therefore, he urges Christians to put away bitterness, wrath, resentment
and malice. Indulgence in anger gives rise to these vices and thus
destroys the unity and peace of the community.[5] Similarly, *gentleness* and *fairness* or reasonableness in all one's relations with
others are essential manifestations of love.

Attitudes and virtues like these may seem to be largely passive,
but they are indispensable conditions of the more active expression
of love in *kindness* and *service*. They curb the selfishness and pride
which stand in the way of sympathy for others and outgoing helpfulness towards them. Therefore, they are brought together with
the active expression of love in the famous praise of love in I
Corinthians 13. Paul begins his praise by declaring that without
love all other spiritual gifts are meaningless. Neither speaking in
tongues, nor prophetic powers, understanding, and faith, nor
boundless generosity and martyrdom can bestow worth upon one
unless he has love. Then Paul shows how love destroys pride and
selfishness, along with the jealousy, rudeness, irritableness, self-
seeking, and resentfulness that spring from them. But it does not
simply destroy these vices; it replaces them with virtues. It makes
one kind, it enables one to bear and endure all evils, and it believes
and hopes all things for others. Thus, love is not only the highest
gift of the Spirit but also the source of all true goodness. That is
why Paul can say at the end of his praise of love that, while all
other gifts such as prophecy and knowledge will pass away because
of their imperfection, love will never end. Along with faith and
hope, it abides, and it is the greatest of the three.

LOVE AND COMMUNITY

The creative power of love as a moral principle is also shown
by Paul's treatment of the problem of unity. Love is the *basis of
harmony in a community*. A community is made up of many

---

[4] Ibid., p. 269.   [5] Ibid., p. 271.

members with different talents and functions; and its members must feel a unity between them that transcends and reconciles all their differences. Paul compares the Christian community to a body composed of many members. "For as in one body," he says, "we have many members, and all the members do not have the same function, so we, though many, are one body in Christ, and individually members one of another."[1] The presupposition of his argument is that the Church is more than an association of individuals for certain limited purposes; it is an organic unity in which each participates in a common life, feels his solidarity with all the others, and contributes to the welfare of the whole body. Therefore, each should strive to preserve the unity of the community and to build up the common life. To this end Paul urges the Romans to "love one another with brotherly affection."[2] Moreover, they are not to think of themselves "more highly" than they ought to think but to think "with sober judgment."[3] "Live in harmony with one another," he says; "do not be haughty, but associate with the lowly; never be conceited."[4] They are to identify themselves in sympathy so closely with one another that they will "rejoice with those who rejoice, weep with those who weep."[5]

It is also in this spirit that Christians should think of the *differences* between them in their spiritual gifts. Paul appeals to the Corinthians, divided by parties quarrelling with one another, to agree and "be united in the same mind and the same judgment."[6] In their "jealousy and strife" they are behaving not as "spiritual" but as "ordinary" men.[7] The source of the trouble, as he sees it, is pride in the form of party spirit that leads each group to boast of its leader and its way of thinking.[8] Moreover, some of the Corinthians were boasting of their peculiar spiritual gift of speaking in tongues and were not showing enough respect for others whose gifts were different. "Now there are varieties of gifts, but the same Spirit, and there are varieties of service, but the same Lord," he

[1] Rom. 12:4, 5.
[2] Rom. 12:10.
[3] Rom. 12:3.
[4] Rom. 12:16.

[5] Rom. 12:15.
[6] I Cor. 1:10.
[7] I Cor. 3:1, 3.
[8] I Cor. 3:21.

reminds them; "and there are varieties of working, but it is the same God who inspires them all in every one. To each is given the manifestation of the Spirit for the common good."[9] The diversity of gifts has its cause in God and the same Spirit is in them all. Diversity is entirely compatible with the unity of the community if each uses his special gift, as God intended, for the good of all. But that is not all. Just as none of the organs of the body can get along without the work of the others, however inferior they may seem, so no Christian can get along without the gifts of his fellows. Therefore, he is not to allow pride in his superior gift to make him deny honor to the gifts of others.[10] Also, he is to be guided by love in his use of his own gift. For example, the gift of ecstatic utterance, "speaking in tongues," must be used, not merely to give expression to the feelings of the person possessing it, but in such a way as to build up or "edify" the whole community.

Thus, if love is present in all the members of the community, the diversity of their gifts will not lead to dissension or confusion but will enrich their common life. Paul is thinking only of the Church, of course, and it cannot be said that he saw all implications of this principle for society as a whole. His ethic of the Church leads him to such an intense preoccupation with the problems of the Christian community that he pays little attention to the problems of the *larger community*. Now and again, he gives advice to Christians concerning their relations to those outside the Church. For example, when he writes to the Romans, "If possible, so far as it depends upon you, live peaceably with all,"[11] he is probably referring mainly to their relations with pagans. Again, the injunction, "Do not be overcome by evil, but overcome evil with good,"[12] is concerned primarily with the method for dealing with pagans who do them harm. But Paul never seems to envisage the possibility of building the whole of society on the foundation of love.

His *conservative attitude* towards social institutions, though doubtless wise under the conditions that prevailed, has sometimes

[9] I Cor. 12:4-7.
[10] I Cor. 12:14-27.
[11] Rom. 12:18.
[12] Rom. 12:21.

been a source of misunderstanding. He accepts slavery without protest, advising slaves to serve and obey their masters diligently and masters to treat their slaves well. His view of slavery, as Enslin says, is that it makes little difference to the Christian whether he is slave or free. "He who is a slave is a slave only according to the flesh. He is on a plane of equality with his master since he is the Lord's freedman."[13] He has little to say about economic questions, except a warning to parasitic idlers that "if anyone will not work, let him not eat"[14] and an assertion that Christians who share spiritual goods should also share material goods through liberal giving to the poor.[15] He says nothing about the danger of riches, perhaps because there were too few wealthy persons in his churches to raise many serious problems.

On political issues, he warns Christians to "be subject to the governing authorities," because they have authority from God to punish evildoers.[16] If this is taken as practical advice for his own time, it is doubtless wise. Paul was well aware of the advantages of the Roman peace and order to the Church and to his own missionary activities. He was also probably concerned lest the early Christians, like their Master, should be accused of revolutionary agitation and should be found to have given grounds for the charge by their independent attitude to the kingdoms of this world. However, he cannot be held responsible for the use by later Christians of his counsel to the Romans in order to justify doctrines of absolute and unquestioning obedience to all secular authorities.

The reason Paul did not see the broader implications of Christian love for society as a whole is easy to find. Like other early Christians, he lived in expectation of the second coming of the Lord to usher in the Kingdom. In view of the shortness of the time, it was natural that he should counsel everyone to "remain in the state in which he was called," even if it was a state of slavery.[17] In addition, his intense concentration upon the problems of the Christian community turned his attention away from the problems of society as

---

[13] Enslin, op. cit., p. 208.
[14] II Thess. 3:10.
[15] Rom. 15:27.

[16] Rom. 13:1-7.
[17] I Cor. 7:20, 21.

a whole. He was, after all, a missionary who saw in the little community of the faithful a "new creation" and a "new life" in the midst of an evil world. Furthermore, Christians constituted a small minority drawn largely from the lower classes and had little or no political influence. It was to be centuries before Christianity would become the dominant religion of the Roman Empire. Christians like Paul must have thought that their task was to maintain and strengthen the life of the Church in a doomed and dying world.

There is a passage in the letter to the Galatians which refers to the levelling of barriers in the Church. "There is neither Jew nor Greek, there is neither slave nor free, there is neither male nor female; for you are all one in Christ Jesus."[18] Though Paul may have been unaware of it, this passage contains the hope of a breaking down of every kind of barrier that separates men in human society and the creation of a community based upon brotherly love. The Church at its best provides the nucleus and the energizing principle for that community.

FAITH AND WISDOM

We have seen that *faith* has an important place in Paul's thinking. We shall see later that *hope* helps to sustain the life of love during its earthly pilgrimage. It is no accident, therefore, that Paul lists faith and hope along with love in his famous praise of love[1] and that he urges the Thessalonians to "put on the breastplate of faith and love, and for a helmet the hope of salvation."[2] Faith and hope are not moral virtues. They are the religious attitudes which awaken love and sustain it through all difficulties. As such, they are the root of all the moral virtues.

When one compares this conception of the basis of morality with that of the Greek philosophers, one sees at once how Hebraic it is. The virtuous life is not primarily a stable set of habits imposed upon the natural impulses by reason; it is an expression of aspiration for a perfect good that is grasped by faith and clung to with

[18] Gal. 3:28.   [2] I Thess. 5:8.
[1] I Cor. 13:13.

hope. It is marked by striving for a good that is invisible and that will be fully attained only in the future. The role of reason is secondary. For the good towards which we strive is revealed to faith rather than discovered by reason. Moreover, the right conduct which is the way to the good is found, not through a process of deliberation by reason alone, but with the help of the Spirit of Christ within.

In his rebuke to the Corinthians who were boasting of their superior wisdom he does not attack wisdom as such; he attacks specious claims to wisdom in the light of true wisdom. "Has not God made foolish the wisdom of this world?" he asks. "For since, in the wisdom of God, the world did not know God through wisdom, it pleased God through the folly of what we preach to save those who believe. . . . Christ the power of God and the wisdom of God."[3] If any of the Corinthians are proud of their own worldly wisdom, they merely show that the true wisdom of God has not been revealed to them by the Spirit. Wisdom, like other spiritual gifts, is nothing without love, and is to be used for the common good rather than for personal glory.[4]

Thus, Paul appeals to the true wisdom in Christ to deflate false worldly wisdom and to persuade Christians to use their wisdom only for the purposes of love. There is also a more positive value in this true wisdom. Paul expects of the Christian, as Dodd says, not "simple obedience to a code," but "a clear and independent insight into moral values."[5] "Do not be conformed to this world," Paul writes, "but be transformed by the renewal of your *mind*, that you may *prove* what is the will of God, what is good and acceptable and perfect."[6] If one's mind has been transformed so that it is in harmony with the mind of Christ in its thinking, one can and should test by his own experience what is of value. Again, in a discussion of the claim that one day is better than another, Paul puts the responsibility for decision upon the individual's own moral insight. "Let every one," he says, "be fully convinced in his own

[3] I Cor. 1:21, 24.
[4] Ibid., 12:4-8.
[5] Sneath, E. H., ed., *The Evolution of Ethics*, New Haven, Yale University Press, 1927, p. 297.
[6] Rom. 12:2 (italics mine).

mind."[7] Similarly, he writes to the Corinthians, "I speak as to sensible men; judge for yourselves what I say."[8]

This should be evidence enough that to Paul *wisdom* is an important factor in the moral life, though it is a wisdom revealed to man by God, and that he expects Christians to use their own *minds* in making judgments of value and specific moral decisions. This is confirmed by an analysis of what he means by "mature" religion. The spiritual gift of speaking in tongues is inferior to that of prophecy, he says, because others do not understand what is said. In order to "edify" or build up the community as a whole, an interpreter must be present and explain that which is being said. He who speaks in a tongue is doubtless inspired, but it would be better if his mind were functioning as well as his spirit. "I will pray with the spirit and I will pray with the mind also; I will sing with the spirit and I will sing with the mind also . . . in church I would rather speak five words with my mind, in order to instruct others, than ten thousand words in a tongue."[9] His conclusion is, "Brethren, do not be children in your thinking; be babes in evil, but in thinking be mature."[10]

Thus, the mind is a necessary and important factor in mature religion and morality. However, it is not the mind without convictions or principles; it is the mind with religious and moral insight based upon the true wisdom revealed in Christ. Since the truth of this wisdom cannot be rationally demonstrated but must be received by faith, Paul's conception remains basically Hebraic rather than Hellenic.

JOY THROUGH SUFFERING

Paul conceives of the Christian life as a life of *joy through suffering*. He never uses the term "pleasure" in writing about the Christian life. He is well aware that suffering is inevitable for the follower of Christ in a pagan world. According to his eschatological point of view, the present age is an evil one and the righteous man must

[7] Ibid., 14:5.
[8] I Cor. 10:15.

[9] Ibid., 14:15, 19.
[10] Ibid., 14:20.

expect persecution from the powers of darkness. The moral life of
the Christian is a continuous battle in which he is bound to suffer
painful wounds. Paul's own experience as a missionary had been
one of sacrifice and suffering. In a striking passage he describes his
experiences: beating, stoning, shipwreck, constant danger, toil, hardship, hunger, thirst, cold, exposure, and anxiety for all his churches.[1]
It is no wonder, therefore, that Paul lays so much emphasis upon
the virtue of *endurance*. "We rejoice in our sufferings," he says,
"knowing that suffering produces endurance, and endurance produces character, and character produces hope, and hope does not
disappoint us," etc.[2]

Yet it is not suffering that is the dominant note in Paul's experience; it is joy and victory through suffering. "For the sake of
Christ, then," he writes, "I am content with weaknesses, insults,
hardships, persecutions, and calamities; for when I am weak, then
I am strong."[3] Certain passages remind us of the paradoxes of the
Beatitudes. "We are treated as impostors, and yet true; as unknown,
and yet well known; as dying, and behold we live; as punished, and
yet not killed; as sorrowful, yet always rejoicing; as poor, yet
making many rich; as having nothing, and yet possessing everything."[4]

Sometimes, Paul uses the language of other-worldly dualism in
describing this experience. There are two worlds or orders of reality,
the spiritual and the material, and the Christian is prepared for
life in the spiritual world by the suffering and wasting away of his
body. "Though our outer nature is wasting away," he writes, "our
inner nature is being renewed every day. For this slight momentary
affliction is preparing for us an eternal weight of glory beyond
all comparison, because we look not to things that are seen but to
the things that are unseen; for the things that are seen are transient,
but the things that are unseen are eternal."[5]

More typical of his attitude, however, is a cheerful and confident

[1] II Cor. 11:24-28.
[2] Rom. 5:3-5.
[3] II Cor. 12:10.

[4] II Cor. 6:8-10.
[5] II Cor. 4:16-18.

acceptance of whatever state he is in. "I have learned, in whatever state I am, to be content," he writes from prison towards the end of his life. "I know how to be abased, and I know how to abound; in any and all circumstances, I have learned the secret of facing plenty and hunger, abundance and want. I can do all things in him who strengthens me."[6] In this passage Paul shows that he has achieved that self-sufficiency and contentment through all the vicissitudes of fortune which was the ideal of the Stoics. But his attitude differs radically from that of the Stoics. He does not claim to have attained his independence of fortune by the strength of his own will, but only "in him who strengthens me."

What was the *secret* of Paul's ability to endure suffering and to accept cheerfully and with contentment anything that befell him? Part of the answer is that "the sufferings of this present time are not worth comparing with the glory that is to be revealed to us."[7] There can be no doubt that *hope of eternal life* plays an important part in the thinking of Paul and gives him strength to undergo suffering. Thus, he speaks of his willingness to "share his (Christ's) sufferings, becoming like him in his death, that if possible I may attain the resurrection from the dead."[8] But another part of the answer is to be found in Paul's complete confidence that the *love of God* can be depended upon in every condition and event of this life. "For I am sure that neither death nor life . . . nor anything else in all creation, will be able to separate us from the love of God in Christ Jesus our Lord."[9] Therefore, he is always expressing his gratitude to God and urging his converts to do the same.[10]

It is worthy of note that expressions of joy abound especially in the letter to the Philippians towards the end of his life. Beginning with rejoicing because his imprisonment had served to advance the gospel, it reaches its climax in an exhortation to rejoice and an assurance of peace. "Rejoice in the Lord always; again I will say, Rejoice."[11] The fact that he was able to find joy and peace in and

[6] Phil. 4:11-13.
[7] Rom. 8:18.
[8] Phil. 3:10, 11.
[9] Rom. 8:38-39.
[10] For example, Phil. 1:3; Col. 1:3-5.
[11] Phil. 4:4.

through suffering is the surest testimony that he had learned the deepest truth of Christ's teaching: self-fulfillment through self-renunciation.

THE CONTRIBUTION OF PAUL

The importance of Paul's conception of Christian ethics can hardly be questioned. In the first place, it brings to light in the clearest possible way the inadequacy of ethical legalism for those who are morally in earnest like Paul. It recognizes the value of law in the moral discipline of the race. But it sees that the major moral problem is not that of moral knowledge but that of moral incentive and power. A way must be found to transform duty from something externally imposed upon the will into something willingly and gladly accepted by it. The duties prescribed by a code of moral law like the Ten Commandments must be fulfilled—indeed, more than any code of laws can ever prescribe is required of anyone who would serve the need of his neighbor in love—but they can be properly fulfilled only if the will is radically changed. It must be brought to accept freely and obey spontaneously that which is right. Otherwise, it will be divided against itself, selfish impulses of the "flesh" warring against the moral aspirations of the "spirit." This is why Paul's defense of liberty for the Christian is so important for Christian ethics. He recognizes that the highest moral achievement is possible only when one goes beyond the requirements of any moral law to follow the promptings of the Spirit within. He sees, too, that the highest moral goodness springs from love of neighbor since love seeks not only to avoid every kind of harm to one's neighbor but also to bestow upon him everything that is good.

In the second place, Paul makes it absolutely clear that the Christian ethic is an ethic of redemption. One's general estimate of this ethic of redemption will obviously depend upon one's conception of human nature and its moral possibilities. A modern Humanist, confident of the rationality and goodness of himself and of mankind in general, is likely to see in Paul only a dark and gloomy pessimism about man, a "failure of nerve" in the presence of man's moral limitations. Therefore, he will regard Paul's doctrine of redemption from sin as only an "escape" from the difficulties of the moral struggle with the help of an imaginary Redeemer. On the other hand, if one has found a sense of forgiveness and moral power through faith in Christ, he will judge Paul's ethic of redemption to be both penetrating and true.

Every man must decide this issue for himself. But one thing must be emphasized: those who contrast sharply Paul's "religion *about* Christ" with the "religion *of* Jesus" are oversimplifying the latter. There is not the slightest trace in Jesus of optimistic Humanism or of the allied doctrine that all man needs is knowledge of what is good. Jesus always assumes that repentance for sin is necessary for membership in the Kingdom, a clear indication of his realism about man. He urges his disciples to pray, "forgive us our trespasses, as we forgive those who trespass against us, and lead us not into temptation, but deliver us from evil." He also stresses the great importance of faith in God, which involves complete trust in him. Above all, he sees men as dependent upon God for all that they need and teaches them to bring their needs to him in prayer. "I tell you, Ask, and it will be given you; seek, and you will find; knock, and it will be opened to you. For every one who asks receives, and he who seeks finds, and to him who knocks it will be opened."[1] Thus, Jesus also stresses the necessity of redemption for man through divine forgiveness and grace to overcome evil.

In the third place, Paul grasps the value of the imitation of Christ in the effort of Christians to attain righteousness. His union with Christ, as we have seen, was a mystical experience in which Paul felt that he was "in Christ." His identification with Christ was so close that he could claim to "have the mind of Christ." But it must not be supposed that this Christ-centered mysticism weakened his sense of his own individuality; indeed, it seems to have strengthened it. Nor did it tempt him to renounce moral effort and evade social responsibility by a flight from time to eternity, as mysticism has often done in the Orient. The proof of this is to be found in his imitation of Christ in his character and conduct. As we have seen, he seeks to imitate Christ above all in his humility, his selfless love, and his suffering. Of all the followers of Christ, only Francis of

[1] Lk. 11:9, 10.

Assisi has shown as clearly as Paul the transforming power of this imitation of Christ. It is true that he speaks again and again of union with Christ as the Risen Lord and that he seldom mentions the historical Jesus. This has led some to say that he was indifferent to the historical Jesus. But his conception of the nature of the Risen Lord and what he requires of his followers is dependent upon his knowledge of the character and spirit of the historical Jesus. Thus, Paul showed once and for all that the Christian ethic consists not only of following the ethical teachings of Christ but also of following Christ.

Fourth and finally, Paul has helped men to see that those who would enter into the Kingdom of God must become loyal members of the Christian community. As we have seen, there are dangers in an ethic that is limited to the problems and needs of the Church, but Paul was surely right in emphasizing the importance of the Church. Though the Church is not the Kingdom, it is the community of those who are seeking to live by the principles of the Kingdom during their earthly existence. They can do so effectively only with the help of others who have the same purpose. Moreover, the Church provides them with an opportunity to work for the further growth of the Kingdom by drawing others into it and building up the new life of those already within it. Thus, membership in the Church enables them, not only to prepare for the coming of the Kingdom in the future, but also to experience its power and joy in the present.

After the death of Jesus, it became more and more obvious that the coming of the Kingdom was to be indefinitely delayed. The Church came into being as a fellowship of those who were awaiting the return of the Messiah and the setting up of the Kingdom. It is one of our greatest debts to Paul that he contributed so much to the establishment and building up of this fellowship. In doing so, he became not only one of the most effective interpreters of the *ethical ideal* of Christ, but also one of those who have done most to make that ideal the dominant factor in the *moral life* of the Western world.

CHAPTER 6

Law and Liberty in Christian Thought

THE PROBLEM IN THE NEW TESTAMENT

ONE of the perennial problems of Christian ethics is that of the relation of love to moral law. We have argued that Jesus' ethical teaching does not constitute a code of laws comparable to that of Moses, but that his sayings which have the form of laws or precepts are simply illustrations of the way love acts in different kinds of situations. But we have also pointed out that he assumes the validity of the law of Moses as a revelation of God's will, despite his independent attitude towards the interpretation of certain ceremonial and ethical laws, and that he means his own illustrative precepts to be taken seriously as indicating the direction his disciples are to go in applying the law of love. Thus, Jesus' ethic is primarily an ethic of love, since all laws must be interpreted in such a way as to be consistent with the law of love. But, though this implies an abandonment of the legalism of his day, it does not imply that love is everything and law is nothing. It leaves a place, though a secondary place, for the Old Testament law and for precepts of the New Testament which illustrate the meaning of the law of love.

Despite Jesus' moderate position on the role of moral law, many of his followers have tended towards extreme views. Some have exalted love at the cost of depreciating law or abandoning it altogether; others have defended the importance of law at the risk of subordinating love to it. Christians representing both extremes could appeal

105

to the authority of Jesus himself. According to the Gospels, Jesus had made different statements in which he seemed to stress now one attitude and now another towards the law without attempting to reconcile them. The best-known example of this is to be found in Matthew's version of the Sermon on the Mount. Jesus says that he has come not to "abolish" but to "fulfill" the law and the prophets and that "till heaven and earth pass away, not an iota, not a dot, will pass from the law until all is accomplished."[1] Yet the verse which immediately follows this strong statement seems to deny the adequacy of the whole conception of righteousness based upon scrupulous observance of the law. "For I tell you, unless your righteousness exceeds that of the scribes and Pharisees, you will never enter the kingdom of heaven."[2]

In the New Testament, these two attitudes are already to be found. Anti-legalism, though not antinomianism, is most brilliantly represented by St. Paul. As we have seen, he expected Christians to fulfill the moral as distinguished from the ceremonial laws of the Old Testament. "Love does no wrong to a neighbor; therefore love is the fulfilling of the law."[3] But Paul's emphasis is upon the fact that Christians now have the Spirit and are able through love to fulfill the law. Consequently, they can rejoice in the liberty of sons who obey their Father willingly from love rather than unwillingly from fear. Thus, the law has been reduced to a secondary place. Righteousness fulfills the law, but it is motivated by love and exercised in liberty.

Unfortunately, Paul was misunderstood by some of his followers who emphasized the negative side of his attitude towards the law. If men are justified by faith rather than works, they argued, works are not essential. The significance of the Epistle of James is that it attacks this dangerous antinomian interpretation of Paul. The key to the epistle is the verse, "But be doers of the word, and not hearers only, deceiving yourselves."[4] The author's chief interest is ethical rather than theological. He is concerned that Christians should "fulfill the royal law," "You shall love your neighbor as yourself."

---

[1] Mtt. 5:17-18.
[2] Mtt. 5:20.
[3] Rom. 13:10.
[4] Ja. 1:22.

If they are to do so, they must obey not some but all of the moral laws. "For he who said, 'Do not commit adultery,' said also, 'Do not kill.' If you do not commit adultery but do kill, you shall become a transgressor of the law."[5] The author sees a danger in the idea that faith alone without good works can save a man. "Faith," he insists, "apart from works is dead."[6] Again, the Gospel of Matthew interprets Jesus' teaching as a new law. "The Sermon on the Mount, simple though it seemed to be, was a formal code which Jesus intended his disciples to observe. The evangelist never failed to remind his readers that they would be judged on the basis of their performance (12:37; 16:27), and the great day might come soon."[7] According to Matthew's view, "Christianity was the perfect morality: hence its laws regarding retaliation, oaths, and sexual relationships."[8]

Thus, we see in the Epistle of James and the Gospel of Matthew the beginnings of an emphasis upon obedience to the "old law" and the "new law," respectively. It is our task in this chapter to consider some of the classical views in the history of the Church with respect to moral law and its relation to love and liberty, and then to make some suggestions of our own on the problem.

ST. AUGUSTINE

In the later development of Christian thought on law and liberty, St. Augustine played a unique role as the father of both Catholic and Protestant thinking about the problem. Stimulated by the controversy with Pelagius, he contributed insights derived from his own moral and religious experience.

St. Augustine, like St. Paul, maintains that the law itself is good. With the exception of the ceremonial laws, he says, the law "contains such precepts of righteousness as we are even now taught to observe." In more than one passage, he makes it clear that the Ten Commandments are binding upon Christians. Thus, he takes it for

[5] Ja. 2:11.
[6] Ja. 2:26.
[7] *The Interpreter's Bible*, Vol. 7, Commentary on Matthew, New York, Abingdon-Cokesbury, 1951, p. 232.
[8] Ibid., p. 232.

granted that the content of the "righteousness of faith" is provided by revealed moral laws. The weakness of the law was not that it did not express God's will, but that men's sinful wills refused to obey it or obeyed it from other motives than love. Thus, the primary problem is not that man does not know what is right and wrong; it is that he does not have the power to act on his knowledge. Hence, man cannot attain righteousness unless God awakens faith and love in him, for righteousness is the fruit of love. It is through the Holy Spirit that this is brought about. The believer, says St. Augustine, "receives the Holy Ghost, by whom there is formed in his mind a delight in, and a love of, that supreme and unchangeable good which is God. . . . Even after his duty and his proper aim shall begin to become known to him, unless he also take delight in and feel a love for it, he neither does his duty, nor sets about it, nor lives rightly. Now in order that such a course may engage our affections, God's 'love is shed abroad in our hearts,' not through the free-will which arises from ourselves, but 'through the Holy Ghost, which is given to us.' "[1] Since it is love of some sort which always moves the will to action, acts will be good or bad as they spring from love of God and neighbor or from love of self. Therefore, the "righteousness of faith" is bestowed by the Holy Spirit by awakening love for God. Such a love makes the doing of one's duty, which before had been impossible, easy. This is Augustine's greatest ethical insight: if the will is to attain true righteousness, it must be transformed by a redirection of love. Through faith, love of self must be replaced by love of God and neighbor.

At the same time, law is indispensable in revealing to man the difference between right and wrong. Though man is justified by grace through faith instead of by good works under the law, he must fulfill the law. "The law was therefore given," says Augustine, "in order that grace might be sought; grace was given in order that the law may be fulfilled."[2] In the famous saying, "Give what Thou commandest; command what Thou wilt," grace and law are held together. There is no depreciation of law in St. Augustine.

In his thinking about freedom he faced squarely a difficult prob-

[1] *On the Spirit and the Letter*, Ch. V.
[2] Ibid., Ch. XXXIV.

lem which moral philosophers have often failed to grapple with: How can the will, which was created free but is now in bondage to sin, be freed from the power of sin and enabled to devote itself completely to the Highest Good? St. Augustine and the Humanists differ radically in their answers to this question. While the Humanists answer it by simply reasserting their optimistic view of man and insisting that he can overcome his sin by more strenuous effort of the will, St. Augustine has a more realistic view of the power of sin over the will. He knows that it is only with God's help that men are given a new moral power and enabled to overcome sin. Therefore, they cannot pride themselves upon their freedom of will, as if it were sufficient by itself for the attainment of goodness. They must be assisted by the divine grace if their freedom is to be effective for good.

Unfortunately, St. Augustine in his controversy with the Pelagians tended to minimize the importance of freedom of will as an indispensable foundation of the spiritual freedom of the Christian life. He was so eager to humble the pride of man and exalt the sovereignty of God that he developed a rigid doctrine of predestination and irresistible grace. As a result, he reduced freedom of the will to man's consent to the determination of his will by the divine will. Thus his profound insight that the motive of true goodness is love bestowed by divine grace was weakened by his deterministic conception of the way the divine grace operates upon the human will.

ST. THOMAS AQUINAS

According to Aquinas, law is an "extrinsic" or external principle by which God directs men to their end and thus aids them to realize their good.[1] Since it is reason that directs a being to its end, law is a product of *reason*. If the sovereign who lays down the laws does not do so in accordance with the rule of reason, his will savors of lawlessness rather than law.[2] Even God's will imposes laws upon His creatures not arbitrarily but in accordance with His intellect.

[1] Aquinas, St. Thomas, *Summa Theologica,* q. 90, a. 1.
[2] q. 90, a. 1.

He is the ultimate source or ground of all law and it is by means of law that He orders all things in accordance with His wisdom. This is what Aquinas means when he says that all law springs from the "eternal law" which is the "notion of the government of things in God."[3] What, now, are the kinds of law by which He governs man and directs him to his end?

The first kind is "natural law" by which man is directed to his earthly end. It is imprinted upon his reason in the form of universal principles. Second, there are "human laws" which are derived by reason as conclusions from the indemonstrable principles of the natural law. Since these are concerned with particular and contingent rather than universal and necessary things, they cannot have the certainty which belongs to the conclusions of the sciences.[4] Third, there is "divine law," which directs man to his supernatural end of eternal happiness. Let us examine briefly each of these three kinds of law.

St. Thomas regards as self-evident to reason the first principles of the *natural law*. The first "precept" of natural law, he says, is that "good is to be done and promoted, and evil is to be avoided," and "all other precepts of the natural law are based upon this."[5] These precepts correspond to the basic natural inclinations of man. To the natural inclination which he shares with all beings, self-preservation, correspond precepts concerning the means of preserving human life. To the natural inclinations which man has in common with other animals correspond precepts having to do with sexual intercourse and the education of offspring. To the natural inclinations of the rational nature peculiar to him correspond such precepts as "to shun ignorance" and "to avoid offending those among whom one has to live."[6] The assumption behind this doctrine is the Aristotelian ethical theory that man's good consists in the realization of the potentialities of his nature by activity under the control of reason. Thus, "natural law" provides principles of moral and political action which are independent of Christian revelation. Since these principles

---

[3] q. 91, a. 1.
[4] q. 91, a. 3.

[5] q. 94, a. 2.
[6] q. 94, a. 2.

are apprehended by natural reason, they are valid for Christians and non-Christians alike.

Human laws are derived from the natural law as "conclusions" from principles or as "determinations" of the way these principles are to be applied to particular situations.[7] The diversity of human laws is due to the fact that "the common principles of the natural law cannot be applied to all men in the same way because of the great variety of human affairs."[8] Despite their diversity, however, all laws must be consistent with the natural law. "But if in any point it (a human law) departs from the law of nature, it is no longer a law but a perversion of law."[9] Thus, the natural law provides a norm by which the justice of "positive" laws may be tested.

Finally, *divine law* has been revealed by God to direct men to their supernatural end. It consists of the "Old Law" and the "New Law." The "Old Law," which preceded the coming of Christ, was good because it forbade sins. But it was imperfect because it could not confer the grace necessary to overcome internal as well as external sins. All the moral precepts of the "Old Law" belong also to the "natural law" because they are in accord with reason.[10] They are reducible to the Ten Commandments in the sense that they are "corollaries" of the latter. For example, "all precepts prescribing the reverence to be observed towards our betters, or kindliness towards our equals or inferiors" are "reducible" to the commandment, "Honor thy father and thy mother"; and "the prohibition of hatred and of any kind of violence" is "reducible" to the commandment, "Thou shalt not kill."[11] Even the precepts requiring love of God and love of neighbor are in a sense contained in the Ten Commandments, for "all the precepts of the decalogue are referred to these as conclusions to common principles."[12]

Despite Aquinas' broad view of the "Old Law," he maintains that it was incapable of "justifying" man. True righteousness could not be brought about by the moral precepts of the "Old Law" but

---

[7] q. 95, a. 2.
[8] q. 95, a. 2.
[9] q. 95, a. 2.

[10] q. 100, a. 1.
[11] q. 100, a. 1.
[12] q. 100, a. 3.

had to be infused by divine grace. This is why the "New Law" was necessary. Through it Christ gave what the "Old Law" promised but could not give. For the "New Law" does not consist primarily of moral precepts; it "consists chiefly in the grace of the Holy Ghost, which is shown forth by faith that worketh through love."[13] Christ in the "New Law" also explained the precepts of the "Old Law" by expounding their true meaning, extending the prohibition of murder and adultery to the "interior acts" of anger and lust and forbidding retaliation altogether. But the main emphasis of Aquinas seems to be on the continuity, not the discontinuity, of the "New" with the "Old Law." Both aim at the same end of eternal life, though the Old Law does so in a preparatory and the New in a more perfect way. One can even say that the New Law is contained in the Old "virtually, as an effect in its cause," "as the corn in the ear."[14] In accordance with this view, Aquinas refutes the objection that Christ taught moral precepts contrary to the Old Law. Moreover, he holds that the New Law made no additions to the moral precepts of the Old Law except those concerned with "interior acts," which simply explain the true meaning of the Old Law, and the "evangelical counsels," which are to be binding only on some Christians.

Thus, the radical character of Jesus' ethical teaching seems to disappear. It is evident only in Aquinas' discussion of the "evangelical counsels" for those who seek Christian perfection. The distinction between a "precept" or "commandment" and a "counsel" is that the one "implies obligation" while the other is "left to the option" of individuals. The "counsels" are concerned with the complete renunciation of "the goods of this world": "poverty" renounces external wealth; "chastity," carnal pleasures; and "obedience," the "pride of life." While the "precepts" deal with "matters that are necessary to gain the end of eternal beatitude," the "counsels" are concerned with "matters that render the gaining of this end more assured and expeditious."[15]

When one compares Aquinas' conception of moral law with that

[13] q. 108, a. 1.
[14] q. 107, a. 3.
[15] q. 108, a. 4.

of Augustine, the first thing one notices is its *optimism* and *rationalism*. It is based upon the conviction that man is a rational being made in the image of God. Consequently, while other creatures fulfill God's purpose blindly, man has been given a share in providence; he is permitted consciously to cooperate with God in fulfilling his destiny. This is most evident in Aquinas' theory of "natural law" and "human law." Man apprehends the principles of the "natural law" by the light of his own reason and deduces from them "human laws" which are adapted to the various and changing situations of his life. Thus, he is capable, apart from revelation, of knowing the fundamental principles of ethics and politics and shaping his personal character and social relationships in accordance with them. Of course, Aquinas is aware of the reality of sin and of man's inability to save himself by his own effort, but he does not emphasize the power of sin over the will as Augustine did. Sin has weakened the inclination to virtue, but it has not destroyed it; and it has left intact the capacity of the reason to grasp the principles of the natural law. Thus, man can attain a measure of moral virtue, political order, and earthly happiness by his own effort.

This rationalistic optimism is the source of one of the most common criticisms of Aquinas' theory of *natural law*. Is it really true that the "precepts" of the "natural law" are the same for all men? It may be granted that the first principle he mentions, that "good is to be done and promoted, and evil is to be avoided," is universally valid. But it is highly abstract and general. If we seek to formulate "precepts" or laws that are more concrete, can we find any that are the same for all men? Aquinas himself seems to recognize the difficulty when he admits that the "proximate conclusions" derived from the "common principles" are only "right in most cases." This implies that specific moral precepts or laws are not universal and unchangeable. Nevertheless, the tendency of Catholic defenders of the natural law is to sanction specific rules like the prohibition of contraceptives. In this way, the appeal to "natural law" makes it possible to rationalize social conservatism and moral custom. This does not imply the uselessness of the theory of "natural law," but it warns us against the tendency to attribute a universal validity to *specific laws* which belongs only to *general principles*.

The fundamental weakness of Aquinas' conception of law, however, is not his theory of "natural law" and "human law," though it is necessary to restate it. His real weakness is that his view of *divine law* is inconsistent with the fact that the Christian ethic is an ethic of love and liberty. Aquinas does not recognize that the "precepts" of Jesus do not constitute a "New Law" but are simply illustrations of what God's absolute will requires of members of His Kingdom. Consequently, he does not see the radicalism of the ethics of the New Testament. As we pointed out, the only differences he sees between Jesus' ethical teachings and those of the Old Testament are that Jesus concerns himself with the "interior acts" or motives of men and adds a few "evangelical counsels" for those seeking a sure and speedy way to salvation.

The basic reason for these errors is his *ethical legalism*. As we have seen, St. Augustine regards the moral laws of the Old Testament as indispensable and insists upon their fulfillment, but he puts his primary emphasis upon the faith and love awakened by God's grace and regards the role of law as subordinate. On the other hand, with Aquinas love becomes one law among many, though doubtless a fundamental one. This is shown, not only by his failure to distinguish the meaning of the two-fold law of love for Jesus from its meaning in the books of Deuteronomy and Leviticus, but also by his view that it is contained implicitly in the Ten Commandments. Was he not aware of the fact that the agape-love of the New Testament must be interpreted in the light of such passages as the parables of the Prodigal Son and the Good Samaritan, the injunction to forgive seventy times seven times, and the thirteenth chapter of First Corinthians?

The only point at which the radicalism of Jesus' ethic of love is acknowledged is in the treatment of the "evangelical counsels." Even here, however, the acknowledgment is only partial because the "counsels" are not for all Christians. Moreover, the restriction of the "counsels" to those who completely renounce the world tends to blind Aquinas to the radicalism of many of Jesus' "precepts" which are obviously addressed to all of his disciples. For example, he argues that the ordinary Christian is obliged by the precept "Love your enemies" only to "be prepared to do good to his enemies and other similar actions when there is need." "But that anyone should actually and promptly behave thus towards an enemy when there is no special need," he adds, "is to be referred to the particular counsels."[16] Thus, while Aquinas' ethical legalism unduly exalts law, it also lowers the level of Jesus' demands for all but a small minority of Christians.

There is little place for *liberty* in Aquinas' legalism. For the Christian who has renounced the world, the "counsel" of "obedience" requires submission to the rule of his order and the advice of his superior. For the ordinary Christian, liberty consists merely in the fact that the New Law does not prescribe or prohibit all his acts but only those that are necessary and that it enables him by grace to "comply freely" with them.[17] This narrowing of liberty is due largely to the fact that the Church had strengthened its authority and elaborated its discipline to a high point by the time of Aquinas. The static and conservative character of the medieval social order which was sanctioned by the natural law also limited severely the freedom of individual action in every sphere of life. As a result, despite the optimism of Aquinas with respect to man and his rational capacity, his legalism prevents him from doing justice to either the radical demands of Christian love or the creative possibilities of Christian liberty.

MARTIN LUTHER

Luther's ethic, like St. Paul's, is usually regarded as an ethic of love and liberty rather than an ethic of law. As such, it is contrasted with the ethical legalism of Aquinas before him and Calvin after him. This view of it is true in the sense that he returns to the emphasis of St. Paul on faith and love, on the one hand, and liberty, on the other, especially in his early treatise *The Liberty of the Christian Man*. But it is inadequate because it is silent about another side of his ethic in which he stresses the importance of both the moral laws of the Old Testament and the secular laws of society. We shall

[16] q. 108, a. 4, reply obj. 4.
[17] q. 108, a. 2.

deal mainly with this second side which is sometimes overlooked or minimized.

Luther tells us in one of his early treatises that the Law must be preached first in order to prepare man for the Gospel. Man needs especially a knowledge of the Ten Commandments, which tell him "what he ought to do and what he ought not to do," in order that he may discover that "by his own strength he can neither do the things he ought, nor leave undone the things he ought not to do."[1] Luther maintains that "the Ten Commandments contain, in a very brief and orderly manner, all the teaching that is needful for man's life."[2] This astounding claim is intelligible only when we remember that before the time of Biblical criticism the unity of all the books of the Bible was assumed and that the less advanced parts were interpreted in the light of the more advanced parts. Thus, Luther argues, like Aquinas, that the Ten Commandments are based upon the two-fold law of love: they "command nothing but love and forbid nothing but love."[3] Consequently, "the law is in itself so rich and perfect that one need add nothing to it" and "no one, not even Christ himself, can improve the law."[4]

Although the law is good and necessary, however, it cannot save. "The commands, indeed," he says, "teach things that are good, but the things taught are not done as soon as taught; for the commands show us what we ought to do, but do not give us the power to do it."[5] The result is that we are brought to despair of our own capacity to justify ourselves by perfect obedience to the law. This leads us to listen to God's promises and throw ourselves upon His mercy for forgiveness. We are justified, not by the law, but by the grace of God through faith. Faith unites the soul with Christ as a bride with her bridegroom, and in this union Christ takes the sins of the soul upon himself and bestows his own righteousness upon her.

But justification by faith does not mean that the Christian may dispense with good works. Good works are necessary in order that

[1] Luther, M., *Works*, Philadelphia, A. J. Holman, 1915, II, p. 354.
[2] Ibid., p. 367.
[3] Ibid., p. 364.
[4] Luther, M., *Commentary on the Sermon on the Mount*, Philadelphia, Lutheran Publication Society, 1892, pp. 124, 125.
[5] Luther, M., *Works*, II, p. 317.

he may subject body to spirit and serve the needs of his neighbors. But he will do good works, not to justify himself before God, but "out of spontaneous love in obedience to God."[6] Thus, "Christian liberty" does not mean freedom from the need to obey the law; it means freedom from the constraint and menace of the law which are felt by us as long as we seek to justify ourselves by the law. This is the meaning of the paradox of the *Treatise on Christian Liberty*: "A Christian man is a perfectly free lord of all, subject to none. A Christian man is a perfectly dutiful servant of all, subject to all."[7] The Christian is dependent for justification upon nothing and no one but his faith as it responds to the Word. Therefore, he is free from bondage to the law, including fear of its penalties. He also possesses spiritual freedom in the sense of power to overcome the world and its evils. But this liberty is a responsible liberty. Though "free lord of all," the Christian voluntarily makes himself "dutiful servant of all" out of gratitude and love.

We come now to one of the most perplexing aspects of Luther's ethics, the dualism between his personal ethics of faith and love and his social ethics of life in the world. In his treatise on *Secular Authority*, he defends secular authority, its law, and its coercion as ordained by God and necessary for social order. Against the Anabaptists, he quotes St. Paul's injunction, "Let every soul be subject to power and authority, for there is no power but from God."[8] But what, then, are Christians to do about Christ's saying, "Resist not evil"? There are two classes of men who belong to two kingdoms: the kingdom of God and the kingdom of the world. The Sermon on the Mount was meant for the former, not the latter. Since Christians live with one another in love, they need no secular law and no sword to enforce it. However, most men are not Christians, and to restrain them from evil, secular law and force are necessary.[9] Therefore, the Christian should not go to law or use the secular sword for his own sake; but he should support the secular authority from love of others for whom it is a necessity. In this dualistic view, the

[6] Luther, *Works,* II, p. 329.
[7] Ibid., II, p. 312.
[8] Rom. 13:1.
[9] Luther, *Works,* III, p. 236.

ethical perfectionism of the Sermon on the Mount is maintained in private life and at the same time a policy of "realism" is followed in public life.

In his later *Commentary on the Sermon on the Mount,* Luther develops further this dualism with the aid of a distinction between a "person" and his "office" and argues that the Sermon on the Mount is relevant to the conduct of the "person" but not to the way he acts in his "office." Every "office" or "calling" is good and everyone who performs the duties of a "calling" approved by God is doing His will.[10] Thus, Jesus' saying, "Blessed are the meek," applies to the Christian as a "person" but not as one whose "office" requires him to exercise authority. How far Luther was willing to carry this dualism is illustrated by a striking passage. "A prince may very well be a Christian, but as a Christian he is not to rule; and insofar as he rules he is called not a Christian, but a prince. The person is a Christian, but the office or princeship has nothing to do with his Christianity."[11] "Are you a prince, judge, lord, lady, etc., and do you have people under you, and want to know what is becoming in you? Then you do not need to inquire of Christ, but consult the law of the emperor or of your state, which will soon tell you how you are to conduct yourself towards your inferiors and protect them."[12]

Luther insists that one must perform the duties of his "office" with the Christian intention of serving his neighbors. Though the duties themselves are determined by the secular law of the state, the fulfillment of them is truly ethical only when it springs from faith. However, the tension between an ethic of love and an ethic of secular law, between an inner intention of Christian service and an outer activity defined by secular law, was difficult to maintain. According to Troeltsch, Luther's tendency was to relax the tension and to emphasize secular law. In any case, obedience towards authority and conformity to the demands of the calling were increasingly emphasized by Luther. The content of social duties was largely

[10] *Commentary on the Sermon on the Mount,* p. 42.
[11] Ibid., p. 294.
[12] Ibid., p. 195.

determined by the calling, and only the disposition or motive was provided by Christian faith and love.

The strength of Luther's position is that he attacked the ethical legalism which had become entrenched in medieval Catholicism. In doing so, he used the weapons put into his hands by St. Paul: justification by faith rather than works; faith active in love as the fulfillment of the law; and Christian liberty. Thus, he restored love and liberty to the central position they had occupied in St. Paul but had lost by the time of St. Thomas Aquinas. There are few passages in Christian literature which describe more eloquently the spirit of Christian love and liberty than certain parts of Luther's *The Liberty of the Christian Man.*

But it cannot be said that Luther realized all the implications of Christian love and liberty for personal and social ethics. With respect to *personal ethics,* he was too much under the influence of the medieval exaltation of the Ten Commandments to see that, important as they are, they do not tell us all we ought to do and not to do. Though he shows in his description of Christian love how much above them are the demands it makes, he insists upon reading into them more than they contain and thus giving them a position in Protestant ethics they hardly deserve. With respect to social ethics, his thinking is even more open to criticism. Doubtless, there is an important element of truth in his *ethical dualism.* It acknowledges the necessity for the Christian to manifest his faith and love within the framework of the political and social order and under the limitations imposed by human sin. He is not to withdraw from the world like the Catholic monk but to work within one of the approved "callings"; and he is not to shun political life like the Anabaptist but to support the state and accept responsibility for office. Furthermore, in his calling he is to respect the technical requirements of the work itself. "As he (the Christian) cannot derive the laws of medical procedure from the gospel when he deals with a case of typhus," says Richard Niebuhr, "so he cannot deduce from the commandment of love the specific laws to be enacted in a commonwealth containing criminals."[13]

[13] Niebuhr, Richard, *Christ and Culture,* New York, Harpers, 1951, p. 175.

Nevertheless, it is disastrous to restrict the Gospel ethic of love to one's life as a "person" and to conform to norms derived from secular law in one's "office" or "calling." The *intention* to manifest faith and love in one's "calling" will make little objective difference if the *acts* one does are determined wholly by secular norms. Of course, it is essential for a person with a political "calling" to take full account of human sin and to do what is practically best in the imperfect situation. In consequence, the Christian ethic does not demand of him literal obedience to "hard sayings" such as "Resist not evil." But he should not allow the duties of his calling to be determined by the imperfect standards of justice operating in his society, for the actual system of justice must constantly be subjected to the criticism of love. Luther is misled at this point by his separation of the good will and its motives from the good works in which it expresses itself. The Christian must concern himself with an act as a whole, both its motive and its probable consequences, and evil acts cannot be justified on the ground of their good motives.

The result of Luther's dualism is that his profound insight into the meaning of love and his vigorous attack in the name of liberty upon the legalism of Catholic Christianity were prevented from producing the social fruits which might have been expected from them. For love which is confined to personal relationships and liberty which cannot express itself in creative social activity are condemned to remain, to a large extent, subjectively precious but socially ineffective treasures of the inner life. It should not be a matter of surprise, therefore, that Lutheran dualism in Germany has fostered blind obedience to political authority and social conservatism.[14]

JOHN CALVIN

Calvin's view of law and its relation to liberty and love has probably had more influence upon Protestant ethics in the Anglo-Saxon world than any other single factor. Along with the ethics of the radical sects of the Reformation, it helped to shape the ethical thinking of larger denominations such as the Methodists and Baptists as

---

[14] Martin Niemöller is reported to have said in June 1945, "My soul belongs to God, my body to the State."

well as of Calvinist churches such as the Presbyterians. It is hardly too much to say that the Puritan ethos was dominant in America down to the First World War, though there has been a sharp re-action against it during the last generation.

Calvin combines Luther's doctrine of justification by faith with a strong insistence that man manifest his faith by righteousness. He maintains both the absolute dependence of man for salvation upon God's grace and the necessity for good works in accordance with the law. The latter bestows upon the *law* a primary importance for the Christian life. Calvin agrees with Luther that the first "use" of the law is negative, to convict man of sin and drive him to fly to God for mercy.[1] The second use is to restrain men from evil by a fear of penalties. This applies not only to the unregenerate but also to the regenerate before they are called, so that they may become "accustomed to bear the yoke of righteousness."[2] The third and "principal" use of the law relates to the faithful after their calling. Though the Spirit of God now lives in their hearts, the law gives them "a better and more certain understanding of the Divine will to which they aspire." Moreover, the saints need to be exhorted as well as instructed by the law. They are "burdened by the indolence of the flesh," which needs the law "as a whip, urging it, like a dull and tardy animal, forward to its work."[3] Therefore, we should not attempt to escape from the law, because it "shows us a goal, to aim at which, during the whole of our lives, would be equally conducive to our interest and consistent with our duty."[4]

This leads Calvin to a very high view of the law of the *Old Testament*. Christ came not to destroy but to fulfill the law. Paul did not wish to abolish the law but the "curse" of the law upon those who fail to fulfill its demands. Thus, "the law has sustained no diminution of its authority, but ought always to receive from us the same veneration and obedience."[5] Consequently, there is no opposi-tion between Gospel and Law. The difference between the Old and the New Testaments is only in the "mode of administration," not

---

[1] Calvin, John, *Institutes of the Christian Religion*, II, Ch. VII, para. VI.
[2] Ibid., para. X.   [4] Ibid., para. XIII.
[3] Ibid., para. XII.   [5] Ibid., para. XV.

in the "substance." Since the demands of the old covenant could not be fulfilled without the power of the Holy Spirit, the old covenant produces fear and leads to condemnation and death. But since the demands of the new covenant can be fulfilled by the power of the Holy Spirit, it leads to confidence and security. Thus, there is no opposition of "substance" between the two; there is only a difference between the ways in which righteousness is supposed to be attained under them.

Accordingly, Calvin refuses to acknowledge a "new law" superior to the "old law." Christ made no additions to the law but simply "restored it to its genuine purity."[6] Like Luther, Calvin extends the meaning of the Old Testament law and claims to find in it much that really belongs to the New Testament. He is able to do this by following the principle that a law includes not only its explicit meaning but all that is implied by it. In determining what is implied by a law we should consider the end or purpose for which it was given. For example, the end of the commandment, "Honor thy father and thy mother," is that "honor may be given to them to whom God assigns it"[7] for the sake of the preservation of order. From this we may see that we should subject ourselves to our "superiors," "whether they are worthy of this honor or not."[8] By this method Calvin attempts to read back into the Ten Commandments even the most distinctive ethical insights of the New Testament. He maintains that "the tendency of the whole law" is to "a perfection of righteousness" and that this perfection consists in love of God and love of our neighbor.[9] For example, since "a prohibition of crimes is a command to practice the contrary duties," the meaning of "Thou shalt not covet" must be that "it is reasonable for all the powers of our souls to be under the influence of love." "Therefore God enjoins a wonderful ardour of love, which he will not allow to be interrupted even by the smallest degree of concupiscence."[10]

Calvin's doctrine of *Christian liberty* is a very limited one. The first "part" or aspect of Christian liberty, he says, is that Christians are freed from the necessity of seeking salvation by the righteous-

---

[6] Ibid., Ch. **VIII**, para. VII.
[7] Ibid., para. VIII.
[8] Ibid., para. XXXV.

[9] Ibid., para. XI.
[10] Ibid., para. XLIX.

ness of the law. The second "part" is that "they yield a voluntary obedience to the will of God." Unlike slaves who are in bondage to the law and are always fearful because they cannot please their master, Christians obey the law willingly and gladly. Like children, they do not hesitate to present their parents with their imperfect works, "in confidence that their obedience and promptitude of mind will be accepted by them, though they have not performed all that they wish." The third "part" of Christian liberty is that we are under no obligation with respect to "external things," such as meats, wine, delicate food, and ceremonies.[11]

It can hardly be denied that Calvin's ethic is primarily an *ethic of law* rather than an ethic of love. This is due to his failure to grasp the radical and unique character of Christ's teaching. He is right in insisting that Jesus did not mean to lay down a "new law"; but he is wrong in holding that Jesus merely "purified" the "old law." As we have seen, Jesus sought to express the absolute will of God which had been only partially revealed in the law of Moses. The fact that he quotes the two-fold law of love from the law of Moses does not imply that love occupies the same place in his ethic as in that of the Pentateuch, or that it is merely a "summary" of the Ten Commandments. The meaning of the law of love for Jesus must be derived from a study of all he said and did, including his death on the Cross. Such a study discloses that his ethic is not an ethic of law, even when love is included as the primary law; it is an ethic of love, which accepts and makes use of laws only insofar as they embody the demands of love.

THE RADICAL SECTS AND JOHN WESLEY

The *Anabaptists* at the time of the Reformation were deeply dissatisfied with the way the Reformation was developing in the new Protestant Churches. They disapproved of the close association of these Churches with the state, their use of coercion in religious matters, the compromise of their leaders with the world, and their failure to produce moral fruits. Consequently, they insisted that the

[11] Ibid., III, Ch. XIX.

Church should not be a comprehensive religious community including all the citizens of the state through infant baptism, but a "holy community" consisting exclusively of voluntary members who had had a personal religious experience and were true believers. For this reason, they insisted upon adult baptism, the separation of true believers from the established Churches, and the establishment of small fellowships with strict moral discipline. Only in this way could they avoid compromise with the world and attain genuine holiness of life in imitation of Christ.

The interpretation of Christian ethics by the Anabaptists differed in several ways from that of Protestant thinkers like Luther and Calvin. We have seen that Luther and Calvin emphasized the moral laws of the Old Testament, especially the Ten Commandments, and the continuity of Jesus' teaching with that of the "Old Law." In contrast, the Anabaptists believed that the "Old Law" had been superseded, and conceived of Christian perfection in terms of the *Sermon on the Mount*. For example, in an anonymous Anabaptist statement from Switzerland a distinction is made between "servile" and "filial" obedience, the one having its source in love of reward, the other in the love of God. "The servile is Moses," it asserts, "and produces Pharisees and scribes; the filial is Christ and makes children of God. . . . The servile is the Old Covenant, and had the promise of temporal happiness; the filial is the New Covenant, and has the promise of eternal happiness, namely, the Creator Himself. . . . The servile endured for a time; the filial will last forever. . . . According to the Old Testament only he who murdered was guilty of judgment; but in the New he also who is angry with his brother . . . The Old permitted swearing if one swore truly, but the New will know of no swearing. The Old has its stipulated punishment, but the New does not resist evil."[1] Thus, the perfect fulfillment of Christ's teachings in the Sermon on the Mount for the sake of holiness was the fundamental principle of Anabaptist ethics. "In practice," says Troeltsch, "this 'holiness' was expressed in the following ways: in detachment from the State, from all official positions, from law, force, and the oath, and from war, violence, and capital

---

[1] *The Mennonite Quarterly Review*, Jan., 1947.

punishment; the quiet endurance of suffering and injustice as their share in the Cross of Christ; the intimate social relationship of the members with each other through care for the poor and the provision of relief funds, so that within these groups no one was allowed to beg or starve; strict control over the Church members, through the exercise of excommunication and congregational discipline."[2] It is obvious that such a perfect fulfillment of the Sermon on the Mount required both a high degree of moral earnestness and a willingness to withdraw from many of the activities of the larger community.

However, it must not be thought that the Anabaptists conceived the "New Law" of Christ exclusively in terms of negations. There was a very strong positive emphasis upon the practice of *brotherly love* in the fellowship. This was manifested in various forms of economic aid to those in need. Menno Simons points out some of the practical ways Christians express their love. "They practice charity and love as much as they have ability; they suffer no one to be a beggar among them; they distribute to the necessity of the saints, receive the miserable, take the stranger into their houses, console the afflicted, assist the needy, clothe the naked, feed the hungry, do not turn their faces from the poor, and do not despise their own suffering members—their own flesh."[3]

Although the Mennonites have maintained their identity as a "sect" to the present time, many of the original "sects" have abandoned the "sect" ideal and become large and powerful "Churches." Despite the fact that they have compromised with the world, the Baptist and Methodist Churches have retained elements of the "sect" conception and have spread widely its influence. The *Methodists* are particularly interesting in this respect. Belonging originally to the "sect" type, in some respects, but seeking to leaven the life of the Anglican Church from within, Methodism led to a religious awakening of the masses and to the organization of large numbers of converts in such a way that its separation from the mother Church became inevitable. After the separation, it moved increas-

[2] Troeltsch, E., *The Social Teaching of the Christian Churches*, New York, Macmillan, 1950, II, p. 696.
[3] Bender, Harold S., *Menno Simons' Life and Writings*, Scottdale, Pa., Mennonite Publishing House, 1936, p. 76.

ingly away from the ideal of the "sect" to that of the "Church."[4] Nevertheless, through the Methodist Church John Wesley's passionate concern for holiness or perfection has had a profound influence in Great Britain and America.

Wesley saw a danger in the tendency to exalt faith at the cost of love and its moral fruits. "We must take care," he said, "to let all men know, we esteem no faith but that which worketh by love. . . . And when we say, 'Believe, and thou shalt be saved,' we do not mean, 'Believe, and thou shalt step from sin to heaven, without any holiness coming between; faith supplying the place of holiness,' but 'Believe, and thou shalt be holy.' "[5] This was why Wesley stressed obedience to the Old Testament law almost as strongly as Calvin. Unlike Calvin, however, he believed that *Christian perfection* or holiness was attainable in this life. It is possible for faith active in love to fulfill the law. "For there is no motive," says Wesley, "which so powerfully inclines us to love God, as the sense of the love of God in Christ. . . . And from this principle of grateful love to God arises love to our brother also. . . . It continually incites us to do good, as we have time and opportunity; to do good, in every possible kind, and in every possible degree, to all men. It is, therefore, the fulfilling of the positive, likewise, as well as of the negative, law of God."[6] Thus, Wesley combines with Luther's doctrine of justification by faith and Calvin's insistence upon strict obedience to law the strong conviction of the radical "sects" that Christian perfection inspired by love is necessary to salvation and possible in this life.

The main *value* of the "sects" is that they break decisively with the traditional Catholic and Protestant tendency to blunt the edge of Jesus' radical ethic of love. The Anabaptists emphasize the contrast between the ethics of the Old and New Testaments and insist upon obedience to the latter rather than the former. As a result, they are more aware than most Christians of the uniqueness of the Christian ethic of love. They also reject the "relative Natural Law"

[4] Troeltsch, E., op. cit., II, pp. 722, 723.
[5] Wesley, John, *Standard Sermons,* E. H. Sugden (ed.), Nashville, Lamar and Barton, I, Serm. XX.
[6] Ibid., II, Serm. XXX.

by which conservative Catholics and Protestants have attempted to justify social evils and injustices. In this way, they escape from the tendency of Luther and others to compromise with the world by conforming to existing social institutions.

The chief *limitations* of the "sects" are their legalism and their separatism. They freed themselves from the legalism of the Old Law only to fall into a *legalism* of the New. In this they had a noble aim before them: to avoid the worldliness of the more inclusive Churches and to follow completely Jesus' way of love. But any attempt to reduce Jesus' ethic to a series of moral rules which are to be literally obeyed is bound to fail. Moreover, the ethical legalism of the "sects" tends to encourage a sense of moral superiority towards Christians who interpret their faith differently. This is closely associated with their *separatism*. In the case of some of the Mennonites, separatism has led to a virtually complete withdrawal from modern society and culture. Such a withdrawal prevents the "sect" from making a substantial contribution, except by example, to the moral transformation of society and culture. It is significant that the radical sect which has had most effect upon the larger community is the Society of Friends, which has refused to withdraw from the world and has attempted to bring to bear forces of reconciliation upon the world from within.

THE REACTION AGAINST LEGALISM AND THE NECESSITY OF LAW

In America there was a reaction against Puritan ethical legalism in the eighteenth century. Inspired by the rationalism and humanitarianism of the time, many insisted that liberty and the pursuit of happiness were "unalienable rights" of man. To those influenced by this idea, the legalism of the Calvinists seemed intolerably narrow and restrictive. In the nineteenth century this rebellion against legalism was strengthened by political and social liberalism, which exalted the individual and sought to free him from every form of oppression. Liberal Protestantism also encouraged Christians to repudiate religious authoritarianism of every kind and appeal to their own reason and experience in matters of religious truth and moral right. Nor has the attack upon moral law been confined to Liberal circles. One of the most powerful recent assaults upon the ethics of law in all its forms is that of Nicolas Berdyaev,[1] a Russian Orthodox philosopher.

The value of this reaction is that it warns Christians against the dangers of ethical legalism. What are some of these dangers?

In the first place, legalistic morality is in large part *negative and restrictive*. It identifies Christian ethics largely with a series of prohibitions and multiplies these far beyond those found in the Bible. For example, since the Gospel tells us to deny ourselves and not to be conformed to the world, a host of specific acts are thought by Christians of some groups to be prohibited, e.g., card-playing, theatre-going, and dancing. The result is that the Christian ethic comes to be associated with narrowness rather than fullness of life, with repression rather than sublimation of impulse, with gloom rather than joy. Moreover, since external acts can be prohibited more easily than states of mind and heart, sins of the flesh are made to appear more deadly than the subtler sins of the spirit such as callousness and pride which cannot be controlled by any law, as in Hawthorne's *The Scarlet Letter*.

The second objection to any legalistic ethic is that it *stifles individuality and creativity* in conduct. Since it interprets duty as simple conformity to general rules, it takes no account of the unique elements in each individual life and each changing situation. The claims of special vocations upon particular individuals are denied. Creativity in action based upon a venture of faith in new possibilities is sacrificed. Prophetic moral insights are discouraged and moral progress becomes impossible. Morality under these conditions becomes a matter of blind submission to patterns laid down in the past whether or not they are suitable for the present.

Third, ethical legalism tends to fall into *externalism*. There is nothing about moral laws or rules that necessarily leads to a neglect of motives and the whole inward side of morality. Sometimes Christians are unjust in their criticism of the morality of the Pharisees at this point. After all, a meticulous observance of all the details of the written and oral Law was quite compatible with love of God as one's primary motive and clearly love of God *was* the

[1] Berdyaev, N., *The Destiny of Man*, London, Geoffrey Bles, 1937, Part II. Ch. I.

primary motive for many Pharisees. But there is always a danger, when men's duties are defined in a code of rules, that it will not seem to matter with what motive and in what spirit they fulfill their duties so long as they fulfill them. For an ethic of law by its very essence requires a constant and unremitting effort to fulfill a large number of rules and this effort tends to crowd out other considerations from the center to the periphery of the moral consciousness. To put it another way, since an ethic of legalism is concerned primarily with man's *doing*, it tends to neglect his *being*.

A final objection to any ethical legalism is that law is externally imposed upon the will, and, when it is contrary to natural inclination, it is unable to secure obedience. Paul was the first Christian to proclaim the *weakness* of the Law when confronted by the rebellion of the "flesh." A new power and incentive must be brought to bear in order to transform the self and enable it to fulfill the Law. To Paul and to all Christians after him, this new power is the divine grace given freely to those who turn in faith to God. With the aid of grace, duty becomes an expression of love within rather than a burden imposed from without, and men gladly obey God in gratitude rather than submit unwillingly to Him in fear.

This raises the crucial question whether Christians, who have repented and turned to God in faith, *need* the guidance provided by moral laws. Are they not able, under the inspiration of love and with the aid of the Holy Spirit, to fulfill all the law's demands spontaneously, without having to be commanded to do so? Will not they produce good works as inevitably as a good tree produces good fruits?

But a moral victory may already have been won in principle without having been fully won in fact. The Christian does not remain on the heights of religious experience and moral power. When he returns to the valleys of ordinary life, he continues to be tempted and must exert moral effort to overcome his temptations. However, Luther's doctrine of the spontaneity of the good will and Calvin's doctrine that the spur of the law is necessary are not incompatible; they simply express different moments or aspects of Christian morality. The will of the Christian has been transformed by faith and is oriented towards love of God and neighbor. As a result, he can spontaneously do good works that fulfill the law.

On the other hand, the transformation has not yet been completed and the good will has still to struggle against temptations. Therefore, it is necessary for the will to exert itself and it is aided by the spur of the law to do so.

In other terms, the motive of *love* and the motive of *duty* are not mutually exclusive but complementary. On the one hand, love needs duty as its ally if it is to move men to do consistently and in the face of temptation all they ought to do. On the other hand, duty alone has little power, and love must strengthen the will before it can do its duty. There is bound to be a tension, of course, between the motive of love and the motive of duty. But as the victory of love over the remnants of sin in the self becomes more complete, this tension is lessened. The Christian becomes more and more able to do willingly and gladly from love what duty demands. Since he cannot expect to attain Christian perfection in this life, however, he should never expect to reach the point where his will and heart will be so completely mastered by love that he will not need to be confronted with the demands of duty.

However, while it might be granted that the motive of duty is essential in the Christian life, it might still be denied that *moral laws* give us any light on the nature of our duty. Christian antinomians tend to emphasize the particularity of moral situations and of the moral acts required by them. This leads them to the nominalistic view that, since moral situations are unique, there are no universal ethical principles or even moral rules which are true "on the whole and for the most part."

Ethical nominalism is justified as a corrective of ethical legalism, which exaggerates the similarities of moral situations and minimizes the differences between them. But the Creation of which man is a part is an ordered whole and man's life is shaped by the structures of that whole. In the first place, the nature of man is universal and permanent in its primary characteristics. Every normal human being has certain needs and capacities. These are the basis of claims on his part. For example, the sexual differentiation of the human species gives rise to sexual needs, and the social nature of man is the basis of a need to give and receive affection. These needs give rise to marriage and to the claims of husbands and wives, parents and children, upon one another. In the second place, men stand in certain types of relationship with one another. These are the source of specific duties or obligations. Confucianist ethics consists in large part of "li," a term which has usually been translated "propriety" but which seems to refer to the sum total of duties recognized by custom as binding in special relationships such as those between father and son, husband and wife, brother and brother, friend and friend, and emperor and subject. The assumption behind "li" is that, while there are obviously differences between fathers or between sons, there are also certain duties common to all fathers and others common to all sons.

The existence of these *universal human needs* and *types of relationship* between persons has been the source of moral rules or laws which embody the experience of men in the past with respect to the kinds of acts which best fulfill these needs and the duties which are required in these relationships. These rules or laws are usually regarded as indispensable in moral education, and are transmitted to each new generation by precept and practice. The assumption of Christian antinomians that without the aid of these moral rules love can discover in each situation what it should do is unrealistic. How can love grasp the needs of a neighbor in a particular situation and discover the best way to fulfill them without making use of the knowledge of similar needs in past situations and of the most effective ways of meeting them? Of course, the Christian must always remember that there are differences between a situation and other situations of the same kind. But the similarities as well as the differences are important, and reason cannot approach each new moral situation as if it were without any knowledge derived from previous moral experience. A love that required this would certainly not be Christian love. Since Christian love of neighbor wills the fulfillment of his needs, it must use all available knowledge embodied in moral laws with respect to the kinds of acts which tend to fulfill needs most effectively.

THE MORAL LAWS OF THE BIBLE

In the preceding section, we have attempted to show the necessity of moral laws for the Christian, but we have not distinguished between different types of moral laws. Indeed, it might have seemed that we were describing exclusively "human laws" derived by reason from human experience and that what we have said has no bearing on the value of the "revealed" moral laws of the Bible. But this is not the case. Unless Biblical laws are completely arbitrary divine commands with no relation to the realities and values of human life, they can furnish guidance to men as to the kinds of acts which best fulfill human needs in different relationships.

Is there any radical difference between the moral laws of the Old Testament and those of the New? Christians have sometimes forgotten that Jesus spoke with approval of the "second table" of the Ten Commandments and that his two-fold law of love was quoted directly from the books of Deuteronomy and Leviticus. But there is a marked difference between Jesus' ethic and that of the Old Testament. Even when he quotes with approval moral laws of the Old Testament, he interprets them in a more radical sense. This is obvious in his treatment of the commandments about murder, adultery, and retaliation; it is equally obvious in the deeper meaning taken on by the two-fold law of love in the total context of his teaching. Thus, the meaning of "Thou shalt love the Lord thy God" becomes different in the context of Jesus' parables about God's love for sinful and lost men and his own submission to the will of God in the Garden of Gethsemane; and the meaning of "Thou shalt love thy neighbor as thyself" is deepened and broadened by the illustrations Jesus gives of the ways this love will express itself, by the parable of the Samaritan, and by his own attitude towards publicans and sinners. The measure of the difference between what love meant to him and what it usually meant in the Old Testament is that under the inspiration of his life and death Paul could write the thirteenth chapter of First Corinthians and the second chapter of Philippians.

With respect to the moral laws of the Old Testament, one of the greatest errors of traditional Christian thought, Catholic and Protestant, was that the whole of the "old law" could be "reduced" to the Ten Commandments. Modern Biblical criticism has shown that the importance of the Ten Commandments is not that they contain all the moral laws of the Old Testament but that they lay down basic conditions necessary for the survival and welfare of any society. Every society must prohibit murder, theft, and false witness; every society must protect marriage and the family. But, indispensable as the Ten Commandments are, they represent an early stage of Hebrew law and the moral laws of the "second table" were shared by the Hebrews with other Semitic peoples. They are indispensable and important, but they describe the *minimum* of moral law necessary for *all* men rather than the *maximum* demands of love upon *Christians*.

Another error of traditional Christian thought with respect to the Old Testament law is the neglect of the ethical principles of the eighth-century prophets and of the moral laws of the book of Deuteronomy which were deeply influenced by them. Yet Amos, Hosea, Isaiah and Micah went beyond the minimal laws of the Ten Commandments to the lofty demands of justice and mercy towards all. And Deuteronomy embodies in a code of laws these human-itarian demands, with a special concern for the poor, widows, orphans, resident aliens, slaves, and even animals. Therefore, the prophets and Deuteronomy are specially valuable for Christians who are concerned with the practical expression of love in social justice. If medieval Catholicism and early Protestantism had empha-sized the prophetic demands for justice and mercy as much as the prohibitions of murder, adultery, and theft in the Decalogue, the Church might have been less politically and socially conservative.

Thus, when Christians seek to judge the value of the Old Testa-ment moral laws, they must distinguish between different books and passages with respect to the different levels of ethical insight repre-sented by them. The same principle must be applied by Christians in evaluating the moral "precepts" and "counsels" of the New Testament. For example, there is great value in the precepts and counsels of St. Paul taken as a whole, very little in those of the Book of Revelation. The unqualified counsel to wives in the Letter to the Ephesians[1] that they should "be subject in everything to your husbands," can hardly claim the universal validity of some of the ethical teachings in the Letter to the Romans: "Rejoice with those who rejoice, weep with those who weep. Live in harmony with one another; do not be haughty, but associate with the lowly; never be

[1] Eph. 5:22-24.

conceited. . . . Do not be overcome by evil, but overcome evil with good."[2]

If distinctions of this kind are to be made, however, a different attitude than the traditional one towards the moral laws of the Bible is essential. The traditional attitude represented by Aquinas and Calvin was a product of the pre-critical conception of revelation. According to this conception, revelation was an external communication of truths in propositional form by God. The minds of men to whom these truths were given were completely passive. The moral laws of the Pentateuch were revealed to Moses and written down without any admixture of human distortion or error. They are binding on men simply because they were commanded by God, and their relation to personal fulfillment and social welfare is irrelevant to their validity. On the contrary, the modern critical study of the Bible has made it clear that the moral laws in the Bible developed during long centuries of moral experience and were formulated by men and groups of different degrees of moral sensitivity. Many of them have commanded the obedience of men through the centuries, not only because they were thought to be commanded by God, but also because they were in accord with the realities of human nature and need. But the minds of men were not preserved from all error in interpreting the meaning of God's revelation to them. "If your brother, the son of your mother," we read in Deuteronomy, "or your daughter, or the wife of your bosom, or your friend who is as your own soul, entices you secretly, saying, 'Let us go and serve other gods' . . . you shall kill him; your hand shall be first against him to put him to death, and afterwards the hand of all the people."[3] Can a Christian really believe that this terrible law was revealed by God and was not distorted by the religious zeal of the writer? Again, in the law of Moses we read, "If a man is found lying with the wife of another man, both of them shall die."[4] Is this law consistent with the saying of Jesus about the woman taken in adultery, "Let him who is without sin among you be the first to throw a stone at her"?[5]

[2] Ro. 12:15, 16, 21.
[3] Deut. 13:6, 9.
[4] Ibid., 22:22.
[5] Jo. 8:7.

Thus, the moral laws of the Bible should be looked upon, not as verbally inspired and arbitrarily imposed commands of a despotic heavenly King, but as men's interpretation of the will of God which was disclosed to them in their historical experience.

LAW AND LOVE

We have attempted to show that moral laws are necessary for the Christian and that the moral laws of the Bible have a special value in his eyes. But we have also pointed out that there are different levels of ethical insight in the moral laws of the Bible, and that there is a human element of error or distortion in the interpretation of God's word by those to whom it came. If this is true, the moral laws in the Bible, with the exception of the law of love as interpreted by Jesus, cannot be assumed to possess absolute and universal validity. It is necessary to test the validity of each of them by the one absolute law, the law of love. This implies that the proper use of the Biblical laws by the Christian is quite different than has usually been supposed by Catholic and Protestant legalists.

The basic difficulty with the legalistic view of the use of the law is that it overlooks the diversity of moral situations and the complexity of the needs which must be considered in many situations. It assumes that to each class of moral situations there corresponds one moral rule which can be applied immediately, except in rare cases, to all situations of the class. In reality, it is seldom, if ever, that only one moral rule is relevant to a particular moral situation. Just as a human body is subject at once to physical laws such as gravitation and biological laws such as heredity, each moral situation is usually subject to several different moral laws. For example, the situation of an unemployed and impoverished father whose wife and children are starving but could be saved by his stealing bread or a sum of money is one to which at least two moral laws are relevant: one, the law prohibiting stealing; the other, the law enjoining responsibility for the maintenance of one's children. Again, a doctor who is asked by a critically ill patient whether he will recover must consider both the rule that he should tell the truth and the rule that he should try to save the life of each patient.

The fundamental reason for the complexity of moral situations like these is that it is necessary to consider all the needs and all the persons in each situation. When there are in the situation several different persons with different needs or when there is a person with different kinds of need, love finds it difficult to decide what one's duty is. In the first of the two examples in the preceding paragraph, should the father treat as paramount the general need that property rights be respected or the need of his wife and children for bread? In the second, should the doctor put first the claim of all men to know the truth or the claim of his patient to be treated in such a way as to help save his life? In such situations, two or more moral rules seem to demand different courses of action and one must either find a way to reconcile them or choose between them. Jesus' precept "Resist not the evil doer" seems to demand one course of action towards *him*; but the law "Love thy neighbor as thyself," when applied to the *victims* of the evil doer, seems to require quite another course.

In view of this complexity of many moral situations, and the applicability of two or more moral laws to them, moral laws which command or prohibit specific kinds of acts are not unconditionally universal in their validity. They may make demands which are valid when considered by themselves but which are not valid when they are overridden by higher demands. They are, as Aristotle says of moral judgments, true "on the whole and for the most part," i.e., generally but not universally. Even a moral law as essential for social order and for the protection of personal worth as "Thou shalt not kill" is true only "on the whole and for the most part." For a Christian policeman may find it necessary to kill a person to prevent him from murdering another person, and, unless he is a pacifist, a Christian citizen may think he should kill an enemy soldier in a war he regards as just.

Therefore, the Christian must distinguish between the law of love, which alone is absolutely and universally valid, and other moral laws, which are generally valid but may have to be set aside on occasion. We do not mean by this that all moral laws except the law of love are "only relative" in the sense that they are products of particular cultures and are valid only within those cultures.

Ethical relativism does not do justice to fundamental moral laws such as the "second table" of the Ten Commandments. Though "Thou shalt not kill" is not absolutely and universally valid, as we have said, it is not valid only within a particular culture. It is valid at all times and in all places when a higher law does not override it. That higher law is the law of love which requires us to fulfill the needs of all our neighbors to the extent of our ability. Therefore, in saying that a particular law is not universally but only generally valid, we are saying that it is valid when considered by itself but that under certain conditions a different kind of act than it demands is required by the higher law of love. For example, the moral law "What God hath joined together let no man put asunder" is generally but not absolutely valid because there are situations in which a permanent marriage cannot be maintained beyond a certain point without violating the higher law of love. But this does not mean that the "law" establishing permanent monogamy as the norm of marriage and prohibiting divorce is only relatively true; it means only that in certain cases the law of love requires that this "law" be overridden. Latitudinarian laxity with regard to moral laws is contrary to the spirit of him who demanded that men's righteousness exceed that of the scribes and Pharisees.

If the law of love alone is absolute and if all other moral laws are valid only when they are not overridden by the law of love, we can give at least a general answer to the question, What is the place of moral law in the Christian life and what is its relation to the law of love? Moral law has an *important* but *subordinate* place in the Christian life; and its value lies in the fact that it *counsels us with respect to what love demands of us.* As Brunner puts it, there is only one "command," the law of love, but there is a variety of ways in which it is to be obeyed according to varying circumstances. "God's Command," he says, "does not vary in *intention,* but it varies in *content,* according to the conditions with which it deals."[1] The various "commandments" of the Bible, from the Decalogue to the Sermon on the Mount, are "expositions" of the one "command" to love, they are "paradigms of love." "Each of these commandments . . . stands, so to speak, in the centre between the infinitely varied

[1] *The Divine Imperative,* Philadelphia, Westminster Press, 1947, p. 134.

reality of life and the unity of the divine will of love. It shows us what love would mean in this or that more or less 'special' but still general case, and it commands us to do this very thing."[2]

This does not mean, however, that the moral laws of the Bible can tell us ahead of time and without question what we have to do. If they could, it would mean that all our relations to our neighbors could be foreseen and be surveyed and every problem of duty arising out of these relations could be decided beforehand.[3] The complexity of human relationships does not permit this except at the cost of treating each of our neighbors as a "case" for the application of this or that law and of evading our "direct responsibility to God" for the way we respond to his particular needs.[4] Thus, moral laws do not enable us to know in advance what our duty is in each kind of situation, but they give us the "right direction" for the route we are to follow and in this sense "guidance" for our conduct.[5] Of course, if the moral laws of the Bible are on different levels of ethical insight, as we have argued, we cannot say that all of them are equally "expositions" of the law of love. But with this qualification, Brunner's view that they are "expositions" of what love requires of us is correct. It is the only view that does justice to the importance of moral laws and at the same time definitely subordinates them to love.

LAW AND LIBERTY

How can Christians make use of moral law for their guidance without destroying Christian liberty? Traditionally, Protestant as well as Catholic Christians have been reluctant to show the same independence in dealing with the law which Jesus showed when he allowed his disciples to pluck grain on the Sabbath and appealed from the Mosaic law permitting divorce to the original law of the Creator prohibiting it. This is natural, since they know all too well that, unlike him, they cannot "speak as one having authority." Yet they should not refuse to appeal to their own reason and conscience

[2] Ibid., p. 136.
[3] Ibid., p. 136.
[4] Ibid., pp. 138, 139.
[5] Ibid., pp. 150, 151.

in interpreting and applying moral laws to their own moral situations.

What should be the Christian's attitude, for example, towards the Mosaic law forbidding the taking of interest on loans? It is well known that medieval Christians regarded it as binding, that Calvin allowed moderate interest on certain kinds of loans but not on others, and that modern Christians pay little attention to the law. Should it be literally obeyed, at least in some cases? Should it be reinterpreted to permit moderate but to forbid exorbitant interest? Does it have any implications for the division of an industry's profits between the capitalist and the laborer? Or is it irrelevant in a modern capitalistic economy very different from the ancient Hebrew economy? There is no simple answer to these questions, but the Protestant Christian can hardly evade the responsibility of asking them and seeking answers to them. Again, does the commandment, "Thou shalt not kill," require the Christian to repudiate capital punishment? or birth control? or euthanasia? These are thorny questions, but they cannot be escaped. Obviously, there is a danger, when one raises questions like these, that one will become involved in elaborate casuistry. This danger can be avoided if Christians clearly recognize that it is impossible to develop a moral science which will give final answers beforehand to all moral questions. Creative morality is incompatible with the mechanical application of moral laws and requires the fullest use of intelligence and imagination in the application of them to particular situations.

It is only when Christians can be independent in their use of moral laws that Christian liberty can have its full meaning for them. As we have seen, Christian liberty has meant several different things in the history of Christian thought: freedom from the ceremonial law of the Old Testament; freedom from the vain effort to win one's own salvation by good works of the law; freedom from bondage to sin and moral power to will the highest good; freedom to obey the law willingly as a son; and freedom to do good works spontaneously from love in one's personal relationships. But Christian liberty has also been limited or attenuated in various ways: by predestination and irresistible grace, as in St. Augustine; by the conception of righteousness as strict obedience to the moral laws of the Bible, as in Calvin; by a restriction of Jesus' ethic of love to personal relationships, as in Luther; and by a literal conformity to the teachings of Jesus interpreted as a new law, as in the Anabaptists.

We have already criticized the first and the last of these limitations, and it is unnecessary to speak about them again. But it may be worthwhile to reconsider briefly the legalism of Calvin and the dualism of Luther in the light of our conclusions about the nature, necessity, and use of moral laws. The ethical legalism of Calvin is due to a false idea of Christian morality as consisting primarily of obedience to the moral laws of the Bible rather than of active love serving the needs of one's neighbors. The assumption behind this idea is that the Biblical law, especially the Decalogue, gives us an accurate and comprehensive knowledge of all God commands us to do. In reality, as we have said, the Biblical law gives us an "exposition" or "guidance" as to what love requires, but does not tell us beforehand what to do. Thus, it cannot relieve us of the responsibility of deciding for ourselves what God wills us to do. When men seek through submission to authority to escape from the responsibility of following their own conscience they do so at the cost of their freedom, as Dostoyevsky points out in his great legend of the Grand Inquisitor in *The Brothers Karamasoff*. On the other hand, if they reject the temptation and accept their moral responsibility, they possess the freedom to participate creatively in the fulfillment of their destiny and that of their neighbors.

The ethical dualism of Luther also rests upon a false assumption. Social institutions and callings, Luther assumes, have been created by God in their existing form and with their present imperfections. As such, they constitute a social order which is fixed and unchangeable and which defines the duties of each "calling." The logical consequence of this is that love is powerless to act *upon* as well as *within* a "calling" and to transform the institutions and "callings" of society in accordance with the demands of a higher justice. But if we reject Luther's assumption and regard social institutions as in part a product of the historical decisions of men, man's creative freedom can be extended from his personal to his social relationships. Christian liberty will then include the capacity to reshape social institutions and "callings" in order to make them more consistent with love.

The discovery of this truth by Christian believers in political democracy in the seventeenth century and social justice in the nineteenth and twentieth centuries is one of the greatest achievements of the history of Christian thought.

The view of moral law we have suggested is consistent with both the primacy of Christian love and the privilege of Christian liberty. We must not forget, however, that we cannot fulfill the moral law without love and that love can be bestowed upon us only by *grace*. Moreover, it is only grace that can destroy the power of sin and restore to us the freedom to choose our highest good. Thus, both Christian love and Christian liberty spring from divine grace. This is the fundamental insight of St. Paul and St. Augustine. Whenever it has been forgotten, the Christian ethic has ceased to be an ethic of love and liberty and has degenerated into a form of ethical legalism by which men seek to save themselves. Whenever it has been remembered, Christians have through faith known the love which fulfills the law but fulfills it in liberty.

Part II

THE CHRISTIAN DOCTRINE OF MAN

CHAPTER 7

Man as Creature and Image of God

IN OUR analysis of the ethical teaching of Jesus, we have pointed out that the standard or norm for man's goodness must be the perfect love of God rather than the imperfect love of men. Man's egoism must be overcome in all its forms and he must deny himself even to the point of death for the sake of the Kingdom. This seems to imply the capacity of man for moral achievement of a very high order. It implies that men can live, even in the present age, as children of light rather than children of darkness. Accordingly, Christians throughout the ages have made perfection their goal. That is the meaning of their quest for "holiness," "saintliness," "sanctification." Though this quest has often led to a naive and complacent perfectionism, it is an integral part of the Christian life. In this respect, Christian ethics rests upon a lofty view of man.

But alongside of this view of the moral goal and possibilities of man there is in the New Testament a realism about man as he actually is that has always seemed to men of the world pessimistic. This realism is usually associated with the name of St. Paul, especially the first few chapters of his letter to the Romans. But Jesus also is fully aware of the terrible reality of sin. "If you then, *who are evil,* know how to give good gifts to your children, how much more will your Father who is in heaven give good things to those who ask him?"[1] In several of his parables he emphasizes the presence of evil along with good in the present age. He attacks again and again the sins of callousness, pride and hypocrisy. He expects

[1] Mtt. 7:11 (italics mine).

145

persecution and suffering for himself and his disciples at the hands of sinful men. He warns the religious leaders of his people that they have betrayed their trust and that God is going to take away their authority from them. True, when he teaches he assumes that his hearers are free to respond in repentance and faith. But the parable of the sower indicates clearly his keen understanding of the fact that forces without and within the hearts of men will prevent many of them from responding.

Thus, the New Testament presents us with a paradox: its perfectionistic ethic seems to assume a high conception of man, but its references to man as he actually is seem to be realistic and at times pessimistic. This paradox, in the minds of some, presents a dilemma. *Either* Jesus' perfectionistic ethic is relevant to man in the sense of being appropriate to his nature, in which case his moral capacities must be great. This would seem to imply a view of man which stresses his dignity, rationality, and potential goodness in the manner of classical and Renaissance Humanism, rather than the "pessimistic" view of much of the New Testament. *Or* Jesus' ethic is irrelevant and unsuitable to human life because man's nature is radically evil, in which case it should be abandoned. If we take the first horn of the dilemma, we retain the Christian ethic, but abandon the Christian doctrine of man or revise it radically. This is what many Liberal Protestants and Christian Perfectionists have done. If we take the second horn, we retain the Christian doctrine of man, but reject the Christian ethic. This is what all worldly cynics have preferred to do.

Is it possible to avoid this dilemma? This is a crucial issue for Christians. They must face squarely the question, Are the *high ideals* of Christian ethics compatible with the fact that men are *sinners*? If we are to answer this question, it is imperative that we have an adequate understanding of what the Christian doctrine of man really is.

IDEALISTIC CONCEPTIONS OF MAN

There has been much disagreement among Christians with respect to the nature of man. One of the main reasons is that the central theme of the Bible is not the nature of man as such but the relation of man to God and his response to the action of God upon him. The Bible is from beginning to end theocentric rather than anthropocentric. It is a record of the divine initiative in history. In the drama it unfolds, God has the leading role, not man. It presents a number of insights about man's nature and destiny, as we shall see; but they are nowhere set forth in systematic fashion. Moreover, it is concerned only with certain aspects of man's nature and conduct, making no attempt at a comprehensive view. These aspects are treated somewhat differently by the various Biblical writers, one emphasizing this aspect and another that. Is it any wonder that Christians have interpreted the Biblical conception in different ways?

The Christian doctrine has often been confused with the conception of Greek and Renaissance *Humanism*. The fundamental principle of Plato and Aristotle was that man is distinguished from other animals by his *rationality*. By the exercise of his reason, man is able to conceive general ideas or concepts. This capacity enables him to free himself from preoccupation with particular objects of sense in his natural environment. He can understand the rational order of the cosmos and attain the highest and purest happiness in contemplating it. By reason he can also free himself from slavery to animal appetite and passion, imposing limits upon them by means of moral virtues. At the same time, he can discover and construct a political constitution or form of society by which he can order the many and diverse interests of his corporate life. Thus, through the exercise of his theoretical and practical reason, he can realize all of his potentialities in a harmonious and happy existence. The task of man as a rational animal is the fulfillment of all his natural powers and functions with moderation.

Renaissance Humanism developed this Greek conception further in certain respects. It insisted above all upon the *dignity* of man as a free and creative being. God created all other species of creatures with determinate natures, said Pico della Mirandola, but he gave man a plastic nature and endowed him with the *freedom* to shape himself in any way he chose. If he used his freedom well, he would raise himself in the scale of being; if ill, he would lower himself. Pico seems to have felt that man could attain to an almost divine level. The Renaissance also stressed the value of man's *individuality*.

The highest good for man was the realization of all the potentialities of the individual in as rich and varied experience as possible. Whereas the Greeks had been clearly aware of the limitations upon human freedom and individuality imposed by fate and society, the Renaissance Humanists tended to deny or minimize these limitations. They stressed above all man's pre-eminence as master of all lower forms of creation.[1] Though he was a microcosm who reflected all the levels of the cosmos around him, he was lifted above other creatures by a soul that was rational and immortal like God Himself.[2] "What a piece of work is a man! How noble in reason! how infinite in faculty! in form, in moving, how express and admirable! in action, how like an angel! in apprehension, how like a God! the beauty of the world! the paragon of animals!"[3]

There can be no doubt that this exalted view of man has been the inspiration of much of the noblest effort and achievement of the modern world. Liberal education owes more to it than to any other conception. For liberal education is based, on the one hand, upon the conviction that every individual has worth and is entitled to the fullest possible development of his personality, and, on the other hand, upon the high estimate of rationality as a guide in this development. Again, modern democracy rests upon the dignity of the individual, his right to liberty, and his capacity as a rational being to determine his own ends. Moreover, political and social liberalism is motivated by belief in the necessity of orderly change, in order to free the individual from all forms of oppression and enable him to develop his personality to the fullest possible extent.

In the early part of the nineteenth century, the optimism fostered by Renaissance Humanism found a powerful ally in *philosophical Idealism*. Philosophical Idealism held that the natural world in space and time is the manifestation to our senses of an absolute reality that is spiritual. Nature is the expression of a universal Mind or Spirit that realizes itself at different levels and in different forms. Man's spirit is a finite, imperfect manifestation of this infinite, perfect Spirit. Each nation and period of human history represents

---

[1] Baker, Hershel, *The Dignity of Man,* Cambridge, Harvard University Press, 1947.
[2] Ibid., p. 236.
[3] Shakespeare, *Hamlet,* II, ii.

the unfolding in time of one phase of the eternal life of the Absolute. The social institutions and laws of a particular state are an objective embodiment of the spirit of a people. Its art, religion, and philosophy are the subjective expression of the same spirit.

Thus, Renaissance Humanism and Absolute Idealism alike have fostered a *high estimate* of man in the modern world. This has shown itself in many ways. Perhaps the most striking of these is the abandonment by modern man of the pessimism of the Middle Ages about this world and the acceptance of a complete "this-worldliness." Modern man tends to think that the "other-worldliness" of medieval man was due largely to the natural and social evils from which he suffered and to his powerlessness to overcome those evils. The discoveries of modern science, the application of these in technology, the development of methods of producing and distributing goods on a large scale, the wide diffusion of knowledge through education, and the growth of free social institutions have combined to convince modern man that he can overcome all evils by the resolute use of the new knowledge and power at his disposal. Consequently, the belief in unlimited progress has characterized modern thought from the end of the eighteenth century to the First World War. The belief that progress is inevitable has also produced the Utopianism of the Western world which has taken forms as different as the hope of the Social Gospel for "the Kingdom of God on earth" and the hope of Communism for a "classless society."

It does not need to be said that during the last generation this sublime but naive optimism about man and his powers has received a series of rude shocks. The inhumanity of man to man has never been more obvious than it is to a generation that has witnessed the destruction and cruelty of two world wars. The explosion of revolutionary discontent and the overthrow of established institutions and cultures in Europe and Asia have revealed the weaknesses of Western and Eastern civilizations. The same reason that has won great triumphs over nature by its scientific discoveries has also put in men's hands the knowledge and power to destroy themselves. Men are groping towards a solution of the gigantic problems created by economic exploitation, racial discrimination, and international anarchy. But they do not have the confidence they once had in their capacity to find or apply the right solution. They know that the source of the evils from which they suffer is their own shortsightedness and selfishness; and they are no longer sure that they can overcome it.

As a result, the modern optimistic and idealistic conceptions of man we have described are no longer in the ascendancy, though they still have great influence upon men. It is now realized that these conceptions have arisen and flourished in the modern world because of an exaggeration of one side of man's nature accompanied by a neglect of the other side. They are not errors, they are *half-truths*. Man *is* a rational being, but his reason is more distorted by prejudice and more easily overcome by passion than modern men have been willing to admit. He *is* a spiritual being capable of devoting himself to the universal ends of the Divine Spirit, but he is also a selfish and sensual being. He *is* a being whose natural impulses and feelings often seem to lead him spontaneously towards goodness, but he also suffers from the most irresponsible and destructive egoism. In short, man is a complex being. The weakness of the humanistic and idealistic conceptions of him is that they have been too simple and abstract. They have seen the higher possibilities of human nature, but they have overlooked the way man seems to turn his back on these possibilities. They have asserted that he is "spirit," but have minimized the fact that he is also "flesh." They have emphasized the conception of him as a rational being, but they have forgotten that he is also a finite creature hedged about with limitations and a sinner that contradicts his higher nature.

NATURALISTIC CONCEPTIONS

It will not be necessary for our purposes to deal fully with modern Naturalistic conceptions of man. The reason is not that they are unimportant—indeed, they are dominant in scientific and philosophical circles at the present time—but that there is little danger of a confusion between them and the Christian view. All Naturalistic philosophies have in common the belief that "nature is all the reality there is." This implies that man is part and parcel of nature and is to be explained wholly in terms of natural laws and processes.

It is true that the older Materialism which attempted to reduce man to physico-chemical and biological terms is now out of favor. The development of the social sciences has made it very clear that man is a product of culture as well as of nature. The raw materials of his biological nature must be developed and shaped by social institutions, patterns, and values. Many contemporary Naturalists, moreover, are prepared to admit that man alone possesses certain capacities such as that of forming symbols and transmitting culture from generation to generation. Julian Huxley thinks that the tendency of evolutionary naturalism to stress exclusively the continuity of man with the rest of nature must be overcome and that the "uniqueness of man" must be emphasized.[1] Nevertheless, the "Higher Naturalism" of today agrees with the "Lower Naturalism" of the late nineteenth century on the most fundamental points. Man is not primarily a spiritual being who has been created by God or in whom an eternal Divine Spirit is manifesting itself and realizing its universal ends under the conditions of space and time; he is a product of blind, purposeless natural forces and his spirit is only a function of his body. His values are not rooted in an objective order of values; they are expressions of his own subjective desires and feelings. He has reason because the evolutionary process has endowed him with a highly complex brain; but he must exercise it in an irrational world. He is responsible to no God above and beyond nature. He follows purposes of his own choosing without reference to any higher and broader purpose. Finally, his existence is bounded by birth and death, and he can have no hope of eternal life.

It seems obvious that this Naturalistic view, which in some circles has dethroned man from the exalted position he formerly held, is simply a product of dogmatism. If a man accepts it, it is only because he has allowed himself to be so dazzled by the successes of the scientific method in dealing with nature that he forgets its limitations in dealing with the spirit and its values. For Naturalism contradicts everything man knows himself to be when he trusts his intuitive apprehension of himself from within. When he thinks rationally, he follows logical rather than natural laws. Through his

[1] Huxley, Julian, *Man Stands Alone*, New York, Harpers, 1941, Ch. 1.

religious experience, he is confronted by a transcendent Divine Being upon whom he is dependent. Through his moral experience, he knows that there is an objective order of right and wrong which is quite independent of his desires and preferences. In short, when he looks within, he knows that he is a spiritual being as well as a child of nature. It is only when he allows his vision to be obscured by the pretensions of those who make an idol of the scientific method or by his own obsession with material things and values that he can doubt this.

In one respect the Naturalistic conception of man is like the Idealistic conception we have already examined: it is a simple and abstract view. It, too, has been developed by exaggerating one side of human nature and neglecting the other side. Man *is* a child of nature, an animal species subject to the laws of nature; but he is also a spiritual being who transcends nature. He *is* an irrational being driven by his appetites and passions; but he is also a rational being capable of gaining a measure of control over them. He *is* a creature of time and he must die; but he is also a being who transcends time and longs for eternity.

The Christian doctrine of man accepts the elements of truth in both the Idealistic and the Naturalistic conceptions, and insists upon their importance. Both the exalted conceptions which spring from Renaissance Humanism and philosophical Idealism and the disillusioned views of scientific Naturalism are justified when they are regarded as partial truths. It is a proof of the greatness of the Christian conception that it can include these partial truths as well as reveal dimensions of human nature of which they know nothing. What *is* this Christian conception?

THE CHRISTIAN CONCEPTION: MAN AS CREATURE

The Christian doctrine of man is based upon the Old Testament affirmation that he is a *creature* who is pre-eminent among the creatures and is entitled to dominion over them. We shall consider first what man has in common with other creatures, and then ask what is distinctive of him and the source of his pre-eminence.

When Christians speak of man as a creature, they mean to contrast him with his Creator. Like all creatures, he possesses only a derivative existence. He exists, not from himself, but from God. He is dependent for all that he is or can be upon his Maker. This is the answer of Christianity to the pride of the modern "self-made" and "self-sufficient" man. Everything man is able to do, he does by using energies and abilities he has received as gifts from God. He also depends for his existence, fulfillment, and happiness upon the love and labor of other persons, as well as upon the properties of natural things and processes; and these persons, things, and processes have also been created by God.

The proper attitude of man, therefore, is that of *humility* and *gratitude*. One who is aware of his complete dependence knows that he has no grounds for boasting. One who realizes that he has received all he is and all he values knows that he owes the deepest debt of gratitude to the Source of his existence. Sometimes the theocentric view of the world is criticized on the ground that it requires man to prostrate himself before God like a slave. But our humility and gratitude towards God are based primarily not upon our recognition of His power, but upon our experience of His goodness in our "creation, preservation, and all the blessings of this life." Of course, if God had brought us into being by a necessary process such as emanation, we might not feel gratitude towards Him. But Christians believe that God created not by necessity but by an act of freedom and that His blessings are bestowed from love. Thus, humility and gratitude are not a sign of the abasement of weakness before His strength; they arise from an acknowledgement and appreciation of His goodness.

The doctrine of man as creature implies not only that he is dependent but also that he is *finite* and *limited*. He is involved in mutability like all things in time. His values and achievements are precarious in the presence of the contingencies of nature. Above all, his days are numbered; mortality is the lot of every man. This is the source of much of the poignancy and tragedy of human life, of bereavement and the incompleteness of all human enterprises. It has always led sensitive minds without a living faith in God and eternal life, e.g., the author of Ecclesiastes and the Buddha, to pessimism about this life. It has stimulated in others a hope for immortality to fulfill the frustrated purposes and undeveloped possibilities of this life. Whether in this life or the next, salvation from the disappointments, losses, and failures of temporal existence has always been one of the primary objects of religious longing.

Man is limited in mental capacity. His knowledge is partial, the wisest being most aware of the fragmentary character of what they know. It is also fallible. Absolute truth is presupposed in the quest for knowledge, but it is never found. That is why dogmatism, intolerance, and intellectual pride are always out of place. Similarly, man's moral capacity is always limited. The effort to attain perfect goodness never fully succeeds and most men are content with conventional morality. Finally, man is limited in his size and strength. Though he can supplement his strength by the physical and human power he can command, he can never attain unlimited power. As the Pharaohs failed to overcome the ravages of time by the pyramids, the great Emperors and Generals have been unable to overcome the limits of physical power by their control of millions of subjects and soldiers.

Man's recognition of the brevity of his existence and the frailty of his powers brings with it *suffering*. But the suffering that is due to man's finiteness as a creature is not regarded by writers of the Bible as the greatest evil. In Hinduism and Buddhism the sense of change and impermanence hangs like a dark cloud over human existence because of the suffering and loss they bring. Salvation consists above all of release from the endless cycle of suffering through enlightenment or the annihilation of desire. Judaism and Christianity, on the other hand, are well aware of the fact of suffering, but they have not believed it to be the ultimate evil. They have learned that pain can be borne, that fidelity and fortitude can be won by "serving God for nought," and that voluntary suffering for the sake of others can be redemptive. Therefore, they do not accept the necessity of annihilating desire or negating the world. It is sin, not suffering, that is man's greatest foe.

But this does not mean that the evil of suffering is minimized in the world-affirmation of the Bible. The Psalms ring the changes on the theme of man's mortality and frailty:

> Put not your trust in princes,
> in a son of man, in whom there is no help.
> When his breath departs he returns to his earth;
> on that very day his plans perish.[1]

> For he knows our frame;
> he remembers that we are dust.

> As for man, his days are like grass;
> he flourishes like a flower of the field;
> for the wind passes over it, and it is gone,
> and its place knows it no more.[2]

When a vigorous faith in the goodness and mercy of God is present, however, the theme of melancholy becomes secondary to that of confidence and trust, as in the great Psalm from which we have just quoted:

> But the mercy of the Lord is from everlasting to everlasting
> upon them that fear him,
> and his righteousness unto children's children.[3]

Finally, to say that man is a creature is to say that his nature and functions are essentially *good* and that his life is *meaningful*. In the myth of creation in Genesis, God looks upon His Creation and finds it good. The fact that the world and man are products of the hand of a good God is an assurance that they also are good and that they have been created in order that some purpose might be realized through them.

This is the basis of Christian *optimism* about the world. It means that the cosmos is not a meaningless welter of blind energies without purpose, it is a sphere for the attainment of ends and values. Sometimes the world has been regarded as the product of an evil power, as in Gnosticism; or as an emanation from an impersonal World Spirit and without meaning, purpose, or even reality in

---

[1] Ps. 146:3, 4.
[2] Ps. 103:14-16.
[3] Ps. 103:17 (A.V.).

itself, as in Hindu Monism. The Christian doctrine of the Creation, however, asserts that the world is the creation of a benevolent God and as such is good. Moreover, every aspect of man's nature, body as well as mind and spirit, is good. This makes it impossible to ascribe man's sin, in dualistic fashion, to his body and its appetites. His body is a vehicle for the life of the spirit, a temple of the Lord, and is to be honored and cared for as such. Thus, the whole of man's nature has value, and he lives his life in a world that is not indifferent or hostile but friendly to him.

The doctrine of man as creature, then, asserts the dependence of man upon God and the finiteness and imperfection of his existence; but it also encourages him to trust in God in the midst of his sufferings and never to forget that his life has value and that he lives in a meaningful world.

MAN IN THE IMAGE OF GOD

The second affirmation of the Christian doctrine of man is that he is *pre-eminent* among the creatures. This is expressed in the great myth of creation by the assertion that "God created man in his own image"[1] and that He gave man "dominion" over other living beings.[2] The influence of this assertion upon Hebrew thinking about man is shown most strikingly by a famous passage in Psalm 8:

> When I look at thy heavens, the work of thy fingers,
> the moon and the stars which thou hast established;
> what is man that thou are mindful of him,
> and the son of man that thou dost care for him?
>
> Yet thou hast made him little less than God,
> and dost crown him with glory and honor.
> Thou hast given him dominion over the works
> of thy hands;
> thou hast put all things under his feet.[3]

In this passage man's puny size and strength are contrasted with the magnificence of the starry skies at night and the greatness of

[1] Gen. 1:27.
[2] Ibid., 1:28.
[3] Ps. 8:3-6.

their Creator. Nevertheless, he is exalted above all the visible creation to a position next to God Himself.

What is the ground of this exalted view of the worth of man?
It is not primarily his superior nature but his special *relationship to
God* that sets him apart. This is clearly implied in the assertion that
God made man in His own *image*. For an image is nothing by
itself; it has its existence and character entirely from that of which
it is the image. This is perhaps the most fundamental difference
between the Christian and the Greek humanistic view of the dignity
of man. To the Greek philosophers, man's dignity belonged to his
nature by virtue of his distinctive capacities and qualities. But the
Bible means by the doctrine of the image of God in man not only
that he possesses qualities like rationality which are similar to those
of God, but also that he can be understood only by his relation to
his Creator.

Thus, man's relationship to God, as one who reflects the nature of
his Creator, belongs to his essence. Just as an image of a thing in
water or a mirror is a reflection of it, so man reflects God's nature.
Similarly, in his action man *responds* to the initiative and call of
another, his Maker. This is not a degradation of man, a denial of his
dignity, as some man-centered modern thinkers seem to feel. For
God, by making man in His own image, has given him alone the
capacity to respond freely and consciously to His will; He has made
him alone a responsible being. Thus, man responds and imitates,
but he also participates in God's creative and redemptive activity
which gives meaning to all existence. Because he was made in God's
image, he can become God's son.

Man's essence, then, should be defined by reference to his relationship of likeness to God, not by analysis of his nature apart from
that relationship. But that does not mean that he has no *nature* of
his own. Though his distinctive qualities and capacities depend upon
his relationship to God, they do exist and are his. An image, after
all, is distinct from that which casts it. According to the doctrine of
Creation, the creatures have a nature and existence distinct from
that of their Creator—they are not mere appearances of Him—and
they have relative freedom in their activity.

What is that nature? What is the content of "the image of God"?
It is possible that the author of the myth of Creation was thinking

in anthropomorphic terms and meant to picture man as like God in his physical form as well as his psychical functions. But in later Judaism and in Christianity the assertion that man is in the "image of God" refers primarily to his *spiritual endowment* as a person. What is this spiritual endowment? Under the influence of Greek philosophy, St. Thomas Aquinas defined the image of God as reason. We must reject this conception. The assertion that man has been created in the image of God refers primarily, not to his rationality, but to his capacity as a spiritual person to respond to God by obedience to Him. Man stands in a personal relationship to God as an "I" confronted by a "Thou." Since he must be able to hear and understand the Word spoken to him in this relationship, rationality is an integral part of his nature. But he is like God not only by his capacity to understand Him but also by his capacity to love and obey Him. Indeed, his capacity to understand, like all his natural faculties, is perverted and becomes the source of evil rather than good when it is not controlled by a will set upon obedience. This implies that the proper response of man to God is *obedience in love*. When he makes this response, he manifests most clearly the image of God in him.

As we shall see, sin distorts the image of God in man. The capacity to respond to God by obedience remains in him and he does not cease to be a responsible being. But he does not manifest the image of God clearly because he is centered in himself rather than God. This is why the New Testament stresses the necessity of being conformed to the "image" of Christ who is "the image of the invisible God."[4] Through faith in him and union with him as the image of God, the Christian is restored to the right relationship with God. By his obedience in love he can then clearly manifest the image of God in him. In short, the image of God remains in man despite his sin but it is in a distorted form; his capacity to manifest it fully must be restored to him by faith in and conformity to Christ.

The Hebrews used the term "ruach," *spirit,* for that aspect of man which is open to God and is invaded and laid hold of by the Spirit of God. It is associated with supernormal phenomena such as the inspiration of the prophet. In the New Testament Church,

[4] Col. 1:15.

possession by the Holy Spirit was the source not only of ecstasy but also of the love, joy, and peace of the new life. The Christian life is "in the Spirit." Since the emphasis falls upon the transforming power of the Holy Spirit or the Spirit of Christ, the spirit of man himself is seldom mentioned.[5] It is difficult, if not impossible, therefore, to discover in the New Testament a description of this spiritual aspect or element of man's personality. It is clear, however, that the spirit is conceived in terms very different from those of Plato's *Phaedo*. It is not a separate immaterial substance which is only externally related to the body. Incalculable harm has been done to Christianity by the identification of its conception of spirit with that of Platonic dualism. This dualism has had great influence upon Christian thought from the time of the Christian Platonists of Alexandria in the second century. It has always led to ascetic attitudes towards sex and marriage. It has fostered contempt of the world as a whole and of the material aspect of the world in particular. It has been responsible for the false explanation of sin in terms of the appetites and passions of the lower animal self.

In contrast, the Biblical view of man asserts the *unity of the personality* as a psychophysical whole. The fact that in the Old Testament various functions of the soul are associated with particular organs of the body, e.g., thinking with the heart, is evidence of this. When the Jews developed a belief in a blessed future life for the righteous, it took the form of resurrection of the body rather than immortality of the soul. In the Gospels there is no dualism between body and spirit, and hence there is no asceticism; the dualism Jesus stresses is a religious and moral one: the present age and the age to come, God and Mammon, heavenly and earthly treasure. St. Paul is responsible for the introduction of dualistic language and for the idea of a conflict between "flesh" and "spirit." But again it is primarily a religious and moral dualism that he has in mind. When he speaks of the flesh as warring against the spirit, he obviously means by "flesh" not the physical body, but the self as corrupted by self-love. Indeed, he lists as "works of the flesh" not only "carnal" sins such as "licentiousness" and "drunkenness," but also "spiritual"

[5] Cf. I Cor. 14:15.

sins such as "idolatry," "enmity," "strife," "jealousy," "selfishness," "dissension," "party spirit," and "envy."[6]

What, then, is the *spirit*? In the most general terms, it is the *capacity of a person to transcend himself and the natural world through devotion to supersensible Reality and Good*. Man is finite but longs for the infinite. Imperfect, he longs for the perfect. Limited and conditioned, he aspires towards absolute Reality and Good. Plato expresses this paradox in the form of a myth about the origin of spiritual love. Love, he says in the *Symposium,* was born of two utterly different parents, Poverty and Plenty. As son of Poverty, he is always lacking and needy. As son of Plenty, however, he is aware of the good he lacks and is always seeking it. According to the Bible, love is not so much an aspiration for an absolute impersonal *Good* which will fill the need of the soul but a response to *God* as Creator and Redeemer. Thus, the spiritual life is conceived by Plato in humanistic terms; it is man's attempt to raise himself above the limitations of time in order to participate in eternal Being and Good. On the other hand, the spiritual life in the Bible is theocentric; it is the life of love and obedience which springs from God's antecedent love for man.

Devotion to supersensible Reality and Good involves devotion to *absolute values*. An absolute value is one which is not relative to one's desires or feelings but claims one's unconditional devotion. For example, truth is an absolute value, when it is more than a means to one's own ends, when it claims one's loyalty at whatever cost to one's personal interests. Similarly, morality has absolute value when duties are performed not for the sake of personal happiness or social reward but because they are believed to be right. However, Christians differ from Humanists in their conception of absolute values. Humanists tend to regard these values as impersonal ideals or "essences" which demand man's devotion for their own sakes. Christians, on the other hand, conceive of absolute values in relation to the needs of persons.

Through the spiritual activity in which man transcends himself,

[6] Gal. 5:19-20.

he is raised to the highest level possible for him. In greater or lesser measure, it brings about a *transformation of the self*. The spiritual life is the creative life. A man's nature is never fully actualized in his character and achievement at any given time. There are many values he has never appreciated, many potentialities he has not yet realized. But his nature is not fixed and static. Of course, he cannot go beyond all limits and attain to infinity and perfection. He is a creature, not the Creator. But he can always transcend in some degree the limits within which he is confined at any given time. He can never know the whole truth, but he can pass beyond the partial truth he now knows. He can never attain perfect goodness, but he can struggle against his vices and seek a higher goodness.

In transcending himself, man also *transcends nature*. This is why the Christian view of man is incompatible with that of Naturalism. Spiritual personality cannot be explained in biological terms alone. The absolute values of the spiritual life, e.g., truth, justice, and love, are radically different from biological values, e.g., health and survival. The realization of them is governed not by biological but by spiritual laws. The quest for truth, for example, is governed by logical norms such as fidelity to fact, consistency, and comprehensiveness. The quest of the will for goodness is governed by moral laws which differ from natural laws in that they tell us what we ought to do rather than describe what we actually do. The radical difference between spiritual and biological values is also shown by the fact that they often come into conflict with one another. When they do, the spirit can limit or deny biological values in order to realize its own distinctive values. For example, no great achievement in the realm of conduct or faith has ever been won without putting restraint upon the sexual impulse. Sometimes the spirit is forced to deny even the impulse to live, the most imperious of all biological drives, as in self-sacrifice for one's country or one's faith.

The transcendence of spirit over nature also implies the *transcendence of time*. The lower animals are able to transcend the present only to a very limited extent. But man is able to preserve in memory the treasures of his past experiences, recall them to consciousness, and survey the whole course of his life. He can extend his knowledge of the past by making use of the memory of his elders and of documents and other records of bygone years. He can even push it back to dim prehistoric ages by a process of inference and trace the course of geological and biological evolution before man emerged. Moreover, he can draw upon his past experience and project plans for the future, choosing a career or undertaking an enterprise which will affect all the rest of his life and have consequences far beyond his death. Finally, the extension of his knowledge of the past and the reaching out of his purposes into the future change radically the character of the present. He experiences the present, not as a discrete unit of time, but as a shifting point in a continuous process of experience. The present is freighted with a significance which is derived from its relation to what has gone before and what is to come after it. Man is a creature of time, involved in mutability and faced with death. But he can endow the moments of his temporal existence with a wider meaning and can even relate them to the eternal.

MAN AS INDIVIDUAL IN COMMUNITY

Although the Bible conceives of spirit as "primarily a capacity for and affinity with the divine," as Reinhold Niebuhr says,[1] it never forgets that man is a creature. As a creature, he belongs to nature even when he is transcending himself and nature. In Niebuhr's words, "he stands at the juncture of nature and spirit; and is involved in both freedom and necessity."[2] This is evident in every phase of his existence. For example, man was created male and female and sexual differentiation is the natural basis of marriage, but he also endows the sexual relationship with a significance which no other animal species knows.

His unique position "at the juncture of nature and spirit" helps us to understand the double fact that he is an individual and that he lives in community with other persons. As a creature, man is an *individual being;* he is himself and no other. But his individuality, which differentiates him from other persons, is more important for

[1] Niebuhr, R., *The Nature and Destiny of Man,* New York, Scribners, 1941, I, p. 152.
[2] Ibid., p. 181.

man than for other animals because he is a spiritual being. "The higher we ascend in the scale of being the more significance does individuality gain," says Brunner. "Individualization only reached its maximum in personal being, in 'personal individuality.' It is not matter that individualizes but life, and still more than life, the spirit. The more spiritual people are the less they can be exchanged for anyone else, the more 'distinctive imprint' they possess."[3] For the free acts and decisions of each man help to shape his individuality.[4] He can confront his actual self with an ideal of what he wants to be, and in a measure can remake himself in the shape of that ideal.

Accordingly, Christianity stresses the *uniqueness* of the individual. "God the Creator," says Brunner, "does not create humanity, but he creates each individual human being separately, He has 'called thee by thy name,' He knows you 'personally,' 'specially.' Hence you are not an example but a person, a self which cannot be exchanged for any other."[5] Since every individual is dear to God, he should be treated as a precious and unique being by other men. This is why Christianity is incompatible with every theory that submerges the individual in a larger whole, as Naturalism submerges him in Nature or Absolute Idealism in the World Spirit. It is why Christians must oppose every social movement that reduces the individual to a featureless member of an impersonal mass. They cannot accept any form of Collectivism, whether of the right or of the left, because it swallows up the individual and makes him merely a means to the ends of the group.

On the other hand, man as a spiritual being is a *responsible* individual. His responsibility *to* God requires responsibility *for* other persons. He is bound up in the closest unity with others. His individuality is not that of an atom which is only externally related to other atoms, as in the view of modern individualism. If he insists upon his absolute independence of others, he not only fails to manifest responsibility for them, he contradicts his own nature. Accord-

[3] Brunner, Emil, *Man in Revolt,* copyright, 1947, by W. L. Jenkins, The Westminster Press, pp. 319-20.
[4] Ibid., p. 321.
[5] Ibid., p. 322.

ing to the Christian view, there is no such thing as independence of others. Man is created for relationship with his fellows. As a finite creature who is dependent from birth upon others to help him fulfill his needs, he cannot live without community.

The *basis of community* is generally blood relationship and the sharing of a cultural pattern. In the city-states of ancient Greece, for example, the natural bonds of unity were strengthened by loyalty to the social institutions and cultural values of the group. Such communities are "closed" societies in which the responsibility of each person is limited almost wholly to the members of his own group. Man, however, is capable of creating a community which is based not upon natural or cultural but upon spiritual foundations. He is called upon to enter into such a community with all those who have accepted the Kingdom of God. The basis of membership in that community is faith and its bond of unity is love of neighbor. While "closed" societies depend upon natural kinship or common values to hold them together, love is necessary to create a universal community. To the extent that such a universal community comes into being, it will limit man's loyalties to the "closed" societies of which they are members and prevent them from becoming absolute.

Thus, the Christian conception of man heightens the worth of the individual and refuses to allow him to be swallowed up in any group. At the same time, it insists that he should be responsible for other men, that he should strive to bring into existence a universal community based upon love for all, and that he should limit his loyalty to less inclusive groups in order to make it consistent with the demands of that community.

CHAPTER 8

Man as Sinner

THE DUAL NATURE OF MAN

WE HAVE pointed out that, according to the Biblical conception of man, his nature is that of a finite creature but that he is pre-eminent among the creatures because of the image of God in him. We have argued that this conception includes the positive truths in both Naturalistic and Idealistic theories. At the same time, it avoids the degradation of man by Naturalism to the status of an ac-cidental product of nature and the exaltation of man by Humanism or Idealism to the status of a rational or spiritual being who can by the exercise of his own powers overcome all the evil that af-flicts him.

The modern thinker who has expressed most adequately the Christian insight into the *dual* nature of man is Blaise Pascal. A brilliant mathematician and scientist, he respected reason. Rejecting the skepticism of Montaigne, he asserted the capacity of the senses and the reason to know the natural world. But he saw that the claims made on behalf of reason by rationalistic thinkers like Descartes were profoundly dangerous. By their pretension to know the essence of matter, mind, and God and to solve metaphysical and theological problems by pure reason, they were encouraging an intellectual pride and dogmatism unsuitable to a finite being. There-fore, Pascal asserted the dignity of man as a "thinking reed" in the face of the infinite space and mighty power of nature, but he also reminded him of the limitations of his reason. Man is in a middle position in the scale of being, "neither angel nor brute." If he thinks only of the higher, rational side of his nature, he falls into pride. As Pascal says, "the unfortunate thing is that he who would act the angel acts the brute." On the other hand, if he thinks only of the lower, irrational side of his nature, he falls into skepticism and despair. He must avoid both extremes, asserting both his "greatness" and his "misery" at the same time.

According to Pascal, man is limited, not only in his physical and mental powers, but also in his moral possibilities. As a rational being, he should be able to discover and follow a universal moral law, the "natural law." But actually his moral judgments are distorted by his prejudices and selfishness and are relative to time and place. Justice should be established in society on the basis of right and might should serve right. But actually justice is based upon might and right is made to serve might. Since man is limited in knowledge and corrupted in will, therefore, his dignity as a rational being must not be allowed to blind him to his misery and his need of help from God. His knowledge of the "order of matter" and "the order of mind" must be supplemented by faith in "the order of charity" which is "infinitely elevated above them"; and his will must be transformed by the divine grace.

This brings us to the third aspect of the Christian doctrine of man: man is a *sinner*. The "misery" of which Pascal speaks is due primarily not to the limitations of his physical and mental powers as a creature, but to the fact that through his sin he contradicts his higher nature and destiny as a spiritual being. This contradiction brings division and discord into his nature. As a result, the will feels powerless to overcome the promptings of evil and to follow the aspirations of the spirit. This is why Christianity has always insisted upon the inability of man to save himself and the necessity of redemption through Christ. Indeed, on any other presupposition than that of the sinfulness of man, the Gospel becomes meaningless. For the Gospel is the good news of God's mercy and forgiveness towards sinners. It offers the blessings of life in His Kingdom only to those who repent of their sins, receive forgiveness, seek to amend their lives, and pray for God's grace to strengthen them.

Many modern persons, it must be admitted, find this doctrine of

sin and redemption wholly unintelligible. As we have seen, modern
man has been taught since the Renaissance to insist upon his dignity
and to minimize his limitations and his sins. Of course, he has been
aware of the evils which assail him from without and within. But
he has tried to convince himself that these are due to lack of knowledge, to faulty social institutions, or to his animal heritage, rather
than to radical evil in his own self. He has believed that he could
overcome them by improving the social sciences, by eliminating
social injustice, by exerting his will a little harder, or by better
education of the younger generation. Consequently, he has attempted to transform the Gospel into something quite different from
an offer of divine redemption through Christ. Either he has abandoned the religious side of Christianity altogether or he has eliminated from its teaching every trace of "pessimism" about the
"natural" man. The Gospel has become for many Protestants a
simple teaching about the Fatherhood of God, the worth of every
human personality, and the happiness of a life of love. Intoxicated
by his scientific and technical achievements and encouraged by
Utopian dreams of future perfection, modern man has turned
away from the Christian doctrine of sin and redemption as if it
were only a morbid and gloomy distortion and degradation of
human nature.

It must be confessed that Christians have been partly to blame
for this, for one of the reasons modern man has turned away from
the doctrine of sin has been the unwillingness of orthodox Christianity to surrender *mythical elements* in the traditional doctrine
which have been discredited by modern science. For example, an
uncritical view of the inspiration of the Bible has caused Funda-
mentalists to defend the historical authenticity of the myth of the
Garden of Eden and the Fall of Adam. Now, anthropologists are
unanimous in denying that there was ever a time of perfect innocence, harmony, and bliss, in a primeval Garden or elsewhere.
Man evolved from animal ancestors and struggled slowly upward
from a condition far inferior to his present state. It is obvious, therefore, that the innocence and harmony of Eden must refer, not to
an actual condition once enjoyed by our first parents, but to an ideal
condition which might have been enjoyed by all men if they had

not denied their higher nature by their sin. Moreover, since a condition of innocence never actually existed, the Fall of Adam must be regarded as a mythical account of man's denial of his higher nature through sin and of the disastrous consequences. It is a story not about the First Man, Adam, but about Everyman, each and all of us.

The uncritical identification of Christian truth with *theological interpretations* of it in the past has also had a harmful effect. Much harm has been done, for example, by the Augustinian idea that the sin into which Adam fell was transmitted by heredity to each and every one of his descendants so that each child is born with a burden of sin and guilt. It should be noted that in the early Church there was a different explanation of the universality of sin among men: Adam was representative of the whole human race in his human nature, so that all sinned "in" him. Even St. Augustine seems to suggest this explanation in a comment on St. Paul: "'For all have sinned'—whether in Adam or in themselves—'and come short of the glory of God.'"[1] Apart from this, however, the fundamental idea of the doctrine of "original sin" is not that of an inheritance of sin and guilt from the first man; it is that of the solidarity of every man with the sin of humanity as a whole. The way in which this solidarity is manifested we shall discuss later. But it should be stressed here that even modern theologians in the Augustinian tradition like Brunner and Niebuhr reject the theory of hereditary transmission of sin. It is not only that it is thought to be biologically impossible but also that it would be wholly irrational and immoral for the descendants of Adam to be regarded as guilty merely because of his guilt. Moreover, the theory tends to relieve the descendants of Adam from their responsibility for their own guilt by attributing it to him.

Finally, the evil consequences of sin have been presented in the traditional Augustinian doctrine in such extreme terms that it has seemed to many a caricature, if not an insult, to human nature. The fearful doctrine of "total depravity," as we shall see, is an exaggeration of a profound truth. For sin has brought radical evil into human nature. But the assertion that there is nothing good in the natural man and that he can do nothing but evil has repelled many

[1] Quoted by Niebuhr, R., *The Nature and Destiny of Man*, New York, Scribners, 1941, V. I, p. 261.

persons not only because it degrades man but also because it seems to be contradicted by the facts. Moreover, it tends to drive man into complete despair by implying that he can do nothing but wait passively for the grace of God to lift him out of his moral impotence.

Thus, modern secularists and Christians alike have been antagonized by literalistic and extreme interpretations of the doctrine of sin. Sometimes it has seemed that those who have insisted upon these interpretations have forgotten the image of God in men. Indeed, they speak of the total "destruction" or "obliteration" of the image of God by sin. As a result they deny that there is any "point of contact" in sinful man by which he can respond to the demands of God or the message of Christ. Consequently, it is necessary for Christians who accept the doctrine of sin but reject these extreme views to restate the meaning of the doctrine in terms that will not be misleading. Let us attempt such a restatement.

THE UNIVERSALITY OF SIN

In the first place, the Bible asserts the *universality* of sin. The natural tendency of men is to admit that some men are flagrant sinners and that other men sin on occasion but to insist that most men in most of their actions are good. It is always possible to maintain one's moral complacency about oneself and one's class or nation by convincing oneself that there are other persons or groups who are morally worse. It is the moral complacency resulting from this kind of comparison which is responsible for the neat and simple division of men into the innocent and the guilty, the wholly righteous and the wholly wicked. It also produces the tendency to find scapegoats upon whom a group can unload all its own guilt and send it away. This way of thinking is to be found in the Bible itself, especially the Old Testament. But Jeremiah pictures the men of Judah as so habituated to sin that they stubbornly refuse to change, and in the Psalms the universality of sin is clearly asserted:
"The Lord looks down from heaven upon the children of men,
to see if there are any that act wisely, that seek after God.
They have all gone astray, they are all alike corrupt;
there is none that does good, no, not one."[1]

[1] Ps. 14:2, 3.

In the New Testament, St. Paul says that "all men, both Jews and Greeks, are under the power of sin."[2] He also puts his finger upon one of the most effective ways by which the "righteous" maintain their moral self-esteem. The Jews, he says, point with pride to the fact that the Law of Moses was revealed to them alone. They not only possess the Law; they profess to follow it. This enables them to rationalize their failure to live up to the Law in their actual conduct. Paul reminds them that the mere profession of allegiance to superior ideals is no proof of superior character. He insists that "it is not the *hearers* of the law who are righteous before God, but the *doers* of the law who will be justified."[3] This tendency to be satisfied with a formal acceptance of a high ideal and to excuse oneself for one's actual sin by paying homage to that ideal is manifested by all of us.

The sense of sin is deeper in those whose moral ideal is very high than in those who are contented with the low standards of conventional morality. In his description of his unsuccessful struggle to obey the Law, St. Paul says, "I should not have known what it is to covet if the law had not said, 'You shall not covet.' But sin, finding opportunity in the commandment, wrought in me all kinds of covetousness."[4] Covetousness is a sin which can be hidden from the eyes of others. To some people it is hardly a sin at all but a spur to effort and success in the competitive struggle with others. But desires as well as actions must be good if one is to fulfill the high demands of a righteous God. After all, covetousness is as clear a sign of self-love as stealing or murder, though it may never find overt expression in external conduct. To put the same point in positive terms, the demand, "You shall love the Lord your God with all your heart, and with all your soul, and with all your mind, and with all your strength,"[5] requires a complete and whole-hearted devotion which is extremely rare. Most persons are contented with a love of God that is half-hearted. But the saint knows all too well the self-centeredness which prevents him from giving *all* his heart, mind, soul, and strength. Though he is a far better man than others, he

[2] Ro. 3:9.
[3] Ro. 2:13, ital. mine.
[4] Ro. 7:7, 8.
[5] Mk. 12:30.

sees himself as a sinner. When one's standard of goodness is the perfect love of God, who will claim that he is *not* a sinner?

Thus, when we cease making comparisons with others that are favorable to ourselves, look at our actual conduct rather than our high ideals, and realize that we are called to perfect goodness like that of God rather than the conventional goodness of men, we see that, in the words of Jesus, "No one is good but God alone."[6]

THE RADICAL NATURE OF SIN

Sin is *radical*. It affects the personality to its very roots. It is not merely particular acts of transgression against this or that moral law. It is more, even, than particular vices or evil habits. If it were only particular transgressions or vices, as most men think, it would be possible to deal with it more successfully. One could discipline oneself to abstain from occasional acts of lying and sexual indulgence; one might even be able to break deep-seated habits of doing these acts. But sin is also a *state* or *condition* of the self due to a fundamentally wrong orientation. Therefore, if one kind of act in which it has hitherto manifested itself is weakened or destroyed, it can easily find another. For example, a person may show remarkable strength of will in mastering "carnal" temptations such as lust and drunkenness, but demonstrate a cold, rigid, censorious, and callous attitude towards others. For this reason, the definition of sin by Augustine as "a word, deed, or desire, contrary to the eternal law,"[1] or that of Aquinas, "nothing else than an evil human act . . . lacking conformity with its due measure,"[2] is inadequate. At the most, these definitions throw light upon the nature of particular sins. But sin is a condition of *sinfulness* as well as a particular *sin*.

The radical character of sin is also evident in the fact that it is a condition of the *self* at its very center. The significance of this can be seen best if we contrast the Christian view of moral evil with that of Greek rationalism. Socrates held that vice is ignorance; it is

---

[6] Mk. 10:18.

[1] Augustine, *Contra Faust.*, XXII, 27.

[2] Aquinas, *Summa Theologica,* I-II, q. 71, a. 6.

due to a defect of knowledge. The merit of this view is that it points to the fact that men do not will evil as such; they will evil in the guise of good. It was Satan, not man, who said, "Evil, be thou my good." Men are capable of willing only that which appears to them to be in some sense good. But it is also true that men often will something they know to be an inferior good. "When an inordinate will," says Aquinas, "loves some temporal good, e.g., riches or pleasure, more than the order of reason or divine law, or divine charity, or some such thing, it follows that it is willing to suffer the loss of some spiritual good so that it may obtain possession of some temporal good," and thus man sins "on purpose because he chooses evil knowingly."[3]

As sin is not a defect of knowledge, it is not an excess of *appetite* or *passion*. True, the will is often moved by a passion, says Aquinas, and the reason may be overcome by it despite its knowledge. For a man may know in general that a certain kind of act is wrong and yet be prevented by passion from applying the general rule in a particular case, or he may know it "habitually" but not consider it "actually" in this case.[4] But this does not excuse him from sin because normally "reason can drive the passion away by turning to other thoughts, or it can prevent it from having its full effect, since the members are not put to work except by the consent of reason, as we have stated above."[5] Thus, sin is not identical with strong passion, because a passion must have the "consent of reason" and be adopted by the will before it can lead to a sinful act.

Therefore, the Greek rationalistic view of sin which attributed it to lack of knowledge or to strength of passion or both cannot be accepted because the whole self is involved. Another proof of the radical character of sin is that it *divides the self* against itself. There is a "higher will" which wills the true good, but the "lower will" mastered by sin contradicts it. This "lower will" appears as an alien force that has taken possession of the self. "I do not understand my own actions," says St. Paul in his classic description of the divided will. "For I do not do what I want, but I do the very thing I hate.

[3] Ibid., q. 78, a. 1.
[4] Ibid., q. 77, a. 2.
[5] Ibid., q. 77, a. 7.

. . . So then it is no longer I that do it, but sin which dwells within me. For I know that nothing good dwells within me, that is, in my flesh. I can will what is right, but I cannot do it."[6] This passage is written from the point of view of the "higher self," the spiritual nature. That is why sin appears as something foreign, "what I do not want." But the tragic fact is that it is precisely what I *do* want insofar as I am dominated by the "flesh," the "lower self." The "higher self" wills the true good, but it is the "lower self" that has the power to get what it wants and what it wants is not the true good. In the *Confessions,* St. Augustine describes his own divided will before his conversion. He points out that there were not really two wills in him, "higher" and "lower," but one will which willed the true good with part of its energy and a lower good with another part. Thus, sin is radical in that it seems to master the self and prevent it from doing what at its best it really wants to do.

Sin corrupts all the functions of the self. The *heart* is perverted. It ceases to love the higher good or loves it feebly and spasmodically, and becomes infatuated with false or ephemeral values. The *imagination* ceases to envisage absolute reality and good, and produces a riot of images of sensuous things and pleasures. The *reason* no longer occupies itself with spiritual reality, thinks only of the sensible world in time and space, and becomes more and more an instrument for the satisfaction of personal desires or the rationalization of class or national interests. Even the *appetites* are perverted. For example, the sexual impulse is limited in animal species; it is merely the servant of the biological need of reproduction. An extreme case of this limitation is found in the bees, the queen bee mating only once and with only one male. With man, however, the sexual impulse, under the stimulation of imagination, becomes inordinate and is used as a means of exploitation. Again, the "instinct of self-preservation" of animal species is transformed in man, the natural "will-to-live" becoming the inordinate "will-to-power."[7]

Thus, the radical character of sin is shown not only by the fact that it has the power to divide the self against itself but also by the

[6] Rom. 7:15, 17, 18.
[7] Niebuhr, R., *The Children of Light and the Children of Darkness,* New York, Scribners, 1944, pp. 20, 21.

fact that it perverts all the functions of the self from their true use as servants of man's spiritual nature and good. This is what orthodox theologians have tried to say in the doctrine of "total depravity." As we have seen, the doctrine is not only false; it has also antagonized many by its apparent degradation of man. To say that man is a sinner in a radical sense is not to say that there is no good in him. Even St. Augustine recognizes the intellectual, cultural, social and moral achievements of man.[8] St. Thomas Aquinas rejects the doctrine of "total depravity" in the clearest possible way. Sin weakens but does not destroy the natural inclination to virtue, he says. "Sin cannot entirely take away from man the fact that he is a rational being, for then he would no longer be capable of sin. Therefore, it is not possible for this good of nature to be entirely destroyed."[9]

Modern Augustinians like Reinhold Niebuhr speak of a *distortion* of all man's faculties by sin rather than of "total depravity." The image of God in him is not destroyed; it remains but in a distorted form. Thus, Niebuhr distinguishes between "the essential nature of man" and "the virtue of conformity to that nature." "Nothing can change the essential nature and structure, just as blindness of the eye does not remove the eye from the human anatomy," he says. "On the other hand the freedom of man creates the possibility of actions which are contrary to and in defiance of the requirements of this essential nature."[10]

This is a more adequate way of describing the radical character of sin. Because of its mastery of the self, sin introduces a *contradiction* into it. It does not destroy the image of God which is the "essential nature" of man or destroy his capacity for cultural and social achievements. But it spoils his achievements and prevents his virtues from being perfect. The moral value of virtues, St. Augustine argues, depends upon the end to which they are directed. An Epicurean, for example, may manifest many of the virtues in his actions, but the end he seeks by means of them is only his own pleasure. Similarly, the virtues of the Romans were vitiated by the fact that

[8] Augustine, *The City of God,* Bk. 22, Ch. 24; Bk. 5.
[9] Aquinas, op. cit., I-II, q. 85, a. 2.
[10] *The Nature and Destiny of Man,* I, p. 269.

they were motivated not by love for others but by love of dominion and glory for themselves. As for the cultural and social achievements of modern men, the tragic fact is that they are accompanied by spiritual hollowness and moral failure on a large scale. Germany was probably the country whose intellectual and cultural achievements during the first generation of the present century were the most outstanding; but it was also the country which under the Nazis produced the most cruel and callous disregard of the rights of others the modern world had known.

THE NATURE OF SIN

What is the *nature* of this universal and radical evil in the self? It is the condition of the self when it has turned away from God and become estranged from Him. It is the disruption of the proper relationship of man to God, that of a creature who acknowledges his responsibility to his Creator and of an image who reflects God in all that he is or does. Thus, sin must be understood, first of all, from the religious point of view as *alienation* from God, the Source of man's existence and good. As we saw, man is a finite creature whose attitude towards God should be one of humble and grateful dependence resting upon trust in His goodness and love. As long as he maintains his dependence and trust, he is in harmony with God, the world, other men, and himself. For he is a finite being who needs to be completed by union with his infinite Maker; he is an imperfect being who needs to attain perfection by imitating God's righteousness; and he is a temporal being who needs the support of God's eternal power and love in his precarious existence. On the other hand, when he abandons his trust in God, this normal relationship to his Creator and Father is broken. He ceases to admit his dependence upon God's Providence and his need to reflect God's perfection in his life. He tries to separate himself from God and live in independence of Him. In short, he makes himself rather than God the center of his life.

Sin is *love of self* in place of love of God, and all particular sins are manifestations of this self-love. Thus, St. Augustine speaks of sin as turning away from the love of God (*amor Dei*) to love of self (*amor sui*) as one's highest good. St. Thomas Aquinas seeks to show that "self-love is the cause of every (particular) sin." Obviously, alienation or separation from God and love of self are one and the same state looked at from the point of view, first, of that *from* which man turns and, second, of that *to* which he turns as his highest good. For the act of turning away from God is also an act of turning towards onself, and vice versa.

What makes this act sinful? Man's nature, as we saw, is that of a derivative being who depends for his creation and preservation upon God. Made in the image of God, the destiny to which he is called is that of a son of God, responding to God's love and serving His will. Therefore, in turning away from God to himself, man denies his dependence and responsibility. He acts as if he depended upon and were responsible to himself alone. Thus, he sets himself in *rebellion* against his rightful Lord and makes himself his own master. This is not only to repudiate God's love; it is also to deny man's own nature.

IS THERE A CAUSE OF SIN?

What is the *cause* of man's tragic alienation from God and love of self? If we mean by the cause of an event another event which is the necessary and sufficient condition of the event, its presence being inevitably followed by the event, no cause can be given for sin. As we have seen, sin is a condition of the self. To seek the cause for it outside the self is to deny the responsibility of the self for the turning away from God to itself which gave rise to that condition. For example, to argue that the *external* cause for it is the temptation of the devil implies that the will is not free to reject that temptation. Even St. Thomas Aquinas denied that he was "directly the cause of man's sinning" and insisted that he only "incites" to sin by offering an object of appetite to the senses or by persuading the reason. Since the will is not moved of necessity by any particular object, "neither the thing offered to it externally nor he that proposes it, nor he that persuades, is the sufficient cause of sin."[1]

[1] Aquinas, ibid., q. 80, a. 1.

If no external cause of sin can be found without destroying the responsibility of the self, can we find an *internal* cause? St. Thomas Aquinas deals with this question at some length. He asserts that "the will in failing to apply the rule of reason or of the divine law is the cause of sin."[2] But *why* does the will fail to apply "the rule of reason or of the divine law"? The answer of St. Thomas is that, while the "proximate" cause of the sinful act is the reason and will, the "remote" cause is the "sensitive appetite" which inclines one towards an object. In this sense, "the cause of sin is some apparent good as motive."[3] However, the apparent good of the sensitive appetite can become the motive of an act only when "the due motive" or "rule of reason" is lacking.[4] Thus, the "internal cause" of sin is complex: "The internal cause of sin is both the *will,* as completing the sinful act, and the *reason,* as lacking the due rule, and the *sensitive appetite,* as inclining to sin."[4]

According to this view, the will is the cause only in the sense that it executes a decision that has been reached by the reason under the influence of an apparent good presented to it by the sensitive appetite. This is in harmony with St. Thomas' belief in the primacy of the reason over the will. But it only forces us to look farther back for the cause of sin. For why does the reason lack "the due rule" and allow itself to be persuaded by the "sensitive appetite"? This seems to be due to the fact that the reason is overcome by passion so that it fails to apply its "universal" knowledge of the good or to "consider actually" this knowledge in a particular decision. This is inadequate because it is equivalent to saying that the sensitive appetite for a lower good is so strong that it forces the reason to approve it.

However, there is another side of St. Thomas' view which is closer to St. Augustine's voluntarism than to Greek rationalism. In a striking passage he says that self-love is the cause of sin. The essential cause of sin, he says, is "adherence to a mutable good." "Now the fact that anyone desires a temporal good inordinately," he says,

[2] Ibid., q. 75, a. 1, obj. 3.
[3] Ibid., q. 75, a. 2.
[4] Ibid., q. 75, a. 3.

"is due to the fact that he loves himself inordinately; for to wish anyone some good is to love him. Therefore it is evident that inordinate love of self is the cause of every sin."[5] This seems to imply that the sensitive appetite or passion for a temporal good would not be strong enough to win the consent of reason unless self-love had already mastered the will. In other words, appetite or passion leads to particular sins but behind these sins stands a sinful state of the will, self-love. Therefore, to the extent that St. Thomas stresses self-love as the cause of every sin, he is true to St. Augustine's profound insight that sin is, first and foremost, the act of the will whereby it turns away from love of God to love of self.

Insofar as one accepts this Augustinian view, one ceases to believe that strength of passion and failure of reason to resist it are the internal causes of sin. But this does not mean that self-love is the internal *cause* of sin. As we have seen, it is the *essence* of sin. Since it is identical with the sinful state of the will, it cannot be the cause of that state. Of course, it is the cause of paticular sins, but that does not make it the cause of sin.

Therefore, we must conclude that *no* internal cause of sin—in the sense of the sinful state of the will—can be given. The will is the "proximate" cause of particular sins, and it is influenced by the strength of the passions and the failure of the reason to resist them. But no cause can be given for self-love, the sinful state of the will itself. As St. Augustine said, sin is a *free act* of the will whereby it refuses to adhere to God, its highest Good, and turns to itself. This may not seem a satisfactory answer from the point of view of the scientific reason, which seeks the cause of every event in something outside itself. But it is the only answer which is consistent with men's experience of themselves as free and responsible beings.

Every attempt to find the cause of sin, therefore, must be rejected. Of course, the rationalistic view of St. Thomas is useful in calling attention to the fact that the appetites or passions incite the will to sin and that rational principles of right are often unable to restrain them. But these appetites or passions can lead to sinful acts only if the will has already been corrupted by self-love. The natural appe-

[5] Ibid, I-II, q. 77, a. 4.

tites are not inordinate in their essence; they become inordinate only because the self has already been corrupted by self-love.

OCCASIONS OF SIN

It is possible, however, to point out some of the *occasions* of sin. Occasions of sin are identical with what has traditionally been called *temptations*. A temptation may be defined as an incitement or stimulus to sin. It is not a sin because it may be resisted.

One of the occasions or temptations to sin most emphasized in traditional Christian thought has already been mentioned: the *natural appetite* or passion of the self which paints its object in the colors of an apparent good. As we have seen, this is not the "internal cause" of sin, if by cause is meant the necessary and sufficient condition of sin. For it may be present without leading to sin, i.e., it may not gain the consent of the will which is required for action. However, it is one of the most common occasions of sin. The fact that it was misinterpreted by some Greek philosophers as the "internal cause" of sin should not lead us to minimize its importance as an "occasion" of sin. As we shall see, however, it is usually bound up with other temptations.

Another occasion or temptation to sin is provided by *social institutions and patterns of conduct*. Modern Christianity realizes more clearly than early and medieval Christianity that the individual is not independent of the culture of his group but is shaped by it from the beginning of his life. Now, in every group there are impersonal forces of evil which are embodied in social institutions, customs and ideals. These forces are so closely interrelated that they supplement and strengthen each other. In their totality they constitute what has been called by Rauschenbusch a "kingdom of evil," i.e., a system of interdependent evils.[1] A child's action and thought are conditioned by these evil forces more than he usually recognizes. Not only is he taught to accept them without question. He is also unaware that they are evil because he has never heard them challenged. The result is that from his earliest years he is completely involved in

[1] Rauschenbusch, W., *A Theology for the Social Gospel*, New York, Macmillan, 1918, Chs. VIII, IX.

them. The solidarity of all the members of a group in a sin such as race discrimination or militarism is partly due to this process. Of course, a child may be told more than once by his parents, the Church, or a teacher that such a social evil is a sin. But the influence of the dominant patterns and ideals of the group is powerful. For example, the economic order in our society has an "immense potency" as a factor in social and moral education.[2]

On the other hand, there is a great danger in our time that men will evade responsibility for their sins by regarding them as inevitable products of the social environment. We are faced with such great social evils that we easily become obsessed with them and blinded to the importance of personal decision. Moreover, the widespread acceptance of naturalistic philosophy and deterministic sociology weakens men's conviction that they are spiritual beings who are free and responsible for their own actions. The social environment must not be regarded as the cause of sin, though it provides one of the most powerful temptations to sin. Man is not bound completely by his culture; as a spiritual being, he is able in some measure to transcend it and resist its evils.

However, the power of the individual to transcend the group and resist its evils is limited. We have been made more aware of this limitation by the regimentation of every phase of life by totalitarian states. We must admit, therefore, that the individual's freedom is never complete but is limited by many factors. Under the conditions that prevail in some societies, the individual is free only in that he can die rather than accept the patterns of the group. But it should be noted that these conditions were produced by choices of members of the group in the past so that men were responsible for them. Also, the opportunity may arise at any time for the members of the group to make choices of a different character. For example, the leaders of the Japanese made certain choices which led them to tragic defeat in the Second World War. It might be argued that, once these choices had been made, individual Japanese were virtually unable to do otherwise than they did and therefore that their responsibility for the evils of militarism and imperialism was slight

[2] Temple, William, *Christianity and Social Order*, New York, Penguin Books, 1941, p. 14.

However, the defeat of Japan presented the Japanese with an opportunity to choose a different ideal and different patterns of conduct. Thus, the relation of individual responsibility to social factors in conduct presents difficult problems.

A third temptation or occasion of sin is *anxiety* in the presence of insecurity. This temptation has been strongly emphasized in recent Protestant thought. "All human sin," says Brunner, "has an element of weakness; it is mingled with anxiety for one's life, a fear of losing something by obedience to God; thus it is a lack of confidence, a fear of venturing all on God alone; it is not simply impudence, but anxiety about onself; it is not merely rebellion, it is a kind of dizziness which attacks those who ought to step over the abyss leaning only on God."[3]

Reinhold Niebuhr has done much to clarify the origin and nature of anxiety. As a creature, he points out, man belongs to nature and is subject to the weaknesses, contingencies, and insecurities of all finite beings. As a spiritual being, however, he is able to transcend nature. He can conceive of an infinite power that would overcome his weakness, an absolute knowledge that would resolve all his doubts, a perfect goodness that would raise him above his moral defects. Sin arises when the anxiety springing from his insecurity tempts him to pretend that he has or can seize supreme power, that he possesses absolute truth, or that he has attained perfect goodness. In other words, it results from the attempt to overcome his insecurity by pretending to be stronger, wiser, or better than he really is.[4] It should be noted that, according to Niebuhr, anxiety is not sin; it is only the occasion of sin. Anxiety is a necessary factor of human existence because of the insecurity of man's life. In contrast, sin is not a necessity of man's finiteness; it is due to his misuse of his freedom as a spiritual being. Moreover, anxiety can be fruitful, the desire for perfection leading men to creative achievements which enrich their lives. It is only when anxiety is not accompanied by faith in God's love that it leads to sin. "The ideal possibility," says Niebuhr, "is that

[3] Brunner, Emil, *Man in Revolt*, copyright, 1947, by W. L. Jenkins, The Westminster Press, pp. 131-132.
[4] Niebuhr, R., op. cit., I, Ch. VII.

faith in the ultimate security of God's love would overcome all immediate insecurities of nature and history."[5]

Paradoxically, this anxiety which is a temptation to sin is possible only because man is a spiritual being that transcends nature, a being "involved in both freedom and necessity." "Is it not the fact that man is a finite spirit, lacking identity with the whole, but yet a spirit capable in some sense of envisaging the whole, so that he easily commits the error of imagining himself the whole which he envisages?"[6] Thus, the source of the temptation of anxiety is not mere animal appetite or creaturely finiteness, it is the fact that man is made in the image of God and can transcend nature and himself. He is tempted by his spiritual capacity, the noblest thing in his nature, to exaggerate his power, his knowledge, and his virtue.

The three temptations to sin we have discussed—appetite or passion, social evil, and anxiety—are often found together, each strengthening and being strengthened by the others. For example, a person naturally desires certain material goods as a means to his happiness. The acquisitive society in which he lives strengthens this desire by presenting him with examples of those who have attained riches and praising them as if they had realized the highest type of success. This leads to an inordinate desire for the satisfactions that money can buy and for the success that is prized most by his society. His desire is strengthened by the anxiety which is inevitable in every human life. As a result, it becomes a consuming passion. In such a person's experience, all three kinds of temptation work together and enhance one another. Again, a weak and dependent child may have his sense of insecurity increased by neglect or harsh treatment at the hands of his parents, by discrimination against him on account of his race, or by the calamities of war. When he arrives at an adult age, he may find a social opportunity to compensate for his sense of inferiority as a leader of a revolutionary party or as a captain of industry. If he succeeds, his ability to satisfy his appetites by power or money may strengthen them further.

[5] Niebuhr, R., ibid., I, p. 183.
[6] Ibid., I, p. 181.

THE INEQUALITY OF SINS

Are all sins equally evil or is there an inequality between them? The predominant view in Christian thought has been that sins are *unequal*, some being more grave than others. This view can claim support from certain passages in Jesus' teaching in which he seems to assert that fuller knowledge of good and evil carries with it greater culpability. "That servant who knew his master's will, but did not make ready or act according to his will, shall receive a severe beating," he says. "But he who did not know, and did what deserved a beating, shall receive a light beating."[1] The same principle is applied by him to whole communities. "Woe to you, Chorazin! woe to you, Bethsaida! for if the mighty works done in you had been done in Tyre and Sidon, they would have repented long ago in sackcloth and ashes. But I tell you, it shall be more tolerable on the day of judgment for Tyre and Sidon than for you."[2]

The danger in the doctrine that sins are unequal in gravity is that it may be used to justify complacency and self-righteousness. What is more subtle than the temptation to justify oneself by comparing one's own sins with what appear to be graver sins of others? Is it not easy to convince oneself that an outburst of anger followed by sharp words is a minor sin when one contrasts it with the murder committed by another? Nevertheless, Christian thinkers have usually seen great value in the doctrine when it is not misused in this way. It gives meaning to the struggle against one's besetting sins and encourages one to seek for moral improvement. It prevents one from falling into despair because of his sins, as he tends to do if he thinks that, no matter what he does, he will continue to be equally sinful. It seems to be in accord with the commonsense view that some acts are to be condemned more than others. Thus, it seems to be presupposed in both our moral efforts and our moral judgments.

Despite this, there has been a strong tendency in orthodox Protestantism to reject the doctrine of inequality of sin on the

[1] Lk. 12:47, 48.
[2] Mtt. 11:21, 22.

ground that it encourages man's pride and self-sufficiency. Most recently, Reinhold Niebuhr has asserted the "equality of sin" while admitting the "inequality of guilt." According to his view, guilt "represents the objective and historical consequences of sin," and it is a plain fact that, while men are equal in their sin, the consequences of their sin are very unequal.[3] This position cannot be maintained. In the first place, there seems to be no Biblical basis for it. For example, the statement of St. Paul, "For there is no distinction; since all have sinned, and fall short of the glory of God,"[4] is not to the point. It asserts that there is no difference between men with respect to the presence of sin in their lives but not that there is no difference between them with respect to the degree of sin, i.e., it asserts the *universality* rather than the *equality* of sin. In the second place, the guilt of a person is more closely related to his sin than Niebuhr's view recognizes. If the guilt of two men is unequal, it can only be because their sins are unequal. For if sin is the ground of guilt, there must be degrees of sin to account for degrees of guilt. To say that the greater guilt assigned to a person is due simply to the fact that his acts have worse consequences for others is to estimate guilt in too external and utilitarian fashion and to transform guilt from a moral into a legal category. The conclusion follows that, if there is inequality of guilt, there must also be inequality of sin.

On the other hand, even "good" people fall far short of the perfect goodness of God, and the fact that they are *less* sinful than "wicked" people does not mean that they are *without* sin or even that their sin is *insignificant*. All men have sinned and all men stand in need of redemption. No one can hope to save himself by gradually improving his moral condition through strenuous effort and becoming progressively less sinful. In this sense, there is an "equality of sin," i.e., all are equally unable to slough off their sinful state and attain the perfect righteousness God requires. Since sin springs from a wrong relation to God, it can be overcome only by a reorientation of the self as a whole away from love of self to love of God, and this reorientation is not a matter of degree.

[3] Op. cit., I, p. 222.
[4] Rom. 3:22, 23.

But the correct way to express this insight is not to speak of an "equality of sin." Though all men are sinful, their sinfulness does not manifest itself as equally evil from the moral point of view. Therefore, we must insist upon the inequality of sin as it manifests itself in human character and conduct, and at the same time recognize that even the "best" fall far short of the perfect goodness of God.

"CARNAL" AND "SPIRITUAL" SINS: PRIDE

Perhaps the most interesting distinction between *kinds of sins* is that between "carnal" and "spiritual" sins. This rests, of course, upon the distinction between the interests of the self which are centered primarily in natural appetites or passions and those which are centered primarily in "spiritual" desires. Thus, of the seven "capital sins" recognized by medieval Christian ethics, "gluttony," "lust," and "anger" may be regarded as "carnal," because they spring from the biological impulses of hunger, sex, and rage. On the other hand, "vainglory" and "envy" may be regarded as "spiritual," because they are obviously rooted in the desire to excel others rather than in biological drives.

This distinction, however, has only a relative value. "Avarice" and "sloth" are difficult to classify; and the biological and spiritual aspects of the self are too intimately related to permit a simple classification of desires. "Anger" has a biological basis; but it may be aroused by a slight to one's self-esteem or by envy at the success of a rival. In such cases, at least, it springs from the "spiritual" sins of "vainglory" and "envy." It will be remembered that Plato regarded anger as an expression of the "spirited element" or "mettle" of the soul which is intermediate between appetite and reason and which leads one to resent injuries and defend himself or his own against evil. Thus, it often seems to have spiritual as well as biological elements in it. Again, "lust" is often a manifestation of pride in the form of the will to power rather than a simple expression of the sexual impulse, while "gluttony" in the form of drunkenness is often an expression of "vainglory." These examples should warn us against the error of thinking that particular sins or vices are separate and independent entities. They are interdependent manifestations of the fundamental sin of self-love. Therefore, any classification of them is bound to be limited in value.

Nevertheless, the distinction between particular sins, especially that between the "carnal" sins which are included under "sensuality" and the "spiritual" sins which are expressions of "pride," corresponds to reality. This is shown not only by the fact that different sins have different objects or ends—the object of lust is sexual satisfaction, the object of vainglory is praise from others—but also by the fact that a person may be mastered by one kind of sin but free from others. Indeed, one's "besetting sin" may dominate one's life so completely that one refrains from other sins which would prevent it from having its way, as avarice sometimes eliminates gluttony and lust.

If there is "inequality of sin," it is meaningful to speak of some kinds of sin as *worse* than others. It is hardly profitable to attempt to rank all forms of sin in an order from the least bad to the worst, indeed, there is danger that the very attempt to do so will lead to the false notion that some forms of sin are trivial and insignificant. But on one point Christian thinkers have usually been in agreement: *pride* is the worst form of sin. Conventional morality, as well as a certain type of "Christian" morality, attaches the greatest blame to certain "carnal" sins and punishes them with virtual ostracism. This is true especially in the case of sexual sins. On the other hand, it sees nothing very wrong in pride when it does not take a blatant form offensive to others. This is easy to understand. It is easier to detect sexual irregularity of certain kinds than the pride which we learn early how to conceal in order to please others. Also, sexual licence leads to consequences such as adultery which society must discourage for the sake of its own health and strength, whereas pride often stimulates creative effort and achievement which benefit society.

Nevertheless, Jesus condemned "spiritual" sins more vigorously than "carnal" ones. Obviously, he did not regard "carnal" sins lightly, as if they belonged entirely to one's "private life" and were to be viewed by others with indulgence. Indeed, he condemns lust as well as adultery. But "carnal" sins, destructive as they are, do not poison the spiritual and moral will at its very center as pride, envy, and hypocrisy seem to do. Also, those who are guilty of "carnal" sins are more likely to know that they are wrong than those who are in the grip of "spiritual" sins. Thus, Jesus contrasted the publican or tax collector with the Pharisee to the advantage of the former and set the sinful woman who wet his feet with her tears over against the Pharisee who had shown little love for him when he entered the house. Again, he denounced hypocrites who do good works and pray long prayers to be praised by men. Thus, pride and the coldness of heart and hypocrisy which are associated with it seemed to him the gravest of sins.

In the first place, these "spiritual" sins *blind* men and stand in the way of their repentance. Those who trust in their own superior ability or righteousness do not humble themselves before God and put their trust in His mercy. Since they are not aware that they need forgiveness themselves, they do not forgive others. Since they do not see that they are under judgment themselves, they judge and condemn others. Their lack of love leads them to callous disregard for the welfare of others. Their hypocrisy, often unconscious, blinds the spiritual eye within them so that they are in darkness. Humility is essential if one is to recognize his sin, repent of it, and seek the help of God in overcoming it. Pride stands in the way of this, leading one to moral complacency and gradually destroying his capacity to see himself as he is. Thus, it is the death of moral aspiration and growth.

In the second place, pride is the most *harmful* of all sins to others. "Carnal" sins are harmful chiefly to those who are guilty of them and those who are directly affected by them. For example, drunkenness is harmful to the individual and those who are affected by his irrational conduct. Sexual indulgence is a source of suffering to those who are exploited to satisfy lust or to the children who may be born as a result of it. But terrible as these are in their effect upon others, they are not as terrible as pride. For pride leads inevitably to injustice, and injustice is one of the sources of the greatest evil in the life of man.

This is most obvious in the case of that form of pride called the *will to power*. Those who enjoy power maintain and defend their privileges, though the result is poverty and stunted lives for others.

Those who crave power strive to overthrow those in possession of it and seize their privileges. Thus, the will to power leads, on the one hand, to callous indifference and oppression, and, on the other hand, to hatred and strife. The struggle for power of nations, races, and classes is made more bitter and uncompromising by the tendency of each to exaggerate the worth of its own interests and values. In this way, it justifies its attempt to dominate, persecute, or even destroy members of other groups. In our day, the collective pride of nations and classes threatens the very existence of our civilization.[1]

However, the destructive effects of pride in the lives of others is fully understood only when we take into account, not only the will to power, but also the more subtle forms of pride. *Intellectual pride* leads to the absolutization of partial truths and the insulation of the mind against new truth. The pride of modern man in the knowledge of the physical world he has attained by the scientific method has blinded him to the importance of insight into spiritual reality and value and of wisdom about the world as a whole. Again, the *moral pride* of the self-righteous, as we have said, is the enemy of moral development in individuals and of moral progress in society. "The good is the enemy of the best" in the moral as well as in other realms. The static, exclusive character of conventional "closed" morality stands in the way of a more universal "open" morality acknowledging duties to all mankind. Above all, the *spiritual pride* of a religious (or quasi-religious) group leads to intolerance, persecution, holy wars, and priestly tyranny. In our day, it is combined in Communism with the will to power of a particular class and nation which claims to be the bearer of a superior culture or the revolutionary champion of true justice for all humanity. Thus, intellectual, moral, and spiritual pride blocks the way to progress and generates fanaticism and cruelty of the most destructive kind.

In the third place, pride is the *root* of some, if not all, of the other sins. For example, luxury often has as its purpose the display of power and the enhancement of prestige by what has been called "conspicuous consumption." Drunkenness may be sought by a per-

[1] Niebuhr, R., op. cit., I, Ch. VIII.

son "in order to experience a sense of power and importance which normal life denies him."[2] Sexual passion in many cases is a means by which one person dominates another.[3] The connection of envy and vanity with pride is also obvious; and in many cases avarice is simply the servant of pride, providing the means of displaying one's superiority over others.

For all of these reasons, pride is the worst of all sins. The proud man will not acknowledge his dependence upon God and responsibility to Him because to do so would be to admit his own inferiority. At the same time, pride destroys the right relationship of a man with other men. Instead of loving his neighbor as himself, he loves himself and seeks to set himself above his neighbor. While he refuses to acknowledge his inferiority to God, he will not admit his equality with men. From the perspective of religion and morality alike, pride is the greatest sin.

IS SIN NECESSARY?

We come now to the crucial question as to whether sin is necessary. Modern Humanism and Idealism have stressed the spiritual nature of man so exclusively, as we have seen, that many have believed man's moral possibilities to be unlimited. Liberal Protestantism has been deeply influenced by this optimistic view. It has sometimes acknowledged no limitation upon man's freedom of choice between good and evil. At times, it has gone so far in this direction as virtually to deny the need of a Redeemer from sin and has regarded Christ almost exclusively as an example and a revealer of religious and moral truth.

On the other hand, St. Augustine and the Protestant Reformers have asserted an inherited propensity to sin that makes sin a necessity. In the terms of St. Augustine, Adam before his Fall had the "ability to sin or not to sin," "posse peccare aut non peccare." After the Fall, however, he and all his descendants have had only the "ability to sin," "posse peccare," and have found it impossible not to sin, "non posse non peccare." Luther spoke of "the bondage of the will" to sin. Under the influence of St. Augustine, Niebuhr refers to

2 Ibid., I, p. 234.
3 Ibid., I, p. 236.

a "bias to evil" in the will which makes sin "inevitable," though he refuses to call it "necessary" because this would imply a lack of responsibility and freedom on the part of the self.

The heart of Niebuhr's doctrine of original sin is that the "bias to evil" in the will is inherent, since every actual sin, even the first, presupposes a sinful condition already present. "Sin posits sin," as Niebuhr puts it; it is only a will that is already sinful that can succumb to temptation and fall into actual sin. It is important to note that this doctrine does not require belief in the hereditary transmission of sin from Adam to his descendants, and Niebuhr definitely rejects it. Hereditary transmission is simply a symbolic way of affirming that, from the beginning of their lives, all men have a bias to sin and the actual sins they commit are consequently inevitable. Niebuhr admits that the apparently contradictory assertion of "responsibility despite inevitability" is a paradox which allows of no further explanation. But he maintains that the complexity of the phenomena can be described only by means of that paradox.[1]

What are we to think of these two positions, the Liberal and the Augustinian? It is now clear that *Liberalism,* in insisting upon the moral responsibility of the individual, exaggerated his independence of society and of history. The dignity of the individual and his capacity for self-determination was one of the fundamental principles of modern Liberalism in every sphere. This principle, unfortunately, was not balanced and qualified by the recognition that the individual is deeply influenced by society in his moral and spiritual choices. The Liberal also tended to minimize the continuity of the present with past generations and the extent to which solidarity with the past determines choices in the present. Walter Rauschenbusch attempted to reinterpret the traditional doctrine of original sin as a symbolic assertion of the solidarity of individuals with society and of the present with the past in sin. He pointed out the way in which evil becomes intrenched in social patterns and institutions, forming a system of evils which support and strengthen one another.[2] Every individual in the formation of his habits and attitudes is deeply

[1] Niebuhr, R., op. cit., I, Ch. IX, secs. IV, V.
[2] Rauschenbusch, W., op. cit., Chs. VIII, IX.

influenced by this system of social evils which is the product of historical forces. In our time, this has become even more clear as depth psychology has delved into the secrets of the self and anthropology has shown how pervasive are the effects of a culture upon human lives. Therefore, we are no longer satisfied with a purely individualistic conception of sin and of responsibility for sin. "What a man is today," says Sir Walter Moberly,[3] "is due in a large measure to all the persons and groups who have influenced him during his life. Of course, he is not only a product; he has not only been acted upon but has been reacting all the time. But the mutual influence between him and others is ceaseless. To unravel it now —to pick him to pieces as it were—to say that so much of him is his own creation and so much is the creation of others—is not only impossible in practice but meaningless."

At this point, the traditional doctrine of original sin, when the idea of hereditary transmission is eliminated from it, is a valuable corrective. It asserts the solidarity of the individual in his sin with the whole of humanity, past and present. He is responsible for his own sin, but others share the responsibility with him and he shares with others the responsibility for their sins.

There is a second point at which the Liberal position has shown itself to be inadequate. According to the humanistic and optimistic view of man which has helped to shape the Liberal position, the will is free at every moment to choose between good and evil. It is admitted that the will may have chosen evil so often in the past that it has established a habit of doing so. But it is held that this habit can be resisted at any time by a resolute effort of the will. Moreover, the reason has not been seriously impaired by sin and can be counted upon to know the good. Thus, evil habits and impulses can be mastered and man can know and obey the moral law if he wills to do so.

The freedom of the will to choose between good and evil, we now see, is more limited than Liberals realized. Here, again, the Augustinian position, if properly qualified, embodies an important insight. While the sinner is "formally" free to choose good instead of evil, according to St. Augustine, he does not have the power to

[3] Moberly, W., *Responsibility,* London, Oxford University Press, 1951, p. 54.

choose the true good so long as he is dominated by love of self. The drunkard is "formally" free to refuse the cup, i.e., he can carry out in action anything he really wills. But unless there is a radical reorientation of his will, he is not likely to resist the temptation. Moreover, his reason is not likely to present to him clearly the claims of his true or highest good. Reason is often only the servant of irrational desires, "rationalizing" acts that will satisfy these desires in order to justify them before the bar of conscience.

Thus, the freedom of the will is not unlimited. Archbishop William Temple has pointed out[4] that the freedom which is essential for moral responsibility is not the freedom of Indeterminism but the freedom of Self-Determination. We are free, not in the sense that there are no causes determining our actions, but in the sense that our own ideas are among the causes that determine them. In other words, our acts are determined, in a measure, by final causes and not solely by efficient causes, by our own ideals or purposes and not solely by external causes acting upon us. We are free in the sense that we can determine our actions by our ideas as to what constitutes our good. We can act, as Temple puts it, in accordance with our "apparent good." But our conception of our good is distorted by our sinful self-centeredness. Because of our sin, our "apparent good" is not our true and highest good. This is what Temple means when he says that our freedom is "perfect bondage," i.e., we can determine our own acts but we can do so only in accordance with our self-centered nature. We are in bondage to our self-love. Moreover, we are unable by striving to overcome this self-centeredness or self-love. We can transcend it in some measure, Temple points out, by devoting ourselves to the higher values of Truth, Beauty, and especially Goodness. But we can never completely overcome self-centeredness by the efforts of a self that is itself self-centered.[5] We may, of course, be able to rid ourselves of particular sinful habits but that is not to rid ourselves of sin. As long as self-centeredness or self-love remains, we may root out one evil habit only to find another grown up in its place.

Therefore, we must accept the *Augustinian* doctrine of original

[4] Temple, W., *Nature, Man and God,* London, Macmillan, Lecture IX.
[5] Ibid., Lecture XV.

sin insofar as it asserts the solidarity of the individual with the race in his sin and the powerlessness of the sinful self to attain absolute goodness. In certain other respects, however, the Augustinian view must be rejected. It is not true that the individual is born with a will that is sinful and therefore guilty antecedent to any actual sin on his part. He is certainly born under circumstances which tempt him to sin from the time he begins to be morally responsible. In infancy he is driven by powerful natural impulses and instinctively claims the help of others in satisfying them. This tendency is natural in view of the fact that each self is so constituted as to be the center of its own world and to seek to preserve itself and exercise its powers. Because of the urgency of his own needs and his inability to imagine the wants and feelings of others as vividly as his own, the child's existence becomes centered in the satisfaction of himself long before he becomes fully self-conscious and morally responsible. Moreover, as he becomes less dependent and begins to exercise his own powers to carry out his purposes, he becomes aware of his weakness and insecurity and he cannot escape anxiety and the temptation to meet it aggressively. If he suffers from the lovelessness of his parents or the harshness of social circumstances, his insecurity will be enhanced and the temptation to self-assertion strengthened. In ways like these, the individual early in his life tends to become centered in himself and is continually assailed by temptations to sin. Before he is fully aware that it is sinful to do so, he is making inordinate demands upon others, giving vent to his anger when he is restrained, and asserting himself before others.

Of course, this description of the development of *temptation* does not explain why temptation leads to *sin* or why sin is universal and radical. It is easy to understand, therefore, why Augustinians like Niebuhr think it necessary to presuppose sin as already present in the will in order to account for its rise. If we can never remember a time when we were not sinning, must we not accept the view that "sin posits sin"? The difficulty with this view is that, as we have already pointed out, one cannot explain sin by reference to an antecedent condition of the will without denying that it is a free act for which we are responsible and asserting that it is a necessity due to an inherent sinfulness in human nature. "How . . . can we expect to find any cause for the universality of sin," asks Wheeler Robinson, "more ultimate than personal freedom? Predisposing influences, i.e., all that we usually include under temptation, we do find; but just as soon as we advance to a universal cause of the universality of sin, we have made moral evil a necessary element in human personality as we know it, and robbed it therefore of its moral quality and religious condemnation."[6]

But if the universality of sin is an empirical fact, as we have maintained, does it not follow that sin is inevitable in the life of every man? And if it is inevitable, is it not necessary? These are baffling questions and they admit of no completely satisfactory answers. Perhaps one might answer that there is no inevitability of sin in the will itself, but admit that, when confronted by the powerful temptations assailing it from the earliest years, it is to be expected that it will fall. This would imply that the will has in itself the freedom to stand or fall, but that the pressure of temptation upon it from within and without is too strong for any will to resist. As we have pointed out, the solidarity of the individual with society strengthens the temptations of natural appetite and anxiety. This may not be a sufficient cause of his succumbing to sin—indeed, we have insisted that no causal explanation of sin can be given—but it makes its occurrence more intelligible.

However, to admit that under the influence of temptation every man may be expected to fall is not to say that the will is under the necessity of sinning or that it is unable not to sin. The Augustinian view that since the Fall of Adam every man has been under the necessity of sinning implies that man's will is completely under the control of sin and cannot avoid sinning in any of its acts. But experience warrants us in asserting only that all men do fall into sin, not that they must remain completely under its power and always be unable to avoid it. While Reinhold Niebuhr rejects the doctrine of a "necessity" to sin, his theory of the "inevitability" of sin comes perilously close to this Augustinian doctrine. The will, he says, is capable of transcending past sin to the extent that it can feel regret for it in a later act of contemplation, but it cannot avoid

[6] Robinson, H. Wheeler, *The Christian Doctrine of Man,* Edinburgh, T. and T. Clark, 1934, p. 304.

sin in any of its future acts.[7] This reduces the spiritual capacity of self-transcendence to a minimum and attenuates man's moral possibilities.

We have emphasized the fact that the freedom of the self is limited by its self-centeredness and cannot attain the perfect goodness which is based upon love. But it need not lie completely helpless under the burden of sin. If it is responsible for its sin, it can and should struggle to overcome that sin. The "image of God" in man has not been destroyed by his sin, though it has been seriously distorted. Therefore, the spiritual capacity for self-transcendence, though seriously weakened, is still present in him. He can struggle against sin and attain a relative virtue. For example, if a self-centered person falls in love, begins to share a larger life with a wife, and is faced with responsibility for children, he may be drawn in some measure out of his self-centeredness. After all, the sinner lives in a world created and providentially directed by God, in a world where the grace of God is at work always and everywhere upon the spirits of men. He cannot lift himself out of the mire of sin by his own moral effort; but his moral effort may prepare him to recognize his need for special divine aid. In such a case, one may speak of a "general" grace of God working upon his conscience, stimulating him to struggle against sin and awakening in him a sense of his need for the "special" grace that comes through faith.

However, the inference to be drawn from this criticism of Augustinianism is far from the Pelagian view that "man is able to be without sin and to keep the commandments of God easily if he wills to do so." Man is not under the necessity of sinning, but he does sin. Man has not lost his freedom to strive for goodnes, but he does not have the power to attain it. For the goodness demanded by Christ is measured, not by the standards of even the best men, but by the standard of God's perfect goodness. The conclusion we must draw from this is that the "image of God," though it has not been destroyed by sin, must be restored if man is to have any hope of obeying the absolute will of God as expressed in the law of love. God has created man for communion with Himself in love. The root of man's sin is that he has been alienated from that com-

[7] Niebuhr, R., op. cit., I, pp. 277, 278.

munion and is seeking to live apart from God. The contradiction in his nature can be overcome and he can be restored to his true self only through reconciliation with God in faith and love. He needs the aid of the divine grace not only for the realization of true goodness but also for the restoration of his true being.

This is why Christianity is a religion of *redemption*. The law of love would stand over against us as a commandment beyond our power and drive even the best of us to despair if there were no way for the power of sin over our lives to be broken. When we are confronted by the love of Christ, manifested in his deeds of mercy and in his death on the Cross, our sense of sin is deepened. Like St. Paul, we say, "I do not do the good I want, but the evil I do not want is what I do,"[8] and we cry out, "Wretched man that I am! Who will deliver me from this body of death?"[9]

[8] Rom. 7:19.   [9] Ibid., 7:24.

CHAPTER 9

Man as Redeemed: The Christian Life

IN THE last chapter we pointed out that there is a contradiction in man. Made in the image of God and capable of loving God and his neighbor, he has fallen into the sin of self-love. Although he is not under the necessity of sinning in every act, he is threatened with despair by his failure to overcome his sin and by his alienation from God and from his neighbor. How can he hope to obey Jesus' commandment to love God with his whole self and to love his neighbor as himself?

Christians believe that it is possible to do so only with the help of God's grace, forgiving their sins and bestowing upon them a power not their own. They affirm their faith that He has redeemed men through Christ and his sacrificial love. In Christ's death on the Cross, the depth and costliness of God's redemptive love for men were made manifest. As St. Paul says, "God shows his love for us in that while we were yet sinners Christ died for us."[1] But that is not all. God continues His redemptive work in the lives of Christians here and now. After Christ's death his disciples became convinced that God had raised him from the dead and that he had appeared to them. On the day of Pentecost, God poured out the Holy Spirit upon them. From these events they received new life and courage, and were bound together firmly in a community of faith and hope. Consequently, they could live together in love and joy while they awaited the coming of the Kingdom. The God who had redeemed them through the death of Christ on the Cross was

[1] Ro. 5:8.

now continuing His redemptive work with them through the Holy Spirit. They could work out their own salvation in the knowledge that God was working in them and giving them the assistance of His grace.

It is obvious that these beliefs about God's redemptive work in Christ and His continuation of that work through the Holy Spirit profoundly affect the interpretation of the Christian ethic. The Christian ethic announces the *gift* of God's love to men in Christ, invites them in gratitude to obey His *command* of love, and offers them a *promise* that He will assist them with His grace. The conduct of a Christian is based upon faith in what God in His love and mercy has done for him in the past and continues to do in the present. Without this faith, the Christian would have no assurance that Christian love is more than an ideal constructed by the human imagination out of the experience of man's love at its best. If it is not rooted in the love of God, there is no ground for confidence that man has support from above in his devotion to it. On the other hand, if God has acted decisively through Christ to redeem man and continues to bestow His saving love upon man, he knows that his effort to obey the law of love will be sustained and strengthened. He knows that, however weak and wavering his own will may be, it will be undergirded by God's loving grace. In that knowledge, he can find the courage to set forth on the way of the Christian life.

FAITH, FORGIVENESS, AND RECONCILIATION

The starting point of the Christian life is *faith* in God's mercy and forgiveness. Christian faith is more than belief in or assent to a truth about the nature of God and His relationship to man. Although it includes such a belief, it is primarily *trust* in God. To have faith in God is to put one's trust in Him rather than oneself or someone else for one's salvation. It is to rely upon Him, rest securely upon Him, put one's confidence in Him for one's Highest Good. Moreover, faith involves complete *dependence* upon God, surrender to His will. It is impossible without humility, without the renunciation of one's self-will and the willingness to receive as a gift at God's hands what one cannot attain for oneself. Finally, faith implies *obedience*. If I am to receive salvation as a gift from God, I must do so on His terms. I must serve Him as a son serves his father, in the knowledge that the service He requires of me is not arbitrary but for my good.

What is the *source* of this faith? Obviously, it cannot be a blind and groundless act. It is true that it involves a "leap." There is no way of demonstrating with certainty the existence of God, or His goodness to all mankind, or His redemptive love in Christ. But faith is not a leap in the dark, a purely irrational and arbitrary thing. Faith in God is grounded in the redemptive act of God in Christ. I can trust in God's love because He has revealed His love to me in Christ's life and death. I can trust that His mercy extends to me because He has shown His willingness to forgive sinners like myself.

Faith is a *gift of God*. Self-centered, self-sufficient man cannot be brought to put his trust in God rather than himself except by the action of God's grace upon him. The act of faith which sets man's feet on the way to salvation cannot be achieved by himself alone; it arises as a response to God's revelation in Christ as the Spirit of God enables him to see it. But faith is also a *free act of man*. He has not been predestined by an eternal decree of God either to accept it or reject it. God has offered His redemptive love in Christ to all men and His mercy is open to all without distinction. Each must accept or reject it for himself. If he accepts it in faith, it transforms his life by reorienting it around God rather than himself as a center. That is why the decision for or against faith is the most crucial act of a man's life.

Faith is the beginning of the process of salvation because by faith man experiences the mercy and forgiveness of God. This is what has been called by Christians *justification by faith*. The meaning of this doctrine, which was first stated by St. Paul and was reaffirmed strongly by Luther, has been unnecessarily obscured by theological controversy. It can be understood only when one remembers what it denies as well as what it affirms. It denies that man is "justified" or saved by virtue of his "good works" performed in obedience to the Law. He *cannot win salvation* for himself by "righteousness" attained through his good works. On its negative side, then, "justification by faith" asserts simply that men cannot save themselves or deserve to be saved by anything they do. On its positive side, it means the *forgiveness of sins* and *reconciliation with God*. Separated and estranged from God by his sin, man has no hope unless his sin is forgiven and he is restored to favor. In Christ, God has taken the initiative to break down the barrier of sin and bring man back once more to Himself. "God was in Christ reconciling the world to himself." Thus, forgiveness means more than a mere "remission of punishment." As Aulen says, it is "nothing less than the re-establishment of that fellowship and filial relation with God which was broken through sin."[1]

Since forgiveness in this sense goes far beyond anything man could have expected in the name of justice, it can be explained only as a spontaneous and undeserved outpouring of God's boundless love. The fact that it seems to transcend justice, however, does not mean that it is an evidence of moral laxity on God's part which cancels His opposition to evil. For the way of manifesting His forgiveness which has been adopted by God, the sacrificial love of Christ upon the Cross, also contains a judgment against evil.[2] From the point of view of Christian ethics, this is highly important. Some sentimental Christians have represented God's forgiveness as similar to that of a weak and indulgent father (or grandfather) who condones and winks at the sins of his children. Such a view neglects the fact that, though God is our loving Father who forgives our sins, He is also the righteous Judge who cannot tolerate evil in His presence. Thus, Paul, who has spoken in such moving terms of God's forgiveness, also warns the Romans not to "presume" upon His forbearance. "Do you not know that God's kindness is meant to lead you to repentance? But by your hard and impenitent heart you are storing up wrath for yourself on the day of wrath when God's righteous judgment will be revealed."[3] If this is the case, there can be no excuse for moral laxity and complacency on the part of a Christian. He must wage a lifelong struggle against

[1] Aulen, Gustav, *The Faith of the Christian Church,* Philadelphia, Muhlenberg Press, 1948, p. 290.
[2] Ibid., pp. 295, 296.
[3] Rom. 2:4b, 5.

the remnants of sin in himself which would break once more his fellowship with God. The Christian, as Luther said, is "at once just and a sinner" ("simul iustus et peccator"). Therefore forgiveness is necessary not merely at the beginning but at every stage of the Christian life.

Nevertheless, the restoration to fellowship with God which takes place through forgiveness is a *new birth* and releases in the Christian a new power to struggle against sin. It awakens gratitude and love of God in his heart which provides a new motive to overcome sin. At the same time, it frees him from his egocentric preoccupation with his own salvation, from his anxiety lest he fail to attain it. Since he can now trust God to grant him salvation despite his unworthiness, he is released from his obsession with himself and from the self-love involved in it. Assured that he is accepted and loved by God in spite of his sins, he can now love God and his neighbors.

SANCTIFICATION

Some Christians have held that justification or forgiveness includes not only the regeneration about which we have just spoken but also what has usually been called *sanctification*. If justification brings regeneration, they ask, how can it be separated from sanctification? Moreover, the conception of sanctification as a later phase of the Christian life seems to imply that a state of holiness or perfection is at some point attained and then can be enjoyed as a secure and permanent possession. In reality, the man of faith continues to be a sinner and to stand in need of forgiveness. If he ever claims to have attained holiness or perfection, he manifests the sinful pride and self-love he thinks he has overcome. Thus, both the fact that justification involves regeneration and the fact that a state of complete sanctification is never attained seem to rule out the idea that sanctification is a state of the Christian life which follows justification.

Despite the strength of these arguments, it is necessary to distinguish, though not to separate, justification and sanctification as aspects of the Christian life. It is true that justification brings regeneration with it. To deny this would be to deny the efficacy of forgiveness in re-establishing the broken fellowship with God. But there is a distinction between regeneration as the act by which the new life comes into being and sanctification as the process by which it grows and produces its fruits. It may be admitted that regeneration begins the process of sanctification but it cannot be identified with the process as a whole. However, the fundamental error in the view we are examining lies in a misunderstanding of the meaning of sanctification. "Sanctification" refers to a *process,* not a *state.* To say that justification and regeneration must be followed by sanctification is not to claim that at some point a state of complete sanctity or holiness will be attained. It is simply to assert that a process of moral and spiritual growth towards sanctity is necessary for the new life to produce its full fruits.

It is true that exaggerated claims to holiness or perfection have been made by some Christians and Christian sects. But sanctification is not a state of perfect holiness; it is a process which aims at such a state as its goal. This seems to be St. Paul's view of the matter. "Not that I have already obtained this or am already perfect," he says, "but I press on to make it my own, because Christ Jesus has made me his own. Brethren, I do not consider that I have made it my own; but one thing I do, forgetting what lies behind and straining forward to what lies ahead, I press on toward the goal for the prize of the upward call of God in Christ Jesus."[1] In a passage in Ephesians the figure of growth to manhood is used, a process which continues "until we all attain to the unity of the faith and of the knowledge of the Son of God, to mature manhood, to the measure of the stature of the fullness of Christ."[2] In both passages, it is a *process* rather than a state which is described and it is not finished until death. It may also be regarded in a sense as a *stage,* since it cannot begin until after justification has occurred. If so, however, one must remember that it is a prolonged stage on a journey or race which continues until death and that the need for justification or forgiveness remains throughout the whole length of the Christian life.

[1] Phil. 3:12-14.
[2] Eph. 4:13.

What is the significance of this for Christian ethics? As we have said, Christian ethics is perfectionistic in the sense that it demands that men should be perfect in their love, although perfection is not understood in the static Greek sense. Unless sanctification aimed at perfection is regarded as essential to the Christian life, however, Christians will not think it their duty to strive for an ever more perfect love, for "the measure of the stature of the fullness of Christ." They will be satisfied with a limited change in their lives. The result will be a spiritual and moral complacency which will paralyze their efforts and lead to the cessation of moral growth. Compromise with their own moral imperfection will be accompanied by a resigned acceptance of social injustice. This is a very real danger in Protestantism at the present time. The current disillusionment with optimistic Liberalism and the strong emphasis of Neo-Orthodoxy upon man's sin have combined to destroy in some circles the doctrine of Christian perfection as the goal of a process of sanctification. The result of this tendency, if unchecked, is bound to be a loss of moral earnestness and ultimately a growth of moral cynicism. The nerve of the modern Christian concern for social justice will also be cut. Perhaps the greatest contribution of the radical sects of the Reformation and of the early Methodists was their criticism of the compromises of the Churches with moral and social evil. The radical sects were wrong in thinking that the Church should include only perfect Christians. The Church does not consist of saints; it consists of men who know they still stand in need of forgiveness. But when the Church ceases to respect saints and does not attempt to produce them, it has forgotten what it means to be a follower of Christ.

LIFE "IN CHRIST" AND "IN THE SPIRIT"

How does God help men who have been reconciled to Him but must struggle to overcome sin and attain a more perfect love? The answer of the New Testament, confirmed by centuries of Christian experience, is that God helps man through the presence and power of the *Spirit of Christ*. We have stressed the fact that the Christian faith and ethic rest upon what God has done for man in Jesus

Christ. But many Christians have depended too exclusively upon the reconciliation or atonement effected through him once and for all in the past. This has been one of the greatest weaknesses of certain forms of Pietism, Evangelicalism and Fundamentalism. Too many Christians have been characterized above all by their "backward look" to the Cross of Christ. They have thought that through "faith in the blood of Christ," conceived as a finished act, they could be assured of salvation and their task would be over.

Strangely enough, they have justified their attitude by an appeal to the letters of St. Paul. Yet a careful reading of St. Paul makes it clear that it is not only Christ on the Cross but also the risen and living Christ who is the center of St. Paul's piety and ethic. Although he sees in the Cross the great manifestation of God's redemptive love and mercy which awakens faith in the Christian, he also enjoys a vivid experience of the living Christ as his risen Lord. This is the source of his "Christ-mysticism" which he expresses in the phrase "in Christ." Whether he speaks of himself as being "in Christ" or of Christ as being "in" him, he is describing an experience of the closest and most intimate union with Christ. The expression "in Christ" occurs again and again in the most various contexts. "There is now no condemnation for those who are in Christ Jesus."[1] "I am speaking the truth in Christ."[2] "If any one is in Christ, he is a new creation."[3] Sometimes his experience takes the form of an identification with the death and resurrection of Christ. "But if we have died with Christ," he says, "we believe that we shall also live with him."[4]

What is the significance of this intimate *union with Christ* for Paul? It is the fact that Christ is not only an historical figure of the past but also a living reality active in the present. If Christ could not be thought of in this way, he would lose his meaning for faith. "Faith lives primarily in the present," says Aulen, "since the inner nature of faith implies being gripped and controlled by something which positively declares itself to be a divine revelation. Without this contemporaneity faith in Christ would be reduced

[1] Rom. 8:1.
[2] Rom. 9:1.
[3] II Cor. 5:17.
[4] Rom. 6:8.

to an intellectual assent to certain events in ancient history, or to certain 'religious ideas' formulated and delivered in the past."[5] The earthly career of Jesus must be regarded as a stage in the process by which the redemptive love of God has always been and now is at work for the salvation of men.

One of the implications of this is that the *imitation of Christ* should never take the form of an unimaginative repetition of the details of his earthly life. The literalism of Christians who have believed they should follow his example even in insignificant details has sometimes led to quaint but appealing practices such as foot-washing. At other times, it has resulted in an insistence upon practices, such as total immersion, which has divided Christian churches from one another. However, the worst effect of this literalistic interpretation of Jesus' teachings has been to restrict Christian liberty. It has made it difficult, if not impossible, for many Christians to base their moral decisions on a careful analysis of the demands of the present time and the particular situation in which they find themselves. Often they fail to see a moral issue confronting them because Jesus had no occasion to deal with it in his time.

Here, again, St. Paul has shown us the right way. There can be no question that the imitation of Christ was of great importance to him. But it was an imitation not of the details but of the *spirit* and purpose of his life. Thus, in the great passage in which Paul urges mutual love and humility upon the Philippians, he cites the example of Christ. "Have this mind among yourselves, which you have in Christ Jesus, who, though he was in the form of God, did not count equality with God a thing to be grasped, but emptied himself, taking the form of a servant, being born in the likeness of men. And being found in human form he humbled himself and became obedient unto death, even death on a cross."[6] The significant thing here is that Paul urges an imitation of the "mind" or spirit of Christ, especially his self-emptying humility, his obedience and his self-sacrifice. Paul gives little indication as to the *method* by which the Christian is to imitate the "mind" or spirit of Christ, but

---

[5] Aulen, op. cit., pp. 242, 243.
[6] Phil. 2:5-8.

it is evident that contemplation of the self-denial and love of Christ is essential.

The Christian life can be described not only as life "in Christ" but also as life *"in the Spirit."* The fact that the New Testament uses these two phrases almost interchangeably indicates that there is no essential difference between the work of the risen Christ and the work of the Holy Spirit. Indeed, St. Paul speaks of "the Spirit of Christ"[7] and "the Spirit of life in Christ Jesus."[8] He does not hesitate to say simply, "The Lord *is* the Spirit."[9]

The presence and activity of the Spirit assures us that God is not a remote Being enthroned on high but is near to us and effective in our lives. It is through the Spirit that love becomes a vital force in the life of the Christian. "God's love has been poured into our hearts," says Paul, "through the Holy Spirit which has been given to us."[10] When God pours his love into our hearts through the Holy Spirit, His love awakens in us a love for Him and a desire to do His will.[11] This explains why St. Paul speaks of the Spirit as bestowing "righteousness" upon the Christian. If the liberty of the Christian is not to tempt him into sin, he must live not "according to the flesh" but "according to the Spirit." Thus, the Spirit is the "Sanctifier." The Spirit also "bears witness" or "testimony" to Christ and his reconciling work, and is the "Lifegiver," the source of the "new life" of the Christian. Paul speaks of "the new life of the Spirit"[12] and says that "the written code (A.V. the letter) kills, but the Spirit gives life."[13]

DIVINE GRACE AND HUMAN FREEDOM

We have described the way in which the Christian life, beginning with *justification by faith* and developing towards perfection through the process of *sanctification,* is a product of *God's redemptive activ-*

[7] Rom. 8:9.
[8] Rom. 8:2.
[9] II Cor. 3:17 (italics mine).
[10] Rom. 5:5.

[11] Augustine, *The Spirit and the Letter,*
[12] Rom. 7:6.
[13] II Cor. 3:6.

ity. It is evident from this that the process of salvation is initiated by God and carried through to the end by Him.

The doctrine of *grace,* first worked out in detail by St. Augustine and reasserted with great vigor by Luther, is fundamental for the Christian faith. It is no less fundamental for the Christian ethic. When Christians think that they can attain goodness by their own efforts or can deserve God's grace as a reward for their own merit, they cease to believe in the necessity of redemption through Christ. The Christian ethic becomes for them merely a sort of moralism which demands that they follow Jesus' example and obey his teachings as a prophet by their own wills alone.

But the assertion of Luther that Christians are saved "by grace alone" has often been interpreted in ways which endanger their moral responsibility and which tend to reduce moral effort to a very subordinate position in the Christian life. It is necessary, therefore, to guard the doctrine of grace against misunderstanding. The purpose of the phrase, "by grace alone," is to eliminate every excuse for pride on man's part, to deny his right to boast about his merits. It reminds him that, if left by God to himself, he centers his love upon himself and makes everything serve his interest, so that the tendency of his own sinful nature is away from salvation rather than towards it. It is also an expression of deep gratitude to God for His redemptive love in Christ and the continuation of His work in the life of the Christian.

However, there is a danger that, in humbling man, it will destroy his freedom, and that, in exalting God, it will make Him arbitrary. St. Augustine was the first to fall into this double danger, and both Luther and Calvin have followed him. St. Augustine had suffered from a weak and divided will before his conversion. As a result of this experience, he argued that, while man had been created by God with freedom of will, his nature had become corrupted by sin after the Fall of Adam and had lost the freedom to choose the true Good. Consequently, it is foolish for man to boast about freedom of will as an inherent capacity of his nature, overlooking the fact that it has been weakened and corrupted by sin. While he still possesses freedom of will, he no longer possesses the power to exercise it rightly by choosing the true Good, just as a man with broken legs may be said to have the inherent capacity but not the actual present capacity to walk.[1] Therefore, unless his nature is restored to health by God's grace, he will not be able to avoid sin. With the help of grace, however, "the evil necessity will be removed and full liberty be restored."[2]

There is a profound insight in this view of the limitations of man's freedom of will and it is one which moral philosophers have not adequately considered. For example, Kant argues that freedom of the will is a "postulate of the practical reason" since the moral imperative, "I ought," implies the possibility of its fulfillment, "I can." The argument is logically valid, but what does it prove? Logically, "I ought" seems to imply "I can." Actually, in the case of a confirmed alcoholic or drug addict, does the fact that he "ought" to abstain mean that he "can"? Psychoanalysts have made us aware also of the fact that conscious effort of the will has no effect upon wholly compulsive actions the source of which may lie below the level of consciousness. Therefore, Augustine is justified in his claim that man cannot make a fully effective use of his freedom of will until the power of sin over him is broken. He cannot will the Highest Good, love of God and love of neighbor, until he has been lifted by God's grace out of his self-love.

But St. Augustine is not content to say that the natural man cannot choose the true Good until his will is healed by grace. He also insists that God's grace is irresistible by man. This assertion, which is bound up with his doctrine of predestination, almost destroys the freedom of the will even after it is healed by grace. St. Augustine insists that free will and grace are both present in the Christian life,[3] and that grace "co-operates" with us when we will.[4] But the freedom of will of a man under "irresistible" grace is, to say the least, a very attenuated freedom. Two passages will make this clear. "It is certain that it is we that will when we will, but it is He who *makes us will* what is good, of whom it is said, 'The will is prepared by the Lord.' "[5] "Not only men's good wills which God

[1] Augustine, *On Nature and Grace,* Ch. 57.
[2] Ibid., Ch. 71.
[3] Augustine, *On Grace and Free Will,* Ch. X.
[4] Ibid., Ch. XXXIII.
[5] Ibid., Ch. XXXII (italics mine).

converts from bad ones, and when converted by Him, directs to good actions and the eternal life, but also those which follow the world are so entirely at the disposal of God that He *turns them* whithersoever He wills and whenever He wills."[6] If God "makes us will" and "turns" our wills wherever and whenever He wills, we obviously have no choice but to will as He wills. St. Augustine can even say of men's wills that "He does *through their agency* whatsoever he wishes to perform through them."[7] Thus the fact that St. Augustine speaks of "co-operating grace" should not blind us to the fact that the only part played by man's will is to consent to acts which are determined by God. Moreover, the faith which is the beginning of the Christian life is attributed solely to God's "operating" grace and man's freedom to accept it or reject it is denied. In short, the theory that God's grace is "irresistible" implies that the wills of men are overborne by His omnipotent will.

This is the danger of the view that man is "saved by grace alone." It is valuable as an affirmation that grace is both a *necessary condition* and the *primary factor* in man's salvation. But it is misleading since it suggests that grace is the *sufficient condition* and *only factor* in his salvation. The assertion that God's grace is "prevenient" or antecedent to anything man can do on behalf of his salvation is true. What man does at any point should be regarded as a response to what God has already done for and in him. Even the exercise of his freedom of will is the exercise of a capacity God has bestowed upon him in creating him and it is possible only as long as God preserves that capacity in being. Thus, man's cooperation with God's grace is not the cooperation of an equal partner but that of a creature with the Creator upon whom he is ultimately dependent for all that he has and can do.

But man's freedom and responsibility should never be depreciated. From the beginning to the end of the process of salvation he must exercise his freedom of will as a responsible person. God's grace does not *coerce* man's will at any point; it seeks to *win* his free response. The best way to conceive of this is by analogy with the self-giving unconditional love of a person which evokes an answering love in

[6] Ibid., Ch. XL (italics mine).
[7] Ibid., Ch. XLII (italics mine).

another person. This kind of love has power to awaken and transform the other person but it is a spiritual power which attracts him
by its own inherent beauty and never compels him to respond. We
must never forget, as theologians in the heat of controversy have
sometimes forgotten, that God is love and that His grace always
operates in a personal way which is consistent with His love.

THE CHRISTIAN LIFE AND THE CHURCH

The Christian life is lived within the *Christian community*. Despite the superficial talk about a "personal" religion among those
who have become disaffected with the Church, there is no such thing
as a purely personal Christianity. It has been so from the beginning.
It is true that Jesus' teaching centers in the Kingdom of God and
that he refers in only two passages of the Gospel of Matthew to the
Church ("ecclesia").[1] But the significant thing is that he associated
with himself a group of men as his disciples and that they constituted a community of believers preparing for the coming of the
Kingdom. After calling them to be his disciples, he sent them out
"to preach the kingdom of God and to heal."[2] As he approached his
death in Jerusalem, he bound them to himself in a solemn act of
participation in his "blood of the covenant," and looked forward to
the time when he would "drink again of the fruit of the vine" in
the Kingdom of God.[3] Thus, while he probably did not establish
the Church as an organized *institution,* he founded a new *fellowship*
("koinonia") which developed into the Church after his death.

The Church has always regarded *Christ* as its Lord. It has considered itself "the Body of Christ" of which he is the invisible
"Head." As such, it continues the work he began during his earthly
career. Fellowship in the Church is fellowship in and with him. This
close relation between Christ and his followers is expressed in the
Gospel of John in terms that express indissoluble unity. "I am the
vine, you are the branches."[4] Also the Church has been from the

[1] Mtt. 16:18; 18:17.   [3] Mk. 14:22-25; Mtt. 26:26-29.
[2] Lk. 9:2; Mtt. 10:7, 8.   [4] Jo. 15:5.

beginning a fellowship of the *Holy Spirit*. The early Church looked back to the day of Pentecost, when the Spirit descended upon it, as a proof that God was present in it and had bestowed His favor upon it. The Spirit was the source of its new life and its love, joy and peace.

Since Christians have always regarded the Church as the sphere in which the redemptive work of Christ is continued and the life-giving and sanctifying activity of the Holy Spirit is carried out, they have always thought of it as a *holy* Church. This does not mean that its members are morally superior to those outside it. Although they should be, they frequently are not. It means only that the Church has come into being as a result of the redemptive love of God in Christ and that God continues His work of redemption through it. "The holiness of the Church," says Aulen, "depends entirely on that Holy Spirit who is active in the Church. If faith is to be certain that there is a 'communion of saints' in the world, this certainly cannot be based on the existence of a relative degree of human holiness, and much less on any human perfection."[5] This view of the meaning of "holy" when applied to the Church safe-guards its uniqueness as a community of grace and at the same time prevents its members from pretending to be more pious or righteous than they really are.

Normally, the Christian life is born and grows within the Church and is nourished at every stage by it. The Church is the bearer of the Gospel, the custodian of the special revelation of God to Israel which culminated in the person and work of Christ, and it transmits the Gospel from generation to generation through its preaching and teaching. It is also the fellowship within which, by the help of God, the Gospel bears its moral fruits in life. Therefore, the Christian is dependent upon the Church for both his knowledge of the Gospel and the power to practice it as a way of life. Through the "means of grace" provided by the Church, the Gospel is first proclaimed to him and awakens his faith. Through the life of its fellowship and of the Christian family, he begins to understand the meaning of love and to respond to its appeal. Thus, the Christian is dependent

[5] Aulen, op. cit., p. 341.

upon the Church for his spiritual and moral life as a child is dependent upon his mother.

For this reason, the modern *individualistic conception* of the Church is completely unrealistic. According to this view, the individual Christian is prior to the Church and the Church depends upon him for its existence and survival. It is simply an association of individual Christians each of whom is independent of the others and of it. This theory of the Church, like the social contract theory of the state, is a product of modern individualism. It is a mistake to think that it expresses the attitude of the Protestant Reformers towards the Church. To them, as to early and medieval Christians, the Church was more than a voluntary association created by an agreement among Christians to form an institution which would further their common religious interests. Of course, each of its members must accept the call of the Gospel by a free decision of faith before he can become a full and responsible part of the Christian fellowship. But Protestant churches urge Christian parents to bring up their children within the Church where they can learn to understand and begin to respond to the Gospel in their formative years. Although the Church is dependent upon the Christian in a measure for its vitality and strength, the Christian is dependent upon the Church in a more profound sense. If he separates himself from it and tries to be religiously self-sufficient, he starves and in the end may destroy his Christian life.

This, in the broadest terms, is the nature of the Church and its relationship to its individual members. It is not necessary for our purpose to discuss "the means of grace" by which the Church builds up the lives of Christians. Among the means of grace, Protestantism has emphasized above all the *Word* and the *Sacraments* of Baptism and the Lord's Supper. It should be pointed out that both the ministry of the Word and the ministry of the Sacraments are essential and that the neglect of either or the undue subordination of either one to the other tends to impoverish the spiritual life of the Church.

Luther speaks of "the mutual conversation and consolation of brethren" as a means of grace.[6] Unfortunately, in many modern con-

[6] Cf. Aulen, op. cit., pp. 355, 356.

gregations there is little "mutual conversation and consolation." Because of the size of the congregation and the impersonal character of the community from which it is gathered, many members of city churches see one another only on Sundays for an hour and know nothing of one another's personal lives. As a result, there is no opportunity for them to share the whole of their lives with one another, to rejoice with one another in their good fortune or to bear one another's burdens. One of the results of this is that in many congregations the conception of a fellowship of Christians who love one another as brothers has been virtually lost. Brunner has argued that in the New Testament the "Church" ("Ecclesia") was primarily not an "institution" but a "Fellowship" ("Koinonia") of persons and that this "signifies a common participation, a togetherness, a community of life."[7] He doubtless exaggerates when he says that the New Testament "Koinonia" "has nothing to do with an organization" and his estimate of the value of the institutional aspect of the later Church is too low. But he is surely right in his contention that *primarily* the Church is a *fellowship of persons* and that it shows the vitality of its faith by the *love and brotherhood* of Christians for one another.

The first ethical task of the Church, as we have seen, is the fostering of the Christian life of its members through the means of grace it provides. The greatness of this task can be appreciated only in the light of all we have said in this chapter about the way God's grace is active as the primary factor in the whole of the Christian life. If the Church is the sphere in which His grace is normally made available to men, it is indispensable for their moral growth. Of course, the Christian life and character of the individual is not *solely* a product of the Church. For the spiritual insight and moral intensity of the individual Christian are also important factors in his development. Nevertheless, even the greatest Christians have heard and responded to the call of the Gospel within the Church and have been loyal and faithful servants of the Church. Therefore, it is one of the duties of the Christian to become a vital rather than a merely conventional member of the Church, to make use of the means of

[7] Brunner, E., *The Misunderstanding of the Church,* London, Lutterworth Press, 1952, p. 10.

grace it offers him for the nourishment of his spiritual and moral life, and to strengthen the fellowship of its members. He needs all the counsel, encouragement and criticism his fellow Christians can give him. And they need his help as he needs theirs.

The second ethical task of the Church is to stimulate the practice of love in all the relations of Christians to their neighbors *outside the Church*. It is natural that Christians should love the "brethren," with whom they share a common faith and life, more easily than those outside the fellowship. However, this does not excuse the *self-centeredness* which is so characteristic of many Churches, but which is in contradiction to the law of love. The Church is "holy" in the sense we have described; but it is also "human all too human." Although it is in its essence a spiritual fellowship within which the divine grace is bestowed on men, it is on its human side one social institution among many others. As such, it often tends to fall into collective pride and to be exclusive towards those outside it. It is also tempted to concentrate its interest upon its own internal life and problems. When it does so, it turns away from the life of the world and becomes preoccupied with the details of its own organization and activities. Withdrawing from the frontier where it is confronted by the needs and problems of the larger community, it becomes introverted and loses its sense of responsibility for the teeming life of the world.

Yet, self-centeredness contradicts the whole nature and purpose of the Church. The Church is not the Kingdom of God. The tendency to identify it with the Kingdom on earth only leads to an absolutization of its claims and ends in a vicious form of spiritual pride and idolatry. The Church is only the community of those who pray for the coming of the Kingdom on earth and hope for eternal life. It is the first fruits of the Kingdom but the full harvest is yet to come. Though Christians have been reconciled to God and are at peace with Him, they have no right to be at ease in Zion. They have a task to perform in the world. The redemptive work of God continues and struggles against bitter opposition from the forces of evil. There are many who have not even had the Gospel preached to them and many others who have fallen away from it. Therefore, the Church is a *missionary community*. It can never be content until the Gospel has been preached to all the peoples of the world and until all have accepted the call. This does not mean that "the Church is only a means, not an end" as is sometimes said. It is a means by which God's redemptive love draws men of all nations into the Kingdom, but it also participates in the life and blessings of the Kingdom itself. This gives it no right to be self-centered. If it is to be worthy of the new life of the Kingdom it proclaims, it must always be looking beyond its own boundaries to the needs of the world outside.

This is of primary importance for the Church not only because of its missionary task but also because of its *social task*. Love of neighbor cannot be confined to relationships between persons but must also be applied in the collective relationships between classes, races, and nations in the form of justice. One of the main reasons for the Church's tragic neglect of this difficult task in the past has been its self-centeredness and withdrawal from the world. This has led it to make a false distinction between "religious" and "secular" needs. All too often it has treated the need for justice on the part of under-privileged races or classes as a "secular" matter because justice is concerned with human life in this world. In this way, it has tended to justify the fear of change and the social and political conservatism of many of its members.

The sharp distinction between "clergy" and "laity" has fostered the same tendency. Whenever the Church centers its attention mainly upon its own internal life and affairs, devoting most of its energy to "saving those who are already saved," the clergy tend to dominate it and most laymen become passive recipients of its benefits rather than active participants in its work. The remedy is not merely to allow laymen to take more responsibility in the internal life of the church, but to stimulate them to carry their Christianity with them into their *"secular" vocations*. Only as they assume this responsibility will they become active and equal partners with the clergy in the work of the Church. Moreover, only as they do so can the difficult problems involved in the application of Christian ethics to political, economic, and other areas of social life be solved. Technical knowledge and practical experience are needed for the solution of the pressing economic problems of our day, and it is usually laymen who can deal with them most effectively. Ministers are a power-less small minority in the Church when they act by themselves, no matter how keenly they may feel the effects of social evils. Another example may be taken from the field of education. If the problem of secularism is to be solved, it must be solved primarily by laymen whose vocation is education, though they must have the advice and support of ministers at every point. Usually, the teaching of history or literature from a Christian perspective can be done most effectively by a trained scholar who is a Christian layman.

If the Church is indispensable for the nourishment of the Christian life of individuals and for the performance of the missionary and social tasks of Christianity, it is obvious that Christians should *respect* it. Actually, they often do not regard it as a holy community of grace, but as a feeble and fallible institution which has an unimpressive and frequently ugly building on Main Street. The main reason for this, apart from the weaknesses we have mentioned, is that Protestant churches have compromised so deeply with our secular culture and society. If the Church is to perform its ethical task of building the Christian life of individuals and applying Christian principles to the social order, it must cease to conform to the ideas and standards of the world. As long as it is content merely to *reflect* the world in its thinking and living, it cannot *transcend* the world and, by prophetic criticism and example, *transform* it. Like the early Church, it must learn once more to be *in* but not *of* the world if it is to bring the light and love of the Gospel into the world.

LIFE IN TENSION

In conclusion, it should be pointed out that the Christian life is lived in *tension*. It often seems paradoxical because it combines and balances opposite attitudes. For example, it is both *this-worldly* and *other-worldly*. It is lived in time and yet it looks beyond time to eternity. From the ethical point of view, both sides of this truth are important. The Christian must strive for holiness or perfect goodness not by withdrawing from the world but by fulfilling the duties that arise in his family, his vocation, and his community. He must never despise his everyday tasks because they seem dull and uninspired. He must pray that God's Kingdom may come on earth; he must also seek to live as a member of it and bring others to it during his life on earth. Early and medieval Christianity tended to neglect this truth under the influence of the apocalyptic hope and of asceticism and it is one of the elements of strength in modern Christianity that it has restored the values of life in this world to prominence.

Nevertheless, the Christian life looks beyond the present to the future and faith is always accompanied by hope. Life is always imperfect and unfinished. The ethical and social aspirations of the Christian are never fully realized. They are limited and often thwarted by his own defects or by the opposition of others. Sometimes he seems to be on the point of realizing them only to be prevented by death. Like Moses, he is allowed to ascend to Mt. Pisgah and behold the promised land toward which he has striven, but he is forbidden to enter it himself.[1] For reasons like these, the modern emphasis upon this world and its tasks, although valuable, cannot be the last word but must be supplemented by hope for the eternal life of the Kingdom.

Again, the Christian life is characterized by *peace* and *joy,* but it is also a life of *struggle* and *suffering.* We have pointed out that one of St. Paul's deepest insights is that joy, one of the fruits of the Spirit, can be won by the Christian through self-denial and suffering, as Jesus passed through death to life. Peace and blessedness are integral aspects of the Christian life. Forgiveness overcomes the anxiety that accompanies sin and, by reconciling man to God, it brings peace with Him, oneself, and one's neighbors. It is also the source of blessedness because it restores man to fellowship with God, his true Good, in whom is his joy.

But this does not mean that the Christian life is marked by continuous feelings of peace and joy. Since it is always imperfect and always struggling against evil within and without, the Christian life cannot be an undisturbed harmony. "The peace of God, which passes all understanding"[2] is a peace in the midst of struggle. "Because the forgiveness which brings peace is an act of God received

---

[1] Deut. 3:27.
[2] Phil. 4:7.

and held by faith, or, in other words because peace depends on fellowship with God, it can exist in the midst of darkness and tumult, and it can dwell in a human heart filled with storm and stress."[3] As Niebuhr says, the peace of the Christian cannot be attained by escaping from the responsibilities and vicissitudes of life in history into harmony with nature or mystical union with God.[4] It comes in the midst of the insecurities and tragedies of life through faith in an ultimate security which remains above and beyond them.

[3] Aulen, op. cit., p. 310.
[4] Niebuhr, Reinhold, *Discerning the Signs of the Times*, New York, Scribners, 1946, Ch. X.

Part III

CHRISTIAN ETHICS AND SOCIETY

CHAPTER 10

Sex and Marriage

SINCE the First World War, a crisis in marriage has developed throughout our Western civilization. The emancipation of women, the impact of industrial change upon the family, the impersonal life of great cities, the rupture of family ties by war, and the widespread use of contraceptives are among the causes of this crisis. It has manifested itself most strikingly in a growing acceptance of pre-marital intercourse and a higher divorce rate.

Men and women have always found it difficult to fulfill the lofty demands of Jesus with respect to sex and marriage. St. Paul's struggle with the sexual lapses of his new converts in Corinth is sufficient proof that the early Christians were tempted by the lax practices of paganism. It would be possible, therefore, to say that there is nothing new in our contemporary situation. But this would be a mistake. There is something unprecedented in our present situation: in the past many men and women have failed in their conduct to measure up to the Christian ideal; in our time there are also many who have come to doubt the validity of the ideal itself.

If Christians are to deal effectively with the crisis, they should not be content to appeal to the authority of particular passages in the Bible. They must interpret the Christian view of sex and marriage in its relation to the Biblical doctrine of man as a whole. They must also re-examine that view in the light of the best modern knowledge about human nature and its needs. In doing so, they must never lose sight of the special problems and difficulties of the present time. There could hardly be any task more important for the Christian thinker today.

221

THE ASCETIC VIEW OF SEX

The task is rendered more difficult by the influence of a *false asceticism* about sex within some branches of the Church. There is no trace of sexual asceticism in the Old Testament. In accordance with the Biblical view of the Creation, sex is regarded as good and marriage is assumed to be the normal state for men and women. The Hebrews were well aware of the dangers of uncontrolled sexual passion, as the stories of Samson and Delilah, David and Bathsheba, clearly show, but they always assume that sex is a natural human function and a source of joy.

On the whole, the New Testament is in agreement with the Old Testament on this point. True, Jesus was unmarried and he spoke of some who had made themselves eunuchs for the sake of the Kingdom of heaven.[1] St. Paul was also unmarried and believed the unmarried state to be preferable for Christians like himself who were capable of remaining continent.[2] But the fact that Jesus and St. Paul were unmarried is no indication that they disapproved of marriage. Indeed, Jesus' saying, "What therefore God has joined together, let no man put asunder,"[3] implies that marriage is ordained by God. Moreover, his saying about those who have made themselves eunuchs is not a law requiring celibacy; "it is simply another extension of Jesus' principle that the Kingom of God takes precedence over all lesser loyalties."[4] It must be admitted that St. Paul's advice to the unmarried has often been interpreted as favoring celibacy for all Christians. "Considering the imminent distress in these days," he writes to the unmarried Christians in Corinth, "it would be an excellent plan for you to remain just as you are."[5] But this is an eschatological counsel based upon his belief that marriage may distract Christians from preparing themselves for the imminent coming of the Lord.

However, a tendency to depreciate marriage soon developed in the Church. Under the influence of Greek and Oriental views of

[1] Mtt. 19:12.
[2] I Cor. 7:8, 32-35.
[3] Mtt. 19:6.

[4] *The Interpreter's Bible,* Vol. 7, p. 481.
[5] I Cor. 7:26 (Moffatt).

matter as evil and in reaction against the licentiousness of paganism, virginity was exalted by St. Athanasius, St. Ambrose, and St. Augustine. In the Middle Ages, celibacy was imposed by Canon Law upon all the clergy. Finally, the Council of Trent anathematized those who said "that the conjugal state is to be preferred before that of virginity or celibacy and that it is not better and more blessed to remain in virginity or in celibacy than to be joined in matrimony."[6] The depreciation of marriage was largely due to the view that sexual pleasure was sinful and that the only justification for sexual intercourse was the propagation of children in marriage, though marriage was also regarded as a "remedy against sin." This view has almost disappeared among Protestants, but the negative attitude towards sex with which it was traditionally associated has survived in the form of the severe "Puritan" condemnation of sexual lapses and the "prudishness" of the Victorians. It is still found among some women in the belief that sexual intercourse is an "animal" or "nasty" thing, to be passively "endured" rather than enjoyed.

Thus, the ascetic view of sex and marriage is foreign to the Bible and has no place in the life of Christians who are true to the Biblical point of view. But it still has a strong influence in the Catholic Church, and has not completely disappeared from Protestantism. Unfortunately, its prevalence in Catholicism and the remnants of it in Puritanism have made it possible for secularists to dismiss the Christian sexual ideal as a survival of ancient and medieval ways of thinking out of place in the modern world.

THE NATURALISTIC VIEW OF SEX

At the opposite extreme from the asceticism of much traditional Christian thought is the _naturalistic_ conception of sex. This conception assumes that man is essentially an animal, though a highly developed and complex one. Accordingly, love is simply sexual desire, and romantic feeling is an illusion woven by the imagination to enhance the value of the loved person as an object of desire. Sex itself is merely a natural instinct like hunger and thirst. Though sexual

---

[6] The Canons and Decrees, Session XXIV, Canon X.

desire can be denied its normal expression for a time, health requires that it be satisfied regularly as soon after adolescence as possible. Therefore, it is undesirable to postpone sexual intercourse until marriage. Since it is pleasant, it is inevitable that men should desire it; since it is natural, there is no virtue in restraining it. Of course, precautions should be taken to avoid evil consequences such as pregnancy and venereal disease; but contraceptives and prophylactics make that relatively easy. Moreover, a certain amount of sexual experimentation before marriage is valuable in acquainting one with the sexual techniques necessary for a successful adjustment in marriage. Promiscuity is foolish, because excessive indulgence of any natural desire leads to satiety and thus defeats its own purpose.

According to this view, when a person finds a member of the opposite sex who can satisfy him sexually and whose tastes are similar to his own, he will usually want to marry and settle down. He will cease to need sexual satisfaction outside of marriage, if he is happily married and has children, but there is nothing morally wrong in an occasional "affair" with a woman who is not his wife, unless he allows it to interfere with his responsibility for his wife and children. For "fidelity" after marriage, like "continence" before marriage, is a duty only to those who still believe in outmoded sexual taboos. By the same token, a man should feel free to divorce his wife, so long as he provides for her and the children. When sexual attraction no longer exists, what is there to bind husband and wife together? Of course, they may share enough common interests and ambitions to make a continuation of the marriage convenient for both of them. If the marriage continues to hold together, it is not because husband and wife feel themselves to be bound together by vows of fidelity, but because, like Edward and Lavinia Chamberlayne in T. S. Eliot's *The Cocktail Party,* they have become necessary to each other's comfort and security.

The naturalistic conception of marriage, however, is not always individualistic. In totalitarian countries the ideal of life—and consequently the ideal of marriage—is collectivistic. Individuals may seek their own pleasure before marriage and may choose their own partners for marriage, but their freedom of action is limited. Loyalty to the state takes precedence over the satisfaction of their own desires. The state may even demand that a man give information against his wife if she is suspected of disloyalty to the party in power and its program. For the rulers of the state value marriage only for its usefulness to society in providing workers for its factories and soldiers for its army. Despite these differences, however, the collectivist agrees with the individualist at the crucial point: the naturalistic view of man and sex is common to both. For the quality of married life, this similarity is more significant than the differences. Since man is viewed wholly as an animal and sex merely as a biological drive, man and woman marry primarily for the satisfaction each can derive from the other. Of course, their comradeship may lead them to cherish affection for one another and to develop a genuine loyalty to one another. But there is nothing in the logic of the naturalistic theory to justify this; indeed, it is one of the main evidences that the theory does not do justice to all the facts of human existence.

THE CHRISTIAN ATTITUDE TOWARD SEX

The Christian attitude toward sex is based upon the Biblical view of man as a creature made in the image of God. On the one hand, man is a *creature*. He is an animal who shares biological needs with other animals. These needs and the activities through which they are satisfied are good. Therefore, there is no reason for him to be ashamed of the sexual impulse. Indeed, since it leads him into a union with another person which dispels the loneliness of his separate existence and is the mysterious source of new life that extends his own existence beyond death, he should regard it as among the most precious of God's gifts. On the other hand, man is a *spiritual being,* created in the image of God. When he relates himself to God in faith and to his neighbors in love, every function of his personality is deeply affected. As a result, his biological functions are enriched with new meanings and endowed with new values.

Indeed, for man even eating and drinking, the most fundamental biological functions, tend to become social and aesthetic occasions. In sexual activity he is involved at a much deeper level of his personality. At its best, the sexual act is a physical expression of the desire of two persons to share their lives and purposes with one another in love. Thus, it is far more than a biological urge. "Sex in the human," says Bertocci, "is so interwoven with his total psychological being that once allowance is made for some physiological similarities, the contrasts are more illuminating than the likenesses. To compare the sounds an animal makes with the poetry of word symbols gives some notion of the range of differences possible."[1] The primary sexual difference between man and the animals is that "persons enjoy deeper, more lasting, and more profound satisfaction when the normal experience of sex lust is not primarily an end in itself but a symbolic expression of other values."[2]

Thus, the distinctive thing about the Christian conception of sex is that it fully acknowledges the reality and importance of sex as a biological function of man, but also insists that it is a function of the total personality which at its highest level is spiritual. In contrast to the ascetic view and the naturalistic view, it acknowledges both the animal and the spiritual aspects of man. It also insists upon the close relationship between these two aspects of his personality. But it does not assert their equality in dignity and value. Though the Bible is not dualistic in its view of the relation of soul and body, it regards the body as subordinate to the soul, an instrument or vehicle for the expression of spiritual values and purposes. For example, when Jesus urges men not to be anxious about food and clothing but to "seek first his kingdom and his righteousness,"[3] he clearly implies that the state of the body is secondary. Consequently, sex is always viewed in the Bible as a function of the whole personality, animal as well as spiritual, but the primacy of the spiritual is never forgotten.

It is only when sex is viewed in this way that Jesus' stern words about *lust* in the Sermon on the Mount can be understood. "You have heard that it was said, 'You shall not commit adultery.' But I say to you that every one who looks at a woman lustfully has al-

---

[1] Bertocci, Peter, *The Human Venture in Sex, Love and Marriage,* New York, Haddam House, 1949, pp. 48, 49.
[2] Ibid., p. 48.
[3] Mtt. 6:33.

ready committed adultery with her in his heart."[4] According to God's absolute will, the lustful thought is as blameworthy as the adulterous act, though society judges it to be less culpable. In looking lustfully at a woman, a man is thinking of her simply as a means to his own self-gratification. As in adultery, he is separating sex from the context of love which alone gives it its true meaning. "The distinction," says A. D. Lindsay, "between desiring something for its own sake or, in simpler language, loving it, and desiring it as a means to our own gratification may seem over-subtle for practical use, but it is a fundamental distinction. For to love things means to think them precious—a judgment as to a quality in them —and upon this judgment as to inherent quality Christianity always inexorably insists; whereas if we let ourselves use other people or things as means only, we soon become grossly insensitive as to their quality."[5] This is the difference people have in mind when they distinguish between "lust" and "love." It is not that love has no sexual desire in it; it is that love, unlike lust, is the desire of a person for another *person*, not for a *thing*, and that it cares for the other person for his own sake.

THE NATURE OF CHRISTIAN MARRIAGE

The teaching of Jesus about *marriage* is closely related to this view of sex. According to the Bible, the sexual impulse should be expressed in intercourse only within the limits of marriage. Consequently, both pre-marital intercourse and marital infidelity are condemned by the Christian ethic. Obviously, this implies a very high view of marriage and a determination to safeguard it against every danger that threatens it. What is the nature of Christian marriage? What are the grounds for it?

According to the Christian view, marriage should be permanent and monogamous. Its permanence differentiates it from the intense but ephemeral relationships between men and women which often precede marriage. Its monogamous character implies the exclusion of sexual relationships with anyone except one's married partner.

---

[4] Mtt. 5:27, 28.
[5] Lindsay, A. D., *The Moral Teaching of Jesus*, New York, Harpers, pp. 148-9.

As evidence of their intention to form an enduring and exclusive relationship of this kind, both partners are required to take *vows of fidelity* to one another.

Why are vows of fidelity necessary if the two partners love one another? The answer to this question takes us to the heart of Christian marriage. Though *love* is an indispensable condition of a happy marriage, as we shall see, it takes more than love to make a marriage. "Marriage is not a natural occurrence," says Brunner, "but a moral act based upon the foundation of a natural occurrence. Marriage does not consist in the mere fact that two persons feel that they are bound to each other in love, marriage only exists where the divine order of marriage is recognized as binding in itself and when two people know that they are bound by it."[1] While marriage has a subjective basis in the feelings of husband and wife, it is an objective state of things. It is a state of being bound together ontologically in a unique kind of union, a union which is created by the free decision of the married partners but which thereafter makes demands upon them. This is why *fidelity* is essential to it. "Fidelity is the ethical element which enhances natural love," as Brunner says, "and only by its means does the natural become personal. It is therefore the only quality which can guarantee the permanence of the marriage relation. Through the marriage vows the feeling of love is absorbed into the personal will; this alone provides the guarantee to the other party which justifies the venture of such a life companionship."[2] As a symbolic expression of the solemn commitment of each to the other and to the new life they are to build together, the vow of fidelity is far more than a "merely formal" matter. It is a sign that each of them is abandoning what Kierkegaard called the "aesthetic" life, with its craving for a continual round of momentary pleasures and its refusal to become involved permanently in the life of anyone, for the "moral" life which commits the self and assumes responsibility in love for another.

The crisis in marriage of our time is largely due to the fact that many have come to doubt whether this ideal, as well as the con-

[1] Brunner, E., *The Divine Imperative,* copyright, 1947, by W. L. Jenkins, The Westminster Press, p. 357.
[2] Ibid., pp. 357, 358.

ception of sex with which it has always been associated, is still relevant and practical under the changed circumstances of contemporary life. Anthropologists have said that marriage ideals and customs are products of particular cultures and are relative to the cultures which produced them. Sociologists have pointed out how radically the economic and social changes of the last few generations have affected marriage and family life. Psychiatrists of the Freudian school have warned that sexual restraints lead to neurosis. And those who hold the naturalistic view of sex try to persuade us that, with the availability of contraceptives, the fear of pregnancy can now be eliminated. Why, then, should men and women deny themselves any longer the satisfactions of sexual intercourse before marriage, especially when they must wait for many years before they can hope to marry? If they marry, why should it be necessary for them to commit themselves to a permanent and exclusive relationship? Would it not be more sensible to acknowledge that love may not last, and that a door should be left open for escape? Why not look upon marriage as an experiment? If one fails the first time, let him try again. Perhaps he will be more successful the second time.

THE BASIS OF CHRISTIAN MARRIAGE

Faced with doubts and questions like these, we must inquire whether the Christian ideal of marriage has lost its validity for modern men or whether it is still rooted in unchanging realities of human nature. The first thing to be noted is that sexual differentiation belongs to the order of the Creation. Sexual differences, which are psychological as well as biological, point to the *incompleteness* of man and woman by themselves. They need each other not only to satisfy their sexual desires but also to complete one another's existence. This is the ontological basis of marriage. After creating the first man, God says, "It is not good that the man should be alone; I will make him a helper fit for him."[1] Following the creation of woman, it is said, "Therefore shall a man leave his father and his mother, and shall cleave unto his wife: and they shall be one

[1] Gen. 2:18.

flesh."[2] In this passage, "it is not good that the man should be alone" refers not only to the psychological state of loneliness, but also to an ontological condition. It is the condition of being less than a complete person, of needing another person to complement and perfect the self. The "helper" man needs is not merely someone to divide the labor with him so that he can hunt or till the soil while she cooks the meals and manages the house; it is someone also to appreciate his efforts, share his interests, and enrich his life by drawing him out of himself into a wider circle of life. Thus, marriage is an adventure in companionship through which each partner stimulates the other and assists the other to complete himself. It is a necessary condition for the mutual fulfillment of personality.

Modern individualism has blinded many to the fact that personality grows through interaction with other persons and that participation in the life of another is indispensable for the enlargement of the self. The loneliness of separate existence is a source of deep unhappiness; it is at the same time a sign that potentialities in the self are not being fulfilled. As such, it drives the self toward the intimate union with another person which alone can overcome his separateness.

Of course, without *love* and the joy of loving and being loved such a union would be imperfect and would fail to accomplish its purpose of mutual fulfillment. The companionship of a man and a woman without love would be a dull, commonplace thing, serving their utilitarian purposes but not drawing them together as persons. With love, their life together is endowed with spiritual significance, for each is enabled by love to transcend his own self-centeredness and identify himself with the concerns of the other. This is the source of the poetry in a happy marriage, and we shall have more to say about it later. But, as full companionship without love is impossible, love which does not lead to *companionship* can never be an adequate foundation of true marriage. The neglect of this is the cause of the shipwreck of many marriages based upon romantic love alone. The romantic idea that "love is enough" exaggerates the emotional aspect of marriage and blinds lovers to the fact that in married life most of the time must be spent in prosaic activities. If love is too fragile

[2] Gen. 2:24 (A.V.).

and exotic to face these activities, as well as the difficulties and tensions that are bound to arise, it is not hardy enough to endure. It will shrivel when the cold winds of misunderstanding and adversity blow upon its blissful harmony.

The mutual completion or fulfillment of two persons through companionship is possible only if there is a sincere intention that it shall be *permanent*. A marriage which is entered upon by either partner with the reservation that he may dissolve the partnership if it does not lead to happiness is doomed from the outset. If he thinks that he may not share the whole of his life with his partner, he will probably withhold part of himself from the union. Only if both commit themselves unreservedly to permanence will they feel sure of each other and give themselves unconditionally to the new life they are planning to build. Without a sense of *security*, they will have neither the courage to venture all they have and are nor the peace that can come only from mutual confidence. It is probable that woman needs this security and confidence more than man. But man needs it also, and he needs it in proportion to the extent of his commitment to his wife and to their marriage.

Permanence is also necessary to permit the slow growth of mutual *understanding* and *sympathy* which is essential for mutual completion. Those who hold the romantic view of marriage seem to assume that when two people fall in love all barriers between them are broken down as if by magic and that they immediately experience unclouded harmony. In actuality, the process by which two lovers come to understand one another is often slow. Unwillingness to undergo this slow process of growth is the cause of many divorces in a period like ours which demands swift solutions of all problems. Mutual sympathy and acceptance may be even harder to achieve than mutual understanding. It is now realized that the sexual adjustment between a husband and wife often requires years. Their adjustment to differences of outlook, taste, or temperament may require still longer. There is nothing strange about this. It is due both to the self-centeredness which prevents them from giving themselves fully to each other and to the infinite complexity of every human being. For this reason, the finest fruits of marriage, if not its most ecstatic joys, are likely to come with advancing years.

In the second place, permanent monogamous marriage provides the best method of *stabilizing the sexual impulse* and *transforming it into a creative energy* which contributes to the spiritual and cultural life of man. In other forms of relationship between men and women sex tends to be a destructive rather than a creative force in its effect upon the higher life of man. Those who advocate pre-marital or extra-marital intercourse sometimes argue that it releases sexual tensions and thus enables a person to use his energies in a creative manner. But the release of tensions through sexual experience is wholly different from the direction of sexual energies to creative purposes. Indeed, when the sexual impulse is expressed without restraint, it tends to become inordinate and to absorb a disproportionate amount of the time and energy of the self. As a result, it interferes with the development of higher intellectual and spiritual interests. It ceases to be a symbolic expression of the mutual love of two persons, one interest among others, and becomes a dominant passion which draws most of the energies of the self into its service.

Romanticists have understood far better than modern Naturalists the power of sexual passion to take possession of the self. Since the Naturalist tends to regard sex as merely a physiological hunger, he assumes that expression satisfies it and puts it to rest. But Romanticists know that sexual desire can monopolize the whole self and sacrifice everything to itself. In contrast, Christian marriage accords a place of importance to sexual desire, but domesticates it and builds it into the total structure of human existence.

This is one of the ways in which Christian marriage contributes to the *moral development* of men and women. The traditional doctrine that marriage is a "remedy for sin" has been associated with the ascetic view of sex as "carnal" and has fostered the idea that marriage is acceptable only because it prevents a worse evil. But there is an insight behind the doctrine which Christians should not minimize. Sex is not in itself sinful, as we have seen; but it is perverted to evil purposes by sinful men. Only insofar as man is able to overcome his self-centeredness, will he be able to love woman for her own sake. Now, monogamous marriage cannot insure the conquest of self-centeredness which makes unselfish love possible. But it offers the most favorable conditions for that conquest. It provides an opportunity for husband and wife to treat each other as persons rather than things, to share their interests with one another, to assume responsibility and to care for one another. Insofar as they rise to this opportunity, they learn to transcend their self-love.

If a marriage is blessed with children, the development of parental affection and the exercise of parental responsibility help to further this process of moralization. As love flowers into marriage and marriage into a family, new incentives arise and wider obligations are assumed. If the responsibilities of parenthood are evaded, there is a serious danger that the self-centeredness of the two individuals may simply be replaced by the "égoisme à deux" of the married partners. This is one of the great temptations of romantic love. Because of the desire of the lovers to cherish their happiness together and safeguard it against threats from outside, they may refuse to risk the complications and troubles that come with children. If they do, they unwittingly thwart their own achievement of moral and spiritual maturity. On the other hand, with the coming of children, husband and wife may both be drawn out of themselves into the widening interests of the family. They are called upon to subordinate their private desires to the interests of their children and even to make sacrifices for them. In the process, their love for one another is not lost; it is purified and deepened. Moreover, as members of the larger community, parents are expected to advise and encourage their children in the process of adjusting themselves to the demands of the group. Their duty to help their children become responsible members of the community and later to establish families of their own strengthens their own sense of social responsibility. Thus, from the time they decide to marry to the end of their lives they are led by the immanent logic of love step by step towards moral and spiritual maturity.

In the third place, monogamous marriage is the form of relationship between the sexes which is most favorable to the *fulfillment of women*. It has often been pointed out that in the ancient world women were generally regarded as means to the ends of men. Treated as the playthings or domestic drudges of men, they had no freedom to determine their own destinies. The main cause of this, of course, was their position of inferiority. Polygamy was the institutional expression of the inequality of men and women, enabling a man to dispose of the lives of an indefinite number of women to suit his own pleasure or convenience. In Doughty's *Arabia Deserta* there is a description of the reaction of some Bedouins to the Christian ideal of marriage. "One said laughing, 'Khalil, we have a better religion, thy rule were too straight for us. I myself have wedded one with another wives fifteen. What say you, companions? In the hareem are many crooked conditions. I took some, I put away some, ay Ullah! until I found some with whom I could live."[3]

A. D. Lindsay has pointed out that, while no institution can be ideal, one institution may encourage the realization of an ideal while another may deliberately deny it. "The justification, for instance, of the Church's condemnation of polygamy," he says, "is not that monogamous marriages are all ideal and polygamous the opposite, but that in polygamy a man definitely commits himself to a course of behavior and to relations which shut out the very possibility of ideal equal relations between men and women."[4] On the other hand, Christian marriage attempts to foster relations of equality between men and women. It is true that women can be treated as means to the ends of men even within the framework of monogamous marriage. For example, it is possible for a man to keep a mistress for his sexual satisfaction while maintaining an outwardly correct relationship with his wife for the sake of social conformity. And there are many marriages in which the husband assumes a patriarchal role and keeps the wife under his thumb all her life. This indicates that monogamy is not always necessarily Christian; it is only when it is based upon love, fidelity, and equality, that it fulfills the Christian ideal. But it does offer women the most favorable opportunity for companionship with men on the basis of equality, and it has contributed greatly to the emancipation of women from men.

In the fourth place, Christian marriage is superior to other forms of marriage in the attitude it fosters towards *children*. The close connection between sexual intercourse and procreation is so obvious

[3] Quoted by A. D. Lindsay, op. cit., p. 136.
[4] Lindsay, ibid., pp. 166, 167.

that many have regarded procreation as the primary or even the only purpose of marriage. This view must be rejected. "Necessary connexion and identity," says Brunner, "are not the same thing. Sexual intercourse is intended by the Creator not only as a means of procreation but also as a means of expressing the love of married people for one another. The very fact that the human need for sex expression is not limited to definitely short periods but is a permanent need, indicates that this, as a characteristic element of human life, is *intended* by the Creator."[5] The question whether procreation is *the* end of marriage or *one* of the ends obviously has an important bearing upon the issue between Protestants and Catholics concerning birth control, since one of the main arguments for birth control advanced by Protestants is that sexual intercourse is an expression of love as well as a means to the procreation of children. However, all Christians agree that normally marriage should lead to the birth of children. The helplessness and dependence of children for their survival, protection, and growth demand that the parents meet the responsibilities they have taken upon themselves. The prolongation of the period of dependence in the human species is an important factor of human existence. As a result, the fidelity of husband and wife to one another entails the faithful concern of both for the happiness of their children.

During the long period between infancy and maturity, children need above everything else the affection of their parents. But they can hardly count upon this affection if either of their parents becomes involved in a sexual relationship with another person. Even if such a relationship does not lead to a complete breakdown of the marriage, it is sure to divide the affection of the unfaithful parent and to distract his attention in some degree from his responsibility for his children. Children also need security, and their security depends upon the continuing love, sympathy, and encouragement of both parents. If the parents are alienated from one another by the infidelity of one of them, this security is jeopardized. If a separation occurs, it may be shattered. One of the best arguments for perma-

[5] Brunner, E., op. cit., p. 367.

nence in marriage is furnished by statistics concerning the effect of broken families upon problem children and juvenile delinquency. It is hardly too much to say that the primary source of the happiness and stability of children is their relation to parents who love them.

Of course, children become less dependent upon their parents for affection, security, and stability after they attain maturity. Consequently, the responsibility of their parents for them is not by itself sufficient ground for a life-long marriage. But even after children marry and become largely independent of their parents a relationship of mutual affection and trust may continue, and parents may be a source of aid and encouragement to their children to the end. It should also be pointed out that, though the children have become less dependent upon their parents, the parents continue to need one another. After twenty-five years of sharing one another's lives, working together for their common purposes and meeting together their joys and sorrows, a husband and wife should have grown together and become in considerable measure one in spirit as well as flesh. If a separation then occurs, it is even more tragic than if it had happened a few years after marriage. It is particularly devastating for the partner who has taken the responsibilities of marriage more seriously and given himself more completely to them. The emptiness and loneliness of old age for both are likely to be great if they do not remarry; and, even if they do, they will be deprived of the joys they might have shared in the homecoming of their children and the fruits of memory they might have gathered as they looked back over a long life together.

These are some of the reasons—there are, of course, others—for believing that Christian marriage is still the ideal relationship between man and woman and between both and their children. It is not only revealed in the Bible as the original will of God in creating man and woman; it is also demanded by the realities of human existence. It may be that, at certain places and under certain circumstances, polygamy or some other form of marriage has been necessary or at least natural. But it can hardly be denied that polygamy has always resulted in the stunting of the personality of men and women, the exploitation of women by men, and the insecurity of children. Christians should have no fear that the Christian ideal of marriage is going to be superseded; it is too deeply rooted in the fundamental and enduring needs of human nature.

CHRISTIANITY AND DIVORCE

Because of its high view of marriage, it is easy to see why the Church has always condemned *divorce*. If permanent monogamous marriage is essential to the mutual fulfillment and moral development of husband and wife, to the treatment of women as ends in themselves, and to the welfare of children, there is every reason to safeguard it. Jesus regarded divorce as out of harmony with God's original will when He created man and woman, and he probably admitted no exception in the case of adultery, though Matthew represents him as doing so. However, it is inevitable that some men and women, due to the frailty and sinfulness of human nature, will not make a success of their marriage. The question arises, therefore, as to whether Jesus' condemnation of divorce must be interpreted as a *moral law* to be enforced by the sanctions of the individual conscience and the Church.

When it is read in the context of his teaching as a whole, Jesus' condemnation of divorce appears to be like other "hard sayings" of his. He goes behind the written Law, as it had been revealed to Moses and interpreted by the scribes, and proclaims the absolute will of God. In doing so he does not make any allowance for the errors and sins of human beings as they are. That he is fully aware of their sinfulness is shown by the fact that he explains the Mosaic law permitting divorce as due to the hardness of men's hearts. The crucial question is whether when the remnants of sin in the hearts of Christians are taken into account, there are cases in which divorce should be regarded as the lesser of two evils. Is the saying condemning divorce essentially different from the "hard saying" which prohibits the resistance to evildoers? In that case, as in the saying about divorce, the difficulty of applying the saying is due to the gulf between the absolute will of God and the realities of sinful human existence. It is generally recognized by Christians that it is impossible, without incurring great evils, to follow the saying literally in a world where there are criminals and predatory nations. In the same way, it would seem that Jesus' condemnation of divorce defines the norm for Christians, but that there may be cases in which divorce should be permitted them in order to avoid greater evil. This is the basis of the Protestant view that, while divorce is a tragic thing, it is advisable under certain conditions when two persons have definitely failed in their marriage.

In one of his essays, C. H. Dodd has opposed the view that Jesus' prohibition of divorce, like the commandment to love one's neighbor as oneself, is so "transcendent" as to be impossible of fulfillment. He holds that Jesus' saying about divorce should be interpreted "as a practical answer to a practical question." "Such a statement resembles a transcendent law no more than does: 'When thou art bidden to a feast, take the lowest room,' or 'Salute no man by the way.' "[1] This is a salutary warning against refusing to take the "hard saying" about divorce seriously. But it overlooks the fact that the commandment not to put away one's wife, unlike the precepts quoted by Dodd, cannot be fulfilled by a single act (like taking the lowest place) or by abstention from a single act (like saluting) which in ordinary circumstances would be easy for everyone. On the contrary, a decision against divorce in extreme cases would require the fortitude to renounce domestic happiness and perhaps to live in continual strife for the rest of one's life. For a literal fulfillment to be possible in such extreme cases, the human desire for happiness, peace, and love must be overcome to a degree which only saints are likely to attain. Moreover, the moral and spiritual values of a successful marriage for husband and wife must be lost. Would this not be to sacrifice the inner substance of marriage for the sake of its outer form?

Moreover, to insist upon literal obedience to the commandment against divorce appears to be inconsistent with Dodd's view that Jesus "did not discuss the 'relevance' of His teaching to the life of the Christian community in the world: such problems were to be dealt with as they arose by the insight of His followers, illuminated by the guidance of the Holy Spirit. . . ."[2] This statement surely puts

---

[1] Nash, Arnold S. (ed.), *Education for Christian Marriage,* New York, Macmillan, 1940, p. 63.
[2] Ibid., p. 65.

the emphasis in the right place. The Christian ethic, we have argued, is not an ethic of law but an ethic of love. It is to be applied by each Christian to his own situation in a spirit of liberty. If so, it is difficult to believe that Jesus, in his teaching about divorce, abandoned this aim and imposed an absolute law. The only principle that can be asserted with confidence is that a person should always enter into marriage with the firm intention of permanence and that he should seek patiently in love to overcome every difficulty that arises. If in spite of this a situation develops which seems intolerable, he should seek to overcome it and should call in anyone from outside who may be able to help. If a final impasse is reached, he should seek a divorce only as a matter of extreme necessity.

If it is unwise to make the prohibition of divorce into a moral law binding upon Christians, it is wholly impractical to make it the basis for a *civil law* binding upon non-Christians and Christians alike. As A. D. Lindsay has pointed out, any law can be effective only if it does not make demands which are far above the moral level of most members of the community. Moreover, any attempt by the state to enforce any part of the Christian ethical ideal destroys the religious character of that ideal. The basic motive for obedience to Christ's ethical ideal is that, in gratitude for God's love for us, we should love Him and obey His will for our lives. If this motive is replaced by (or mixed with) the radically different motive of conformity to a law from fear of the state's punishments or hope for its rewards, obedience ceases to be a religious and becomes a purely social act.

We have argued that divorce is opposed to the original will of God, since the norm for man is permanent monogamous marriage. But we have insisted that this norm should not be transformed into an ecclesiastical or civil law prohibiting divorce or permitting it only for a few specified causes. But we must be on our guard lest this interpretation of the Christian view of divorce should be used by Christians as an excuse for laxity. Many Protestants, in rejecting the Catholic legalistic view of divorce have adopted an attitude towards it which is almost as lax as that of secular Naturalists. The individualistic and hedonistic conception of marriage appeals to them because it chimes in with the modern emphasis on freedom from restraint. But Protestantism does not advocate the freedom of the individual from restraint; it insists upon a responsible freedom, a freedom to obey God's will and to serve one's neighbors. It is not a freedom to pursue one's happiness in one's own way; it is a freedom to fulfill the demands of love, demands which are not less but more rigorous than those of any code of laws. If so, the desire for greater satisfaction for the self or the unwillingness to face ordinary difficulties can never be an adequate ground for divorce. The Christian will be prepared to endure unhappiness so long as there is any chance of overcoming the obstacles that endanger his marriage, especially when the happiness and security of his wife and children are at stake. When he is tempted to resort to divorce as an easy way out, he should remember his solemn vow to take his partner "for better for worse, for richer for poorer, in sickness and in health, to love and to cherish, till death us do part, according to God's holy ordinance."

PRE-MARITAL INTERCOURSE

The Church has always regarded *pre-marital intercourse* as one of the major threats to Christian marriage. In the past, the argument against such intercourse has usually stressed the danger of physical effects, especially pregnancy and venereal diseases. This danger is still real and should not be minimized. Since the spread of the knowledge of contraceptives and methods of preventing disease in the Western world, however, it is considerably smaller than it once was. As a result, many have come to wonder whether there is any longer a valid reason for chastity before marriage.

But the primary arguments against pre-marital intercourse have nothing to do with its physical dangers, whether great or small. They are based upon its more intangible psychological and moral effects upon persons who are regarded as having infinite worth. First, the habit of exploiting others for the sake of one's own satisfaction "hardens the arteries of tender feeling."[1] Bertocci describes the "progression of sex" which results from the use of others as

[1] Bertocci, P., op. cit., p. 47.

means to one's own satisfaction. "When a person decides that he is going to get all he can out of sex *as sex,* he is driven into an almost endless progression: he must find a new fancy, a new variety of sexual experience, real or imaginary, for he soon tires of the last mode of sexual exploitation."[2] This is one of the main dangers of "heavy petting." When a young couple are strongly attracted to one another, it is entirely natural that they should wish to express their affection by physical contact. But if they form the habit of deliberately stimulating one another sexually by "heavy petting," their friendship will soon be spoiled. If they resist the temptation to go still further to actual intercourse, they will be aroused to a high degree of sexual excitement and tension which is not relieved. On the other hand, if they proceed on to actual intercourse, the habit of satisfying sexual desire soon becomes established and makes it virtually impossible for either of them to enjoy a normal friendship with the other or with any person of the opposite sex. Since sex has become an end in itself apart from love, it is stripped of the tender feelings that accompany it when it is an expression of love, and transforms members of the other sex from persons into objects of prey.

Second, pre-marital intercourse makes more difficult the attainment of a happy and harmonious sexual adjustment in marriage. When sexual experience before marriage has become, like eating and drinking, a means to the regular satisfaction of a biological need, one loses the sense of the mystery and wonder of sex. He will be fortunate if he does not also lose his respect for members of the opposite sex whom he has learned to treat as means to his own end. Such a person can hardly approach sexual experience in marriage with the respect for his partner or the feeling for the experience itself which he would have had if he had not learned to take them for granted. "The person whose past experience with sex," says Bertocci, "has been that of the hungry animal, or that of the egotistic philanderer who has thought of his partner essentially as a means to his enjoyment, will not have an easy time meeting a new situation in which his highest nature wants expression for the sake of his beloved."[3]

[2] Ibid., p. 47.
[3] Ibid., p. 70.

Third, the practice of pre-marital intercourse makes it harder to maintain fidelity in marriage. If one has become accustomed to the periodic satisfaction of his sexual desires, it is more difficult for him to impose the prolonged restraint upon himself which may be necessary from time to time in marriage. He is not as likely to endure the long periods of abstinence required by the serious illness of his partner, separation from her for vocational reasons, or service abroad in time of war. Apart from such unusual strains, he will not find it easy to resist the temptations offered by occasional encounters with sexually attractive persons, especially after the sexual appeal of his married partner becomes less intense. If a person has not learned before marriage to sacrifice an immediate satisfaction for the sake of a more remote but greater good, will he be able to trust himself or be trusted by his partner after marriage?

Up to this point we have been dealing mainly with the evil effects of pre-marital intercourse upon others and upon the marital relationship. What are its effects upon the individual himself? Pre-marital intercourse strengthens the hold of sexual desire and tends to weaken the interest of the self in the higher spiritual values which are necessary to the development of personality. It is almost impossible to develop a strong interest in intellectual activities, for example, without imposing restraint upon one's sexual desires. One does not need to accept a Platonic dualism of soul and body, reason and appetite, to recognize this truth. Intellectual achievement is impossible for one who cannot direct his attention away from the objects of the senses and appetites to the objects of reason. While some military and political leaders have curbed their sexual desires as little as their will to power, the achievements of statesmen like Lincoln would be inconceivable without self-control. And every great religious founder or moral prophet had to master his own sexual desires before he could become a spiritual leader of mankind.

However, we do not need to go to the lives of great men to prove the point. It is rare that a person even attains a high level of education without restraining the sexual impulse. Interesting evidence of this is furnished by the first Kinsey "report," which indicates that American men whose education does not extend beyond grade or high school have a significantly greater "total sexual outlet" than those who go to college.[4] Kinsey also offers considerable evidence that religious devotion has a restraining effect upon sexual activity. As he puts it, "devout acceptance of the church's teaching is correlated with sexual frequencies which are two-thirds or less than two-thirds of the frequencies which are found among males of corresponding age and educational level who are not actively connected with the church."[5] Despite Kinsey's view that "sublimation" of sexual energy is "only an academic possibility rather than a demonstrated actuality," it is clear from facts like these that it is an actuality in the lives of many persons.

It is difficult to conceive of a stronger challenge to our schools, churches, and families than that which is implicit in these facts. The failure of the schools to arouse a strong intellectual interest is partly responsible for the fact that a large proportion of our young people terminate their formal education as soon as possible and fall into the sexual pattern of the large group who do not go on to college. The failure of the churches to stimulate a deep religious concern and to present effectively the Christian conception of sex contributes to the same result. Nor can parents excuse themselves by pointing to the defects of the schools and churches. Since the attitude of parents toward education and religion profoundly affects the attitude of their children, their failure to encourage by their example an active interest in the things of the mind and spirit may make the task of the school and the church all but impossible.

CONDITIONS OF SUCCESS IN MARRIAGE

Clearly, the decision to marry is a very solemn one. It should be made only after both parties have thoroughly searched their hearts

[4] The statistics for pre-marital intercourse are striking. "About 98 percent of the grade school level has (sexual) experience before marriage, while only 84 percent of the high school level and 67 percent of the college level is involved. . . . The frequency figures show still greater differences between educational levels. In the age period between 16 and 20, the grade school group has 7 times as much pre-marital coitus as the college group. There is not much drop in the differential even in the older age groups." (Kinsey, A. C., *Sexual Behavior in the Human Male,* Philadelphia, Saunders, 1948, p. 347.) Of course, there are other differences involved besides those of education, e.g., the occupational status of the parents, but there is little doubt that the time and energy devoted to intellectual and cultural activities by the college group is one of the main causes for their lower sexual activity.

[5] Op. cit., p. 472.

to determine whether their marriage is likely to be a successful one. There are three essential conditions of success in marriage which young couples should always have before their minds.

The first of these conditions, of course, is *love*. We have argued that love as a "natural occurrence" is not a sufficient basis for marriage, and have pointed out the dangers of the "romantic" conception of marriage. Nevertheless, love is indispensable to a happy and successful marriage. It is a very dangerous thing to marry without love, though love sometimes develops after marriage. Friendship and common interests are not enough. "For a marriage without love," as Brunner says, "is a misfortune which can only be borne by those who possess great moral force, and it demands such an heroic attitude towards life that most people feel it to be a task 'beyond their strength.'"[1] This love should include both sexual attraction and romantic feeling. The former is usually stressed so strongly that there is little danger of its importance being forgotten. The greatest danger lies in the tendency to think that by itself it is a sufficient basis for marriage.

For it is often assumed that sexual attraction always includes romantic love in itself. Actually, it is quite distinct from romantic love. In its impatience to possess and enjoy its object, it can blind a person and persuade him that romantic feeling is also present. The sign of romantic love is the idealization of the loved one in her uniqueness and individuality. In romantic love, as Bailey says, there is a "vision of perfection" of the loved one. "Obviously the beloved is not and cannot be perfect in the strict meaning of the term,"[2] but "the perfection disclosed in the vision is no romantic illusion."[3] "It is a potential perfection—a perfection to which the beloved has not attained, but to which, by the grace of God, she may be brought," and in it the lover sees reflected "something of the perfection of God."[4] It may be doubted whether romantic love is usually interpreted in such religious terms, and when it is there is always a danger of idealization of the beloved passing over into idolatry. But it is legitimate for Christians

[1] Brunner, E., op. cit., p. 361.
[2] Bailey, D. R., *The Mystery of Love and Marriage,* New York, Harpers, 1952, p. 14.
[3] Ibid., p. 15.
[4] Ibid., p. 16.

who see the immanence of God in His creatures to regard the potential perfection of the beloved as a partial revelation of the actual perfection of God or at least as pointing beyond itself to that perfection.

The second essential condition of successful marriage is the possession by the lovers of *common beliefs and ideals* more basic than the differences between them. It is a truism that marriage requires a measure of diversity between husband and wife. If one of the main purposes of marriage is the mutual completion or fulfillment of husband and wife, as we have asserted, it is easy to see that differences of interest and temperament enable them to complement one another. On the other hand, if their fundamental beliefs and ideals are radically opposed, it is difficult if not impossible for them to find companionship with each other and to live together in harmony. For companionship is more than the enjoyment of each other's "company"; it also involves sympathetic understanding of each other's major interests and an approval of each other's primary values.

The third essential condition of a successful marriage is *character*. Neither the sharing of common beliefs and ideals nor the inspiration of love nor both together can prevent misfortunes, difficult problems and tensions from arising. It will be impossible to meet these successfully unless both partners can call the distinctively Christian virtues to their aid. They will need patience in the face of provocations and adversities. They will need to forgive and be forgiven when they hurt one another. They will need the humility to acknowledge their shortcomings. They will need the kindness that manifests itself in simple acts of helpfulness. Above all, they will need the love, greater even than the natural love that first brought them together, which "bears all things, believes all things, hopes all things, endures all things."[5]

[5] I Cor. 13:7.

CHAPTER 11

Love and Justice

MANY in our time are willing to admit that Christian ethics has produced the highest ideal of personal character and goodness in the history of the Western world. But they are perplexed, sometimes even irritated, by their inability to find in Christian ethics definite answers to their questions about social institutions and social justice. As a result, in a time of rapid social change and critical social problems like ours, Christian ethics seems irrelevant to them. How, they ask, can an ethic which stresses love between individual persons have anything to contribute to the solution of the difficult and urgent social issues that confront us? May it not be that the Christian ethic, suitable for an earlier period when the relationships between men were personal, is no longer adequate for our age in which relationships have become more impersonal and collective?

These questions are acute, and they can hardly be answered by saying that Christianity is a religion of personal salvation rather than a social theory. This answer satisfied many Christians in the earlier phases of the modern period when individualism was in the ascendancy, but we can no longer believe that personal regeneration is all that matters or that it will automatically bring about the social transformation that is obviously needed. The social evils of our time are so great and the human suffering that results from them is so widespread that Christians with any compassion for their less fortunate brothers at home or abroad cannot be indifferent to or complacent about the effects of the social order upon human lives.

JESUS' ATTITUDE TOWARDS SOCIAL JUSTICE

But when we ask what light is thrown upon social issues by Christian ethics, the first thing that strikes us is that little or no specific guidance is to be found in the teachings of the New Testament with respect to the form of *social institutions*. Jesus says little or nothing about the state, the economic order, the penal system, or the restraint of aggressive nations for the sake of peace. In some respects this is an advantage, since it enables the Christian to exercise his liberty in dealing with social problems and in adapting social institutions to changing social needs. The real difficulty is that, whereas Jesus offers us ethical principles to guide us in making our personal decisions, he seems to provide us with no *principles of justice* by the aid of which we may solve our social problems. He says nothing about liberty, equality, and their relations to one another, or the right distribution of goods, or the relation of the individual to society. If he had laid down the fundamental principles of social justice with respect to such matters, it might be possible to deduce from them answers to our political, economic, and international questions. But he is as silent about principles of social justice as he is about social institutions.

Indeed, Jesus seems at times to think that from the point of view of love justice is of no importance. When he was asked to arbitrate a dispute between two brothers over a division of the family property, he refused to do so and warned against the covetousness that sets even brothers at variance with one another.[1] In the parable of the laborers in the vineyard,[2] he implied that God does not reward men according to their work but according to His good pleasure. It is true that this parable is concerned not with the economic problem of reward for work done in human society but with the reward given by God to members of His Kingdom. But the question cannot be avoided: if God deals with His children without regard to the principle of reward according to merit and if men are to imitate Him in their conduct, should not the distribution of rewards in society be without reference to merit? Moreover, it will be remembered that

[1] Lk. 12:13.
[2] Mtt. 20:1-16.

men are required always to love their neighbors without regard to their merit or lack of it. If so, there would seem to be no room for justice in their dealings with one another.

An illustration of the way the demands of justice seem to be swept away by Jesus is his setting aside of the "lex talionis" or law of retaliation in favor of the principle of non-resistance to evildoers. One need not approve of the law of retaliation to be troubled by the apparent implication that the principle for dealing with those who do us harm is that of not resisting them. As we have seen, he did not have in mind the treatment of criminals by society but the reaction to wrongdoers by persons who have been hurt by them. But the social philosopher or statesman is bound to ask whether the effect of not resisting wrongdoers would not be to encourage aggression on a large scale and thus endanger social order and security.

Thus, Jesus seems not merely to offer us no principles of social justice, but to be completely indifferent to social justice. This is not all. In his ethical teaching, he always seems to conceive of a moral situation as one in which one person stands in relationship with another *person* or with each of several other persons. He seldom or never speaks of a moral situation in which a person stands in relationship with a *group* of other persons, e.g. a class, race, or nation. In other terms, he always seems to have in mind moral problems that arise in *personal* or "face-to-face" relationships rather than those that arise in *impersonal* or "collective" relationships. Now, moral problems that have to do with the form of social institutions and social justice are usually problems of the latter sort. For example, the question whether dictatorship or democracy is the better form of government, whether capitalism or socialism is the better economic system, or whether murder should ever be punished with death is one which concerns the whole of society. Again, the question whether it is just to segregate the colored from the white citizens of our country or to tax the rich in order to provide benefits for the poor is a question which concerns the relation of a whole class to another whole class, i.e., colored to white or rich to poor. If I vote on the issue of democracy or dictatorship, or if I take a stand on the issue of segregation, my act will affect the lives not of one but of many persons.

Moreover, even when I do not seem to be acting at all, I am often involved in the actions of the group to which I belong and am in some measure morally responsible for the social consequences of those actions. For example, if I live in the better residential district of my town, I am involved in the whole system of residential segregation which restricts colored people to the poorer sections of the town, though I may personally be opposed to segregation. Similarly, if my country goes to war, I become to all the citizens of that country an "enemy" and they become "enemies" to me, though I may disapprove of the war. Even if I refuse to participate in the system of segregation or the war, I am still involved in them. As a white person, I belong automatically to a privileged race and share the advantages of discrimination; and the only way I can stop sharing these advantages —and the guilt that accompanies them—is to stop being a member of that race, i.e., to die. Even if I renounce some of the advantages, e.g., residential segregation, I still retain the priceless advantage of being a white person in a society dominated by the white race and having the prestige and security of that race. Similarly, even if I refuse to participate in a war, I cannot avoid accepting the advantages that accrue to my country from a victory as long as I live and remain a citizen of it. Do I have no responsibility for acts which bring me advantages like these?

Thus, while love of neighbor as Jesus describes it seems to be directed towards persons, many of my acts affect the welfare of a whole class, race or nation. Is it possible to love a whole group of persons, most of whom one has never seen and will never see? Of course, one can love each of the members of the group whom he knows, but he cannot possibly know more than a very small proportion of the fifteen million members of a race or the seventy million members of a nation. He can also cultivate a feeling of general benevolence towards the group as a whole. But love of neighbor requires not merely feeling but practical service.

THEORIES OF LOVE AND JUSTICE

These difficulties have led many to think that Christian ethical principles cannot be applied to social institutions and to the relations between races, classes, and nations. Socially responsible Christian thinkers, however, have drawn a quite different inference. They have held that, though Jesus is silent about social problems, Christians can derive from his ethical teaching fundamental social principles by means of which they can find answers to these problems. Obviously, these social principles must take the form of principles of justice. This raises the question, What is justice, and what is its relation to love?

The question is an important one because love and justice are often regarded as either opposed to or at least radically different from each other. While justice, it is asserted, is concerned with the *rights* of all, love is concerned with the needs of the neighbor. Or, while justice renders to each the rewards or punishments *due* to him, love bestows upon him more than he deserves and overcomes his evil by good. Or, while justice is prepared to use *force* to secure obedience, love bestows its benefits freely and effects its purpose by persuasion. Do these alleged differences between love and justice prove that they are opposed to each other in their nature and purpose? If so, it will be impossible to make justice serve the ends of love. Or is there a fundamental similarity between the ultimate purposes of the two? If so, it may be possible for love to make the ends of justice its own and to transform justice into an effective instrument of its own ends. In order to decide between these alternative views, we must first consider two theories of the relation of love and justice, one of which stresses their mutual opposition, the other their radical difference.

(1) Some Christian thinkers have held that love and justice are *radically opposed* to each other. Therefore, a society that is to take love of neighbor seriously must dispense with the whole system of social justice. Leo Tolstoy was one of the most distinguished of these thinkers. He held that sayings like "Resist not the evil one" and "Judge not" rule out for Christians punishment of criminals by courts of law, resistance to aggressive nations, and the existence of the state which uses force for these purposes.[1] If necessary, society should return to a primitive economy, each person working with his own hands in order not to be a burden to others and to contribute to the fulfillment of the needs of all.

This extreme view is based in part upon a legalistic and literal-

[1] Tolstoy, Leo, *A Confession and What I Believe,* London, Oxford University Press, 1932, Chs. II, VI.

istic interpretation of Jesus' teaching, in part upon a highly optimistic theory of human nature which is closer to modern Romanticism than to Christianity. The result is an interpretation of Christian ethics which turns the Gospel into a new law based on love and insists upon the ability of everyone to live up to it if he will only exert his moral will. It is worthy of notice that the literal application of this perfectionistic ethic of love would be possible, as Tolstoy saw, only at the cost of destroying the whole structure of the state and culture that has developed under civilization. If Tolstoy had been more realistic in his view of human nature, he would have realized that this meant, not a state of love between all, but "a state of nature," a "war of all against all." It should be clear, therefore, that love of neighbor is not an alternative to justice, enabling us to do away with the latter. There is no place for political anarchism and Utopianism in Christian ethics.

(2) Brunner's theory is more realistic in that it acknowledges the necessity of justice. However, it stresses the *radical difference* between justice and love. According to Brunner, justice renders to each person what is "due" to him, what is "fitting" for him in view of his place in the "primal order" of right.[2] If we are to decide what the rights of men are, whether they should be equal, how the individual and the community should be related to each other, or make up our mind about any other problem of justice, we must refer to this "primal order" of creation and man's place in it. "That is the deepest reason," he says, "why a certain impersonality clings to the idea of justice. In every case, what 'belongs' to me, what is my due, is definite, fixed. Hence, if I treat a man justly, and only justly, I regard him as fitting his place in the structure, as one whose place has been decided upon and so decided that this or that is his due or property. I do not see him himself. I see his 'claim,' his right, we might even say his 'share' in the whole structure. As contrasted with love, justice has this statutory quality, this sense of things fixed. . . . I have to do, not with him, but with his right."[3] Brunner recognizes that what justice requires is relative to the particular situation, that "justice must change with changing life."[4] Thus, his theory of justice has room for the

---

[2] Brunner, E., *Justice and the Social Order*, New York, Harpers, 1945, pp. 19, 20.
[3] Ibid., pp. 19, 20.
[4] Ibid., p. 96.

"dynamic," as well as the "static," aspect of justice. Nevertheless, the "sense of things fixed" by their place in the "primal order" of creation dominates his whole thinking about justice.

One of the dangers in Brunner's way of thinking is to be found in his assumption that without love of our neighbor we can determine what is just for him. Brunner seems to think that even "natural" men whose vision is blinded by individual and class egoism can see what is due to others. This was the error of Christians who accepted without qualification the Graeco-Roman concept of a "natural law" of right which can be discovered by the reason of man without the aid of faith and love. For the reason of man is confused, as his will is corrupted, by sin. How can it be expected to discover what is in accordance with the "primal order" of right unless it is illuminated by faith and purged of egoism by love? How can it understand the purpose of God manifested in the "primal order" of Creation without reference to the revelation of that purpose by the Redemption of men through Christ? In short, how can it know what is just for man without taking into account not only his place in the creation but also what love wills for him?

Moreover, Brunner has not freed himself from the dualism of love and justice. As he puts it, "the nature of justice is *radically different* from that of love, yet, deriving from the one God, is very *closely akin* to it."[5] Justice, he holds, is concerned with a person not in himself but only in relation to the system; love is always personal. On the one hand, justice is not "an inferior thing"; it is "always the precondition of love; justice must never be neglected by love;"[6] on the other hand, love transcends justice, its free gift is "beyond justice."[7] Justice must first be done, and a love which did not respect another's rights would be mere sentimentality. But love must then do more than justice requires because it is given freely and without regard to merit or desert.

Despite his recognition of the importance of justice, Brunner does not see the close relation between justice and love. The reason is to be found in his view that justice must be impersonal in its purpose because it is impersonal in its form as law. "Justice can make no use

[5] Ibid., p. 125 (italics mine).
[6] Ibid., p. 129.
[7] Ibid., p. 130.

of this love," Brunner says, "nor does it need to—Justice belongs to the world of systems, not to the world of persons."[8] Therefore, love comes into play only *after* the demands of justice have been met, supplementing them by its own free gift. It can play no part in shaping the system of justice itself. Surely, this is an error. As we shall see, the key to justice is not to be found in its impersonal form but in its purpose, and love can transform a system of justice so that it meets its purpose more effectively.

JUSTICE AS AN INSTRUMENT OF LOVE

This can be shown by an independent analysis of the nature of social justice and its relation to love. What is *social justice*? No society can maintain order or freedom without a system of *laws* or *rules* that define the rights and duties of its members to one another. In order that these laws or rules may be effective, they must be approved and obeyed by the great majority of its members. A must know that, if he abides by them, B, C, and D will do the same. B, C, and D must have a similar assurance about A and about one another. In other words, the effectiveness of the system depends upon a tacit agreement of all or almost all that they will do their duty as defined by the rules. Now, laws will not be accepted and obeyed by the majority if they make higher and harder moral demands than a large majority are willing to follow. Therefore, the laws in which social justice is embodied must lay down duties towards other persons which fall short of those demanded by love of neighbor. Lawmakers must take account of the fact that many of the members of a society will seek primarily to protect and further their own interests. Hence, law can only limit the egoism of men by defining the rights of all and by enforcing them against those who encroach upon them.

Thus, the purpose of a system of social justice is to establish and maintain an order of rights and duties and the method by which this purpose is attained is to lay down laws. These laws must be general, a particular law applying to all members of the class for which it was designed. A law is also, at least in theory, impartial. It is meant to be applied to all the members of the class in the same way, without discrimination in favor of or against any of them. Because of its

[8] Ibid., p. 128.

generality it disregards the difference between the persons to whom it applies and the special needs of each of them. Moreover, the law pays no attention to the motives from which a person fulfills his duties, so long as he fulfills them. Thus, it sets up a framework of order within which each person may carry out his purposes.

What is the *value* of such a system of social justice under law? It is easy to see its negative function: it restrains the egoism and aggressiveness of each member of society and makes social order possible. But this negative function is subordinate to a positive function: it provides the structural conditions for the fulfillment of purposes by all the members of society. It enables each of them to know what sort of conduct he may expect from the others and enables others to know what sort of conduct they may expect from him. Without it, the members of society would not be able to predict one another's behavior and carry out their purposes in harmony with one another. Without it, the freedom of each person to make his own decisions and seek his own ends without being frustrated by the actions of others would be impossible.

Now, if this is a correct analysis of the purpose and nature of social justice, it is obvious that *what it seeks is also sought by love:* the fulfillment of the ends of all persons in community. Therefore, one of the main aims of love should be the establishment and maintenance of social justice. Social justice is—or should be—that manifestation of love which aims directly at the good of a *group of persons* but only indirectly at the good of *each person* of the group.

This view enables us to deal with the difficulty that, while Jesus always seems to picture neighbor love as directed towards a single person, it seems impossible to direct neighbor love towards a class, race, or nation. We can now see that neighbor love is far from powerless to guide us in our relations with groups like these. Since love of neighbor is all-inclusive, it must be given to all persons who are affected by our actions. But it cannot be given to each of the members of a large race, class, or nation *directly* and *individually*. Therefore, it must be given to them *indirectly* and *collectively*. The most effective way to do this is to seek the common good of the group by furthering justice for them.

It may be objected that love of neighbor is meaningless except in an "I—Thou" relationship between two persons, in which each enters into the life of the other and identifies himself directly with the needs of the other. But love of neighbor, unlike romantic love or love of friendship, does not require direct relationship *with a person,* it requires only the willingness to treat another, directly or indirectly, *as a person.* Of course, love of neighbor arises more naturally in a direct relation with a person than in an indirect relation with him as a member of a group. This is one of the most important causes of the difficulty of applying love to collective relationships. But it must be remembered that love of neighbor is not primarily a sentiment or feeling; it is a practical disposition to affirm the welfare and serve the needs of others. As such, it does not depend upon a personal relationship with each of them.

An example may help to clarify this conclusion as to the relation of love and justice and show how love can be applied to a group of persons by seeking justice for them. One may deal with the problem of discrimination against Negroes not merely by refusing to practice it oneself, but also by trying as a citizen to change the economic and other conditions which are products of it. One may seek more equal opportunity for Negroes in economic life, in politics, in education, in housing. The determination to secure justice for them may be carried out in many ways. One may be able as an employer of labor to employ more Negroes, pay them the same wages as whites, and give them the same opportunities for advancement. One may be able as a member of the administration of a school or college to press for the admission of Negroes as students. In the political sphere, one may lend his support to every effort to remove discrimination by speaking and voting for wise "fair employment practices" bills, for the removal of segregation in the public schools, and for full political and legal equality. Each of these acts would be aimed directly at the improvement of the lot of a large class of persons, but indirectly at the welfare and happiness of every person in that class. If these acts are motivated by a disinterested concern for Negroes as neighbors and brothers, the justice promoted by them is an instrument and expression of love.

It should be noted also that justice is an *indispensable* means to the welfare of a race or other group. For example, if my fellow-citizens and I refuse to make full use of the method of justice to express our love for our colored neighbors, the system of economic, educational, political, and social discrimination will continue. My personal disapproval of it or refusal to conform to it will not avail to overthrow it. All efforts to change it by converting individual white persons will also fail, unless conversion leads on to social action. The system of discrimination will continue unless it is overthrown by action designed to replace it by a more just system. Gradually or rapidly, the social structures of law, custom, and institutional pattern must be changed. No amount of love of whites for Negroes as individuals will bring this about. If love does not change the structures of justice, it will be socially ineffective. This is doubtless what Archbishop William Temple meant when he wrote that it will not do to "bleat fatuously" about love and that what is needed is plain justice. The point is not that love is unimportant in dealing with social problems; the point is that love is not love but sentimental talk unless it manifests itself practically in seeking justice for all.

This is not to say, of course, that one's efforts to attain justice for Negroes or any other class *as a group* should be the only expression of one's love for them. One must also, in one's dealings with them *as individuals,* seek to fulfill their needs and further their welfare as persons. Social justice, though an indispensable, can never be a complete and adequate expression of love. The reason lies in the nature of social justice itself: social justice is concerned with the *general* or *common* good shared by all the members of a group but it pays no attention to the *special* needs of the members. But love is concerned with all the needs of persons, special as well as common. Therefore, love must seek social justice for *all* but must also go beyond this to seek the welfare of *each* as an individual.

IDEAL VS. ACTUAL JUSTICE

Up to this point, we have considered the ideal rather than the actuality of social justice. We have seen that insofar as this ideal is realized in actual systems of social justice, there is no dualism between the requirements of justice and those of love; indeed, justice becomes an indispensable expression and instrument of love. The distinction between ideal social justice and love is simply that justice establishes the general conditions for the good life of a group and represents the demand of love for *all* the persons of the group, while love also seeks to fulfill the special needs of *each* person.

When we consider social justice as it actually has been, however, our account must be different. The content of the actual system of social justice has usually been determined in large measure by the dominant class of society rather than by the society as a whole and it has been determined mainly with a view to the interest of that class rather than the interest of all. In the early stages of its development, particularly, social justice is more the product of the will to power of the dominant class than of the practical reason of all seeking to further equally the freedom and security of all. At the best, it is a compromise between the rational demands of morality and the arbitrary demands of power. Thus, it fails to protect the freedom or provide the opportunities needed by all in an equal and impartial way.

This is the source of the resentment and bitterness of under-privileged classes and races all through the course of history against the actual social justice under which they have had to live. Since Ahab's confiscation of a poor subject's vineyard in the time of Elijah, appeals have been made from the arbitrary "justice" of the king to a higher justice of God. This is why moral philosophers distinguish between "legal" and "moral" justice, between "legal" and "moral" rights. Sometimes legal justice has denied to a whole class fundamental rights, as Athens denied both freedom and political rights to its slaves. Sometimes it has bestowed upon a class a limited freedom but has treated them so unequally in the distribution of opportunities as to make their freedom hollow, as America treated her Negroes after their emancipation. Sometimes it has theoretically given all freedom and equality of opportunity, but has favored the rich or the well born in such a way as to render the freedom and equality of others less effective, as in most Western democracies today.

Thus, the actual system of social justice that has usually prevailed has seemed to many to be a mere mockery, a cloak for oppression of the weak by the strong. This is what St. Augustine had in mind when he disputed Cicero's contention that one of the foundations of a commonwealth was justice. If justice was a necessary condition of the existence of a commonwealth, he argued, there had been and was no commonwealth in the ancient world. Justice is impossible with men who do not love God and, in loving Him, love their neighbors as themselves. The systems of "justice" established by such men will be products of the will of the strong to dominate the weak in their own interest. Thus, the "justice" of Rome, after the Romans had lost their early love of liberty and their temperance, was imposed upon her conquered provinces by force. Like her other virtues, her justice was motivated largely by love of dominion and glory for herself. For the sinful pride and self-love of men prevent them from loving their neighbors as themselves and consequently from seeking their neighbors' welfare as well as their own. This "pessimistic" view of St. Augustine has something in common with the view of Marx and Lenin that the whole legal system of the state is only a means whereby one class oppresses another.

However, most actual systems of justice in history have had good as well as evil in them. They have been neither products of an impartial reason serving a moral purpose, nor mere instruments for the domination of the weak by the strong. They have usually arisen from compromises between the will to justice and the will to power, between moral principle and the egoism of the ruling class. Partly to satisfy their own consciences, partly to secure the willing obedience of the oppressed classes, the ruling class has bestowed some rights and privileges upon the ruled. These have been increased from time to time by further concessions. Thus, "might" has often determined "right," but "right" has won limited victories over "might." This warns us against the extreme of pessimism no less than that of optimism in our view of the moral quality and possibilities of social justice.

When the Idealist contemplates the discrepancy between justice as it ought to be and justice as it is, he is able to preserve his equanimity because of his highly optimistic view of human nature. He looks upon the denial of true justice in history as provisional and tentative. It is only a temporary failure which has been overcome in a measure already through the course of progress and will be overcome altogether in the future. Or it is a necessity due to the finiteness of the human spirit but capable of being transmuted into a larger good in the life of the Absolute Spirit. The philosophical Naturalist is also able to accept the discrepancy as a "natural" and therefore pardonable expression of man's animal nature, due to the survival of aggressive and brutal impulses which may be outgrown in the further course of evolution. But the Christian is bound to feel deeply the tragic gulf between ideal and actual justice. He sees in it, not a necessity due to man's finiteness or his animal ancestry, but a result of his egoism and pride which is not necessary and should be overcome. Therefore, though he must avoid pessimism with respect to man's capacity to achieve justice, he must never cease to feel a *tension* between ideal justice and the actual justice man has attained.

THE CHRISTIANIZATION OF JUSTICE

This brings us to our final point about the relation between justice and love: the gulf between ideal and actual justice should be a constant challenge to Christians to *transform* the actual system of social justice under which they live in order to bring it into harmony with the ideal justice demanded by love. If they believe that love requires the welfare of all persons in the community, they cannot be satisfied with a system of distributive justice which sanctions privileges for one class and denies them to another. If they believe that love requires mercy, they cannot approve a system of penal justice which deals harshly and unsympathetically with criminals. Therefore, they will bring social justice under the criticism of love and seek to make it more consistent with the demands of love. Even when the actual system of justice of their society seems closer to ideal justice than the systems of other societies, as democratic justice is closer than totalitarian justice, they will not allow themselves to become complacent about it. For the law of love which provides the perspective for their criticism is a transcendent, absolute principle, and the actual justice of every society in history will always fall far short of the perfect justice demanded by love.

That love requires this criticism and transformation of actual justice into ideal justice is obvious from an analysis of the nature of love itself. It can also be shown by an examination of the history of the Western world that love has already effected substantial changes in actual justice. We see these changes most clearly when we compare the theory and practice of justice that have developed since the beginning of Christianity with the justice of the Greeks. Greek distributive justice denied altogether the benefits of citizenship to slaves. Aristotle asserted the principle of equal benefits for equals but unequal benefits for unequals, i.e., the aristocratic principle that superior status entitles one to greater benefits. The early and medieval Church did not seriously challenge this way of thinking because of its own other-worldliness as well as the social circumstances under which it lived. But modern democracy, under the influence of Christianity, has insisted upon the dignity of all men and has made more of their fundamental equality. It has done away with slavery. It has not challenged the principle that rewards or benefits to different members of society must be unequal, despite the rise from time to time of equalitarian theories like that of the "Diggers" in seventeenth-century England. But it has been more and more insistent that inequality of rewards should be based upon inequality of merit, and it has interpreted merit less in terms of the birth or status of individuals than in terms of their work or contribution to society. Moreover, modern democracies have tended more and more to assume that equality in the enjoyment of political rights is not enough and that society should seek to bestow economic, educational, and other rights upon all the citizens. In recognizing their responsibility to raise the standard of living and cultural opportunity of their underprivileged citizens, they have taken a long step in the direction of equality of treatment.

It would be foolish, of course, to claim that all of these changes in distributive justice during the Christian era have been due to the influence of Christian love. The concern of the modern world for greater equality has also been fostered by other forces such as the Age of Reason, the Industrial Revolution, and Socialism. But there can be no doubt that Christ's teaching that love should be bestowed upon all, serving the needs of all in a practical way and given to all alike without regard to merit, has contributed much to the modern movement towards equality. Christianity has also insisted from the beginning that all men are equal as sinners and as potential sons of God, and that inequalities of birth or social status are of secondary importance. It has asserted that all men were created in the image of God. In doing so, it has raised common men to a dignity they did not enjoy before. At the same time, it has humbled the pride of the rich and mighty, reminding them that prosperity is not necessarily a sign of the divine favor. It has taught men to regard all superior ability as a divine gift to be used, not for their own advancement, but for the service of their fellows. In view of facts like these, who will question the statement that Christian love has effected a transformation of the Western theory, and to a lesser extent the Western practice, of justice? Thus, what Reinhold Niebuhr calls the "relevance" of Christian love to the problems of society is shown by its effect upon actual systems of justice.[1]

Accordingly, the recognition that ideal justice is an instrument of love should never be allowed by Christians to make them either complacent or despairing about the systems of actual justice under which they live. The gulf between ideal and actual justice is due to the sin of man, and it will never be completely bridged in human history. The tension in the Christian's conscience between the demands of love and the demands of the system of justice under which he lives must never be relaxed. His task is to modify the system of actual justice at every point where it is not in accord with ideal justice.

He can undertake this task with the knowledge that he is fulfilling one of the most important demands of neighbor love and that there is nothing in the nature of justice itself that sets it in opposition to love. For justice, as we have seen, should be a manifestation and instrument of love for the service of persons in a group. Since the eighth-century prophets, the genius of Judaism and Christianity has insisted that religion must be expressed in morality and morality must be embodied in social justice. This should never be forgotten by Christians as they seek justice for all their brothers within the nation and for all the nations. Love is not only compatible with justice; it cannot be made effective in collective relationships except by means of justice.

[1] Niebuhr, R., *An Interpretation of Christian Ethics,* New York, Harpers, 1935, Ch. IV.

CHAPTER 12

Christianity and Politics

"THINGS THAT ARE CAESAR'S"

JESUS says as little about the state as about other social institutions. In reply to the question, "Is it lawful to pay taxes to Caesar, or not?"[1] he pointed to the image of Caesar on a coin and said, "Render to Caesar the things that are Caesar's, and to God the things that are God's."[2] This saying is of great value because it implies both the validity of the authority of earthly rulers in their own sphere and the illegitimacy of their claims to an absolute obedience that belongs to God alone. It justifies the tenacious insistence of the Western Church, Catholic and Protestant alike, upon the independence of the Church in relation to the State. When Thomas More went to his death at the order of Henry VIII rather than compromise the authority of the Church, he appealed to this principle. He was, he protested, "the King's good servant, but God's first." Thomas Jefferson applied the same principle in a more revolutionary fashion and in the name of the individual conscience when he said, "Rebellion to tyrants is obedience to God." The Christians who went to concentration camps in Germany rather than accept the paganization of the Church by the Nazis have rediscovered in our own time that the saying of Jesus provides the basis for resistance to any form of totalitarianism which exalts Caesar to the throne of God.

However, there is nothing in the saying that can enable Christians to distinguish in concrete situations between "the things that are

[1] Mk. 12:14. [2] Mk. 12:17.

Caesar's" and "the things that are God's." Consequently, it is not surprising that they have differed from one another with respect to the way to apply it. Even in the New Testament there is a radical difference between the author of the Book of Revelation and St. Paul. The former, writing after a persecution of the Christians, speaks of Rome as "Babylon the great, mother of harlots and of earth's abominations," "drunk with the blood of the saints and the blood of the martyrs of Jesus."[3] St. Paul, writing under more favorable conditions, urges upon the Christians at Rome obedience to the authorities of the state. "Let every person be subject to the governing authorities. For there is no authority except from God, and those that exist have been instituted by God. . . . Pay all of them their dues, taxes to whom taxes are due, revenue to whom revenue is due, respect to whom respect is due, honor to whom honor is due."[4]

From the early Church down to the modern period the dominant attitude of Christians to the secular authorities was closer to that of Paul than to that of the Book of Revelation. Christians took it for granted that kings derived their authority from God and should be obeyed, though on rare occasions they might have to be resisted if they sought to lay impious hands upon "the things that are God's." Indeed, the general attitude of most Christians to all established institutions was a conservative one. They did not believe that Christianity had a responsibility to transform political and social institutions in order to bring them into harmony with the teachings of Christ. What were the reasons for this conservatism?

The most obvious was that Christianity began as a small and weak minority movement with no social prestige or political power. Until the fourth century when it became a legal religion in the Empire, it had little opportunity directly to influence political life. The early Christians also entertained a strong hope for the imminent return of Christ to destroy the present evil age and establish the Kingdom of God. As a result, it did not occur to them that it might be God's will for them radically to transform the political and social institutions of the Mediterranean world. After all, Jesus had summoned them to prepare for the coming of the Kingdom within the framework of

[3] Rev. 17:5, 6.
[4] Rom. 13:1, 7.

the present world-order. Their attitude after his death, therefore, was that described by the author of the Letter to the Hebrews. Like Abraham, they "looked forward to the city which has foundations, whose builder and maker is God."[5] "For here," says the author, "we have no lasting city, but we seek the city which is to come."[6] Though the existing institutions were accepted, they were regarded "with a spirit of inner detachment and independence, since, after all, these things belong to a perishing world and are everywhere steeped in paganism."[7]

The influence of this Christian social and political conservatism has continued into modern Protestantism, though in a different form. Troeltsch points out how German Lutheranism, for example, allied itself with social and political reaction after the French Revolution. However, Calvinism had a strong sense of responsibility for the community and held that the Church should seek to Christianize the community in every aspect of its life, cultural, social, and political. In combination with other forces, this has led to a modern way of thinking about the state quite different from that of early and medieval Christians. The state is no longer passively accepted by Christians as something given, willed by God, despite all its imperfections. It is something human, though it exists in accordance with the will of God. Like all things human, it is subject to criticism by reason and conscience. Wherever it is found wanting, it is to be reformed, or, if necessary, overthrown. For it is an instrument designed by men for the attainment of certain purposes and shaped in such a way as to attain them as effectively as possible. If so, it may be transformed under the influence of Christianity until it serves in larger measure the purpose of God for mankind.

THE NATURE AND PURPOSE OF THE STATE

The *state* is the organization developed by the community to protect its members and harmonize their activities. The method it

[5] Heb. 11:10.
[6] Heb. 13:14.
[7] Troeltsch, Ernst, *The Social Teaching of the Christian Churches,* London, Allen and Unwin, 1950, I, p. 83.

uses to perform this function is to establish and maintain a system of laws. Since these laws must be enforced if they are to be effective, there must be a center of authority with a monopoly of force at its disposal. But the authority of the state is always to be used as an instrument of the *community*. Therefore, we might define the state as the organ of the community which lays down laws and enforces them with supreme power for the purpose of furthering the common life.

This view of the state is diametrically opposed to that of political absolutism. Political absolutism, which is based upon the idea of the absolute sovereignty of the state, acknowledges no limits to the authority of the state but pictures it as an omnicompetent Leviathan. But the state presupposes the existence and autonomy of voluntary associations within the community. The family, the school, the Church, the labor union, the philanthropic society, and other associations serve important interests of the community, and must be free from political domination if they are to serve these well. This limits the function of the state to the coordination and harmonizing of the free activities of its citizens as individuals and as members of voluntary associations. Moreover, since the state performs this function by means of law, it can only provide external opportunities and control external conduct by means of its laws. While it can compel obedience, it cannot control the motives of obedience. This means that the inner life of feeling, conscience and thought is beyond its province, except insofar as its external action indirectly affects that life.

The *purpose* of the state is two-fold: order and justice. Obviously, order or peace is more fundamental. Political absolutists like Hobbes have pointed out that in the absence of order there is certain to be anarchy, "the war of all against all." Under such circumstances, life is "nasty, brutish, and short." But if life is to be not only lived but lived well, justice is equally essential. Man is a moral being, and he can never be content to live under an order which is not based upon justice. This is the reason for the tension, previously described, between actual social justice and ideal social justice, and for the constant attempt to transform the former. It is misleading, therefore, to say as Brunner does that "the essence of the state is not justice but power" or to speak of a first "stage of political justice"[1] characterized by coercive power alone without any concern for justice. An order based upon sheer power alone and wholly lacking in justice may have existed at certain times in history, but it should not be called a "stage of political justice." Justice presupposes order, as Brunner argues; but the order of a state must be, however imperfectly, an order of justice. Thus, the purpose of the state is not only to protect the lives and liberties of its citizens by its *order,* but also to further their common good by its *justice.*

If social justice may be an instrument of love, as we have maintained, and if one of the main purposes of the state is social justice, Christians have no excuse for political indifference. They should be constantly striving to make the state under which they live more just in order that it may be a more adequate medium through which they may express their love for all their neighbors.

LAW: ITS USES AND ABUSES

We have pointed out that social justice must be embodied in laws which are general in their scope, impartial in their application, and external in their action. We must now examine more closely the values and limitations of law in the state.

Since law is general in its scope, it determines the basic conditions of social order in the state. By defining the expectations of the citizens with respect to one another, law makes it possible for a person to predict the future and to enter confidently into agreements with others in carrying out his purposes. The vital *importance* of order based upon law is seen most clearly when one reflects upon the mutual suspicion, fear, and anarchy which prevail in international relations where there is a minimum of order. Again, law enables the citizens to settle their disputes by the application of rules rather than by an appeal to brute force or the arbitrary decisions of judges. Thus, law is essential not only to the order of the community as a whole but also to the progressive development of the purposes of its members. As such, it provides a basic condition for the perfection of men's higher faculties. Even the "City of God," St. Augustine argues,

[1] Brunner, E., *Justice and the Social Order,* New York, Harpers, 1945, pp. 196, 198.

needs the order and peace of the state, however imperfect, for its historical development.

But there are also *limitations* of law, and to say that law is always a condition of moral and spiritual development is a dangerous half-truth. Why should order and law be contrasted so often with freedom and progress? Why should it be regarded by so many Christians as the antithesis of love? There are three main reasons for this. First, if laws are not impartial or are not impartially administered, they may strengthen the chains that bind the weak and poor to the strong and prosperous. They may favor privilege and provide a front of respectability behind which true justice may be evaded. Unjust laws may come to be accepted uncritically as just because they are parts of a legal system which is a necessary condition of order. In the name of order, the weak who suffer from unjust laws may be persuaded to endure them and the strong may be encouraged to defend the privileges derived from them. For the laws of the state, as we have said, are only in part dictated by justice for the common good of all; they are also shaped by the economic interests and social pride of the dominant class. Moreover, even when they are impartial in themselves, they may be administered by policemen and judges in such a way as to favor the interests of the dominant class.

It was facts like these, of course, which provided the basis for Marx's cynical view of the state and its laws as merely an instrument of oppression wielded by the ruling class.

A second limitation of law is the difficulty and tardiness with which it changes in response to new needs. Dull imagination makes it hard to conceive any alternative to the social institutions or relationships of the present. Timidity magnifies the dangers that would attend any change. It is easier to see the values that would certainly be lost by change than the values that would probably be gained. As a result, law often preserves continuity with the past at the cost of subservience to it. Professor Walton Hamilton describes the way a verdict by an English judge in 1837 laid the basis for "a doctrine of 'employer's liability'—or, more accurately, nonliability—which was destined to outlive, by some decades, its usefulness."[1] Reflecting the bias of the country gentry of the time, the verdict was used a few

[1] Ward, A. D. (ed.), *Goals of Economic Life,* New York, Harpers, 1953, p. 255.

years later by an American judge to support a decision quite inconsistent with the realities of the new factory system.[2] However, it is possible to exaggerate the static and inflexible character of the law. The legislators who make law and the legislators who apply it belong to a society that is always changing. When new situations arise and cases come forward for which there are no precedents, judges find ways of adapting the law to meet them. "Old concepts are given new contours; old rules are fitted out with 'exceptions' which grow in number and eventually cause the rule to be recast or even set in reverse."[3] For example, the verdict on employer's liability mentioned above did not stop the movement for workmen's compensation and finally employers accepted responsibility for the payment of benefits according to a fixed rate.[4] It must also be remembered that continuity with the past is important and may be threatened by rapid changes in the law.

The third limitation of law is the most fundamental one, and it is the ultimate cause of the failure of law to be completely impartial and to adapt itself more quickly to changing needs. It is the fact that law must rest upon the imperfect moral opinions and sentiments which are dominant in the community. A law is likely to be obeyed only if it does not make demands which are too far above the moral level of the community as a whole. Since it is the creature of the morality prevalent in a society, it can hardly be expected to embody a higher ethical ideal than that accepted by most members of the group.

The conclusion we would draw from all of this is that Christians should, on the one hand, honor and obey the law, but, on the other hand, refuse to endow law with a sanctity it does not possess. Despite its limitations, they must honor and obey the law because it is an instrument of justice. The justice it embodies may be rough and defective, but it is the indispensable basis of social order. Moral idealists and social reformers find it hard to be fair in their estimates of systems of law. The former are repelled as they see how far short the law falls of the highest ethical ideal, the latter are impatient at

[2] Ibid., p. 256.
[3] Ibid., p. 249.
[4] Ibid., p. 257.

its conservatism. But law cannot be expected to reflect an ethical ideal which is above that of the community as a whole or always to keep pace with the rapid rate of social change in a dynamic society like ours. Therefore, Christians should manifest a sober realism in their attitude towards the law, appreciating its benefits but not expecting from it a perfection possessed by nothing human. On the other hand, they should never regard human laws as sacred or submit passively to social evils merely because they are permitted by law. Christians have sometimes accepted without protest unjust laws which should have been modified or resisted. This political passivity has been encouraged by pessimism about man and all his works. It has played into the hands of political conservatives who have defended the whole system of things as they are. Since law is capable of being a powerful instrument of social justice, men should not be permitted to make it merely a servant of their own personal or class interests.

POWER

We have pointed out that the state, as the political organ of the community, seeks to further the common life by means of law. We have also analyzed the nature of law, and have indicated both its values and its limitations as an instrument of social justice. We must now deal with the *power* of the state which is necessary for the enforcement of its law.

In recent years, there has been much realistic, not to say cynical, analysis of the primary motives for political action. Disillusioned by the appalling abuse of political authority in totalitarian states, many have accepted the view that men seek political power exclusively from egoistic motives. According to this view, the basis of the state is might, not right. Marx has had much to do with this way of thinking, because he held that modern states are nothing but engines of oppression devised by the dominant class to exploit the workers. Christian social thinkers have not accepted this cynical view, but there is often a deep strain of pessimism in them. The use of force as a means of coercion, Brunner thinks, is "entirely immoral" because it turns a person from a subject into an object, from a "Thou" into an "It." However, though "not itself good," the coercive power of the state becomes a "moral entity" through its relation to law.[1] Brunner's oscillation between these two views of force is the main source of his ambivalent attitude towards the state. There are, he says, "two faces" of the state. On the one hand, the state is an irrational "natural growth" like a primeval forest; it is always "organized selfishness," "the instrument of sinful, selfish, secular forces."[2] On the other hand, it is "a manifestation of spiritual forces and purposes, the bearer of culture, the guardian of justice and of human values against arbitrary violence, and the creator of community."[3]

Though this is paradoxical almost to the point of absurdity, there is an important truth in it. While the state has a moral purpose and its power is justified by that purpose, it often falls under the sway of men who distort its purpose and capture its power for their selfish ends. But it is not correct to say that it is a "natural growth" and that it "cannot be controlled by ethical considerations." Though natural forces play an important part in its growth, it is also a product of human wills. If it were not, there would be no possibility of realizing a "moral purpose" in it at all. It is also untrue that states have been merely products of "organized selfishness." Throughout history, both moral purpose and selfishness have been at work, struggling against each other, in the origin and development of states. As a result, political power has been used in different ways by different states. It has never served a completely moral purpose in any historical state; but it has been used partly for a moral purpose in many historical states. Furthermore, some states have served a moral purpose to a greater degree than others; and some forms of government, notably democracy, are designed to serve a moral purpose.

Insofar as the state exercises its power to enforce just laws which serve the purposes of the community as a whole, its power is good; insofar as it fails to do so, bad. Moreover, coercive power is indispensable to the realization of the purposes of the state, though it should be exercised as little as possible. It is naive and sentimental

[1] Brunner, E., *The Divine Imperative,* copyright, 1947, by W. L. Jenkins, The Westminster Press, p. 453.
[2] Ibid., p. 460.
[3] Ibid., p. 443.

to suppose, as Tolstoy did, that love can dispense with justice or that justice can be maintained without physical power. However, physical power is not the essence of the state; it plays only a secondary role. As A. D. Lindsay points out, a state is able to control its subjects only because most of them approve of its purposes and voluntarily obey its laws. "The state can have and use organized force because most people usually want common rules and most people want those rules to be universally observed; there must be force because there are rules which have little value unless everyone keeps them, and force is needed to fill up the gap between *most* people *usually* and *all* people *always* obeying."[4]

However, Christianity has always insisted that power is not an end in itself but a means to an end, and it has always recognized the dangers of power. The power of the state should be used only for the common good of the people and in accordance with law. When power becomes an end in itself, it poisons those who seek and those who possess it. This is the meaning of Lord Acton's famous saying, "Power tends to corrupt; absolute power corrupts absolutely." Jesus was completely realistic about this. When James and John requested him to grant them seats at his right hand and at his left in his glory, Jesus made the request an occasion for one of his most striking sayings to the disciples. "You know that those who are supposed to rule over the Gentiles lord it over them, and their great men exercise authority over them. But it shall not be so among you; but whoever would be great among you must be your servant, and whoever would be first among you must be slave of all."[5]

St. Augustine saw clearly that Christians must not use their citizenship in the City of God as an excuse for refusing to accept political responsibility in the city or state of which they are citizens. They must be prepared, for example, to assume the difficult duties of a judge or juror who must determine the guilt or innocence of others without adequate knowledge. If they refuse to do so, others with no more knowledge and with less sympathy for their fellows may be given the responsibility. But Augustine insists that the Christian

[4] Lindsay, A. D., *The Modern Democratic State,* New York, Oxford University Press, 1947, p. 206 (italics mine).
[5] Mk. 10:37, 42, 43.

should never seek to acquire power for himself and will accept it only if he is requested to do so, and that the use of power as a means to domination over others is sinful. The first of these counsels is not always practicable. To follow it literally would prevent men from preparing themselves for public service by long study and apprenticeship in the difficult art of politics. In a democracy, especially, it is important that some Christians should devote themselves to politics as a Christian vocation. If so, they must study the most effective ways of attaining and exercising power.

The second of St. Augustine's counsels is as valid and necessary today as it was in the Roman Empire of his time. Though it may be desirable in some cases to seek power for oneself, especially when many of one's fellow-citizens are urging one to do so, it is sinful to seek it in order to dominate others. As St. Augustine pointed out, the love of domination by the Romans was motivated by the love of glory for themselves, a form of self-love. It is not different in our own time. Though leadership in a democracy is exercised by men who claim to serve rather than rule their fellows, it involves the use of power over others and power is almost as dangerous for those who claim to represent others as for those who do not. A partial safeguard against its abuse is a realistic recognition of the presence of self-love in one's heart and a determination not to allow it to make one ruthless. But one must also be motivated in his dealings with his fellows by love and compassion, if he is not to lord it over them but to be their servant.

Power is never just when it is exercised in the interest of only a part of the state, even a large majority. This raises the question whether a government which exercises its power as a means of oppression should ever be overthrown by violence. Many Christians would condemn the use of violence against the established order under any circumstances. The reason is that order is a basic social value and that revolution is a catastrophe which not only unleashes violence but also disrupts continuity with the past and tempts reckless men to establish a reign of terror. All too often, revolutionists are cursed with an impatience which leads them to destroy more effectively than they can rebuild. Embittered by resentment at existing evils and lacking the wisdom to reform, they can only destroy.

As Edmund Burke said, they consider bloody revolution such a small matter that they would make of it not the last bitter medicine of the state, but its daily bread. Therefore, all rational men and all Christians will avoid violent revolution by every means possible, knowing that even an imperfect social order may be better than the anarchy followed by tyranny which revolution so often brings.

But there are extreme cases where law and order are on the side of injustice rather than justice and where repeated attempts to remedy the evil have failed. In such cases, the moral right of revolution cannot be denied. Conservatives like Burke as well as Liberals like Locke have asserted this right. Though Burke wrote some of the most scorching passages in political literature against the French revolutionists, he never thought of denying the justice of the English Revolution of 1688. If liberty is to be defended, there may be times when revolution is unavoidable. When such a time comes, a country is blessed if, like England in 1688 or the United States in 1776, it can carry out its revolution under the leadership of moderate men. Then the destruction will be as small and the new order as stable as possible. Since revolutions are seldom moderate, however, they should not be advocated as long as there is even a small hope of orderly change. One of the advantages of democracy is that, unless it is rent asunder by class or sectional conflict, it offers the opportunity for gradual and peaceful change.

The rise of totalitarian states in our time warns us that when a people has become demoralized it is difficult to prevent the seizure of absolute power by a ruthless dictator. This tragedy can be avoided only by preventing the evil conditions which lead to it and by maintaining a sturdy love of liberty on the part of the citizens. Above all, the citizens must have a sense of their own political responsibility and a healthy distrust of the pride and pretensions of demagogues. But the fear of political absolutism should not blind us to the fact that there are other forms of power which are also dangerous. In the Middle Ages, the authority of the state was frequently too weak to curb the power of ambitious nobles and for some time it could not successfully resist the pretensions of worldly popes. In more recent times, the major challenge in the democracies has come from the concentration of economic power. Indeed, they have not yet found a way to check this danger. Americans have been extremely conscious of the dangers of "big government" from the beginning of their national life. They have learned during the last few generations to be afraid of "big business" also and to insist upon the control of it by the government. The fact that during the last twenty years the rights of organized labor have been legally recognized and that "big business" is now balanced by "big labor" has only increased the responsibility of government. For the power of both must be checked in the interest of the community as a whole. This makes it necessary for the state to have power adequate to control economic power and prevent it from exploiting the people. It is unrealistic to hope for a return to weak government in a society where capital and labor have attained the stature of giants. At the same time, it would be fatal to assume, like the Communists, that economic power is the root of all evil and that political power becomes innocent when it is taken out of the hands of one group and put into the hands of another. The task of the citizens is to endow the state with as much power as is necessary for its purposes but to hold it strictly responsible to themselves for the use of its power.

EQUALITY

We come now to one of the most crucial questions of politics: What are the major *principles of justice* on which the state and its laws should be based? Upon the answer to this question will depend, in large measure, the answer to the further question: What is the form of government which most fully embodies these principles?

The fundamental principles of justice in the state are *equality* and *liberty*. These principles are often opposed to one another, and it is supposed that a community must choose between them. In our time, there is a tendency in some circles to say that democracy rests upon liberty and communism upon equality. In these circles, any attempt to stress the importance of equality in a democracy is regarded as dangerous. This view springs from a complete misunderstanding of the nature of both equality and liberty. One cause of this misunderstanding is the conception of the state as a product of a social contract entered into voluntarily by individuals in order to preserve their liberties. Locke's social contract theory has been utilized by individualists of the privileged classes to thwart every effort of less fortunate classes to raise their economic and social status by appealing to the principle of equality. This is indefensible. Historically, equality as well as liberty has been crucial in the development of modern democracy. Moreover, equality, when it is rightly conceived, extends rather than destroys liberty because it insists upon equal opportunity for all.

"Christianity," says A. D. Lindsay, "stands for the equality not of all members of this or that community but of all men."[1] This conception of universal equality is implied in the saying of St. Paul, "There is neither Jew nor Greek, there is neither slave nor free, there is neither male nor female; for you are all one in Christ Jesus."[2] Unfortunately, Christians have all too often contented themselves with the belief that all men are equal only in the sight of God. They have rationalized this restriction of the meaning of equality by preaching that men who are inferior in wealth or social status may be as good and happy as their earthly superiors.

Modern Christians have realized more and more that this is an error, and the Social Gospel has emphasized the profound effect of social conditions upon the spiritual life. "There can be no fundamental faith about human nature," says Lindsay, "which will not somehow express itself in institutional form."[3] Faith in the equality of all men is no exception. The test of one's sincerity in professing this faith is whether he is prepared to translate it into personal conduct and social institutions. Throughout the Middle Ages and at the beginning of the modern period, inequality in all social institutions was taken for granted. It was only in the middle of the seventeenth century that the radical Puritans of Cromwell's army insisted upon the application of the principle of equality to the political sphere. The radical Puritans were organized in small voluntary congregations or societies on a democratic basis. All were regarded as equal in the sense that all were equally called by God. "That fundamental fact," says Lindsay, "outweighed their differences

[1] Lindsay, op. cit., p. 251.
[2] Gal. 3:28.
[3] Lindsay, op. cit., p. 256.

of ability, capacity, character and wealth so completely that these differences could be freely recognized and made use of. The Puritan congregation is a fellowship of equals who are recognized to be different. They are all alike called by God and guided by Him, and therefore all equally called on to contribute to the common discussion about the purpose and actions of their small society."[4] This belief in religious equality and this practice of democracy in the congregation soon produced, in the Putney debates between the radical Puritans and Ireton, a demand for universal suffrage. The principle to which they appealed was stated by Colonel Rainborough in an unforgettable sentence: "Really, I think the poorest he that is in England hath a life to live as the greatest he."[5] This implies that the life of the poor man has an intrinsic worth equal to that of the rich man and that he has an equal responsibility for the living of his life. We shall examine the political and economic implications of this principle in later chapters.

LIBERTY AND RIGHTS

According to John Locke, a state is the product of a social contract entered into by individuals to safeguard their life, liberty, and property. Its function is purely instrumental: to secure the rights of the citizens. This theory of the state has deeply influenced American political theory. As a result, Americans have tended to think of *liberty* as the highest social value and to depreciate government as little more than a necessary evil, necessary as a means of protecting the rights of the individual but evil because it interferes with his doing as he pleases. The assertion, "That government is best which governs least," expresses not only the fear of absolute power in the government but also the desire to be left alone by it. This conception rests upon an individualistic view of man and a *negative* view of liberty as absence from restraint by anything or anyone outside the self. Consequently, the government and its laws are regarded as limitations upon the liberty of the individual. The lack of respect for

[4] Ibid., p. 117.
[5] Woodhouse, A. S. P. (ed.), *Puritanism and Liberty,* London, Dent, Debate of Oct. 29, 1647, p. 53.

law, even lawlessness, which has been characteristic of many Americans is largely a product of this way of thinking.

But there is also a *positive* conception of liberty: liberty is the capacity to choose and to carry out one's purposes. Of course, liberty in this positive sense presupposes a measure of liberty in the negative sense. If the self is completely limited by external restraints, it may retain its freedom to choose its own purposes but it will not have the freedom to carry them out by its actions. Nevertheless, there is a great difference between the negative and the positive conceptions of liberty, and the difference leads to very different attitudes towards government. For when liberty is conceived as positive self-determination through the choice and fulfillment of purposes, the state and its laws may be regarded as not only necessary but also good.

According to this view, the authority of the state is justified because it establishes a limited but responsible liberty under laws. These laws define a system of *rights* whose purpose is to make the liberty of the citizens effective. A right is what Lindsay calls a "guaranteed liberty." Legally, it is a claim which is recognized and enforced by the state. Since a legal right is of no value unless it is respected by all, there is a duty corresponding to each right. If the state recognizes my right to drive an automobile on the public roads, it expects me to respect the right of others to do the same. Consequently, I must acknowledge my duty to stay within the speed laws, to drive carefully, and, in some states, to have my car periodically inspected for safety. The right, with its corresponding duty, creates an area of freedom for each citizen while requiring him to respect the similar area of freedom of each of his fellow-citizens. Thus, the system of rights and duties embodied in law is the basis of an effective and responsible liberty for all.

However, it is a mistake to suppose that there are no rights except those which are recognized and enforced by the state. A distinction must be drawn between *legal* and *moral* rights. A "moral" right is a claim made by a person which *ought* to be recognized by others. Whether it *is* recognized and enforced by the state is irrelevant to a moral right. When Antigone claimed the right to bury her brother, she was appealing to a moral law higher than that of the state which forbade her to do so. When the factory workers in the early stages

of the Industrial Revolution claimed the right to work under more
healthful conditions and for shorter hours, they were putting forward a moral rather than a legal right. Without this distinction, it
would be impossible to effect social changes under the spur of moral
criticism and to embody new moral insights in law. On the other
hand, there are "legal" rights which do not embody moral rights
because they are inconsistent with the best moral consciousness. Thus,
the distinction between legal and moral rights is indispensable for
both the establishment of new legal rights and the modification
of old ones.

This distinction implies that there is a *basis for rights* which is
deeper than the will of the state. Brunner holds that rights are rooted
in the "order of creation" which determines what is justly due to
each person. There are certain "primal rights" which are derived
directly from this "order of creation." There are other rights which
are secondary, because "they can be deduced from the primal rights
only indirectly, and with the aid of certain historical assumptions."[1]
"Primal rights" are those which are "due to man in *all* circumstances
and hence may *never* be withheld from him by the community."[2]

The value of this view is that it bases the rights of man not merely
on his own natural desire for happiness or on political expediency,
but on the will of God for man as it is manifested in his nature and
needs. It implies that man has a right to whatever is necessary for the
fulfillment of God's purpose for him. Thus, when man demands a
right that is not yet recognized by the state, he can appeal not merely
to the *fact* of his personal desires, but to a *responsibility* laid upon
him by God through his conscience. However, the particular form
that should be taken by a right, e.g., private property, can hardly be
determined by a direct inspection of the "order of creation." It must
be decided in relation to a particular society at a given time. Moreover, there is no real distinction between a "primal right" like private
property and a secondary right like freedom of the press. Both are
rooted in the creation, but both have been discovered and their form
determined in the course of history. The fact that one right may
have been recognized before or more widely than another does not

[1] Brunner, E., *Justice and the Social Order*, p. 63.
[2] Ibid., p. 63.

necessarily mean that it is more "primal" in the sense of more "essential."

One of the main differences between political Liberals and Conservatives is that the former are usually more sensitive to the need for *new* legal rights. Liberals have been influenced by Christianity at this point. Liberals see the unrealized possibilities of man and demand that he be accorded the rights necessary to realize them. Unlike justice as it is usually conceived, the ideal justice which is an instrument of love is creative and hence is willing to entrust man with rights he may not yet seem to deserve, in the faith that by their help he may be able to realize his possibilities more fully. In the modern world, three new rights have been legally recognized under the influence of this creative attitude: religious, political, and economic rights. It is necessary at this point to speak briefly of each of these rights.

Religious liberty demands the right to believe and worship according to one's own faith. It was recognized as a legal right only after years of religious dissension following the Reformation. Until the seventeenth century, most Protestants as well as Catholics assumed that religious uniformity was necessary for the sake of both political unity and eternal salvation. Gradually, however, it came to be realized that religious faith must be freely accepted if it is to be sincere and that the attempt to enforce it contradicts the spirit of Christian love. It also became evident that religious diversity, if it was accompanied by toleration, was not incompatible with political unity. As a result, religious liberty became more widely established in the West in the eighteenth century. Although it has been violently attacked by the totalitarian states of our time, it is the most fundamental of the rights which are necessary for spiritual development, because religion provides a basis of orientation to the whole of reality and value.

Political rights are rights which are required for participation in the affairs of the state. Though they began to be recognized as necessary for all citizens by the seventeenth century, it was only in the eighteenth century that they came into their own. In the nineteenth century, there was a tendency in the democracies to emphasize political rights so strongly that the importance of economic rights for the welfare of all was depreciated. It has come to be realized in our time, however, that political rights have little meaning to people who are economically impoverished and insecure. As a result, among exploited classes and in economically undeveloped countries the value of political rights tends to be minimized. Nevertheless, it is clear that political rights are as essential to social welfare as religious rights are to spiritual fulfillment.

If the seventeenth century was the age of religious rights and the eighteenth and nineteenth centuries the age of political rights, the twentieth century is the age of *economic rights*. Although there was equality of opportunity in theory in the nineteenth century, there was little economic opportunity for most workers in practice because of the unfavorable circumstances which handicapped them from childhood. This gave rise to the most bitter criticism of capitalistic democracies by the Marxists. They charged that the exploitation of the workers under capitalism reduced them to the status of "wage slaves" and that the offer by democracy of political rights to them was only a sop of no value to them. Though this criticism was exaggerated, the experience of the last hundred years has made it obvious that without economic rights and opportunities for all classes, the political rights bestowed by democracy are bound to seem unimportant.

We have spoken of the rights that make liberty effective as if they belonged to individuals by themselves. In reality, liberty is realized in large part through participation in the activities of *voluntary associations*. We have already pointed out that the state is an organ of the community for certain limited purposes and that the community realizes other purposes through voluntary associations such as the family, the church, the university, the labor union, and the professional association. Some of the rights of which we have spoken find their most natural expression within these associations, indeed, they would have little meaning for most people apart from participation in group activities. For example, religious liberty for most of us means the right to worship in accordance with the beliefs and practices of our church. Economic liberty means not only the right of the individual to choose his own vocation but also the right to strike with his labor union or to engage in the activities of a business partnership. Participation in the life of a church or university in which compulsion is absent and spontaneous interest is strong, affects the lives of many people more profoundly than their association with their fellow-citizens in the state. It is concerned, not with the general structure and laws of the community, but with the personal appreciation and realization of the highest spiritual values, and it makes possible a close fellowship, with mutual understanding and sympathy.

This is why a state which is concerned with the liberty of its citizens must respect the autonomy of voluntary associations. Functioning as intermediaries between the individual citizen and the all-inclusive state, they provide opportunities for the free development and exercise of personal capacities and for the enrichment of the life of the community. Thus, they make the liberty of the citizens effective by stimulating them to use their energies creatively beyond the control of the state. In contrast, the totalitarian state inevitably destroys or renders powerless all voluntary associations. Since its aim is to control the activities of its citizens in every sphere, it can brook no rival institution. Therefore, it must eliminate or paralyze any intermediate association which attracts the interest of a substantial group of citizens and divides their loyalty with the state. The result is a mass of individuals as homogeneous as possible, under the complete control of the state, and with no outlet for their creative energies but that provided by the state.

It cannot be denied that Americans have often been more eager to defend their liberty against interference from society than to use it for the benefit of society. They have asserted their own rights against the community more willingly than they have acknowledged what Brunner calls the "rights of the community" against them. Because of the conditions of frontier life and the influence of economic individualism, they have tended to confuse liberty with a rugged independence. The qualities most needed by the pioneer were resourcefulness and self-reliance. Valuable in themselves, these qualities often fostered unsociableness, aggressiveness, and indifference to the gentler qualities and higher values of human life. The qualities that led to economic success and power in the era of expansion after the Civil War were in many respects similar. Indeed, they were heightened by ruthlessness towards competitors and a narrowly materialistic scale of values. The results in many cases were unloveliness of character and social irresponsibility. The "liberty" of the industrial buccaneer to assert himself without outside interference often led to the exploitation or unemployment of thousands. Individualism produced the widespread belief that social progress depended upon the ruthless assertion of individual wills and the domination of the weak by the strong. As a result of large-scale depression and social revolution during the last generation, it has become clear that *limitations* must be placed on the rights of individuals and groups. Perhaps the greatest political task of the next generation will be to discover the most effective way of doing this without destroying freedom.

Though human liberties are among the most precious achievements of the modern period, they are by no means secure, even in democratic states. In times of war, when national unity is essential, they are always threatened. Even in times of peace, fear of external aggression or social change often drives men to deny or weaken them. In the presence of arbitrary power of every kind "eternal vigilance is the price of liberty." Christians must always be prepared to say in the face of any state or group that encroaches on liberty: "We must obey God rather than men."[3]

[3] Acts 5:29.

CHAPTER 13

Christianity and Democracy

THE greatest political achievement of modern Western civilization is democracy. Though it was discovered by the Greeks, democracy has assumed a form in the national states of Europe and America very different from that of Greek city-states like Athens. Christianity has played a crucial part in the development of modern democracy and is largely responsible for some of the characteristics which distinguish it from Greek democracy. Indeed, many have been so impressed with the affinity of democracy with Christianity that they have regarded it as simply the application of Christian ethics in the political sphere. But there is much in the secular democratic states of the West which is opposed to the Christian ethical and social ideal.

At the beginning of the twentieth century, democracy seemed to be firmly established throughout the West and destined to triumph everywhere. Indeed, according to the Social Gospel of Rauschenbusch, democracy was the political expression of the Kingdom of God on earth. There was a boundless faith in it and an unclouded optimism about its future. But since the First World War there has been a sharp reversal. Democracy has been openly attacked in the West. The brief experiment with democracy in Germany failed when Hitler came to power in 1933 and the newly established democracy of Czechoslovakia was destroyed by Communist power in 1948. Moreover, there is real danger that the newly awakened peoples of Asia will reject democracy and embrace its most deadly enemy, Communism. At the height of its influence before the First World

War, democracy is now on the defensive everywhere. Can Christians continue to believe in the political and moral superiority of democracy in the face of this world-wide challenge?

THE NATURE AND PURPOSE OF DEMOCRACY

As the term implies, democracy is government *by* as well as *for* the people. As such, it is contrasted with monarchy, or government by one man, and aristocracy, or government by the "best" people. Of course, it is impossible for the people as a whole to govern themselves in the literal sense of the term. In the "natural democracy" of the New England town meeting there was an approximation to direct government by the people as a whole. But the town was usually quite small, the citizens knew one another personally, and they could understand easily the simple problems of their common life. When we speak of government "by the people," we do not mean that the people literally govern themselves; we mean that they have the final authority and that those who govern them are responsible to them. They govern themselves in the sense that they select and consent to the rule of those who govern them. There is no such thing, of course, as government by the consent of all. If the consent of all were required, no candidate could be elected, no policy adopted. But democracy is government by consent in the sense that it is government by *representatives* who have the general approval of the majority or at least a plurality.

The *purpose* of democracy is to serve the common good of all the citizens without bestowing advantages upon any privileged group. It conceives of the common good as belonging to individual persons, not as something that exists above and beyond them. Therefore, democracy differs from every form of state which subordinates the good of the individual person to a superpersonal entity. It rejects the collectivistic theory that State, Class, or Race transcends in importance the persons who are its members, for it does not believe that the worth of persons is wholly derived from their membership in a superpersonal whole of any kind. On the other hand, democracy is not based upon the individualistic theory that the end of the existence of each individual is to be found in himself and his happiness alone.

This theory, which denies the social nature of man, is incompatible with democracy because it fosters an irresponsible attitude on the part of the individual towards the community. The purpose of democracy is not to exalt individuals as independent and self-centered beings, but to further the good of persons as members of the community.

The major *political device* through which democracy functions is *majority rule*. This is sometimes regarded as the essence of democracy, but it is possible to maintain the outer form of majority rule even under a totalitarian government. However, majority rule is important if general lines of policy are to be determined by as large a portion of the citizens as possible and be accepted by all of them. It is necessary to the success of any government and its laws that as many citizens as possible should consent to them. The state can hardly enforce a policy which most of its citizens are not prepared to support and obey. Majority rule is simply a practical device to enable the community to make decisions approved by as many citizens as possible and at the same time to maintain the unity necessary to its continued existence. Thus there is nothing sacred about majority rule. In any given election there is no assurance that the majority is right and the minority wrong, even when the majority is a large one. Moreover, since there is a possibility that the voters may reverse themselves on an issue or a candidate, the minority in one election may become the majority in the next. In this way, the minority may hope to have its way some time in the future. Also, the minority, though defeated in an election, can continue to express its opinion afterwards and have its voice heard as the "loyal opposition." If the minority is a substantial one, it may even be able to affect legislation not only through criticism of the program of the majority but also through its own votes in the legislature. Finally, the rights of individuals and of racial, religious, and other minorities are protected.

The *election* is only one moment in the continuous, ongoing political activity of the people. The importance of the election should not be minimized because it provides an opportunity for the people periodically to manifest their authority and make fundamental decisions on policy. But its value depends upon what goes on before and after it. During the process of deliberation preceding the election, as well as after it is past, there must be *discussion* of the candidates and issues by the people. In this discussion, the people must be permitted to think and express their opinions freely. In a totalitarian state, there is no free discussion in which different opinions are expressed, since it is assumed that only one opinion is possible for a loyal citizen—that of the party in power. In a democracy, free discussion is protected by the rights of free speech, press, and assembly. The denial or weakening of any of these rights for the sake of imposing conformity upon the people is dangerous in a democracy, precisely because it makes free discussion impossible. Why is this process of free discussion necessary? It is not merely to provide a safety valve through which dissenters may express their grievances without harming anyone. It is, rather, to provide an opportunity for everyone to participate in the process by which the community makes up its mind what to do. The community is often uncertain as to the best way to manifest its spirit in general policies, or, if it has already decided upon general policies, as to the best means of realizing them. Its uncertainty may be due to conflicts of interest between different classes, threats of aggression from without, new problems produced by social change, or other causes. Whatever the causes, full discussion is necessary before the community defines its policies or the methods of carrying them out.

To summarize, democracy is government not only for the people but by the people through representatives responsible to them. Its purpose is to serve the good of individual persons in the community, not subordinate them to a superpersonal entity such as the State or Race. Majority rule is not the essence of democracy; it is a practical method adopted to secure the responsibility of representatives to the people and to make possible the determination of general policy by as large a proportion of the citizens as possible. Finally, it is of primary importance that there be a full and free discussion before and after the election in order that everyone may have an opportunity to make some contribution and to have his voice heard in the discussion.

THE CASE FOR DEMOCRACY

There are valid reasons for thinking that democracy is superior to other forms of government from the ethical as well as the political point of view.

The first is that *it is less likely than other forms of government to overlook or neglect the good of any individual or group*. If the moral justification of the state is to be found in the good of the community as a whole, a government in which all members of the community may be heard and may have a share in determining policy would seem to be the best. "Political democracy," says Professor Perry, "is founded on the belief, supported by experience, that the best guarantee that any given individual's interests will not be neglected is to give to that individual both the voice and the power with which to obtain a respectful hearing. He, at least, will not forget his interests, and is their most vigilant and untiring advocate."[1]

A similar argument has been stated by A. D. Lindsay with special reference to the need for the people to make their grievances known. "The common life is the life lived by all members of the society. It cannot be fully known and appreciated from outside. It can only be known by those who live it. Its disharmonies are suffered and felt by individuals. It is their shoes that pinch and they only who can tell where they pinch . . . and without that knowledge the wisest statesman cannot make good laws."[2] This argument at first sight seems to require only that government should be sensitive to public opinion. But Lindsay points out that the government must also be controlled by the people if their grievances are not merely to be heard but to be taken seriously. "Unless there is power behind the expression of grievances, the grievances are apt to be neglected."[3] For the rulers may not only lack knowledge of the needs and grievances of the people, but also be arbitrary in the use of their power. "No man," said Lincoln, "is good enough to govern another man without that other's consent."

[1] Perry, R. B., *Puritanism and Democracy*, New York, Vanguard, 1944, p. 483.
[2] Lindsay, A. D., *The Modern Democratic State*, New York, Oxford University Press, 1947, pp. 269-70.
[3] Ibid., p. 271.

Second, *democracy furthers the development of practical intelligence and moral virtue among the people by entrusting political responsibility to them.* Since the development of modern democracy, it has been recognized that political activity opens up a broad field for the exercise and growth of intelligence and character. John Stuart Mill was one of the first to emphasize this as one of the main advantages of democracy. He held that, despite the popular preference for the "submissive" and "passive" type of character, it was largely the "energetic" and "active" character that was responsible for "improvement in human affairs."[4] The fullest opportunity is afforded by a democracy for the exercise of social responsibility and consequently for the development of character. True, only those who make a career of politics or have considerable leisure to devote to public affairs have a continuous opportunity to assume political responsibility. But even the private citizen has the responsibility to keep himself informed on major political issues and to perform special political duties from time to time. To the extent that he does so, his social sympathies may be enlarged and his sense of moral responsibility deepened.

Third, *man is a rational being and should share in the process of formulating the policies through which the purposes of the community are to be realized.* To deprive him of this opportunity is to truncate his freedom and deny him the possibility of functioning as a fully human being. It is to violate his dignity by treating him as a thing rather than a person, or, at the most, a child rather than an adult with an independence and initiative of his own.

The assumption that man is a rational being capable of self-determination has been vigorously attacked during the last few generations under the influence of naturalistic ways of thinking. As a result, there has been a reaction against the high view of man upon which democracy is based. Freudian psychologists and Marxist historians have stressed the irrationality of the thinking as well as the conduct of man, and some biologists have reduced him to the status of a complex animal. This conception of man must be rejected by secular as well as Christian defenders of democracy, for democracy rests in part upon faith in the dignity of man and in his creative possibilities. In meeting the challenge of naturalism and

[4] Mill, J. S., *Representative Government,* Oxford, Blackwell, 1946, p. 145.

irrationalism, however, some democratic thinkers have failed to acknowledge the element of truth in it. They have simply repeated the exaggerated claims for man made by eighteenth century Rationalists and nineteenth century Romanticists and Liberals. Even Professor Perry, whose claims for man are more moderate on the whole, says without qualification that man is "educable, that is, capable of having his deficiencies removed" with the help of "popular education" and free "institutions of public information" such as the press and radio.[5] In view of the widespread ignorance about elementary political facts and the low average level of information provided by the press and radio in America, this is a rather optimistic statement.

But the argument for democracy based upon the dignity of man as a rational being need not exaggerate his rationality. It asserts simply that the rationality which gives men dignity and entitles them to participate in political activity is not confined to one class of the people. It is not the technical, specialized knowledge of the expert that is required of the political leader, but "common sense" or "sound judgment" about human affairs. This may be found in any class, poor as well as rich, uneducated (in the formal sense) as well as educated. Of course, the emergence of men from all classes with the "sound judgment" that qualifies them for leadership is not all that is required in a democracy. It is also necessary that most of the private citizens should have enough judgment to recognize and follow these men when they appear. In view of the fact that they do not always do so, it cannot be argued that they always and under all conditions have the degree of rationality necessary for the success of democracy. Indeed, in an industrialized society, Lindsay admits, the great mass of men live specialized and narrow lives which make it difficult for them to develop a high degree of rationality and virtue. This poses one of the most difficult problems for modern democracies like our own. "How can we keep a modern industrial society from becoming not a community but a mob, not a society of persons capable of judging for themselves, discussing and criticizing from their experience of life the proposals

[5] Perry, R. B., op. cit., pp. 480, 481.

put before them, but a mass played upon by the clever people at the top?"[6]

It would be folly to pretend that under unfavorable conditions like those of our industrial society—narrow specialization of work, impersonal urban life, vulgarized and standardized recreation, unstable family life, and fear of war—the people will always make wise political decisions. But this is not fatal to the argument for democracy we are presenting. For there is no evidence that a privileged class of any kind is politically wiser than the people as a whole. Of course, the complex issues faced by modern governments require the technical knowledge of ways and means possessed by highly trained experts. But what is required of the private citizens in a democracy is not technical knowledge about the most efficient *means* to the attainment of ends; it is judgment about *ends* and about *persons*. Judgments about ends are essentially judgments of value; and judgments about the ends which ought to be realized in particular situations are moral judgments. But judgments of value and moral judgments depend upon experience of life and soundness of character rather than technical knowledge. Judgments about persons are based upon similar factors.

Of course, practical wisdom on political issues also requires knowledge of the community, its institutions, its way of life, and its most crucial problems. This is the reason democracy must educate its citizens beyond any other form of government, and it is doubtful whether any democracy has yet raised the average level of education high enough. But universal free public education in England and America, though far from perfect, is at least a start in this direction. Already, it has provided empirical evidence that the rational capacity of many is higher than was thought when education was a privilege reserved for the upper classes. As poor and underprivileged people have been offered educational opportunities, many have responded in a remarkable way. It is not uncommon in America to meet men whose parents were illiterate and uncultured but who have themselves attained distinction. And the example of Abraham Lincoln reminds us that, even with the benefit of only the slightest formal education, common people can

[6] Lindsay, A. D., op. cit., p. 280.

educate themselves and prepare themselves for outstanding political leadership.

Thus, the argument that the dignity of man as a rational being entitles him to a share in determining the policies of the community does not rest upon an idealization of the wisdom and virtue of "the people" as a whole. But it does assert that they are as competent as any privileged class to make judgments of value and moral judgments about the ends of the community and judgments about persons who are to lead them. Also, it maintains that, with the aid of universal education, they are as likely as the rich or the highly educated to make sound political judgments about the general policies needed to realize these ends.

Fourth, *democracy gives more scope to freedom and the creativity of individuals than any other form of government, while at the same time it does not minimize the necessity of order.* Contemporary totalitarianism regiments the individual for the sake of order. Submission and uncritical obedience to authority rather than independent thought and initiative are required of him. Social change is regarded with fear and suspicion as a threat to the established order. On the other hand, democracy safeguards the *freedom* of the individual in every possible way and encourages him to use fully his creative energies. It expects him to be independent in his thinking and critical of anything that seems to him wrong. It regards social change as inevitable when new problems arise and new opportunities beckon; and it looks hopefully for social progress in the future. But it demands that social change and progress should take place in an orderly way by means permitted in the constitution. "Man requires freedom in his social organization," says Niebuhr, "because he is 'essentially' free, which is to say that he has the capacity for indeterminate transcendence over the processes and limitations of nature. This freedom enables him to make history and to elaborate communal organizations in countless variety and in endless breadth and extent."[7] Moreover, the community, as well as the individual, needs freedom for the potentialities of man to realize themselves as fully as possible. For freedom is the root of

[7] Niebuhr, R., *The Children of Light and the Children of Darkness*, New York, Scribners, 1944, pp. 3, 4.

social progress, and without it social progress cannot occur at all or can occur only by violence.

At the same time, the individual, as well as the community, needs *order* and must express his freedom within the limits of order. For man is a social being. He cannot fulfill himself in isolation from his fellows. He can be truly human only in mutual relations with his fellows, and this is impossible except within a framework of order. However, the aim of order in a democracy is the welfare of individual persons, and, since freedom is essential to their welfare, order is not exalted above freedom and allowed to become static. The necessity of maintaining a balance between freedom and order was fully recognized by the seventeenth-century Puritans of Cromwell's army who accepted the medieval Christian view that men must act in accord with Natural and Divine Law. Similarly, the debates during the Constitutional Convention in 1787 showed a deep concern for order and fear of anarchy. It was only under the influence of economic individualism in the nineteenth century that freedom was exalted at the expense of order and law. Certainly, the Christian conception of democracy is at least as much concerned with the responsible exercise of freedom within the framework of order as with freedom itself.

THE MORAL WEAKNESSES OF DEMOCRACY

The most obvious weakness of modern democracies has been the *individualism of the citizens.* Many have thought that in democracy the liberty of the individual is everything, while equality and fraternity are mere Utopian fancies. This view is largely the product of nineteenth-century economic liberalism. According to it, democracy is simply a political system whose essence is universal suffrage and majority rule. Each class votes for its own interests and acts as a pressure group to influence legislation favorable to itself. Conflicts of interest between different classes are compromised on the basis of enlightened self-interest. In order to bestow the greatest possible freedom upon individuals and to avoid interference with their economic rights, the government must not be allowed to become too strong.

This individualism has led to a disillusionment of the masses with democracy, especially in less prosperous countries than our own, because it seems to sacrifice the equality of all to the economic liberty of the privileged classes. Even Brunner reflects this disillusionment in some measure. "Formal political democracy," he writes, "offers not the least guarantee of the justice that is the crying need of the day both in the social and economic spheres. . . . But if social justice cannot be obtained by democracy, the social class suffering most from injustice will unhesitatingly prefer the dictatorship of the proletariat in the totalitarian state to formal democracy."[1]

Underlying the individualism of modern democracies is the *moral weakness of the citizens*. Democracy is a venture of faith which rests upon a high, though realistic, conception of man. It assumes, as we have seen, that man is a rational being capable of participating in political activity; it also requires that he accept the responsibility which goes with that privilege. In other terms, democracy affirms man's dignity; but it also expects him to conduct himself in a way that befits his dignity. In fact, however, the majority in our Western democracies are content with commonplace values and standards. Many seek nothing higher than pleasure and comfort for themselves and their families. The more ambitious aim at success in business and superior social standing. In consequence, there is a widespread indifference to social and political issues. Despite universal public education and the rapid communication of news, there is a striking ignorance about political facts and problems. This political indifference and ignorance allows political bosses with powerful machines to control elections and makes many citizens susceptible to the appeal of demagogues to their fears and prejudices. There is little respect for those who make politics a career and comparatively few men of outstanding ability are elected to office.

The *corruption* of political appointees is one of the most obvious manifestations of the moral weakness of American democracy. Professor Graham has recently pointed out the paradoxical fact that, while from the beginning "the nation has avowed the highest moral standards known to man," yet "ethical questions are treated

[1] Brunner, E., *Justice and the Social Order*, New York, Harpers, 1945, pp. 206, 207.

as subordinate, secondary, or inconsequential."[2] He finds the explanation of this paradox in the general conditions of American life and in the dominant attitudes and habits which have developed during the last century. For example, there is an assumption that economic problems as such have no "moral aspects" and that moral issues arise "only in the political methods and processes by which they are handled."[3] This assumption reflects the idea that the economic system is "a machine largely automatic in quality," that competition "so integrates the efforts of all that no matter what each does or tries to do for his own benefit, the effect is to benefit all."[4] As a result, while political appointees are severely condemned for accepting bribes, businessmen or others who bribe them are hardly blamed at all. Professor Graham believes that the neglect of ethical considerations may also be due to the "impersonality" of American life and to the lack of genuine community in great cities.[5]

Thus, there is a glaring contradiction between Christian ethical standards and the standards which guide men in their economic and political activities. This contradiction is largely due to the impatience of Americans for immediate rewards and their ambition for outstanding success. "There is in American life a double standard, one highly responsible in its warm feeling for the welfare of our fellows, and the other coldly irresponsible in its single-minded devotion to direct personal advantage. The ruthless standard is epitomized by the traditional comment that 'business is business' or 'politics is politics.' "[6]

Precisely because democracy gives more responsibility to the citizens than other forms of government, it demands for its success a higher level of moral virtue from them. Under the influence of economic and social forces, modern democracies are not adequately meeting this demand. This is the source of the failure of private

---

[2] Graham, George A., *Morality in American Politics*, New York, Random House, 1952, p. 26.
[3] Ibid., p. 29.
[4] Ibid., p. 33.
[5] Ibid., p. 50.
[6] Ibid., p. 60, quoted from *Ethical Standards in Government*, printed by U. S. Senate Committee on Labor and Public Welfare, pp. 8-10.

citizens to meet their political responsibilities, as well as of the political corruption of officials to whom they entrust authority.

THE CHRISTIAN CONTRIBUTION

We have analyzed the nature of democracy and given reasons for thinking that it is the best form of government. We have also described some of the weaknesses of modern democracies. When we face the discrepancy between the theory of democracy and the "spotted actuality" of modern democracies, we are driven to ask: Does Christianity have a contribution to make which can help the modern democracies overcome their weaknesses?

(1) The first and most obvious contribution of Christianity to democracy is its *faith in the dignity and worth of every person.* This faith was lacking in the democracies of ancient Greece. Though it was assumed that the free citizens of the city-state had dignity, slaves were excluded from the privileges of citizenship and foreigners were regarded as "barbarians." The Stoics believed that all men shared in the World Reason as rational beings and they recognized the same rationality in the slave Epictetus as in the emperor Marcus Aurelius. But their estimate of those whose reason was undeveloped was quite different from their estimate of the few truly wise men. Christianity, on the other hand, ascribes dignity and worth to every man, apart from any inherent capacity in his own nature, as a creature made in the image of God. Moreover, those whom men regard as inferior—for example, the poor, slaves, and those of other races—possess dignity and worth equal to that of others. This is the fundamental assumption of democracy about man, and whenever it is denied the door is open to totalitarianism which treats individuals as means to the ends of State, Class, or Race.

As we have seen, there is much in modern democracies that makes it difficult to retain faith in the dignity of man and therefore to treat him as an end in himself. Therefore, Christianity must assert this faith more strongly. In its doctrine of Creation, it affirms that man was made in God's own image; in its doctrine of Redemption, it affirms that it was for man, for every man, that Christ died; and in its doctrine of Eternal Life, it affirms that at the highest level of the spirit each individual transcends the state of which he is a member in time and is a citizen of the Kingdom of God in eternity. It must proclaim these doctrines uncompromisingly in opposition to both the naturalistic philosophy which denies man's spiritual nature and the impersonal social forces which reduce him to the level of a thing.

(2) The democratic *belief in the fundamental equality of all men* is in part derived from this Christian belief in their dignity and worth. In the preceding chapter, we maintained that equality is as essential as liberty in a democracy. But we pointed out that modern democracies have in practice subordinated equality to liberty and that many members of the privileged class regard equality as little more than a Utopian dream.

The reason for this discrepancy between democratic theory and practice is not merely the egoism and pride which lead the privileged to defend their advantages. It is also the fact that they can justify themselves in doing so by pointing to the existence of actual inequality. In most respects, men are not equal. Physically, intellectually, and morally some are superior to others. This actual inequality of men has been one of the major causes of the subjection and oppression of the weak by the strong during the whole course of history. It has also provided the basis for the justification of slavery, monarchy, and aristocracy. Plato, for example, defended rule by an aristocracy of intellect and virtue on the ground that there are inborn differences between classes of men as there are baser and finer metals. In the nineteenth century, Nietzsche maintained that the strong should not be prevented by moral scruples from ruthlessly asserting their will to power and dominating the weak. As nature has differentiated beasts of prey from their victims by superior strength, it has raised the "masters" above the "herd" of slaves by their superior ability and courage. Consequently, they are justified in brushing aside pity, mercy, and other virtues and using the "herd" for their own higher purposes. Though Nietzsche was neither a nationalist nor a racialist, his glorification of a master class and justification of a fundamental inequality made him the intellectual forerunner of those in our time who have exalted the superior Race and its Leader above the people. Unfortunately, his way of thinking, though bitterly opposed to democratic thought, has its counterpart in the democracies. For example, in America, even after more than a century and a half of democracy, there are still many who believe in the inherent and permanent superiority of the white to the Negro race.

It is clear, therefore, that the equality which is essential to democracy cannot be defended by empirical arguments based upon the actual equality of men. It must be justified on the basis of belief in a fundamental equality which transcends all the actual inequalities between men. For example, the existence of *actual* inequality due to past discrimination against the Negro is used as a major argument by defenders of an inherent and *permanent* inequality of the two races. It is necessary, therefore, to justify genuine equality of opportunity and equality of consideration for Negroes not primarily by empirical evidence for their actual equality but by a conviction of their ultimate equality. This conviction is a product of the Christian faith. It springs from the Christian belief in the dignity of man as created in the image of God and the equal need of all men for His forgiveness and grace as sinners. The Nazi and Communist totalitarianism of the last generation has shown us that when this belief is destroyed, men cease to respect the dignity of other men, especially members of other races, classes, and nations, and that the claim of all men to equality ceases to have meaning for them.

(3) The Christian contribution with respect to *liberty* and *rights* is somewhat different. It cannot be maintained that the demand for liberty originated with Christianity. The Greek democracies accorded to citizens, if not to slaves, a high degree of liberty; indeed, one of the main criticisms of democracy by Plato was that it gave men too much liberty. The Greeks also discovered that liberty must be embodied in political rights if it is to be effective. But the Greek democracies could not prevent their citizens from pushing liberty to excess and exercising their rights in an arbitrary fashion. As we have seen, modern democracies have also suffered from individualism and from the subordination of duties to rights.

In opposition to this tendency, Christians must insist upon the responsibility of the individual to the community. In the Bible, the individual is always regarded as a member of the community as a whole. When Elijah, Amos, and other prophets defend a private citizen against the arbitrary action of king, nobles, or priests, they appeal to his rights as a member of a people who stand in a special relationship to God. The individual, they assume, is a social being and can fulfill himself only by sharing in the common good of the community. Similarly, Christian love of neighbor demands a *responsible liberty*. It impels the individual not so much to assert his own rights as to care for his neighbor and his neighbor's needs. Moreover, it attacks irresponsible liberty at the roots by insisting that freedom to follow one's impulses and do as one pleases is really a kind of bondage, while perfect freedom is to be found only in the service of God. Thus liberty is rendered responsible by love of neighbor and by obedience to God's will. It should be noted that it is only this kind of liberty which is compatible with equality. Irresponsible liberty destroys both equality and fraternity by encouraging the ruthless self-assertion of the individual against others.

(4) The *realistic view of man* in the Bible and in Protestant Christianity has contributed deeply to the development of government responsible to the people. It has helped men to see the necessity of imposing a limitation of power upon the representatives of the people. Thus, the radical Puritans of Cromwell's army demanded not only universal suffrage without any property qualification but also the election of Parliament every two years and the limitation of its meetings to definite periods of time. In this way, they sought to keep Parliament responsible to the people and "prevent the many inconveniences apparently arising from the long continuance of the same persons in authority."[1] They also appended a list of "native rights" which were to be "reserved by the represented to themselves." These rights included freedom of worship, freedom from compulsory military service, and strict equality before the law.[2] Behind all of these demands is a clear recognition that political power is dangerous and liable to abuse because of the sin of man.

Christian realism about man can also help to prevent conflicts

[1] Woodhouse, A. S. P., *Puritanism and Liberty,* London, Dent, 1951, "An Agreement of the People," p. 444.
[2] Ibid., p. 444.

between different groups in the community. Faith in a majestic and holy God, accompanied by a deep realization of the finiteness and sin of man, generates a humility which deflates the individual and collective pretensions of men. Reinhold Niebuhr has pointed out that humility is an indispensable basis of the mutual toleration of religious, racial and economic groups. For example, under the conditions of modern religious pluralism, modern democracies without mutual toleration would have been rent asunder by religious strife. The true basis for toleration is "humble and contrite recognition of the fact that all actual expressions of religious faith are subject to historical contingency and relativity."[3]

Finally, the Christian doctrine of man as sinner warns us that every society is bound to be corrupted in some measure by sin. The example of Communism proves that Utopianism which overlooks the fallibility and sinfulness of all men can tempt a revolutionary party to use the most ruthless means to attain its ends. A democracy that is based upon Christian realism about man will be more moderate in its expectations for the future. It will be suspicious of absolute and final solutions of economic and social problems. It will be content to be, in Niebuhr's words, "a method of finding proximate solutions for insoluble problems."[4]

(5) The *existence of the Church as an autonomous community* alongside the State limits the power of the State. As Lindsay says, "the existence and prestige of the Church prevented society from being totalitarian, prevented the omnicompetent state, and preserved liberty in the only way in which liberty can be preserved, by maintaining in society an organization which could stand up against the state."[5] Though the relation between Church and State presented a difficult problem, the partisans of neither denied the claims of the other to a sphere of its own. "The Christian always knew that he had two loyalties: that if he was to remember the Apostle's command 'to be subject unto the higher powers,' he was also to remember that his duty was 'to obey God rather than men.' "[6]

The existence of the Church has also maintained the Christian

---

[3] Niebuhr, R., op. cit., p. 134.
[4] Ibid., p. 118.

[5] Lindsay, op. cit., p. 60.
[6] Ibid., p. 60.

ethical ideal within its own community and has sought to permeate the wider community with its leaven. The only basis of the laws or rules of a community is the ethical standard the great majority of people are prepared to accept. "This implies," as Lindsay says, "that there must always be a distinction, even a tension, between the average accepted standard of society as expressed in its laws and moral codes, and the call to a more perfect standard. As the challenge to perfection gradually changes the average standard to which men are prepared to conform, the standards and rules of society will change— but because the Christian challenge is to perfection, the distinction of the two moralities remains."[7]

The importance of this can hardly be overestimated. The fact that the Christian ethic of love is too severe in its demands to be fully accepted by most people in a society and made the basis of their laws does not prevent Christians from striving to live by the Christian ideal themselves and using it as a norm for criticism of the moral standards, laws, and institutions of the state. In this way, a tension is maintained between the actual justice of the state and the ideal justice required by the law of love. The ethic of love, though impossible of complete fulfillment by any individual or group, provides a moral leaven which works within the community and becomes a source of social progress. Since it *transcends* all the moral and social achievements of the community, it is a norm by which they are judged and found wanting; but, since it is also relevant to all human activities, it can also *transform* and raise the level of social morality and of the system of social justice.

(6) The greatest contribution Christianity can make to democracy is to provide a *deeper basis for the unity of the community*. One of the greatest weaknesses of modern democracies is the individualism which stresses rights rather than duties and assumes that each person will exercise his rights in his own interest. The result of this is not only gross inequality but also the conflict of classes, races, and other groups which divides the Western democracies and makes them vulnerable to Communist attacks. This individualism and class conflict destroy the sense of community which is necessary to bind together all individuals and groups.

[7] Ibid., pp. 61, 62.

When a vital sense of community is lacking, the process of discussion which precedes an election can hardly be expected to produce real agreement on the common good. It was this lack of a sense of community between conflicting groups in the Weimar Republic which stultified the process of discussion among the citizens and turned the Reichstag into a mere "debating society." As a result, it was impossible to arrive at an agreement with respect to the common good and the people in desperation listened to the blandishments of a strong "Leader" who could impose upon them the unity they could not achieve themselves. In similar fashion, since the Second World War France has been unable to maintain a stable government because of the unwillingness of individuals and parties to subordinate their interests and claims to the common good. Thus, the process of discussion in a democracy can produce agreement only if there is a sense of unity more fundamental than the differences between various groups. Discussion will be fruitless unless most of the citizens share similar basic assumptions and values and feel a sense of common destiny. This is why "party spirit" is so dangerous in a democracy. If each party pushes its principles to the limit and makes absolute claims for its program, it will refuse to compromise and government will be paralyzed.

At this point Christianity makes its supreme contribution to democracy. The Gospel implies that *love of neighbor* is the only ultimately satisfactory basis of community. As love created a sense of unity in the Church so intimate that Paul could use the analogy of a living organism to describe it, it can create a sense of unity within the larger community which can help to reconcile all differences between its members and groups. Of course, there can never be the same kind of unity between the members of the political community as that which should bind together the members of the Church. Nor does the state require the high degree of unity that should prevail in the Church, since it is concerned only with the order and justice which can be furthered by general laws sanctioned by force. Nevertheless, love in the sense of mutual respect and good will between the citizens is essential to the unity of a democratic state, since democracy does not rely upon fear and force for its unity. The slogan of the French Revolution should never be forgotten in any democratic state: "liberty, equality, and"—though the word is seldom mentioned in our secular democracies—"fraternity."

There are those who hold that good will or fraternity is not essential and that enlightened self-interest is a sufficient basis of community in a democracy. Since man's motives are egoistic, they maintain, the self-interest of individuals and groups must be expected always to determine their political conduct, but if they can be shown that their own interest is bound up in a measure with that of their fellow-citizens, they can be brought to respect the rights of others. This conception is false. It may be possible to maintain simple economic relationships between men, though hardly the very complex relationships of our modern economic order, purely on the basis of their mutual advantage. But a political community must have a deeper and stronger foundation. Enlightened self-interest may lead men to respect the rights of others where it is clearly to their own advantage to do so; it can never generate that devotion to the common good which leads public-spirited men to serve their country in time of peace or to risk their lives in time of war.

In addition to enlightened self-interest, the sentiment of nationality has usually been depended upon since the time of Rousseau as the basis of community. Burke emphasized the importance of bonds of sentiment which have been forged by association through centuries of history. Indeed, he sometimes seemed to regard the solidarity of the state as merely a matter of habit and feeling, sustained by the momentum of the past. But social sentiments, though deeply rooted in the natural feelings and habits of men, are not enough. The citizen must respect the rights of many citizens with whom he feels little natural sympathy or solidarity. This is especially true of a country of such vast size, brief history, and diverse cultural traditions as our own. Moreover, the sentiment of nationality does not necessarily foster the kind of unity which is suitable for a democracy. It may lead to a uniformity which is hostile to liberty, as in Fascism, or to a national solidarity stimulated by hostility to other nations, as in Nazism. Thus, the sentiment of nationality cannot always be depended upon to provide a strong foundation of community; and, when it does, it may produce unity at the cost of oppression at home and aggression abroad.

Is it not clear from this that the unity of a democracy must rest, not merely on enlightened self-interest or the sentiment of nationality, but on the disposition to establish and maintain a community of persons with *good will* towards one another? Is it not obvious also that this mutual good will must be *all-inclusive*? If common people, or people of other races, classes, or religions than one's own are excluded, the unity of a democracy will be destroyed, especially when it is composed of heterogeneous groups like the United States. Without good will towards all groups, one will not be willing to seek equality and liberty for them. It is difficult, if not impossible to respect the rights of individuals or groups, if one is indifferent to their welfare. If one belongs to a privileged class or race, one may be prepared to grant to members of another class or race the legal and political rights which are the indispensable minimum in democratic government; but, without good will, one will have no desire to grant them real equality of opportunity and equality of consideration. Thus, fraternity or good will is an essential condition not only of community but also of equality.[8]

Since the majority of citizens in the Western democracies either are not Christian or are very imperfectly Christian, it would be Utopian to expect Christian love to become the primary moral basis of the democratic state in our time. For the state, as we have seen, must be based primarily upon the moral standard which most of the citizens are prepared to accept. But this does not mean that Christian love is irrelevant to the life of the democracies, or that it is powerless to help them solve their practical problems. Christian love is a powerful leaven which attracts others by its perfection, its effectiveness cannot be measured by the number of those who consciously practice it or by its tangible results, and the liberal democracy of the last hundred years would have been impossible without the vast store of humanitarian good will which had been produced by Christianity in the past.[9] It both leavens the community with good will,

[8] For the argument contained in the last three paragraphs, I have drawn upon an earlier book of mine, now out of print: *Spirit and its Freedom*, Chapel Hill, University of North Carolina Press, 1938, pp. 143-47.

[9] Cf. Thomas, G. F. (ed.), *The Vitality of the Christian Tradition*, New York, Harpers, 1944, p. 354.

and, by opening men's minds to social evils they had taken for granted, it brings about a gradual improvement of social justice.

(7) Finally, Christianity can inspire the democracies with the *hope for a world community based upon brotherhood*. The Christian is a member of a religious community which transcends the boundaries of race and nationality. But he also dreams of a more inclusive community in which all men will be able to live together in peace and love. He knows that this dream can never be fully realized on earth because man's sin stands opposed to it. But his ultimate loyalty is to it and he seeks as far as he can to realize it within his own community and among all nations.

This dream of a world brotherhood has been closely related to the universalism of democracy since the eighteenth century. Though Americans and Frenchmen were struggling primarily for their own rights, they also spoke of "the rights of man." They were convinced that all men were entitled by the moral law to the same rights. Similarly, nineteenth-century patriots of "the land of the free" believed that America should be "a beacon light of liberty" to all the oppressed peoples of the world. There was, of course, much proud nationalism and naive optimism compounded with this political idealism. But it has always given meaning and direction to our national life and hope to less fortunate peoples of the world. Can we dispense with it today when our responsibility for the welfare of mankind is greater than it has ever been and when the foes of liberty are more determined and ruthless than at any other time in our history?

The disillusionment of our generation with nineteenth-century optimism and Utopianism has led some Christian thinkers to decry idealism. This is valid as a criticism of the sentimental and Utopian idealism which is blind to the tragic realities of human existence. But the spread of democracy in the nineteenth century would not have been possible without the democratic dream. Moreover, if democracy is to attract men's loyalty in the twentieth century, it must be supported by a practical but strong idealism. Of course, Christians must be realists, if their political decisions are to be based upon knowledge of things as they are; but they must also be idealists, if they are to make the justice of the state reflect more fully the demands of love and are to strive with all their power for a world community.

But the political idealism of Christians must differ from that of Communists. Their hope should be more sober than that of the Communists. Communism holds out to the poor and oppressed peoples of the world the hope that historical forces are inevitably moving towards the overthrow of their oppressors and the establishment of a classless society. The historical determinism upon which this hope is based is false; the Utopianism with which it views the future is naive. Since Christians acknowledge the power of sin, they cannot compete with Communism by holding out to men such illusory hopes for the future. The Kingdom of God, or the brotherhood of man, will never come on earth in its fullness. But this does not mean that Christians must be content to offer men only an other-worldly hope and leave them without hope for this world. The democratic ideal is superior to other forms of government and ways of life, because it is more in accord with the Christian conception of man and community. This should provide us with no excuse for pride in the actual democracies of the West. But it should give us a strong incentive to overcome the weaknesses of democracy in order that it may commend itself to other peoples of the world. Thus, democracy based upon Christian faith and love offers to mankind both a *sober* and a *revolutionary* hope.

CHAPTER 14

Christianity and the Economic Order

THE GOSPEL AND ECONOMIC INDIVIDUALISM

DESPITE the crucial importance of economic issues in our time, some Christians still deny that Christian ethics throws any light on problems of economic life. When a minister confines himself to vague generalities about stewardship in the use of wealth, he usually gains the assent of those in the pews. But if he ventures to speak of the living conditions of migrant workers or the need for better low-cost housing in the neighborhood, he is likely to meet with a cold reception from some members of his congregation. Most "liberal" ministers have learned after a few disillusioning experiences that they are not expected to "interfere" in matters having to do with business or labor. Why are so many Christian laymen opposed to ministers or church leaders "taking a stand" on economic issues?

At first sight, the answer seems simple: these laymen do not believe that the Gospel has anything to say on economic issues. "Did not Christ concern himself with religious and moral rather than economic questions?" they ask. "Did he not refuse to intervene in a dispute between two brothers over the division of an inheritance? It is true that he warned men against the danger of riches. But he also commended the men in the parable who added to their talents by investing them. Therefore, he must have believed that there is nothing wrong with wealth unless it is improperly used. When he said that men were not to lay up treasures on earth, he must have been warning them against the love of money, 'Mammon,' rather than the lawful acquisition of it. Although Christian radicals have sometimes regarded him as a social revolutionary, leader of the poor and oppressed 'people of the land' against the religious and economic ruling class, there is no evidence that he was interested in economic reform."

Now, it is true that Jesus shows little interest in social institutions and reforms, economic or political. But, as we have seen, his criticism of those whose main concern is with riches is unsparing and his law of love has implications for social justice in every area. May it not be, therefore, that many Christian laymen resent the "interference" of the Church on economic issues, not because the Gospel has little to say about them, but because what it does say is so disturbing? Although the Gospel champions no economic system, it challenges some of the fundamental attitudes and practices of modern economic life. We shall here mention only two of these.

In the first place, Jesus explicitly denies the *primacy of material values* over spiritual ones. He warns men against anxiety concerning food and clothing, and insists that they put first the Kingdom and its righteousness. Whatever he may have meant by calling the poor "blessed," it is clear that for him economic activities which are concerned with the production and distribution of material things have only a secondary value. Yet, to a large extent, modern economic life has been based upon an inversion of this order of values. It is not correct to say that the main concern of most Western men is money. But their main concern *is* with the material things and pleasures money can buy or with the power and prestige which can be attained through it.

In the second place, the theory of modern economic individualism has emphasized the *autonomy of economic activities*. It has held that economic decisions are governed by economic laws and that moral considerations are secondary or even irrelevant. This is the meaning of the saying, "business is business." The basic assumption behind the theory is that the primary, if not the only, motive for economic activity is self-interest. Of course, this theory, like the concept of the "economic man," is based upon an abstraction of economic activity and interest from other aspects of life. Actually, responsible business men or labor leaders *are* influenced by other than economic considerations and motives. They do not act in accordance with the principle of economic autonomy because they are not only economic but also moral beings, loyal members of society, and, in many cases, Christians. The motives of men are usually mixed. They may be motivated simultaneously by self-interest and desire to serve the community. Moreover, the prudent businessman is concerned about the future as well as the present and knows that he must satisfy his workers and customers if he is to retain the loyalty of the former and the patronage of the latter.

Nevertheless, the principle of economic "autonomy" corresponds to reality, even if it is only an aspect of reality. For the assumption that the economic system is a mechanism which operates according to its own laws dominated the thinking of "laissez faire" businessmen during the nineteenth century and still has great influence. Yet the whole spirit of Christianity is opposed to the exclusion of ethical principles from any area of life. If Christ is the Lord of life, he is the Lord of all of it. To remove an area of life as important as the economic from the control of principles of justice and to surrender it to unrestrained self-interest is to contradict the Christian ethic. The root of most of our modern economic trouble is that this truth has been forgotten by those who have accepted the theory of economic individualism.

THE CHRISTIAN CONCEPTION OF PROPERTY

What is the Christian conception of property and how does it differ from that of economic individualism? In the *early Church,* the right of property was taken for granted, although there was a voluntary sharing of possessions for a time in the Church at Jerusalem and the claims of brotherhood insured generous help to those in need. According to certain Fathers of the fourth century, property was originally held in common, and private property was established only after men fell into sin. Thus, the right to private property, though legitimate, does not belong to men by natural law.[1] In the *medieval period,* St. Thomas Aquinas insisted that private property was in accordance with natural law, but his view of the rights of property did not differ greatly from that of the early Fathers. Although prop-

[1] *Property, Its Duties and Rights,* London, Macmillan, 1915. Essay by A. J. Carlyle, p. 122.

erty should be privately owned, it should be for common use, the individual ministering from what he has to the necessities of others.[2] It is evident from this that early and medieval Christians did not acknowledge an unconditional right to private property. Indeed, the medieval Church branded "avarice" as one of the capital sins, prohibited "usury" or interest on loans, and attempted to enforce a "just price" on merchants. As Tawney has pointed out, there was a gulf between the ideal and the actuality in the Middle Ages; but the ideal was that economic activities should be controlled by ethical principles and subordinated to spiritual ends.[3]

The effect of the *Protestant Reformation* upon Christian thinking about property was profound. Although Luther violently attacked the new Capitalism, Calvin accepted the economic activities of the middle class as legitimate. For example, he justified the taking of interest on loans, although he insisted upon a reasonable rate. The Christian life, he held, is to be lived not in contemplation apart from the world, but in activity in the vocations of the common life. The will must be disciplined by self-denial if the flesh is to be mastered and the work of one's vocation is to be done well. Such a practical and severe conception of the Christian life naturally produced men of strong character with a bent toward strenuous activity and with a willingness to forego immediate pleasures for more remote ends. As a result, Calvinistic "asceticism within the world" did much to prepare the way for modern Capitalism. But it would be a mistake to speak of Calvin or his early followers as defenders of economic individualism in the modern sense. Calvin attempted to prevent Geneva merchants from securing monopolies on essential products and selling them at unjust prices. In the same spirit, Richard Baxter and other Puritan writers attacked excessive interest on loans, insisted upon just prices, and stressed the principle of stewardship in the use of wealth.[4]

In certain respects, however, the *later Puritanism* did tend to foster economic individualism. The Puritans held that private property is implied in the prohibition of stealing in the Decalogue and thus has

[2] Aquinas, Thomas, *Summa Theologica*, II-II, q. 66, a. 2.
[3] Tawney, R. H., *Religion and the Rise of Capitalism*, New York, Harcourt Brace, 1926, Ch. I, sec. III.
[4] *Property, Its Duties and Rights*, essay by H. G. Wood, pp. 141-143.

a divine sanction. They spoke of the blessing of wealth and regarded it as ordained by God. They justified class distinctions and standards of living. Although they insisted strongly that economic activities should be in accord with ethical principles, they put the responsibility upon each Christian to apply these principles for himself and repudiated the economic restraints imposed by Church and state. As long as they subordinated their worldly interests to the attainment of eternal life, their moral scruples imposed a check upon their economic ambitions. But they tended increasingly to seek the riches of this world and to regard prosperity as a sign that they were among the elect. Businessmen could make the best of both worlds, reaping the rewards of success here as well as being assured of heavenly blessings hereafter. Thus, the later Puritans prepared the way for what Tawney calls "the triumph of the economic virtues."[5]

At the end of the seventeenth century, the new middle class found their most effective spokesman in *John Locke.* His theory of property was a turning point in Christian thinking on the subject. The right of private property, he maintained, rests upon the law of nature. Every person has a natural right to that with which he mixes his labor. This right belonged to men before they established civil government. Indeed, the purpose of government was to protect the right to life, liberty and property. Locke qualified this natural right of property in two ways: a man could appropriate only as much land as he could use, and only where "there was still enough and as good left" for others.[6] For Locke assumed that the individual would be a responsible member of the community and would not assert his property rights in such a way as to injure others. However, by stressing the origin of property rights in natural law and by conceiving the state as an instrument for the protection of these rights, Locke prepared the way for the modern theory that property rights are absolute.

These historical facts make it clear that the Church has usually recognized the right of property as *legitimate,* but has been keenly aware of the moral and social *dangers* of property and has imposed *limitations* upon it to protect the welfare of the less fortunate. Later

[5] Tawney, op. cit., Ch. IV, sec. III.
[6] Locke, John, *Second Treatise on Civil Government,* Ch. V, pp. 30, 32.

Puritans like Locke prepared the way for the modern belief that the right of property is absolute and unlimited. But that belief itself was a product of the economic individualism which culminated in the nineteenth-century "laissez-faire" economics of the Manchester School in England and the "Gospel of Wealth" in America. Despite the fact that it was strongly asserted by many Christians during the last century, it stands in contradiction to the spirit of the New Testament and to the main tradition of economic thinking in the Church. There are scarcely any outstanding Christian social thinkers in our time who would defend it.

What then is the Christian conception of property? (1) The dominant tradition of Christian thought has always accepted the *necessity of private property*. Although some of the Fathers regarded it as a result of the Fall, as we have seen, they considered it legitimate. Communistic sects of Christians like the "Diggers" in seventeenth-century England have always been small minorities. There have been good reasons for this general acceptance of private property, although they have not often been expressed clearly. One is an economic and social one of a very practical kind. The ownership of property, as Aquinas pointed out, is an *incentive* to diligence in work. It is not always true that men will labor more diligently for what is to belong to themselves than for what is to belong to all.[7] If it were, it would be difficult to account for the diligence of monks like Aquinas himself who were allowed to possess no private property. Insofar as man is a spiritual being, he will devote himself to the cause of truth or justice or religion without thought of material reward. But there can be no question that many, perhaps most, men are stimulated to work with regularity and to the full extent of their capacity by the promise of material possessions which they can use as they see fit. More particularly, it is unlikely that, without some measure of material reward, society would ever be able to persuade enough men to do the more monotonous, difficult and dangerous tasks which must be done if the needs of all are to be fulfilled. Perhaps material rewards would not be necessary if men were free from all self-interest. But, as Temple says, "until the vast majority of us are almost perfect saints,

[7] Aquinas, op. cit., II-II, q. 66, a. 2.

self-interest will play a large part in governing society and shaping character."[8]

The individual can realize meaning and value in his life only by adopting and carrying out purposes of his own. Since material things are necessary as instruments through which personality may express and realize itself, private property is essential to *self-determination* and *self-fulfillment*. The full force of this argument does not become clear until the effect of Communism in denying all private property is appreciated. If all property which is not actually being consumed is owned and controlled by the state, those who administer it have virtually unlimited power to direct the lives of their fellow-citizens and to prevent them from fulfilling any purposes and needs which are not approved by the government in power.

(2) But this does *not* justify any person in claiming an *unconditional right* to acquire property and dispose of it as he pleases without regard for the consequences to others. The theory that property rights are absolute has been of crucial importance in the development of economic individualism. It has led to incalculable evils in the lives of men. It has provided a moral justification for the theory that the state cannot legitimately limit property rights even when the common good demands it. In this way it has been used by property owners for generations to attack every proposal of social legislation for the benefit of poor and underprivileged citizens.

There is no ground whatever for the claim that property rights are absolute; it is nothing but an arbitrary and dogmatic assertion. This can be shown by a brief analysis of the *nature of rights*. While a legal right belongs to an individual, it exists only as it is recognized and enforced by society. Society also helps to create property. Much private property was not created by those who own it, e.g., inherited property. Indeed, private property is seldom, if ever, created by the individual alone; the creation of wealth is a cooperative process in which the community takes part. Thus, both the recognition of the right to property and the creation of property depend upon society. Now, what society does it does for a purpose; and what it does it can undo or modify, if its purpose is not being properly fulfilled.

[8] Temple, William, *Christianity and Social Order*, New York, Penguin Books, 1941, p. 78.

Since it recognizes the right to property for the sake of the common good, it may limit or qualify the right of each in order to accomplish this purpose for all.

An analysis of the *nature of the individual* who possesses property points to the same conclusion. Individual persons are not discrete and atomic beings but members of a community. They do not exist alone and in isolation one from another; they share a common life with one another. This interdependence of individual persons requires the rights of all to be limited by society if they are to serve the common good. Ultimately, this is for the good of the individual person whose rights are limited, as well as for the good of his fellows, for a person is a social being who can fulfill himself and attain true happiness only along with other persons. If he cuts himself off from his fellow-citizens and refuses to seek their good as well as his own, he narrows his life and empties it of meaning and value.

(3) We have pointed out that private property is essential for the realization of the self, but that the right to property is not an absolute right. This leads to the thorny question: *how much* property does a person have a moral right to possess?

The simplest but also the least unsatisfactory answer is that a person has a moral right only to as much property *as he actually needs.* The difficulty with this answer, of course, is that it is difficult to apply. Since the needs of persons differ, that which would be a "necessity" for A might be a "luxury" for B and that which would be a "necessity" for B might be a "luxury" for A. Therefore, the principle that each person has a moral right only to as much property as he actually needs, although valid, can never be made the basis for a *law* which would define the amount of property everyone should have. Nevertheless, the principle has some value as a *"regulative ideal"* to be applied by each individual for himself. In applying it, he should remember that his "needs" include more than the bare "necessities" required to maintain life. As Brunner points out, the demand of some "levellers" that men should "first of all procure the necessities of life and only then (after this has been achieved) the higher goods of civilization and culture"[9] would defeat its own pur-

[9] Brunner, E., *The Divine Imperative,* copyright, 1947, by W. L. Jenkins, The Westminster Press, p. 437.

pose. "Only where there is freedom for research, only where people have time and leisure to cultivate art and science and education will it be possible to create an economic order in which what is actually necessary for life will be provided for every one."[10]

This seems to confirm the ancient insight that men should seek neither poverty nor riches. On the one hand, the medieval idealization of *absolute poverty* is indefensible. Like the mortification of the flesh by ascetics, it was usually a product of Greek dualism with respect to the body and a legalistic interpretation of Jesus' teachings. There can be no doubt, as we have said, that Jesus demanded rigorous self-denial of his disciples, including the renunciation of their possessions; and this may still be necessary in some Christian vocations. But there is no evidence that he meant to lay down a rule requiring absolute poverty of all Christians or even of all seeking to live the perfect Christian life. On the other hand, modern Christians do not need to be told that absolute poverty is not required of them. It is against *riches,* as in Jesus' day, that Christians still need to be warned. In a materialistic civilization like ours, men are tempted to think that they cannot be happy or make their loved ones happy unless they have a large income and can afford a "high standard of living." Many have postponed marriage for years until they were assured of having enough for comfort and a measure of luxury. When material things and satisfactions are prized so highly, men forget that the sources of the deepest and purest natural happiness are not material things but things like beauty, friendship, and creative work.

Besides materialism, there is another and deeper source of the desire for riches. Men desire wealth, beyond the amount which is necessary for the fulfillment of their physical and cultural needs, as a symbol of superior achievement and as a means of domination over others. They want wealth, not only for use, but also for power and glory. The will to power over others is accompanied by the will to glory in the eyes of others. The desire to impress others with one's wealth and success may be manifested in the form of boasting, but it is more likely in our society to take the form of "conspicuous consumption." Large houses, expensive automobiles, lavish entertainments and

[10] Ibid., p. 437.

showy jewelry are only a few ways in which men and women display their riches before others.

It has often been said that Christians in the past have been concerned too much with excessive and harmful consumption and too little with unjust distribution. Probably more sermons have been preached from Protestant pulpits against the drinking of alcohol than against the exploitation of workers or exorbitant prices. However, it must not be thought that moderate consumption is unimportant. Since it would permit men to be content with property sufficient for their needs, it would destroy one of the main roots of the feverish pursuit of riches. Moreover, if there was less demand for the luxuries which are now consumed by the privileged class, a larger proportion of business enterprise and labor could be devoted to the production of the necessities and amenities of life which are now unavailable to millions of people at prices they can pay. Instead of great mansions and fleets of automobiles for the few, more food and better housing and education could be produced for the many. As a result, one of the greatest barriers which separate men and nations from one another would be broken down.

Of course, the principle that each should seek only the amount of property which is sufficient for his needs cannot be applied with precision. The amount of property which is needed by a particular individual depends not only upon his personal needs but also upon his responsibility for others. The father of a family, for example, requires property sufficient for the needs of his wife and children as well as his own. Since the needs of individuals are always changing and cannot be accurately predicted there is no simple and certain way of determining the exact amount of property necessary to fulfill their needs. It is also obvious that the principle must not be applied in such a way as to prevent the accumulation of capital necessary for the process of production. In short, it can provide guidance only of a broad and general kind.

It also raises a difficult technical question which the Christian moralist is not competent to answer: How can the goods produced by factories and farms in our economy be absorbed unless there is a high level of demand? And how can a high level of demand be maintained if men acquire only enough property to satisfy their actual needs? In our dynamic economy which produces an increasing amount of goods through the use of new machines, it seems that men must develop new needs if these goods are to be bought and the wheels of industry are to keep turning. It cannot be said that a solution of this problem has been attained. But it seems obvious that men should not be made slaves to the productive process and to the machines which make it possible. This would invert the true order of values by turning the means of living into its end. It would be to subordinate even further the inner life of the spirit to the satisfaction of "needs" which require material things for their satisfaction. Men *cannot* be required to dehumanize themselves in order to keep the wheels of industry running at full speed, especially in a world in which so many millions are in desperate need of food and other necessities.

THE PROBLEM OF EQUALITY

If the right of *all* to property sufficient for their needs is to be made effective, a *wider distribution of property* will be necessary. This will require a different attitude toward equality in the economic sphere. In the nineteenth century, it was believed that *equality of opportunity* was sufficient. According to this view, the function of government was to provide a fair field for all competitors and refuse to interfere with the free play of economic forces. This would provide equality of opportunity for all, because no one would enjoy legal privileges in the competitive struggle and men would rise to the top by virtue of their own merit alone.

The principle of equality of opportunity has had a special appeal in America where natural resources have been abundant and an expanding economy has offered scope for the exercise of a great variety of abilities. These favorable conditions have fostered a spirit of optimism. Men have been confident that their abilities were sufficient to enable them to rise to a higher level of attainment than their fathers. They have been aided in the attempt to rise not only by favorable natural and economic conditions but also by the provision of free public education. Though this advantage has not overcome inequalities of wealth and social position, it has offered an unusual opportunity to develop whatever abilities a youth possessed. For these reasons equality of opportunity has corresponded to reality in America more nearly than in European countries. "It spurs a man to 'make the most of himself'," says Perry, and "enriches collective life by bringing to light talents which would otherwise go unused."[1]

But equality of opportunity is fictitious without equality in the *circumstances* under which men have to develop and exercise their capacities. Inferiority of birth, wealth, and social environment handicaps the great majority of children from the start. As a result, it is only a small proportion of persons, except in societies where there is an unusual degree of social mobility, who are able to rise from a lower to a higher class, for opportunities to rise can hardly be equal in a society where the conditions surrounding different persons from birth are quite unequal. From the ethical point of view, there is a still more fundamental limitation of equality of opportunity. The fact that some exceptionally able individuals manage to escape or rise above unfavorable circumstances does not make the lot of those who continue to suffer from them less bitter. Moreover, it often fosters a callous indifference on the part of exceptionally able "self-made" men towards those who are less successful than themselves. Indeed, in a competitive society equality of opportunity puts a premium upon ambition and aggressiveness rather than moral qualities like gentleness and kindness. "All orderly competitions," says Perry, "encourage something. Competition for wealth puts a premium upon the qualities of acquisitiveness . . . it sanctions greed and guile as well as industry and invention."[2]

Because of these limitations of equality of opportunity Christians must reject the view of laissez-faire individualists that the state should not seek by positive action to further equality among its citizens. They must seek to raise the economic level of the poor and underprivileged classes by social legislation, using weapons such as taxation to bring about a redistribution of wealth and opportunity. Thus, they must supplement the individualistic ideal of equality of opportunity with the more humane ideal of *equality of consideration*. This is the principle that everyone should be genuinely taken into account in

[1] Perry, R. B., *Puritanism and Democracy,* New York, Vanguard, p. 569.
[2] Ibid., p. 573.

the distribution of social benefits and should be helped by the state to develop his capacities and fulfill his needs as far as possible.

It is difficult to define equality of consideration more precisely. It differs from the principle of abstract or mathematical equality in that it acknowledges differences between the needs of persons. Consequently, it does not demand that all should be given identical benefits but insists that the special needs of each class or group be considered in the distribution of benefits. At the same time, it differs from the principle of equality of opportunity in demanding that the state accept positive responsibility for the welfare of all classes of its citizens. In practical terms, this means that a resolute attempt should be made to raise the economic and cultural level of underprivileged classes by more adequate housing, education and medical service. Even a comparatively small expenditure on public health or education raises the level of life for the poor out of all proportion to the cost.

Obviously, equality of consideration for the general and special needs of all is consistent with a considerable measure of *inequality*. As we have said, abstract equalitarianism would lead to the treatment of persons as homogeneous units and neglect their individual differences. It also refuses to recognize the fact that persons who make different contributions to the community may have to be rewarded unequally in order to secure an adequate flow of persons into the more dangerous or difficult but important vocations. This may be called "functional inequality" since it is an inequality which serves a useful social purpose. But it provides no excuse for the appalling economic and cultural inequality that still exists in most capitalistic societies, an inequality that manifests itself in housing, medical facilities, education, and other areas. "Too great disparities of wealth, too great difference in education and upbringing, too great differences in function make a common life in any proper sense of the word impossible. When there is nothing which can be called a common life in which all members of society participate, to assert the doctrine of Christian equality can only be a mockery. The believers in true democratic equality will want to remove such differences as make the expression of equality unreal and impossible."[3] Any inequality which

---

[3] Lindsay, A. D., *The Modern Democratic State,* New York, Oxford University Press, 1947, p. 260.

stunts the lives of the underpriviledged and destroys community between them and their more fortunate fellows is inconsistent with
Christian love.

WORK AND VOCATION

Modern man is confronted not only with the problem of property
and its just distribution, but also with the *problem of work*. What is
the purpose of work? What is the proper relation of the worker
to the employer? What are the most suitable conditions of work
as a Christian vocation? What are the factors in our present economic system which distort the purpose of work, the relation of
the worker to his employer, and the conditions of his work?

There are two major *purposes* of work. The primary purpose of
work is *the production of things necessary for life* in the broadest
sense of the term. Men work in order to live and to live well. The
physical and spiritual needs of man could not be satisfied without
the production of things by work. Man is endowed by nature with
capacities but it requires effort to exercise them. He is provided by
nature with raw materials or resources, but he must gather them
and usually he must transform them before he can use them to
satisfy his needs. If a man is always idle, his capacities are not developed and the resources around him go to waste. As a result, he
contributes nothing to the fulfillment of his own or others' needs.
The crucial question is whether he should carry out this purpose
from a motive of self-interest or from a motive of service to others
or from both. According to the Protestant doctrine of vocation, the
dominant motive of a Christian in any vocation is to serve God by
serving one's neighbors in love. In actuality, most men have some
interest in the good of their fellows and desire to add something to
the life of the community as a whole. They are also motivated by
self-interest, loyalty to their employers and fellow-workers, and
desire for social approval.

The second purpose of work is the *realization of the self through
creative activity*. As we have said, man is born with capacities which
can be developed only through effort. The process by which these
capacities are developed is also a process in which the self realizes

itself and discovers meaning in its life. Thus work is not only a means to the fulfillment of needs, it is also an end in itself. Through it the worth of personality is developed and manifested. A man never knows the nature and extent of his powers until he exercises them upon a task, and his neighbors can never know his worth until he has created something objective by mental or physical labor. According to the Biblical view, each man is given certain talents and is held responsible for the way in which they are exercised. However, they are to be developed and used not primarily for the advancement of the self, but for the fulfillment of others' needs. In seeking to fulfill the needs of others, the self is realized; but this is the secondary, not the primary purpose of work.

The effect of modern economic attitudes has been to turn this Christian doctrine of vocation upside down. Instead of choosing his vocation and carrying out the tasks imposed by it primarily for the purpose of fulfilling the needs of others, a man who is imbued with the spirit of individualism does so from the motive of pleasing himself, or, at the best, realizing himself. Since he chooses a vocation which he thinks he would "enjoy most" or "be most interested in" his primary motive is a self-centered one and service of his neighbor's needs is at best secondary and incidental. William Temple speaks of the choice of a vocation as the choice of a sphere of service. "To make that choice on selfish grounds," he says, "is probably the greatest single sin that any young person can commit, for it is the deliberate withdrawal from allegiance to God of the greatest part of time and strength. A young man who is led by his inclination to take up teaching or business or whatever it may be, must none the less make his choice because in that field he can give his own best service."[1] The neglect of this truth has also led to the subordination of vocations like the ministry and teaching to business and the more lucrative professions. For many persons, it has also transformed professions like medicine and nursing from "service" vocations into impersonal ways of making a living. All too often it corrupts even the vocation of the Christian ministry until it becomes only a "career."

The *dignity of work* is closely associated with the purpose of

[1] Temple, William, op. cit., p. 52.

work. It is well known that Greek thinkers tended to despise *manual work* and to regard intellectual activity as far superior. This was doubtless due to the fact that much of the manual labor was done by slaves, but it was also a product of the dualistic conception of the relation of body and soul. There is nothing corresponding to this attitude towards manual work in the Bible. When it has arisen among Christians, it has been due to Greek influence or to the substitution of a contemplative for a practical conception of religion. When the motive of service is stressed in relation to work, the dignity of all useful work is acknowledged. Christians should never forget that Jesus and his disciples worked with their hands and that Paul supported himself on his missionary journeys by working at a trade.

On the other hand, there has been a tendency in some Christian circles to depreciate intellectual, artistic, and, more generally, *cultural work*. In reacting against the social irresponsibility of the upper class, Leo Tolstoy insisted that everyone should work with his own hands at least part of the day. Like St. Francis' refusal to allow his friars to own books of any kind, this was useful as a protest against an existing evil. But if Tolstoy's example were followed literally by all scholars, writers, artists and scientists, the loss to society would be great. The division of labor has made possible many of the finest fruits of civilized life by enabling these groups to devote their full time to the development and exercise of their special talents. In America, the depreciation of intellectual and cultural work arises mainly from the suspicion that it is not as useful as more "practical" kinds of work. Because of the great importance of technology in our age, most Americans tend to put a higher value on technical than on intellectual or artistic work. This is the fundamental cause of the fact that public school teachers are usually paid less than skilled workers such as electricians and plumbers.

Against those who depreciate either manual or intellectual work, the Christian doctrine asserts that all kinds of work have dignity and that no kind of work which is undertaken from a motive of service should be regarded as inferior. Whether a particular person should choose one kind of work or another for his vocation depends, first, upon the need of the community at the time, and, second, upon his special talents.

The *economic individualism* of the nineteenth century weakened and in some circles virtually destroyed this Christian conception of the purpose and dignity of work. The main reason was that the primary, and often the sole, motive of many employers in laissez-faire Capitalism was *profit* for themselves rather than the service of others. The needs of the consumer were subordinated to the profit of the producer: "the consumer is treated," says Temple, "not as the person whose interest is the true end of the whole process, but only as an indispensable condition of success in an essentially profit-seeking enterprise."[2] The dominance of the profit motive over the service motive also distorted the right relation between the employer and the workers in industry. The employer regarded his workers not as his partners whose welfare and happiness he should seek as his own, but as his hirelings to whom his only obligation was to pay wages.

This was the basic cause of some of the worst *evils* of industrial work, evils which still pervert the purpose and destroy the dignity of the work of millions. The first of these is that the *products* of many industries are either of trivial value or positively harmful. When production is primarily for the sake of profit rather than service to the community, many industrialists are willing to cater to desires of actual or potential buyers which correspond to no real need and may even be desires for harmful things. They do not hesitate to create a desire for useless or even harmful products by skillful advertising. Habit-forming drugs and salacious magazines may be taken as examples of products which are physically and morally injurious. The effect of these products upon the consumer is to demoralize his character, vulgarize his taste and fill his life with cheap and tawdry things. But it is their effect upon the industrial workers that we are considering here. If the primary purpose of work, from the Christian point of view, is to fulfill the needs of men, what must be the effect of producing such things upon the mind and character of the worker?

The second evil of industrial work is the fact that many workers

[2] Temple, ibid., p. 58.

have little or no *voice* in the industry for which they work. Although organized workers now have gained considerable power over wages and hours through collective bargaining, they often have little to say about the conditions of their work. "The individual participates, if he is a good citizen, in the politics of his city, his county, and perhaps even his state. But decisions taken by the mayor, the city council, the county manager, the governor of the state have comparatively little bearing on the daily life of the average citizen. It is his relation to the business for which he works that conditions his whole life. About this relationship he has little or nothing to say, particularly if he is one of the many millions of Americans who work for corporations enploying a thousand or more workers."[3] Workers should participate at the very least in "the management of the plant community" with respect to "matters of cleanliness and order, routines of work and relaxation."[4]

The third evil is that of periodic *unemployment*. Although great strides have been taken toward the mitigation of its evil effects through unemployment insurance and old age pensions, the threat of unemployment can be removed only if a way to prevent depression is found, for the danger of periodic inflation and depression is inherent in an unregulated economy. If work is a necessary condition of the realization of the self and of service to others, protracted unemployment is bound to narrow and demoralize the lives of men. When they cannot exercise their powers, they begin to feel that their lives are meaningless and uncreative. Even when they are protected by unemployment insurance against physical want, the worst of the trouble remains: they feel that they are useless to the community and therefore unwanted.

We have attempted to state the fundamental principles of the Christian doctrine of work and have indicated some of the ways in which economic individualism has tended to distort the purpose and destroy the dignity of work for millions of men and women. The problem of work cannot be solved as long as employers are indifferent to the dignity of the worker. Fortunately, during the

---

[3] Childs, Marquis and Cater, Douglass, *Ethics in a Business Society,* New York, Harpers, 1954, p. 162.
[4] Ibid., p. 164.

last generation employers have been learning to treat their workers better. It is becoming clearer to them that their employees will work better and will be more contented if they work in clean, sanitary, and attractive surroundings. Personnel managers have been appointed and efforts have been made to treat the workers not as mere "hands" but as persons.

In a recent article, a Christian businessman has pointed out some of the ways in which employers can improve their relations with their workers. "Christ did not deal with people primarily as members of a class or group," he writes, "but as individuals, each important in the sight of God. So also in business, men must not be classed as drill-press operators or riveters or truck drivers, but must be treated as individual personalities. . . . Another important point in dealing with employees is working conditions. . . . Washrooms and lunch rooms should be well kept and attractive. Conditions of safety need much study and careful planning."[5] This seems to reflect the attitude of an increasing number of industrial employers towards their workers. It is also accompanied by a growing sense of responsibility towards the community: "Modern management is interested in the public school system, the recreation facilities, and all the other factors in a community which are vital to its employees."[6] This is one of the most promising developments in recent Capitalism.

CAPITALISM, SOCIALISM, AND THE MIDDLE WAY

The *achievements* of Capitalism have been great. It increased production to a level far above what would have been thought possible a few centuries ago. It built up a vast world market and a complex system of distribution for the goods it produced. It stimulated the discovery and exploration of new territories and facilitated the exploitation of their natural resources for the benefit of men. It made it possible for a greatly enlarged population to be fed, clothed, and maintained in existence. It encouraged the development of tech-

[5] Wilson, Albert D., Jr., "Faith Revitalizes Business," in *The Christian Century*, April 15, 1953.
[6] Childs and Cater, op. cit., p. 93.

nology and lightened the heavy burden of labor for millions of workers on farms and in factories. It raised the standard of living for all classes of the people. It stimulated the initiative and released the creative energies of bold and resolute men. Finally, it encouraged people to face with courage and confidence the obstacles which frustrated their purposes and the evils from which they suffered. Of course, modern science and other factors also had much to do with this, but without Capitalism it would not have been possible. There should be no question, therefore, of trying to turn back the hands of the clock to some idyllic period of the past. It is necessary to preserve the great gains we have made and to go forward from where we are.

But these achievements of Capitalism have been won at a great *cost*. For unregulated Capitalism has given rise to evils which have been sources of suffering and bitterness for millions of people and which are still producing social revolutions all over the world. Fortunately, many of these evils have been recognized during the last few generations in Great Britain and America and resolute efforts have been made to overcome them. But Christians must not allow themselves to be lulled into complacency by the fact that in certain respects the Capitalism of the middle of the twentieth century is not the same as that of the latter part of the nineteenth century. Moreover, they must not yield to the temptation to defend everything in Capitalism on the ground that Communism is worse.

Perhaps the greatest source of danger in American Capitalism now is not economic inequality but the *concentration of economic power*. A comparatively small number of giant corporations wield vast power over workers, consumers, other producers, and even government. It has been said that the power of some of our largest corporations is greater than that of many of the states. We have become so dependent on these corporations that it is doubtful whether the government could allow them to fail. If it was forced to prevent their failure by taking them over, the result would be a form of collectivism. Meanwhile, they exercise great power over thousands of small subcontractors and distributors who are dependent upon them.

It has recently been argued by Professor Galbraith that the widespread fear of giant business is largely unjustified.[1] The concentration of industrial power, he points out, has led to the development of "countervailing power" by other groups. Among the examples of this development are giant labor unions and retail companies. These protect the interest of workers in higher wages and the interest of consumers in lower prices. Of course, there are still some millions of Americans who are without organized expression of market power, for example, hired farm workers, clerical workers and municipal employees. But Galbraith holds that these can and should organize for the protection of their interest and that whenever necessary the government should assist them to do so. "Countervailing power" can then be depended upon to bring about efficient production, fair wages and reasonable prices. The major responsibility of the government is to assist unorganized groups in organizing "countervailing power" and to preserve the economy from depression or inflation.

This argument has the merit of facing squarely the fact that the classical theory of competition no longer fits the facts and that the vast power of giant business makes necessary the development of vast power elsewhere to balance it. However, one may doubt whether giant power in the hands of one group is rendered socially innocuous by pitting against it the giant power of other groups. Apart from the dangers of monopoly, two of the groups may form at least a temporary alliance against a third. Professor Galbraith himself admits that organized labor may become an ally of an industry instead of acting as a "countervailing power," the industry agreeing to a demand from labor for higher wages but passing on the cost in the form of higher prices to the consumer. The vicious circle of higher wages, higher prices, still higher wages, and still higher prices is familiar in America. Again, any balance of power which is based upon nothing more than the self-interest of conflicting groups is precarious. It may be endangered at any time by the inordinate demands of one of the groups or by its stubborn resistance to the demands of another group, and this may lead to a bitter class struggle and ultimately to social revolution. One of the contending groups may seek to strengthen its position by gaining con-

[1] Galbraith, J. K., *American Capitalism*, Boston, Houghton Mifflin, 1952.

trol of the government, as the great industrialists of Germany sought to ally themselves with Hitler. Finally, any satisfactory solution of the problem of economic power must take into account not only economic and political factors like these but also moral factors. While giant business may favor technical development and a high standard of living, as Galbraith argues, many social thinkers are convinced that it gives autocratic power to a few executives at the top of each corporation, destroys the initiative and self-reliance of many of those beneath them, and results in impersonal relationships because of the vast size of the corporation.

As a result of the inequality of the rich and the poor and the concentration of economic power in the propertied class, a *class struggle* has developed in some capitalistic countries which threatens to destroy the unity of the community. The bitterness of the class struggle has been mitigated in America by high wages and by the opportunity to rise from the lower to the higher classes. In less fortunate and prosperous countries, the propertyless classes feel almost completely alienated from the community. They feel that they have been denied not only justice in the distribution of social benefits but also brotherhood with their fellow-citizens. Often, they have a stronger sense of solidarity with their own class in other countries than with other classes in their own country. This is one of the secrets of the strength of international Communism and of the willingness of many Communists to betray their own countries.

As economic individualism tends to disrupt the relations of men with one another in the community and to empty their lives of meaning, it also distorts their *relation to nature*. Urban man has been cut off from his roots in nature. He lives largely in a world of his own making, surrounded by human artifacts rather than natural things and processes. He is more aware of what he has done to his environment than of what he has received from it, of his power to transform nature than of the limitations she imposes upon him. He does not feel himself to be a part of nature but a master who stands outside and above her. Consequently, he *uses* nature, *exploits* her for his own purposes, without any thought of her claims upon him. This is evident, not only in his lack of appreciation for her beauty and her bounty towards him, but also in the ruthless way in which he wastes and destroys the *natural resources* she offers him. He devastates the forests without replanting them. He mines out the soil by foolish methods of plowing and planting. He refuses to curb his consumption of precious minerals and fuels. In ways like these, he neglects to conserve the natural resources upon which he and his children are dependent. The basic causes for this neglect are his greed and his short-sightedness. The one drives him to exploit nature as rapidly as possible for the sake of quick profits. The other prevents him from thinking about the future. As a result, he is irresponsible to the community as a whole, especially to the oncoming generations which are dependent upon nature for survival and for civilized life.

According to the theory of economic individualism, the economic system is a *self-regulating and self-adjusting mechanism* governed by economic laws. Although each individual in a system of competition is motivated by his own economic interest, the operation of economic laws such as the law of supply and demand will bring about a harmony of interests. Unfortunately, this theory is no longer in accord with the facts. The most striking proof of the breakdown of the traditional theory is the fact that every economic group has demanded government aid when its own interest has required it to do so. Although government "interference" is supposed to be undesirable, manufacturers have insisted upon protective tariffs and farmers have cried out for price subsidies. The breakdown of the theory of a self-regulating economic system was most evident during the Great Depression. Every group of citizens from unemployed workers to great bankers clamored for resolute action by the government to rescue them. Ever since that time the fear of depression and unemployment has haunted Americans of all classes, and they have come to expect the government to do whatever is necessary to promote economic security, preserve economic stability, and prevent the recurrence of depression. In spite of this, many are still unwilling to abandon an economic individualism which does not correspond to the economic realities and needs of the present time.

Because of these weaknesses, Capitalism has been undergoing substantial change during the last generation and further change is necessary. The concentration of economic power, the danger of social disunity, the waste of natural resources, and the necessity of preventing depression require resolute *action by the state* to protect the common good. For example, in agricultural countries like Egypt, India, and Italy, a powerful class of great landowners extorts high rents from the peasants and dominates their whole life. In such countries, a redistribution of the land must be enforced by the state if the poverty and misery of hundreds of millions of people are to be effectively dealt with and the threat of Communism is to be overcome. In industrial countries like the United States, resolute action by the state is necessary to deal with giant business. "One of the hardest tasks of modern government," says Professor MacIver, "is to keep within proper bounds the various monopolistic forces, the expansive organizations that subdue competition and can thus dictate their terms unless they are held in check by a vigilant political authority."[2] Despite the dislike of economic individualists for government "interference," economic regulation by the state for the general welfare is indispensable.

The real question is, how much and what kind of regulation is desirable? Some Christian thinkers have maintained that the socialization of industry is necessary. They have held that only through the social ownership of great industries which deeply affect the general welfare can the dangerous concentration of economic power be overcome, justice be done to the claim of workers for a fair share of the profits, and the concern of consumers for a reasonable price be safeguarded. They believe that the managers of those industries can be and should be made responsible to the people by democratic methods.

Most American thinkers fear that Socialism would necessitate a highly centralized government and a kind of economic planning which is impractical. For this reason, they reject Socialism as well as laissez-faire Capitalism and are seeking for a *middle way* between them. They point out that property which does not involve excessive power over others is not dangerous, e.g., a home, a family farm, a store, or a small factory. In relation to property of this kind, they believe that the aim of Christians should be a wider and more

[2] Ward, A. Dudley (ed.), *Goals of Economic Life,* New York, Harpers, 1953, p. 200.

equitable distribution and that government should help to further such a distribution by its tax policies, by loans, and in other ways. Public ownership, they hold, may be necessary in a few vitally important industries which are monopolistic in character, but it should be resorted to only if they cannot be regulated under conditions of private ownership. Advocates of the "middle way" differ among themselves with respect to the best solution of the general problem of the concentration of economic power, some maintaining that concentration is unavoidable but that strict government regulation of giant business can prevent many of its evils, others holding that an effective way must be found to break up the great industrial empires. But all of them attempt to combine the advantages of private enterprise and efficient production with the advantages of government regulation and equitable distribution.

One argument for the "middle way" is that it is impossible to dispense with *self-interest* as a motive for economic activity. The individual must have an adequate incentive to develop his talents and use his energies. While service of the needs of others should be the primary motive of the Christian in his work, many of those engaged in economic activity are not Christians and Christians themselves are motivated in part by self-interest. Consequently, a reward in the form of profit is necessary to persuade men to assume the risks and responsibilities involved in economic enterprise. The aim of Christians should be, on the one hand, to increase the number of persons who are motivated primarily by the desire to serve, and, on the other hand, to find ways of directing self-interest into activities which will contribute to the common good as well as the good of the individual. Moreover, economic progress depends upon the bestowal of rewards on those who make innovations and apply them to the process of production. "As a dynamic process," says Professor Boulding, "economic progress means the development of better ways of doing things; this implies as a corollary that worse ways must be abandoned."[3] Insofar as competition makes this possible, it is a condition of economic progress. This is the more important because the abolition of poverty and the achievement of

[3] Ward, A. D. (ed.), ibid., p. 63.

greater equality depend, at least in part, upon the increase in productivity made possible by economic progress.[4]

On the other hand, advocates of a "middle way" recognize that there is constant need for *political power* to limit the encroachments of economic power. "It is primarily the task of government," says Professor MacIver, "to prevent these encroachments, by setting limits to price agreements, by curbing tendencies to monopoly, by broad regulation over credit and banking, by preventing the destructive waste of natural resources through competitive exploitation, by intervening when the strife of worker and employer threatens the public welfare, by setting up standards and limits of various kinds in the public interest, and so forth."[5] In other terms, *economic freedom* must be qualified and limited by the claims of *social justice* enforced by the state as the political organ of the whole community.

At the first Assembly of the World Council of Churches in Amsterdam in 1948, a significant report was adopted on "The Church and the Disorder of Society." "The church cannot resolve the debate," says the report, "between those who feel that the primary solution is to socialize the means of production, and those who fear that such a course will merely lead to new and inordinate combinations of political and economic power, culminating finally in an omnipotent state. In the light of the Christian understanding of man we must, however, say to the advocates of socialization that the institution of property is not the only root of the corruption of human nature. We must equally say to the defenders of existing property relations that ownership is not an unconditional right; it must, therefore, be preserved, curtailed or distributed in accordance with the requirements of justice."[6] After an analysis of the "points of conflict" between Christianity and Marxian Communism and between Christianity and Capitalism, the report adds: "The Christian churches should reject the ideologies of both communism and laissez-faire capitalism, and should seek to draw men away from the false assumption that these extremes are the only alternatives.

[4] Ibid., pp. 76, 77.
[5] Ibid., p. 190.
[6] Reprinted by permission of *The Christian Century* from the issue of October 6, 1948, p. 1048.

Each has made promises which it could not redeem. Communist ideology puts the emphasis upon economic justice, and promises that freedom will come automatically after the completion of the revolution. Capitalism puts the emphasis upon freedom, and promises that justice will follow as a by-product of free enterprise; that, too, is an ideology which has proved false. It is the responsibility of Christians to seek new creative solutions which never allow either justice or freedom to destroy the other."[7]

THE ECONOMIC TASK OF THE CHURCH

The primary task of the Christian *moralist,* we have assumed, is not to propose a concrete program for the solution of economic problems, but to formulate Christian ethical principles which can guide men in their attempts to solve these problems. But what is the task of the *Church as a whole?*

It is obvious that the Church as a whole cannot and should not identify itself with any particular economic system or program not only because of the difference between Christians on economic issues, but also because the Church as such does not possess the technical knowledge necessary for the solution of economic problems. But this should not prevent individual Christians and groups of Christians from seeking solutions to the economic problems we have raised, solutions which will be both technically sound and in accord with Christian principles. Indeed, Christian businessmen, labor leaders, social scientists, and politicians have a special responsibility to do this. In addition, every Christian citizen has the obligation to cast his vote in support of the political party or the candidates who seem to him to offer the best solutions of pressing economic issues. He cannot avoid taking sides on these issues. If he fails to support efforts to achieve a better economic order through political action, he merely supports the existing order.

While Christians live and work within the framework of the present system, they should strive to create a different "economic spirit." The Church has the great educational task of creating anew the idea of community between men which has been almost destroyed

[7] Ibid., p. 1049.

by individualism and its encouragement of self-assertiveness. A better, more Christian economic order can be built only on the idea of love manifesting itself as justice, the idea of the responsibility of all for all. The task will not be an easy one. Under the influence of the economic individualism of the nineteenth century, the Church neglected the teachings of Christ and the greatest Christian thinkers. The result was suffering in the lives of millions of poor and underprivileged people, on the one hand, and callous and complacent indifference to that suffering on the part of the well-to-do classes, on the other. More than that, the Church usually identified itself consciously or unconsciously with the privileged classes. As a result, it antagonized the working class, and the workers in certain countries became secularized.

In America and Great Britain, fortunately, there has been a gradual awakening of the Protestant churches to their responsibility for social justice. However, it cannot be denied that some of the Protestant churches of America are still largely "class churches." They are predominantly middle or upper class in their membership, leadership, and thinking. This will make their task of creating a new economic spirit extremely difficult. Nevertheless, they must not refuse to undertake the task. Although economic reform in our society can be achieved only through the exercise of economic and political power, it will be ineffective unless there is also a fundamental change in the minds and hearts of the people. Despite her modern compromise with materialism and individualism, the Church can never quite forget the words of her Master, "You cannot serve God and Mammon."

CHAPTER 15

Race

THE RACE PROBLEM

RACIAL prejudice, discrimination, and exploitation are the source of one of the most serious social problems of our time. In America, discrimination against racial minorities, especially Negroes, constitutes one of the gravest threats to our unity and stands in flagrant contradiction to our democratic ideal. In Germany, the persecution of Jews under Hitler was one of the most cruel examples of racial hatred in all history. In Asia, the exploitation of Orientals under Western imperialism has led to a sharp reaction against the West and may well tip the balance in favor of Communism in its struggle with Democracy. In South Africa, recent governments have been following a policy of racial segregation which is utterly unrealistic and is certain to be self-defeating. These are only a few examples of the evil effects of the racial beliefs and attitudes of Western peoples.

One of the most ironical aspects of the race problem is that most of the white Westerners who have imposed their wills upon the yellow and dark-skinned peoples of Asia and Africa have professed to be Christians. As a result, Christianity has come to be associated in the minds of many Asiatics and Africans with the enslavement or exploitation of weaker peoples. Fortunately, Christian missionaries have often supported the efforts of subject peoples to achieve independence from the imperial powers, and have won the gratitude of many by their unselfish devotion to the welfare of these peoples. On the whole, however, the record of the "Christian" peoples of the West in dealing with the peoples of other races has been extremely bad. During the Middle Ages, they forced the Jews into crowded ghettos and periodically expelled them; in the modern age, they tolerated Negro slavery until the nineteenth century; and they have exploited the "backward" peoples of Asia and Africa up to our own day. Is it surprising that Western nations are regarded among these peoples as materialistic, aggressive, and ruthless? Is it any wonder that, while many among them are attracted by the glittering promises of the Communists, they seem to be indifferent to the propaganda of the Western democracies?

Of course, excuses could be found for the white Christians of the West. It could be pointed out, for example, that slavery has been practised since ancient times by many races and that it would have been economically difficult to dispense with it before new methods of production were introduced by the Industrial Revolution. It might be argued that persecution of religious minorities such as the Jews was inevitable as long as men believed that the unity of society depended upon religious uniformity. And imperialistic exploitation might be laid at the door of Westerners who were so blinded by the love of wealth or power that they virtually abandoned their Christianity. There is an element of truth in these excuses, but they are, after all, only excuses. The fact remains that Christians of the West have betrayed their Master again and again by their racial attitudes and practices.

Why have they done so? How was it possible for English Christians to be slave traders and American Christians to be slave owners until the nineteenth century? How is it possible even today for South African Christians to keep millions of black and colored people in a position of inferiority? Some have failed to understand that Christian love demands justice, however costly it may be, in the relations of one race with another. Others have understood, but have stubbornly refused to heed. Still others have partially understood, but have been prevented by rationalizations from seeing clearly.

FORMS OF RATIONALIZATION

How have Christians attempted to justify their denial of justice to people of other races? In the first place, many Christians may profess to *believe* that all men without distinction of race are equal in worth, but find it difficult to *feel* it. To a member of one group, those of another group seem strange because they are unfamiliar. If he does not see them often enough to enter into their life, he cannot possibly understand and appreciate them. Moreover, when he seldom sees them, he almost forgets them. For this reason, he finds it difficult to realize that God is as much concerned with them as with those of his own race. If the men of another race are *separated* from us geographically, they are completely out of sight and therefore it is easy to forget their existence. It is not even necessary that they should be separated from us by distance. They can live among us or near us and yet be all but invisible to us and absent from our thoughts. It is safe to say that, although there are slums within a few blocks of Park Avenue in New York—the same thing could be said of a fashionable street in many another city—many of the privileged families who live on it are hardly ever aware of their existence. Again, the appalling conditions under which Negroes are forced by residential segregation to live are not realized by the whites because they are seldom seen, and even when they are seen are seldom appreciated. Thus, separation, whether by geography or by segregation, can make one race almost oblivious to the misery it inflicts upon another and blind it to its guilt.

In the second place, Christians have usually convinced themselves of the natural and inescapable *inferiority* of the races against which they have discriminated. They have done so in many cases because of the primitive character of these races at the time of the first contacts with them, e.g., the black-skinned peoples of Africa and the red-skinned tribes of America. It has been easy to infer from the primitive culture of a people to its racial inferiority. Moreover, even after a primitive people has been brought into contact with a civilized people, it is natural that it should continue for some time to seem inferior to the latter. Thus, many white Americans continue to regard Negroes as inherently inferior because at present some of them appear inferior in certain respects to most whites. But this apparent inferiority seems to be due not to the racial inferiority of Negroes, but to the discrimination against them throughout our history. May not the fact that until recently Negroes were restricted to unskilled manual labor and were denied the opportunity for higher education explain the fact that many of them are still unqualified for highly skilled and professional work? Gunnar Myrdal speaks of this as the "vicious circle."[1] The fact that at present many Negroes seem to be inferior in certain respects, he points out, is made an excuse for denying them equal opportunities; and yet the denial of equal opportunities to them in the past was probably the main cause of any present inferiority there may be.

According to democratic theory, there is actual inequality between the citizens in many respects, but this is not an adequate reason for denying equality of opportunity to any of them. The assumption is that all should be granted equal opportunities in order that each may be able to develop and exercise his talents as fully as possible. The fact that many white Americans are unwilling to follow this principle in their relations with Negroes is strange. For many Negroes have taken full advantage of their economic and educational opportunities during the last few generations and have achieved equality with most whites and superiority to many. In some fields, e.g., education, music, literature, and statesmanship, Negroes have attained positions of high distinction. These and other facts seem to confirm the view of competent social scientists that there is no adequate evidence of the racial inferiority of Negroes to whites, mentally, morally, or physically.[2] The fact that, in spite of all this, many whites are still reluctant to grant equal opportunities to Negroes seems to indicate that their belief in the inherent and inescapable inferiority of the Negro race is only a rationalization. It is as if, deep down, they suspect that Negroes are not racially inferior and are determined to deny them equal opportunities in order to prevent them from demonstrating it.

In the third place, Christians of the dominant white race have justified their subjection of another race on the ground that it was necessary to the maintenance of their own *superior culture*. Since a high level of culture requires leisure for creative activity, this argument has a certain plausibility. Before the Industrial Revolution

---

[1] Myrdal, Gunnar, *An American Dilemma,* New York, London, Harpers, 1944, Ch. 3, sec. 7, "The Theory of the Vicious Circle."
[2] Ibid., Ch. 6.

made it possible to speed up the production and distribution of goods by the use of machinery, it seemed impossible for all classes to enjoy the leisure necessary for creative activity. Consequently, many have maintained that the art, science, and philosophy of the Greek city-states rested upon the foundation of slavery, and some of the spokesmen for the Southern aristocracy before the Civil War justified the maintenance of slavery on similar grounds.

The basic flaw in this argument, from the Christian point of view, is that the cultural superiority of one class or race, however great, does not justify the use of another class or race as a mere means to its own ends. The reason Christians have often accepted it despite this flaw is that they have desired to exploit another race but have had to justify themselves to their own consciences. Belief in their own cultural superiority, which is easily associated with belief in their racial superiority, provides them with a rationalization for their conduct. As Myrdal says, such racial beliefs are "beliefs with a purpose,"[3] i.e., they are not based upon evidence but are products of the interest of the exploiting group.

This does not mean that the only purpose behind such racial beliefs is that of economic advantage. It is difficult to separate the economic motive of a man or a group from other motives. Men and groups do not work merely to earn a living or to acquire wealth; they work also to maintain their whole pattern of life. For example, slaveholders owned slaves not merely for the sake of profit but as a symbol of social superiority and as a support of the privileges and values which accompanied that superiority. Thus, exploitation is motivated not only by the economic interest but also by the social and cultural *pride* of the dominant race.

It should be noted that, while collective egoism and pride play an important role in all racial discrimination, they may take different forms in relation to different racial groups. Because the dominant majority in America have regarded races such as the Negroes and Indians as racially and culturally inferior, they have been able to justify their exploitation of them on this ground. But they have not usually thought of Jews as racially inferior and they have not considered them culturally inferior to themselves. Although

[3] Ibid., Ch. 4, sec. 7.

Jews have often been poor, they have generally been industrious and energetic. They have also frequently manifested superior intellectual and artistic ability and have achieved outstanding success in many fields, e.g., business, law, education, art, and science. Thus, it has usually been impossible to justify discrimination against them on the ground of racial or cultural inferiority. It has been necessary, therefore, to justify it on the ground of their economic and cultural achievements. These achievements are a source of danger to the Gentile majority, it is claimed, because they have led to a disproportionate influence of Jews in society. Anti-Semitic leaders even profess to see a danger that Jews will dominate the country and change its culture if they are allowed to attain more key positions of power in economic and professional life. Consequently, discrimination against them takes the form of refusing to admit them on an equal basis to universities, excluding them from socially desirable clubs and residential areas, and, in most states, keeping them out of high positions in political and educational life.

All of this suggests that the discrimination against Jews is not for the purpose of exploiting a supposedly inferior group, but to prevent the rise of an energetic and able group to a higher position in society. Like all racial discrimination, it is a product of collective egoism; but that egoism is manifested primarily in the form of *fear* and *envy*. Undoubtedly, economic motives play a part in this, especially jealousy of the success of Jews on the part of their Gentile competitors in business and the professions. Also, religious intolerance still plays a part. Since the eighteenth century, however, it has been recognized that religious diversity is not fatal to the solidarity of a society. The growth of religious toleration has combined with modern secularism to eliminate religious differences in America as a primary source of anti-Semitism. Among narrow and bigoted Christians, however, religious intolerance is still an important factor.

We have attempted to describe some of the ways in which Christians have attempted to justify racial prejudice and discrimination, and have pointed out that the racial beliefs they use for this purpose are rationalizations. Their primary motive, hidden by these rationalizations, has been to exploit weak and primitive races or to hold back strong and civilized ones whose competition they fear. In both cases, collective egoism in the form of racial and cultural pride is a powerful factor. Even when the economic motive is strong, it is usually associated with claims of racial and/or cultural superiority which are expressions of collective pride.

From this it is clear that, while the race problem may be rooted in *natural* conflicts between social groups which are struggling to survive and improve their lot, it is primarily a psychological and social problem. It is a *psychological* problem in the sense that racial beliefs and attitudes are largely products of collective egoism and pride. The race problem is also, of course, a *social* problem, because it arises in the interaction between social groups and because the beliefs and attitudes of a social group embody themselves in social patterns. Consequently, any attempt to solve the problem must be aimed at both the psychological and the social manifestations of it. In other terms, the race problem cannot be solved until both personal attitudes and social patterns are changed.

THE STRATEGY OF CHRISTIANS

What can Christians do to solve the problem? How can they help to overcome the racial beliefs and attitudes in people's minds, on the one hand, and the racial discrimination in our society, on the other?

First, they should come to terms with false racial beliefs and attitudes in *their own minds* which they have absorbed from society. They should realize clearly that these are radically opposed to the Christian affirmation that all men are worthy of respect because they have been created in the image of God. It is not enough that they should know this as an abstract truth; they should also understand its practical implications. It implies that however inferior a race may seem to be in certain respects, it should not be regarded with contempt or excluded from community. It also implies that such a race should not be subjected to unjust treatment by the denial of equal opportunities and rights to it. Thus, racial prejudice and racial discrimination alike are incompatible with the Christian doctrine of the *dignity* of man. The idea that another race may be made a mere means to the economic prosperity, cultural achievement, or power of one's own race, therefore, should be abhorrent to every Christian.

The Biblical doctrine of man also emphasizes the *unity* and *solidarity* of all men. In the great story of the Creation in the first chapter of Genesis, God makes "man" in His own image. All men are descended from a common father, Adam, so that the many and diverse peoples of the earth are one in origin. In the New Testament, the unity of mankind is also affirmed in terms of the solidarity of all men in sin and the universal need for redemption. St. Paul says, "all men, both Jews and Greeks, are under the power of sin."[1] In His love God has sent His only Son to redeem all men. "God was in Christ reconciling the world to himself."[2] In reconciling all men to Himself through Christ, He also reconciled them to one another. In the letter to the Ephesians, it is asserted that Christ "has broken down the dividing wall of hostility" between Gentiles and Jews in order "that he might create in himself one new man in place of the two, so making peace, and might reconcile us both to God in one body through the cross, thereby bringing the hostility to an end."[3] Consequently, there is no place in the Christian community for the barriers which divide men. "There is neither Jew nor Greek, there is neither slave nor free, there is neither male nor female; for you are all one in Christ Jesus."[4] Neither the natural difference between the sexes, nor the social difference between freemen and slaves, nor the racial and cultural difference between Jews and Greeks should separate those who acknowledge Christ as their one Lord.

But, second, it is not enough for Christians to eliminate from their own minds racial beliefs that are incompatible with the Christian conception of the dignity and unity of all men; they should also do everything in their power to combat these beliefs in *others*. One of the most effective methods, though not the quickest, is that of education. It is the responsibility of all Christians to correct false rumors about other races by quiet appeal to the facts. Race riots in

[1] Rom. 3:9.
[2] II Cor. 5:19.
[3] Eph. 2:14-16.
[4] Gal. 3:28.

America, like pogroms in Europe, have often been started by the circulation of rumors without any basis in fact. In addition, Christians can do much to make it known to others that, according to social scientists, there is no substantial evidence for the native inferiority of Negroes and that there is much evidence that any present inferiority there may be is due primarily to the many handicaps from which they suffer.

However, it must be borne in mind that, when interests and prejudices are involved, education in the sense of verbal communication of facts and correction of errors is not sufficient. Since racial beliefs are rationalizations of half-hidden desires and fears, as we have seen, it is necessary to make ourselves and others more clearly conscious of these irrational forces at work in our minds. The desire of whites to exploit the Negro—or at least their willingness to profit by the exploitation of him in our society—should be brought into the full light of consciousness. The fear that if he is granted equality of opportunity he will become a powerful economic competitor, or will lower the level of our culture and morality, or will seek intermarriage with whites must be frankly faced and examined. For example, is there any real ground for the fear of intermarriage? Or is Myrdal's opinion correct that what Negroes desire most is economic and other forms of opportunity and what they desire least is intermarriage with whites?[5] If they continue to make good use of their opportunities and gradually overcome any inequality there may still be between them and ourselves, will intermarriage still seem a dreadful thing to be avoided by the white race at all costs? Questions like these should be considered by Christians on their own merits rather than evaded.

It must also be remembered that direct contact with members of another race, if accompanied by a genuine desire to understand them and a willingness to change our opinions, is one of the most effective methods of education in the realities of the race problem. Of course, unfortunate contacts with a few of the least admirable members of another race may deepen a prejudice against it rather than create an appreciation of it. On the other hand, contacts with only a few of its most admirable members may give rise to an

[5] Myrdal, op. cit., Part I, Ch. 3, sec. 4, "The Rank Order of Discriminations."

unrealistic enthusiasm and an uncritical optimism about it which may blind one to weaknesses and defects. But repeated and continuous contacts with members of a race, at all levels and of all kinds, is surely essential to any adequate understanding and appreciation of them as they really are.

Third, Christians should take every opportunity to *defend the rights* of other racial groups, as well as to urge the *extension* of their rights as rapidly as possible. Every violation of the political or legal rights of Negroes, e.g., by intimidation at the polls or by an unjust verdict in a court, fastens more firmly the shackles of discrimination. On the other hand, every successful protest against such a violation helps make these rights more secure and effective. Again, every extension of economic or educational opportunities to them, e.g., through a state fair employment practices law or admission to a college or professional school, enables them directly to improve their position and indirectly prepares the way for future gains. While Negroes themselves can do much to protect and extend their rights by agitation and other forms of protest, the primary initiative must lie with the whites. Since they were the original source of the whole system of discrimination and still constitute the group which enforces it, they must take primary responsibility for bringing about necessary social changes.

It will frequently require courage to do this, especially in countries like South Africa or states like those of our Deep South where the inequality of the races is deeply entrenched and strongly defended. However, the forces making for social justice are often stronger than they appear on the surface and there are usually more persons who are ready to support a proposed change than is realized. Frequently, all that is needed is a spokesman to voice feelings which others are too timid to express. In any case, Christians are counselled by St. Paul, "Do not be conformed to this world but be transformed by the renewal of your mind, that you may prove what is the will of God, what is good and acceptable and perfect."[6] One of the main reasons they have accepted racial attitudes which contradict their Christian faith is that they have not followed this counsel but have passively conformed to the world from fear of being different. Yet

[6] Rom. 12:2.

it is idle to pretend that American Christians are just to Negroes or any other racial minority so long as they do not have complete equality of rights, economic, political, educational, and social.

Fourth, Christians should oppose *segregation* as strongly as discrimination. Indeed, segregation, the enforced separation of one race from another, is itself one of the worst forms of discrimination. It is peculiarly painful and highly unjust to the Negro. For one thing, the principle of "separate but equal" facilities for the two races, which is often defended by whites as just to Negroes, is impractical. In education, for example, it would be quite impossible to provide equal opportunities for Negroes and whites without senseless duplication and intolerable financial burdens. In practice, "separate but equal" facilities means that the dominant whites take possession of and exclude Negroes from the best seats on public vehicles, the good hotels and restaurants, and the most desirable residential districts. One result of this policy is to keep Negroes out of all but the poorest houses. This condemns them to all of the evils involved in bad housing, e.g., overcrowding, unattractive surroundings, inadequate sanitation, lack of space for play, and long distances from work.

Segregation is not only a source of great privation and suffering; it also involves the exclusion of the segregated race from almost all normal social relationships with the dominant race. For the motive of segregation is to confine relationships with the minority race to the necessary minimum. The refusal to live in full community with them is a source of great humiliation to sensitive and self-respecting members of the minority race, since it is an ever-present reminder that they will always be regarded as inferior in spite of all they can do. It also makes it possible, as we have seen, for the majority race to remain in ignorance of the evil effects of its discrimination. This ignorance breeds mutual suspicion and misunderstanding and makes cooperation between the races far more difficult.[7]

Fifth, the *Church* should set its own house in order. It has been charged that the Church is as completely segregated as any other institution in America. Nor is there as much difference between

[7] For a broad study of the forms of Negro segregation and the reaction of Negroes to it, see Charles Johnson's *Patterns of Negro Segregation*, New York, Harpers, 1943.

the North and the South in this respect as many people suppose. In many churches of the North there are a few Negroes in the congregation. But whenever the proportion of Negroes to whites goes beyond a certain point, the whites tend to transfer their membership to other churches or to build a new church. Segregation of Negroes is also practised by many church schools and colleges.

It must be stated uncompromisingly that racial segregation in the Church is in contradiction to the spirit of Christ, the teaching of St. Paul, and the nature and purpose of the Church. Of course, it will not be easy to change the situation in parts of the country where segregation is practised in all other institutions and public places. When the members of a congregation insist upon the segregation of Negroes in the schools, hospitals, public vehicles, and restaurants, it will be difficult for them to abandon it in the churches. Also, it must be admitted that it would be rather artificial to sit in a pew or kneel at the altar with a man on Sunday and then deny normal fellowship to him outside the church during the rest of the week. Doubtless, this has much to do with the apparent preference of many Negroes for worship by themselves. For it is more natural to worship with people who set up no barriers against one than with those who exclude one from most of their lives. Moreover, it is well known that there is considerable fear of integrated churches on the part of many leaders of Negro churches because they might lose much of their influence in a united church in which the majority of members would be whites. Thus, there are difficulties in the way of integrating the Negro and the white churches. Nevertheless, the task must be undertaken. It would be ironical if the Christian Church should be one of the last, rather than one of the first, institutions to abandon Negro segregation.

Finally, Christians should seek to eradicate *racial and cultural pride* from their hearts. Pride of race and culture, as we pointed out, provides one of the main sources for the rationalizations by which a group justifies racial discrimination and exploitation. A race, like a state, can become an idol, especially when it is associated with a high level of culture.[8] Christians should never allow themselves to

[8] One of the most striking and tragic examples of this idolatry of a race is that of the Nazi movement in Germany.

fall into racial pride. The realistic view of man's finiteness and sin in the Bible should remind them that all the virtues and achievements of any race are relative, not absolute.

Humility about their own race and culture will also help them to appreciate better the qualities and attainments of other races. Humility about ourselves and charity towards others go together. As long as we hold another race at arm's length from ourselves in our pride, we cannot learn to appreciate its virtues and care about its welfare. On the other hand, when we are humbled by a vivid insight into the foolishness of our pretensions, we can open ourselves to the needs of others and concern ourselves for their welfare. Once we have learned to repent of the wrongs which have been inflicted upon other races by our fathers and ourselves and have begun to feel compassion for the unknown millions of defenseless persons who have suffered from these wrongs, we shall see better what we should do to right them. Like Mr. Jarvis in Alan Paton's *Cry the Beloved Country*,[9] we shall be able to lift some of the heavy burdens by which we still oppress many of our less fortunate brothers and find practical ways to help them help themselves.

[9] Paton, Alan: *Cry the Beloved Country,* New York, Scribners, 1948.

CHAPTER 16

War and Peace

THE BIBLE AND PEACE

THE longing for peace and the vision of a time when the evils of war will have ceased are very old. In the eighth century before Christ the prophet Amos pronounced doom in the name of Yahweh upon the surrounding nations which had been pitiless in war. Damascus had "threshed Gilead with threshing sledges of iron;"[1] Gaza had "carried into exile a whole people to deliver them up to Edom;"[2] Tyre had also "delivered up a whole people to Edom, and did not remember the covenant of brotherhood;"[3] Edom had "pursued his brother with the sword, and cast off all pity;"[4] Ammon had "ripped up women with child in Gilead, that they might enlarge their border;"[5] and Moab had "burned to lime the bones of the king of Edom."[6] It is a terrible picture of folly and cruelty. When we remember it, the vision of peace in two other eighth century prophets, Isaiah and Micah, takes on deeper meaning:

> For out of Zion shall go forth the law,
>   and the word of the Lord from Jerusalem.
> He shall judge between the nations,
>   and shall decide for many peoples;

[1] Amos 1:3.
[2] Ibid., 1:6.
[3] Ibid., 1:9.
[4] Ibid., 1:11.
[5] Ibid., 1:13.
[6] Ibid., 2:1.

> and they shall beat their swords into plowshares,
>   and their spears into pruning-hooks;
> nation shall not lift up sword against nation,
> neither shall they learn war any more.[7]

It is significant that this vision is preceded by a picture of many nations going up to the temple of the Lord in Jerusalem that He may teach them "his ways" and that they may "walk in his paths."[8] The prophets realized that the root of war is injustice and that peace can come to men only when they are governed at home and abroad by God's moral laws.

Christianity is heir to these prophetic hopes and insights. In his life and teachings alike, Jesus showed himself to be truly the Prince of Peace. From the beginning he proclaimed the "good news" of a new age in which men would love one another and forgive their enemies. He said "blessed are the peacemakers." At his arrest in Gethsemane, he refused to allow his disciples to defend him with their swords.[9] On the Cross, he asked God to forgive those who were torturing and killing him.[10] Thus, he was consistent to the end with the attitude he had shown during his whole career. St. Paul was surely reflecting the spirit of Jesus when he wrote: "Repay no one evil for evil, but take thought for what is noble in the sight of all. If possible, so far as it depends upon you, live peaceably with all. . . . Do not be overcome by evil, but overcome evil with good."[11]

Thus, those who would follow Christ's teaching and example must seek to live in harmony with others and to make peace between men wherever they can. They must seek to reconcile men with one another, overcoming evil with good.

But Christians have not fully agreed among themselves with respect to the best method of seeking peace and with respect to their responsibility in relation to those who do evil. Some of them have believed that peace can be obtained only by refusing to participate in any war. Others have maintained that it is their duty to support a "just war" and that the best way to promote peace is to build a stable

---

[7] Is. 2:3-4; Mic. 4:2b-3.
[8] Is. 2:3; Mic. 4:2.
[9] Lk. 22:49-51.

[10] Lk. 23:34.
[11] Rom. 12:17, 18, 21.

international order under law. However, the two groups are by no means in total disagreement. Members of the first group admit—indeed, in many cases insist upon—the necessity of supplementing the negative method of non-participation in war with active efforts to prevent war and to further the reconciliation of nations after war. Most of them also believe that an international order based on law is necessary to prevent war. Some of them agree that this will require an international armed force analogous to a police force to restrain belligerent nations. Most members of the second group, on their side, agree that pacifist Christians have a moral right to refuse military service and they maintain that the Church should defend them in every possible way as they bear their witness to the way of peace. Like the pacifists, they acknowledge that war is a great evil and that it should be abolished. Finally, they emphasize the importance of measures to prevent the outbreak of war and of processes of reconciliation after a war is over. Thus, the fundamental difference between the two groups is that the first refuses to participate in war in any circumstances, the second believes that it should do so in certain circumstances. Let us examine the positions of the pacifists and the non-pacifists in turn.

THE CASE FOR PACIFISM

There are two main arguments for Christian pacifism. The first is that it is required by the teaching and example of Christ, which Christians are committed to follow. The second is that, in the long run, it is a more effective method of dealing with the conflicts between nations than war. These may be called the religious and ethical argument and the political or pragmatic argument.

The first of these arguments is the fundamental one, though it is often difficult in our time to separate it from the second. It is a *religious* argument in the sense that Christian pacifists believe war to be contrary to God's will and inconsistent with faith in Christ. It is an *ethical* argument in the sense that they also regard war as morally wrong, contrary to man's conscience as well as God's revelation. The essence of the argument is that, whether or not Jesus had in mind nations as well as persons when he said "Do not resist one who is evil"[1] and "Love your enemies,"[2] these precepts are as applicable to national enemies and evildoers as to personal ones. Some Christian pacifists like Leo Tolstoy have held that Jesus himself was thinking of nations, but the case for Christian pacifism does not rest on this interpretation of Jesus' original intention. It rests on the fact that the distinctive method used by Jesus and his early followers in dealing with personal hostility and injury was not to resist it by force but to submit to it and seek to overcome it by love. From this the conclusion is drawn that the same method should be employed in situations of conflict between nations. It is usually admitted that the method has not always been successful in transforming evil men and that it might not always succeed in changing the attitude of an aggressive nation or its rulers. But it is maintained that Christian love must be prepared to suffer as Christ himself had to suffer on the Cross.

The second or *political* argument, which is a more pragmatic one, is that war has failed and must be replaced by a more effective method of dealing with conflicts between nations. Pacifists hold that war has not only brought great evils upon humanity; it has also failed completely to solve the problems which set nations against one another. The causes which result in an armed conflict usually remain when it is over, it is said; they are not removed by the mere fact that one side has shown itself to be stronger than the other. Moreover, the settlement which follows the conflict is likely to be based primarily upon the superior force of the victor rather than upon justice to the vanquished. As a result, it simply produces new causes of future wars. Although an aggressive nation may be temporarily restrained and weakened by defeat, the punishment imposed upon it arouses bitter resentment and a deep desire for revenge. Moreover, one of the victorious nations may emerge from the war in a stronger position than before and assume the role of aggressor itself. Driven by pride in its newly discovered power and by continued fear for its security, it may become a major threat to the peace it sought to preserve. Thus, war breeds war.

[1] Mtt. 5:38.
[2] Mtt. 5:44; Lk. 6:27.

This argument has a special appeal in our time, for the West has suffered two devastating world wars within a generation and there is a clear connection between them. Germany was defeated in World War I by the Allies in what the latter regarded as a war to defend freedom and democracy. But peace terms were imposed upon her which she regarded as unjust, and economic suffering caused by inflation and depression deepened her resentment. In World War II she was defeated again, along with her ally Japan. This time the defeat was more decisive as the armed forces of Germany and Japan were badly beaten in the field and many of their cities were devastated from the air. But the fruits of victory have once more eluded us, and our situation now seems worse than it was before. Although Germany was beaten to her knees in the West, Russia and America have both emerged from the war much stronger than they were before and are already engaged in a mighty struggle which at any time could erupt into a third world war. In the East, Japan was also decisively beaten and there was hope that she might be induced to abandon her militaristic nationalism. But in the meanwhile China has undergone a social revolution and now confronts us as another menacing great power. Perhaps the supreme irony is that, having fought the war to destroy German and Japanese militarism, we are now frightened by the threat of Russia and China into re-arming Germany and Japan! Is not the history of our time the crowning proof that war solves one problem—or appears at the moment to do so—only to create another?

The argument becomes even more plausible when one takes into account the fact that modern war has become more and more destructive. Those who win suffer the destruction of their cities as well as those who lose; indeed, it has become a truism that in modern war there are no victors. American cities were mercifully spared in World War II; there is not the slightest possibility that they will be spared again. Furthermore, in "total war" all the energies of the citizens are devoted to the war, the arts of peace languish, and civilians suffer as much, often more, than the soldiers. With the coming of the atom and the hydrogen bomb and the dreadful threat of bacteriological warfare, it is doubtful whether Western civilization could survive another world war. As a result, some Christians who reject the position of the absolute pacifist that all war is wrong hold that modern "total war" cannot be justified. Any humane person, whether he is a pacifist or not, is bound to feel horror at the thought of another world war in which weapons of mass destruction may kill millions of civilians and destroy whole cities. Surely, all will agree that the prospect of such a disaster makes the necessity of finding a way to prevent war far more urgent than it has ever been before.

THE CASE FOR NON-PACIFISM

What can the non-pacifist Christian reply to these arguments of the pacifist? To the first argument, which maintains that Christ's method of non-resistance should be applied to conflicts between nations, it is not enough to reply that in all probability Christ had in mind personal rather than national evildoers when he said "Do not resist the evil one" and "Love your enemies." The reply of the non-pacifist should be, rather, that there are some international conflicts in which *justice* seems to require him to take sides. When a powerful nation seeks to conquer and dominate another nation, it is right that the citizens of the latter should defend their lives and liberties. Of course, it may be difficult at times to determine which of two nations is the aggressor in a war, e.g., one nation may attack another to free itself from domination. In such cases, the apparent aggressor may not be the real one. In other cases, the two nations may both be aggressors and justice may lie on neither side. The difficulty of determining right and wrong in an international conflict, therefore, should never be minimized. Nevertheless, it remains true that there have been and continue to be cases of unjustified, unprovoked, and deliberate aggression by one nation against another, such as the conquest of Manchuria by Japan in 1931, the assault of Germany upon Poland in 1939, and the attempt of the Communists to seize South Korea in 1950. In these cases, the concept of the "just war" is as valid today as it was in the Middle Ages, although it needs to be reformulated in the light of modern experience.[1]

It may be admitted by the Christian pacifist that *justice* may seem

[1] For a discussion of the development of this concept, see Lee, Umphrey: *The Historic Church and Modern Pacifism*, New York, Abingdon-Cokesbury, 1943, Ch. 3.

to be on the side of the victims of national aggression, but he may question whether *love* allows them to defend themselves by force. When they do, they certainly have to act in a way quite different from the way Jesus acted and their act hardly seems to be an expression of love. This is true if their act is looked at *by itself,* apart from the *purpose* they have in view. A man does not seem to be loving his enemies when he attempts to kill them. But if his purpose is considered, his act may appear quite different. In the case of an unprovoked attack, his purpose is to prevent harm from being done to the people of one nation by the people of another. It is to defend and protect them, even at the risk of his own life. His act, when it is viewed in this way, is not only in accordance with justice; it is also a manifestation of love. In relation to the soldiers of the attacking nation, of course, his aim will not seem to express love. Nevertheless, his primary motive is love, love of those whom he is seeking to protect from harm. For what would a love of one's neighbors be which refused to defend them from injury and suffering?

The fact that in protecting one's neighbors one may be required to kill enemies who are also one's neighbors, in Jesus' sense of the term, is tragic and it presents a *mystery of evil* that is as difficult to understand as the problem of evil in general. Perhaps if one could see more clearly the relation of love to justice in God's providence, if one could see why love for some of one's neighbors sometimes seems to require justice in the form of punishment for others, one could penetrate this mystery of evil. But although one cannot understand these things, he cannot evade the responsibility laid upon him by love to protect the lives and liberties of others.

This argument is based on the assumption that an aggressive nation can be prevented from inflicting injury and suffering upon the people of another nation only by resistance. This assumption is challenged by many Christian pacifists who maintain, as we have seen, that non-resistance is not only the morally *right* method of dealing with an aggressive nation but also a more politically *effective* one than resistance. Now, it cannot be denied that, when non-resistance has been motivated by love and persisted in with patience, it has often been successful in dealing with aggressive persons. The crucial question, of course, is whether non-resistance would also be successful in dealing with an aggressive state and its rulers. If Christian non-pacifists were convinced that it would, they would probably become pacifists themselves. But it is more difficult to bring about a radical change in a nation than in a person. This is not due to the supposedly "immoral" character of nations. It is due to the fact that a state, unlike a person, possesses no single center of decision and action, that the process by which a decision to go to war is reached is often a complex one, and that the problem of bringing about a change in such a decision, once made, is a slow one. It is not sufficient to change the attitude of the soldiers in the field. It was asserted by some pacifists at the outbreak of World War II that if an invading German army were not resisted but were received with kindness, it would soon abandon its aggressive intention. This overlooked the solidarity of the German army with their rulers and their people. Moreover, even if the army had been converted by the kindness shown them, the war would not have been stopped as long as their officers and rulers were determined to carry it on, dealt ruthlessly with those opposed to it, and could count upon the support of most of their people.

Some Christian pacifists point to the success of Gandhi's non-violent resistance in India as evidence of the effectiveness of non-resistance. Apart from the fact that non-violent resistance is not the same as non-resistance, however, it must be pointed out that its effectiveness in India was partly due to certain factors in the situation there which were unique. The British army and civil service in India were relatively small and had to have the cooperation of substantial elements of the native population to maintain their authority. For this reason, while violent resistance would have been futile because of the lack of a native army, the non-cooperation of the vast native population was a very powerful weapon. Moreover, the British were not ruthless in dealing with Gandhi and his movement. For example, they did not execute or keep Gandhi permanently in prison, as they might have done. The British Empire had for some time been evolving into a Commonwealth of free and independent nations and there was strong support of the aspiration of India for freedom among the people of Great Britain. Finally, the financial and military burden of holding her in subjection by force at the end of World

War II would have been intolerable. Thus, the relative weakness of the British ruling class in India, their unwillingness to be ruthless in their use of force, the sympathy of many Englishmen for India's aspirations, and the costliness of continuing the struggle played an important part in Gandhi's success. This is not to minimize in any way the wisdom and effectiveness of his strategy under the conditions that existed in India; and non-violent resistance may play an important part in future movements of liberation on the part of oppressed peoples who have no other weapons but their determination and courage, e.g., the black and colored peoples of South Africa. But Gandhi's success in India is no proof that Christian non-resistance, even if it were on a large scale, would succeed in stopping a powerful and ruthless nation bent on aggression.

In short, Christian pacifism, in a world where sin is deeply entrenched in the lives of men and manifests itself in a peculiarly demonic form in the will to power of nations, cannot hope to succeed as a political strategy for overcoming national aggression. Pacifism as a special vocation for some Christians who are able to stand firm and bear witness against the evils of war has its value. But pacifism as a national policy for dealing with an aggressive national enemy is not sufficiently realistic about man as a sinner and does not recognize that the collective pride of nations is one of the most stubborn expressions of his sin. Thus, the Christian pacifist's argument that the method of nonresistance to evil can be extended successfully to aggressive nations breaks down. At times Christians are confronted with the bitter necessity of choosing between two evils: resistance by force or abandonment of the victims of an aggressive nation to tyranny. If they choose the first, they do so with reluctance and only because it seems to them the lesser of two great evils.

But are they correct in thinking that sometimes, at least, war is the lesser of the evils? *Is* it, in fact, ever the lesser evil? In our day, this is perhaps the most crucial issue between Christian pacifists and non-pacifists. As we have seen, the Christian pacifist believes that war is always a failure as a means of settling conflicts between nations, that it solves no problems and indeed creates new ones. If so, it seems unrealistic to say that it may sometimes be the lesser evil. Does the Christian non-pacifist have any answer to this argument?

It must be admitted that war does not solve international problems. Conflicts are settled and problems solved only by negotiation, persuasion, compromise, and other peaceful methods. But the inference drawn by the pacifist from this fact may be questioned. For a war may succeed in the more limited purpose of restraining an aggressive nation and preventing it from doing serious injury to another nation; and by doing this it may create more favorable conditions of life for millions of persons.

Let us take as an example World War II. As we contemplate the world situation which has developed since the defeat of Germany and Japan, we naturally feel a sense of disillusionment and wonder whether the war was not fought in vain. But a choice had to be made by the Western democracies between a frightful war and an indefinite extension of the power of militaristic nationalism which negated the most cherished beliefs and values of Western civilization. In choosing the former alternative, they were under no illusion about the war "solving the problem" of German and Japanese nationalism. Their aim was quite simple: the restraint of German and Japanese aggression and the destruction of the governments which were responsible for it. This aim was at least partially fulfilled by their victory in the war. The fact that other evils have arisen since the end of the war cannot undo that fact. It may be that Russian Communism is an even greater danger to the free world today than German Nazism was in 1940. Nevertheless, the evil which had to be dealt with in 1940 was a great evil. It is difficult to escape the conclusion that the war, frightful as it was, was less evil than the triumph of German and Japanese militarism over large parts of Europe and Asia would have been.

The Christian pacifist may reply that temporal evils such as the loss of liberty are only relative and that Christians should suffer them rather than be guilty of the absolute evil of disobedience to Christ. But this reply simply begs the question at issue: What *does* obedience to Christ and the law of love require of Christians when they are threatened with the loss not only of a piece of territory or some other material possession, but also of their national independence, their freedom of thought and action, and the right to devote themselves to the values they cherish most? It will not do to depreciate these rights and values, or the evil involved in the loss of them, as merely temporal and relative. If history is the sphere in which the divine purpose is being fulfilled, time and its values have significance and God is not indifferent to them. Political and intellectual freedom has been won by the Western peoples only at the cost of centuries of hard struggle; and the spiritual values of Western civilization have been developed and transmitted only through a long and laborious process that began with the Hebrews and Greeks three thousand years ago. From the point of view of God's absolute wisdom and will, these human achievements may be relative; but they are a precious heritage and if they are lost they will not easily be recovered.

It may be objected that in most wars of the past the moral issues have been more confused and justice has usually been no more with one side than with the other. In sober fact, the history of past wars is darkened by human folly and sin and Christians should look very critically at any proposal for war before supporting it as just. Indeed, they should be prepared at any time to refuse participation in a war which seems to them unjust. This is important because in our time the evil of war has been increased enormously by its wider extension and greater destructiveness. If a third world war should break out, Christians would have to face the terrible question whether the evil against which they were being asked to fight was greater than the evil which would result from a world war waged with the new weapons of mass destruction. The decision would probably be a more difficult one than Christians have ever been called upon to make before. They would have to consider not only the question whether justice seemed to be on their side but also the brutalization of men, the appalling devastation, the destruction of life, and the difficulty of rebuilding after the war the shattered patterns of life on both sides. For the development of weapons of mass destruction, especially the atomic bomb and the hydrogen bomb, presents us with a new situation. Hitherto, the destruction which nations could bring down upon one another has been limited. With the recent development of the hydrogen bomb, men now have it in their power to destroy all life over a wide area and as yet they cannot defend themselves successfully against the new weapons.

In the light of this, the frequent assertion that weapons of mass destruction present no new moral problems to the Christian seems superficial and even frivolous. It is true that it is no more evil to kill a million persons with one bomb than with a thousand bombs. But this does not mean that there is only a quantitative difference between the destruction wrought by a hydrogen bomb and that wrought by a conventional bomb or shell, for this quantitative difference in destruction implies a more far-reaching difference in the total consequences which may be expected. Traditionally, the intention of each side engaged in a war has been to defeat the enemy nation rather than to destroy it. It has been assumed that after the conflict has been resolved by the victory of one side, the victor and vanquished will be reconciled to each other, and resume the normal life of peace. Thus, limited evils have been visited upon the vanquished for the sake of limited gains by the victor. But total war waged with the new weapons will result in nothing less than the virtual destruction of one, or more probably both, nations. Under these circumstances, it is extremely difficult to apply the principle of the "just war."

This makes the idea of a "preventive war" abhorrent. It also makes imperative the mutual renunciation, guaranteed by international inspection, of the new weapons of mass destruction. Above all, it confronts us with the absolute necessity of finding a way at all costs to establish an international order which can prevent war.

THE POLITICAL BASIS OF PEACE

The dream of peace which has haunted the minds of men since the eighth-century prophets has become a possibility only in our time. The economic and cultural interdependence of the world has become evident in our generation. The great distances which have kept the peoples of the world apart and indifferent to one another have been largely overcome by the development of rapid transportation and communication. Two world wars within a generation, followed by the threat of a third, have made the peoples of the world realize as never before their solidarity in good and evil alike. The sufferings inflicted by these wars and the dread of a still more terrible one have created a longing for peace in the hearts of men everywhere. Are not the conditions present for the coming into being of "one world"?

The establishment of the United Nations after World War II was proof of the new hope for peace and security. Unfortunately, it came into existence only under the most unpropitious circumstances. The war had left behind a great bitterness and resentment. Although it had demonstrated the folly of extreme nationalism, the war had also strengthened it in some countries. As a result, it was impossible to form anything more than a confederation of nations in which all retained absolute sovereignty and the great powers had the preponderant power. Authority to deal with matters involving security was reserved to the Security Council and each of the great powers was given a seat on it and the power to veto any of its decisions. The right of all nations to security and to a voice in the new organization was recognized by giving them representation on the Assembly. But the Assembly was given little power and was subordinated to the Security Council in vital matters. No international armed force was created by the charter to enforce decisions affecting peace. These structural weaknesses of the new organization, however, might not have prevented it from functioning fairly effectively if there had been a basic unity among its members. But it has been rent asunder from the beginning by the open and bitter struggle between the Communist bloc led by Russia and the non-Communist nations led by the United States. As a result, it has been unable to function effectively in cases where the interests of a great power were involved.

One of the major duties of Christians is to do everything possible to support and strengthen the United Nations. If it is to have the authority to settle disputes in which one or more of the great powers are involved, the right of veto will probably have to be done away with. The authority of the Assembly on which both the great and the small powers are represented will have to be increased. However, these and other structural changes are likely to be effected very gradually and only after there is a relaxation of the tension between Russia and the United States and a substantial measure of disarmament on the part of these great powers and their major allies. The difficulties in the way of strengthening the authority of the United Nations, therefore, are great.

Political idealists are likely to become impatient and disillusioned in the face of these difficulties. In their desire to establish a strong world government, they overlook the fact that a government presupposes a community, that a community comes into being only through a gradual process of development, and that a world community exists at present only in embryonic form. At the end of World War II, Reinhold Niebuhr warned that "whatever unity may be achieved in the coming decades must be attained by the coalescence of power and the development of a core of international community among the great powers."[1]

But realism with respect to the difficulties should not prevent us from seeking to transform the United Nations from a confederation of sovereign states which has little power over its strongest members to a federation of states with the authority to enforce its decisions. The fact that there are sharp racial, economic, cultural, and ideological differences dividing many states from one another and preventing them from developing a sense of community with one another warns us that the way to a World Federation is steep and strewn with difficulties. It is an error to suppose, as federalists sometimes do, that there is a close analogy between the sovereign states of the world today and the states of America in the eighteenth century when our federal union was established. The American states were already united by language, social institutions, religion, and common experiences. Serious obstacles had to be overcome and it was not until the union had passed through the fires of civil war that it proved itself strong enough to endure. The achievement of a World Federation, therefore, will probably come, if it does come, after many disappointments and failures. Consequently, Christians should regard a World Federation as the ultimate, not the immediate, goal. Their immediate task is to support the United Nations and defend it against attacks, misunderstandings, suspicions, and, above all, indifference.

But they have a right to hope that, as the United Nations proves itself to be indispensable to security, the member nations will see that they must give it more authority. Moreover, they should not be so cautious in the presence of difficulties that their will to act boldly and decisively becomes paralyzed. Political cynicism and defeatism are as dangerous as political Utopianism. As we have pointed out in an earlier essay, "it is not necessary to wait for a perfect world commu-

---

[1] Niebuhr, R., *The Children of Light and the Children of Darkness,* New York, Scribners, 1944, p. 171.

nity before laying the foundations of world order; indeed, an indispensable condition of progress toward world community is the laying of these political foundations."[2] This is an argument, not for World Federation *now,* but for resolute steps towards it *whenever* they become possible.

THE MORAL BASIS OF PEACE

The doctrine of absolute *national sovereignty* is one of the main obstacles to the growth of a world community. Under its influence, the citizens of modern states like our own are reluctant to enter into international agreements which involve any surrender of authority to an international body. Yet it is clear that a World Federation with adequate authority and with sufficient power to enforce its decisions is impossible until national states like America are willing to accept a limitation of their freedom of action.

However, the doctrine of national sovereignty is only a symptom of a far deeper disease of the modern national state: the belief that the state has no obligation to consider the interests and welfare of those who are not its own citizens. The frequent assertion that a government must base its foreign as well as its domestic policy upon the "national interest" alone is an expression of this belief. It is a manifestation of a national egoism and irresponsibility which is fundamentally opposed to Christian love. Obviously, the doctrine of absolute national sovereignty can be overcome or modified only if the citizens of one national state will acknowledge their responsibility for the citizens of other national states and will insist that their government do the same.[1]

This poses the most crucial question in the sphere of international

[2] Essay on "American Ideals and the Peace," in *The Second Chance,* edited by John A. Whitton, Princeton, Princeton University Press, 1944, p. 218.

[1] There is a sense, of course, in which national sovereignty is indispensable. For there must be in each state a supreme authority of government. But as this does not prevent the state from making treaties which are binding upon it and limit its freedom of action in certain respects, so it would not hinder it from voluntarily entering into an agreement with other sovereign states by which all surrender authority for certain specified purposes to an international organization, e.g., a world federation. The source of the trouble is not the *fact* of sovereignty in this sense but the *dogma* of absolute sovereignty in the sense we have discussed.

relations: can *national egoism* be sufficiently overcome or limited to make a world order based upon equal justice to all nations possible? On the answer to this question the possibility of enduring peace depends. Some political "realists" maintain that a stable world order can be founded upon the enlightened self-interest of the nations. But national self-interest, however "enlightened," can never generate a genuine concern for the welfare of other nations, and without such a concern a nation will never be willing to modify its policies when its own interest conflicts with the interest of other nations. It is not necessary that national egoism should be replaced by a national altruism which would *sacrifice* the interest of the nation to the interests of other nations. But it is necessary for each nation to *be concerned with* the interest of other nations as well as its own.

Since concern for the interest of other nations is seldom or never as intense as concern for that of one's own, the scope of men's *sympathy* must be enlarged. This is one of the points at which Christians can make an important contribution to world community and peace. As we have seen, the modern national state has been largely egoistic in its foreign policy, governing its conduct by the rules of a "closed morality" which is concerned solely with the welfare of the group. Christian love, on the other hand, demands an "open morality" which is concerned for the welfare of all mankind. For love impels men to do justice to the claims of all. Therefore, an important task of Christians as peacemakers is to strengthen the moral foundations of world community by preaching and teaching a universal "open" morality based upon love.

This task, however, should be conceived in the most practical terms. Although the Church has preached love and peace from its pulpits for nineteen hundred years, it has not succeeded in making them effective forces in the conduct of nations. Of course, the primary reason is the egoism and pride of nations. But an important secondary reason is that the Church has not made it clear that Christian love is not primarily a sentiment but a practical disposition of the will and that justice to the claims of others always requires one to limit his own claims. If a nation is to do justice to the claims of other nations, it must learn to limit its assertion of its own interests. The test of its devotion to peace is its willingness to do this. If it is prosperous and has a high standard of living, it must be willing to grant assistance to poorer countries and further their economic development. If it is powerful, it must be willing to cooperate with weaker nations rather than dominate them.

It would be idle to pretend that great powers like America will find it easy not to regard smaller powers as inferior to themselves. For this reason, the former have a special need of *humility*. It is the duty of American Christians, therefore, to remind their fellow citizens that their prosperity and power would have been impossible if it had not been for their good fortune in possessing great territory, boundless natural resources, a large population, and the gift of freedom. Therefore, they have no right to boast. They should not try to keep their prosperity for themselves alone but should seek to share it with less fortunate peoples; and they should regard their power not as a source of pride but as a responsibility to be used for the benefit also of peoples weaker than themselves. They should remind themselves that, according to the Gospel, greatness consists not in being served by others but in serving others. The test of the greatness of a nation, therefore, is not the degree of its power and prosperity but the use it makes of them. Great powers should never forget that the judgment of a nation's greatness by its contemporaries is usually reversed by posterity. It is not the "Great Powers" of the ancient world like Assyria and Babylonia, it is the "small powers" like Israel and Athens, which we now look upon as great. It is a sobering thought that posterity might pass a similar judgment upon some of the "Great Powers" and the "small powers" of today. If "Great Powers" like America do not humble their national pride and complacency and devote themselves to the welfare of humanity as a whole, it almost certainly will.

Part IV

FAITH AND REASON IN ETHICS

FAITH AND REASON IN THINGS

CHAPTER 17

Christian Ethics and Moral Philosophy

MORAL PHILOSOPHY: ITS NATURE AND LIMITATIONS

MORAL philosophy arises among those who have become dissatisfied with the moral judgments and practices imposed by their society. When they reach intellectual maturity and have sufficient leisure for independent thinking, they discover that many of the moral rules and virtues inculcated by their society are irrational and inconsistent with one another. They begin to analyze critically the accepted moral judgments and practices and to clarify the meanings of moral concepts such as courage and justice. This process can be studied by any careful reader of the Socratic dialogues of Plato. One can watch Socrates' mind at work as he subjects the moral *opinions* of his fellow-Athenians to searching criticism in the attempt to arrive at genuine *knowledge*.

But philosophers are not content merely to refine and clarify the morality of their group; their ultimate aim is to establish morality on a more solid basis of *general principles* which are consistent and comprehensive. They cannot be satisfied with a plurality of rules which are not based upon fundamental principles approved by reason, and, since reason is common to all men, these principles must be *universally valid*.

What are the *presuppositions* of the moral philosophy which results from this interest in universal principles of moral conduct? The first is the *autonomy of the reason*. In group morality, man's duties are imposed upon him by his society; in rational morality, they are determined by himself. There is no place for any moral authority but that

367

of reason and the only moral obligations that are binding upon a man are those he imposes as a rational being upon himself. For example, a moral law may have originated in a religious "revelation" and may have been transmitted by the Church. But it is accepted by the philosopher, if at all, because it commends itself to his reason, not because it has been thought to be revealed. The dignity of man as a rational person requires him to lay down principles to determine his own conduct rather than let others prescribe his duties for him. This implies that reason has the *capacity* to discover ethical principles which are true and that the work of reason can be carried through without serious interference and distortion by the philosopher's social affiliation, moral defects, and other irrational factors.

While group morality is the work of a society, moral philosophy is developed *by individuals*. The ethical theory of a philosopher may have been influenced by the thinking of many other persons, but it is formulated by him on his own responsibility. The fact that he claims universal validity for its principles is not incompatible with this fact. It means only that he appeals to the reason of other individuals like himself to approve of his conclusions. Moreover, his ethical theory is intended *for individuals*. Although a philosopher may hope that his work will have some influence upon his society as a whole, he knows that he can directly affect the thinking only of individuals. He cannot claim to be a spokesman for the whole of his society, since his ethical theory differs from the dominant group morality. At the most, he may claim to be a spokesman, like Aristotle, for the wise and good men of his society. In this respect, he differs from the Christian moralist, who does not speak merely as an individual but as a member of the Church and for the Church as a whole. This is one of the main reasons for the fact that moral philosophy has not affected the lives of most men, even educated men, as much as religious morality. It is an *ideal* proposed by one individual for adoption by other individuals, not a *way of life* which has been accepted and become a reality in a community.

Since the time of Aristotle, it has been recognized that philosophical ethics is *normative* rather than merely descriptive in character. The primary purpose of ethics is to determine what men "ought" to do and to formulate it in terms of "norms" or "standards" of conduct.

There is, of course, a descriptive science of ethics which confines itself to the actual moral judgments and practices of men. This "descriptive" ethics is of great value to moral philosophers because it provides them with moral data. But they are primarily concerned not so much with what men in various societies *have done* as with what they *should do*. A description of the moral judgments and practices of men, past and present, cannot answer the question as to how men ought to act. Not only have the moral judgments of men been in conflict with one another, but also many of them have been absurd or evil. There is no way by which a purely descriptive analysis can disclose which of them, if any, are true and worthy of acceptance as moral norms.

What is the *method* of ethics? According to Aristotle, the method employed in a field of knowledge should be determined by the nature of the subject. Now, the function of the moral philosopher is not to create or discover new values; it is to clarify and evaluate the moral judgments of men, to uncover the truths contained in them, and to organize these truths with the help of fundamental principles into a consistent ethical theory. This determines the nature of his method. He usually begins with an empirical analysis of the moral judgments of men, and seeks to develop generalizations about the values and virtues they have prized and the duties they have recognized. Unlike the descriptive scientist, however, he seeks through this empirical analysis to arrive at intuitions or insights of his own with respect to the values, virtues, and duties necessary for the best life. In other words, while he goes to the moral consciousness of men as reflected in their moral judgments for his data, he must depend upon his own moral consciousness, broadened and deepened by his study of these data, for his conclusions. Thus, his method is to start with an *empirical study* of the moral judgments of men, to derive from this study *basic intuitions* concerning the right and the good, and to develop these into a comprehensive *ethical theory*. At every stage, of course, his thinking is deeply influenced by his world view and his conception of man.

The *value* of moral philosophy is obvious. As a rational being, a man cannot be content to follow blindly the morality of his group. When he begins to think for himself and realizes that there is much arbitrariness and inconsistency in the acccepted moral rules, he is bound to ask, "What is truly good and right?" The moral philosopher has analyzed the virtues which deliver men from impulsive and foolish acts by providing them with an armor of habits against the assaults of passion. He has shown up the vanity of many values prized by his fellows, pointing out that wealth and power and glory are not as noble as justice and truth. He has appealed to them not to conform to customary practices which are cruel or meaningless.

Is moral philosophy, then, an adequate basis for the good life? Many moral philosophers have thought so, especially in our secular age. But there are *limitations* of moral philosophy which have always prevented most men, even educated men, from regarding it as by itself sufficient. What are these limitations?

First, moral philosophers are concerned with the discovery of what is good for men and right for them to do, but they have seldom been able to awaken in men a love of the good or to stimulate their wills to do the right. This is the familiar problem of moral *incentive* or *motive*. It may be admitted, with Sidgwick, that there is a desire in man to do that which is right and reasonable. But that desire, by itself, is not strong enough in most men to overcome the natural passions and social forces which are opposed to the right and reasonable. It is not enough to appeal to the reason; the will and the affections must somehow be brought into line with the dictates of reason. Plato realized the importance of moral education through associating pleasure with the good and pain with the evil, and Aristotle emphasized the necessity of forming right habits. But philosophers have seldom probed this problem very deeply. They have tended to assume that if we know our true good we will seek it and if we know our duty we will do it. Therefore, they have thought that when they have defined the good and the right, their task is over. But man's will is divided and he cannot love his true good with all his heart. Again and again, he finds himself in the tragic situation of St. Paul: he knows what is good but he chooses the evil. He is powerless by himself to acquire the virtues or perform the duties which are required of him by moral philosophy. If he is to attain true goodness, he must be radically transformed. His desires must be redirected and his affections fixed firmly upon the good.

Second, man's effort to attain virtue by himself is often a source of *moral dangers*. Although the greatest moral philosophers insist upon a disinterested devotion to the good, the realization of higher values often leads to moral pride and complacency. Man's self-centeredness even perverts his virtues and turns them into means of furthering his own interests. Without faith and love, the attempt to attain virtue and do good works often leads to self-righteousness. Apart from this tendency of natural egoism to corrupt the achievements of the moral will, the excessive dependence upon moral striving is accompanied by serious dangers. It sometimes produces inner tension and anxiety concerning the success of one's efforts. Moralism in the sense of strenuous effort by the will to "live up to" high ethical ideals without the power to do so may be the cause of inner conflict and failure. The result may be psychological frustration or even breakdown. More often moralism leads to a stern, unlovely character with strength but without graciousness and spontaneity. Some of the finest moral qualities cannot be attained by conscious willing at all but must come from the unconscious influence of other persons and from participation in the life of a moral community.

Third, there is no *imaginative vision* in moral philosophy capable of inspiring spontaneous love and devotion. The principles of moral philosophy are expressed in concepts rather than images. This is necessary for the sake of clarity and precision; but it prevents most moral philosophers from moving the heart and stimulating the will. One of the reasons Bergson does not recognize the morality of philosophers as a third type of morality along with "closed" and "open" morality is that its concepts seem to him to have little power over the will.[1] His tendency to anti-intellectualism leads him to minimize unduly the function of reason in morality, for reason can survey the various ends sought by men and organize them into a unified ideal. But it is a timely warning against the opposite tendency to neglect the non-rational factors in the moral life. What is there in moral philosophy which can stimulate aspira-

---

[1] Bergson, H., *The Two Sources of Morality and Religion*, New York, Holt, 1935, p. 57.

tion like the Christian vision of a universal community based upon love of God as Father and love of all men as brothers?

Fourth, the ideals of moral philosophers also lack the appeal that comes from the *incarnation* of a way of life in a living person and the inspiration that is derived from *imitation* of him. One of the greatest sources of appeal in Platonism, which is close to religious morality in many ways, is the embodiment of its ideal in Socrates. The power of Buddhist ethics is due largely to the fact that the followers of the Buddha are called upon to "take refuge" in *him* as well as in his *teachings*. Certainly, the reason Christian ethics has been able to transform the lives of men is to be found not only in the teachings of Christ but also in his life and in union with him. While a moral philosophy presents men with an *ideal* to be followed, it seldom offers them the *example* of one who has followed it. Nor is its ideal embodied in the way of life of a *community* or *church,* whose members strengthen and encourage one another in their efforts to realize it. Is this the reason why the greatest rival of Christian ethics in our time is not philosophical ethics but the secularized religious ethics of Communism, with its imaginative vision of a classless society embracing all men, the embodiment of its ideal in great leaders like Lenin, and its dependence upon an organized party to make its vision come true?

While moral philosophy has undoubtedly been one of the major sources of the ethical tradition of the Western world, these limitations force us to raise the question whether the attempt of many modern philosophers to separate moral philosophy from Christian ethics is not a fatal mistake. Should not moral philosophy and Christian ethics be regarded as complementary rather than mutually exclusive? May not the limitations of moral philosophy be overcome and its insights made more effective by the acceptance of Christian faith and love? May not Christians be aided by the insights of moral philosophy to obey God and serve their neighbors more wisely? The purpose of this chapter is to suggest that these questions should be answered in the affirmative, and to indicate a way in which the breach between Christian ethics and moral philosophy can be overcome.

THE AUTHORITY OF REVELATION AND THE
AUTONOMY OF REASON

In carrying out this purpose, however, we shall be confronted with *objections* from moral philosophers and Christian theologians. Some moral philosophers repudiate Christian ethics on the ground that it is based on revelation rather than reason and consequently is "authoritarian." Some Christian theologians refuse to accept any of the theories of moral philosophers on the ground that they are useless and unnecessary for men of faith. It is essential to deal with these two objections before we attempt to show how Christian ethics and moral philosophy should be related to each other. We shall begin with the objection of secular moral philosophers that Christian ethics is "authoritarian."

With respect to the source of authority, Christian ethics and moral philosophy seem at first sight to be in absolute opposition to one another. Christian ethics derives its principles from the revelation recorded in the Bible. Liberal as well as orthodox Christians insist upon the authority of this revelation. In contrast, secular moral philosophers seem to reject every authority but that of reason. Moral philosophy, they insist, must be "autonomous"; the moralist must depend upon no source of truth beyond reason. This raises several important questions: In what sense does Christian ethics rest upon the authority of revelation? Insofar as it does so, is it necessarily "authoritarian?" Again, what do moral philosophers mean by the "autonomy" of the reason? Is this autonomy absolute or limited? Finally, is it possible to accept the "authority" of revelation without sacrificing the legitimate "autonomy" of the reason?

First, in what sense does Christian ethics assert the *authority of revelation*? Christians differ in their answer to this question. In Protestantism, Christian ethics is based upon the authority not of the Church but of the Bible. Since the Bible is the record of a divine revelation in history, this means that Christian ethics is ultimately based upon the authority of that revelation. However, the revelation cannot be simply identified with the words of the Bible in which it is expressed; the "Word" of God is not the same as the words in

Hebrew and Greek by which it is mediated to us. Moreover, as Temple has said, it does not consist of dogmas and commandments stated in propositional form. It is a revelation of God and His redemptive activity, not of dogmas about God; of new life in love, not rules of conduct. For it is a revelation in historical events as interpreted by prophets and apostles, and the full meaning of historical events can never be exhausted by the words of any of its interpreters.[1] If so, the responsibility for interpreting the meaning of the revelation belongs to the individual person as a member of the Christian community. Does not God address men in the Biblical revelation as beings who can listen, understand, raise questions, and judge for themselves?

When understood in this way, the authority of revelation is wholly inconsistent with religious "authoritarianism." Religious "authoritarianism" is usually based upon belief in a visible authority, e.g., Church or Bible, as the source of dogmas which must be believed and rules which must be obeyed. Moreover, the pronouncements of this authority are unquestioned. They are felt to be binding whether or not they are approved by the reason and conscience of the individual. The free acceptance of revelation, as we have described it, is incompatible with this authoritarianism. According to our view, the acceptance of the authority of revelation by a Christian not only permits but demands that he use his reason fully in determining its meaning and its implications for his life.

This brings us to the question, what is the meaning of *"autonomy"* in moral philosophy? Positively, it asserts that man should determine his moral conduct by laws or principles approved by his own reason. Negatively, it denies the dependence of the rational will upon any external authority such as a church or state. According to Kant, it is "the property of the will to be a law to itself,"[2] and "the will possesses this property because it belongs to the intelligible world, under laws which, being independent of nature, have their foundation not in experience but in reason alone."[3] This view of the "autonomy" of the

[1] Temple, William, *Nature, Man and God,* London, Macmillan, 1940, Lecture 12.
[2] Kant, I., *The Metaphysics of Morals,* tr. by T. K. Abbott in *Kant's Theory of Ethics,* London, Longmans, Green, 1909, p. 66.
[3] Ibid., p. 72.

reason seems to assert that the reason lays down moral laws in complete independence of moral experience. However, Kant argued that his fundamental ethical principle was only a precise formulation of what is presupposed in the common moral consciousness. In any case, the usual method of philosophical ethics is to develop its principles through an examination of the moral experience of men as reflected in their moral judgments. Thus, "autonomy" means only that reason should not passively submit to an external authority, but should derive its ethical principles from reflection upon moral experience. If "autonomy" is interpreted in this way, reason may and should take into account every kind of moral experience, including that of religious men, in formulating its ethical principles.

When the "authority" of revelation and the "autonomy" of reason are interpreted in this way, the absolute opposition between Christian ethics and moral philosophy is seen to be unnecessary. On the one hand, the Biblical revelation of moral truth was not imparted to men whose minds and consciences were passive, but was mediated to them through their moral experience. Moreover, it continues to be accepted by Christians because it seems to be confirmed by their own moral experience. Thus, there is nothing arbitrary or irrational about it. On the other hand, the moral philosopher depends upon the facts of moral experience, and since the value of his conclusions is determined largely by the depth and breadth of the moral experience from which he derives them, it is reasonable for him to take seriously the moral experience recorded in the Bible.

In fact, however, there is a fundamental *difference* between Christian ethics and secular moral philosophy in their interpretation of moral experience. Christian ethics is inseparable from the Christian faith that God has revealed His will in Christ. A philosopher who does not share this faith cannot accept Christian ethics as a whole, although he may incorporate into his own thinking certain ideas derived from it. Consequently, he cannot give the moral experience recorded in the Bible a "privileged position" in his examination of the facts of the moral consciousness. He may acknowledge that important and valid ethical ideas originated in this moral experience, but he cannot acknowledge their primacy in his ethical thinking.

Thus, while there is no logical necessity for an absolute opposition between Christian ethics and moral philosophy *as such,* there is a radical difference between Christian ethics and a *secular* moral philosophy. However, the Christian moralist can do much to bridge the gap. Although the secular moral philosopher refuses to give primacy to ethical insights derived from the Christian moral experience, the Christian moralist should acknowledge the truth of some of the ethical insights of moral philosophers and adapt them for the use of Christians. We shall indicate later in this chapter why he should do so and how he can do so in the most fruitful way.

In addition, he can seek to remove a common misconception from the minds of moral philosophers which stands in the way of their acceptance of the Christian faith and ethic. This is the idea that, while Christian ethics is based upon the moral experience of a particular people in the past, moral philosophy is a product of universal reason reflecting impartially upon the moral experience of all humanity. Because of this supposed difference between them, the secular moral philosopher believes that his method and conclusions are superior to those of the Christian moralist. But is his examination of moral experience as all-inclusive and impartial as he thinks? Does he actually analyze the moral judgments of *all* peoples of every time and place? Does he analyze moral judgments from the perspective of an *impartial* reason unconditioned by his own time and place?

The moral philosopher is incapable of such an analysis. The limitations of his knowledge and the effect of his culture upon him cannot be overcome. In his analysis he usually limits himself to the moral judgments of his own people or civilization. Even when he deals with the moral judgments of other peoples and other times, he is naturally influenced more deeply by those of his own. The ethical theories of Plato and Aristotle would have been impossible in any country except ancient Greece, and Kant's ethics is clearly a product of the Age of Reason. Thus, the perspective of the moral philosopher is not that of universal reason reflecting impartially upon the *general* moral experience of mankind; it is that of his own reason conditioned by the *particular* moral experience of his time and place. In reality, he accords, a "privileged position" to the particular moral experience of ancient Greeks or modern Europeans, as the Christian moralist accords such a position to the experience of Hebrew prophets and Christian apostles.

If so, the moral philosopher should not claim superiority for his method. Like the Christian moralist, he gives the "privileged position" to those whom he believes to have been the wisest and best; and if he is pressed for the reason why he believes them to be so, it will be seen that his belief really rests upon metaphysical and ethical assumptions which he cannot demonstrate but accepts by a kind of faith. In brief, there is no such thing as an ethic which has been developed by pure reason without the aid of presuppositions. The difference between Christian ethics and secular moral philosophy is not that the former has presuppositions while the latter is free from them; it is that they derive their presuppositions from different sources. Can the moral philosopher prove that his presuppositions or the sources from which he draws them are superior to those of the Christian moralist? If the test of ethical presuppositions is their fruitfulness in ethical theory and their value as a guide in moral decisions, Christian ethics has stood this test successfully during many centuries. Can more be said of the ethical presuppositions of any philosopher?

FAITH AND REASON

The preceding argument concerning the relation of Christian ethics to moral philosophy presupposes a certain view of the nature of the Christian faith and its relation to reason. We must now make this view more explicit. Some philosophers suppose that faith has no cognitive value but is a wholly irrational act which springs from the will or the feelings. Now, it is certainly true that faith is not only intellectual assent; it is also a response of the whole self, including the will and heart, to the reality of God. But this does not destroy its *cognitive value*. For faith involves an apprehension of the reality and goodness of God as He has revealed Himself. It is not a blind faith, but a response to God as He has confronted man in his experience. It differs from reason when the latter is conceived as the faculty of discursive thinking. Faith *affirms* the reality and goodness of God as He is experienced and it leads to a commitment to Him. Reason, on the other hand, critically *examines* a judgment to determine whether there are adequate grounds for asserting it and it frequently leads to a refusal of commitment. Thus, faith is more adventurous than reason, reason more cautious than faith. But while faith goes beyond reason, it need not contradict any knowledge which has been definitely established by reason. And reason, which has a constructive as well as a critical task, cannot complete its task unless it is willing to accept premises or presuppositions which it cannot demonstrate. Thus, while faith without reason is uncritical, reason without faith is uncreative.

Of course, reason can attain to knowledge of certain kinds without the aid of faith. In the form of common sense, it can enable men to cope with problems of everyday life. In the form of science, it can describe natural phenomena, make predictions about future events, and design machines for exploiting natural resources. But it cannot attain to wisdom about the world as a whole or the highest good of man without *presuppositions* derived from faith.

The mind can understand reality, says Niebuhr, "only by making faith the presupposition of its understanding."[1] This is the Augustinian view of the relation between faith and understanding. "Credo ut intelligam," "I believe in order that I may understand." Since every world view rests upon presuppositions which cannot be rationally demonstrated, each of us must face the problem as to whether he is to start with presuppositions derived, at least in part, from the religious experience of God as transcendent Reality and Good. If we try to avoid the problem by denying the possibility of a world view and contenting ourselves with the description of relations between natural phenomena, as in Positivism, we refuse to heed the highest demand of reason and to meet the deepest need of life itself. If we try to find the meaning of the whole of reality in some aspect of nature, e.g., matter or life, we are merely explaining the whole by one of its finite parts to which we have arbitrarily accorded a privileged position over other finite parts. But if we have had a vital religious experience, we can never be satisfied with anything less than a religious world view based upon an affirmation of faith in God as transcendent Reality and Good.

Of course, in laying hold of God by faith, man's "reach exceeds his grasp." Though God has revealed Himself in religious expe-

[1] Niebuhr, R., *The Nature and Destiny of Man*, New York, Scribners, 1941, I, p. 158.

rience, He remains hidden in His transcendent otherness. Nevertheless, faith ventures out beyond the world of finite and contingent things and affirms an infinite and supersensible Being as the Ground of its existence, its nature, and its value.

Thus faith is a *source of truth* about reality, not a subjective fancy. As such, it involves, not only an act of trust, but also an intellectual act, an act of insight. That is why it is the source not only of religion but also of any philosophy which does justice to the transcendent element in experience. Every world view, irreligious as well as religious, is based upon a principle of meaning, a vision of truth, which is accepted by a kind of faith as the key to reality as a whole. In the words of Bradley, "metaphysics is the finding of bad reasons for what we believe on instinct."[2] A religious world view differs from naturalistic world views in that the principle of meaning upon which it rests is a transcendent principle, God. The fact that it is transcendent, however, does not mean that it is irrelevant to our understanding of the finite and contingent things of the world in which we live and to our life in that world. Indeed, finite and contingent things, especially the life and spirit of man, find their meaning and explanation only in relation to it and apart from it they become unintelligible.

This is not a mere dogmatic assertion of religion alone; it can be confirmed by reference to other spiritual activities and values also. Plato points out in the "Symposium" how the experience of beautiful faces and forms leads on to the experience of beautiful souls and finally to the experience of Beauty itself as the transcendent principle which is invisible but is present in all visible things of beauty and is the ultimate source of their beauty. One does not have to accept the Platonic theory of Ideas as universal Forms which subsist in a realm of their own to see that he is describing the experience of all those who love beauty as something more than the "aesthetic surface" of a physical object. The sense of frustration of every great artist because he cannot capture perfectly the vision that hovers before him points in the same direction. Similarly, all moral striving seems to presuppose an absolute and perfect goodness that is never fully realized in men's conduct but

[2] Bradley, F. H., *Appearance and Reality*, New York, Macmillan, 1893, p. XIV.

that haunts them and beckons them on. Thus, the aesthetic and moral experience of man, like his religious experience, points to a transcendent Reality and Good beyond the natural world. But since religious faith apprehends directly this Reality and Good, it is the source of the highest knowledge. Without faith, all knowledge of finite reality through common sense or science becomes distorted and loses its crown of wisdom.

This is the theoretical significance of faith; its *moral significance* is equally important. Without faith the will of man is directed towards values that are near **and immediately accessible because** they belong to the world of actuality. He finds it hard, if not impossible, to conceive of a life radically different from his own or values radically different from those of the society in which he lives. But the man of faith has caught a vision of possibilities that go far beyond anything in the world of actuality, of a new life and other values which are richer and more blessed than those he knows around him. Thus, it is faith in the Christian sense which envisages a universal, "open" community in the place of the exclusive, "closed" societies in which men actually live. It sees the possibility of a more perfect love than that of even the best men. Moreover, it trusts in the mercy and power of God to bring into reality that universal community and that perfect love in the lives of men. In this way, faith transforms the moral will by setting before it higher and broader purposes than those of the self or the group and strengthening it in its efforts to realize those purposes. By subjecting the self to the will of God, faith rescues it from its self-centeredness and self-love. It frees the self from its fears and anxieties about itself and enables it to give itself in love to others. Thus, faith not only apprehends God as the transcendent Reality who gives meaning to all existence, but also awakens devotion to Him as the absolute Good which is the source of all the higher values of the moral life.

Modern rationalism has denied the necessity of faith. It has divorced reason from faith in philosophy and has not hesitated to attack faith. As a result, there has been a sharp *reaction against reason* itself on the part of certain Christian theologians. These theologians argue that modern man rejects faith in the Biblical revelation at his peril. If God is transcendent and other than man,

they say, why should man's finite and puny reason hope to demonstrate His existence or comprehend His nature? Some of these
theologians go even further. They attack the effort to know God
by reason as a sign of man's infidelity and pride. Man must set
aside the pretensions of reason and depend upon the Word of God
alone.

This is a serious error. It is true that intellectual pride is one of
the most widespread manifestations of modern secular Humanism.
But the source of this intellectual pride is not to be found in the
"pretensions of reason"; it is to be found in the pretensions of man.
Reason should not be regarded as an entity in itself, personified, and
regarded as capable of making pretensions. Reason is simply a
function of the human self. It is the function by which the self
seeks to understand reality in all its aspects, opening itself to all
of them impartially and letting each of them speak in its own way.
If so, reason should not deny revelation or dispute the right of
man to faith. It should seek to understand what has been revealed
by God in the historical events recorded in the Bible, as it tries
to understand the phenomena of the senses or the imperatives of
conscience. It should open itself to reality as a whole and try to
interpret every phase of experience without prejudice against any.

Only when this is recognized does the true relation of reason
to faith become manifest. Reason should accept the evidence of religious experience and faith for God and then seek to *understand* faith
as clearly as possible, to express its meaning in terms that are intelligible to others, and to draw out its implications for conduct.
Reason purifies our thinking about faith of false ideas, superstitions,
and inconsistencies. It relates it to our experience as a whole. In short,
reason seeks to understand faith, to relate it to the world, and to
apply it to life. Reason needs faith to enable it to affirm the
transcendent; faith needs reason to interpret the meaning of its
affirmation.

THE REPUDIATION OF MORAL PHILOSOPHY:
EMIL BRUNNER

If this is true, the objection of secular moral philosophers that
Christian ethics is authoritarian and that Christian faith is incom-

patible with reason is unwarranted. But we must also consider the objection of some *Christian theologians* against any attempt of Christian moralists to appropriate the conclusions of moral philosophers. This objection arises in large part out of a reaction against the tendency to accommodate Christian truth to secular thought or to form a synthesis between them.

The reaction against these tendencies in recent Protestant theology has led to a virtual *repudiation of philosophy* by some Christian theologians. Like Tertullian, they ask, "What has Athens to do with Jerusalem?" Perhaps the best example of this attitude in Christian ethics is to be found in Emil Brunner's *The Divine Imperative*. Since Brunner has usually shown himself more hospitable than Barth to secular thought, it might be supposed that he would be sympathetic with the efforts of moral philosophers to deal with problems of conduct. But his conclusions with respect to "philosophical ethics" are almost entirely negative. After a very brief survey of a few systems of "philosophical ethics," he concludes that each system has its values but also its defects and that any kind of "synthetic ethics" is also unsatisfactory.[1] All "natural morality," he says, necessarily leads to contradictions because of the cleavage of human life due to sin. When man makes himself independent of God, God becomes to him an alien power and His commands seem external and arbitrary. Therefore, he tries to free himself from them by means of a purely rational morality of universal laws and falls into ethical legalism. Or he develops an ethic of happiness which regards life as good in itself apart from God. In both cases, "natural morality" is a product of man's sinful rebellion against God's will. Though there are "fragments" of truth in it, each fragment "by its isolation from the whole, is itself twisted, distorted into a caricature of the original," so that "the picture presented by natural ethics is a heap of ruins."[2] Thus, philosophical ethics is virtually useless to the Christian. But this does not matter, since Christian ethics needs no help from any other source. Its own answer to the questions raised by morality is all-sufficient. "Does

---

[1] *The Divine Imperative*, copyright, 1947, by W. L. Jenkins, The Westminster Press, p. 43.
[2] Ibid., p. 67.

the Christian faith," Brunner asks, "give *the* answer, the *only* answer, and the *whole* answer to the ethical problem?"[3] His reply is an uncompromising "Yes."

This negative attitude towards "philosophical ethics" is determined, in part, by Brunner's conception of Christian ethics. Obedience to God's will, he holds, requires only one thing: love of God as expressed in love of one's neighbor. But how are we to determine what *duties* love of our neighbor requires? Brunner replies that we cannot be guided by any "principle" in deciding what the divine command of love requires in a situation. In this sense, Christian ethics has no "content." Its "content" must be discovered anew in each situation by listening to the voice of the Spirit.[4] Again, the *virtues* are possible not as a result of human achievement, but through a "new birth" in faith. Though they constitute a "permanent element" in character and possess some value, they have no positive content and consist simply in "having one's mind and heart open" to fulfill the needs of one's neighbor. Finally, the command of love is that we should serve our neighbor, Brunner says, not that we should realize *values*. Though he recognizes that values are necessary to human life, he does not attempt to make a Christian analysis of values. Thus, without rules or even "principles" of duty, virtue, or value, we are simply to open ourselves to the claims of our neighbors in each situation and listen for God's command.

Now, the real question for the Christian is not whether moral philosophy has the whole truth but whether it has important insights that must be included in the truth. As we have said, secular philosophers have often made exaggerated claims for moral philosophy, insisting that reason can discover the highest good without the aid of faith. Christians must reject these claims. But this does not justify the conclusion that, because moral philosophy does not have *all* the truth, it has *none* of the truth. Although Brunner has pointed out defects or weaknesses in a number of ethical theories, it hardly justifies him in rejecting them altogether. It is also true that there are serious contradictions between different ethical theories. There is a

[3] Ibid., p. 51.
[4] Ibid., p. 111.

contradiction, for example, between the Hedonist's view that pleasure is the only good and Kant's view that the good will is both a good and the only unconditional good. But when we are faced by such a contradiction between two theories are we simply to throw up our hands and refuse to think further about the question? Or are we to try our best to decide whether one theory is right and the other wrong, or whether both are wrong, or whether, as is often the case, one is right in a certain respect and the other is right in another respect? If we take the former course and stop thinking about the problem, we shall never arrive at or even come closer to the truth, for the road to truth lies through the patient and critical examination of opposing views. If we take the latter course, we shall find ourselves involved in philosophical reflection with all its difficulties as well as its rewards. Anyone, Christian or otherwise, may refuse to become involved in it if he wishes, but if he does refuse he has no right to an opinion on the question whether the difficulties can be solved.

Thus, Brunner's criticisms of the weaknesses and contradictions in moral philosophy are not so much false as irrelevant. Like all branches of philosophy, ethics is a continuous, cumulative intellectual enterprise, and those who engage in that enterprise may hope to broaden their understanding of moral truth even if they do not arrive at final solutions of moral problems. The fact that there is error along with truth, chaff among the wheat, does not change this fact. Indeed, not the least fruitful part of philosophical reflection is that which consists in discriminating between error and truth.

Another serious error of Brunner is his assertion that any ethical synthesis of the true insights of different theories must be eclectic and therefore superficial. Most persons who have read the classical moralists carefully and with an open mind have felt that each of them has one or more valuable insights, though their insights are often obscured by their errors. There are insights even in a moralist with a distorted vision like Epicurus or Nietzsche. Since many moralists have tended, under the influence of intellectual pride or narrowness of vision, to deny the insights in other theories than their own, it is precisely through a synthesis of insights derived from different moralists that we shall arrive at a more comprehensive ethical theory. Brunner fails to see this because he thinks that the only kind of synthesis is an eclectic one, a mere patchwork of ideas pieced together artifically without any fundamental principle to give them unity. But this is only one kind of synthesis, as the history of thought shows. Moreover, every philosophical system is in some measure a synthesis. Absolute originality in philosophy, as in other fields, is a figment of the imagination. Every philosopher must use materials furnished him by his predecessors, and some of the greatest thinkers have been primarily synthetic thinkers. Plato could hardly be called eclectic in his thought, and yet he wove into the fabric of his philosophy practically all the basic insights of his predecessors.

Despite the fact that he has such a negative attitude towards moral philosophy, Brunner himself is influenced by moral philosophy at more points than one. For example, he has a strong sympathy for Kant's ethics of Duty, though he rejects Kant's legalism. Again, he holds that principles of political and social action must be derived from reason, and he makes use of a modified version of the concept of "natural law" himself in his analysis of justice.[5] The truth is that it is impossible to avoid being influenced by moral and political philosophy whether one tries to formulate abstract principles or wrestles with concrete problems. The only question is whether one will come to terms with it consciously, or whether one will be shaped in his thinking by it unconsciously. Many a person finds himself talking philosophy without knowing it. But it is likely to be better philosophy if he knows it.

We have seen that Brunner's conception of moral philosophy is unjust. What are we to say of the adequacy of his *interpretation of Christian ethics?* His ethical insights are often so penetrating and his statement of them is so persuasive that a serious defect of his interpretation as a whole has not been sufficiently noticed. The divine command of love, he says, should not be regarded as a "principle" and what it requires in each situation cannot in any way be determined "beforehand" but must be discovered in the situation itself. He holds that if we come to a particular situation with a "principle" in our minds, we will not be sensitive to the claims of our neighbor and will not listen to the divine command coming to us in that

[5] Brunner, E., *Justice and the Social Order,* New York, Harpers, 1945, Ch. 8.

unique situation. The "principle," like a "law" or "rule," will stand between us and our neighbor as an impersonal barrier and prevent a fully personal relation with him. Consequently, we will be in danger of sacrificing his welfare to our "principle."

Now, there is undoubtedly a danger of this kind in acting from *principle*. It is well known that "men of principle" are often too calculating and that they sometimes lack sensitiveness to the unique elements in a particular situation. But this is due to the way in which they conceive and apply a principle. If a principle is conceived in a narrow and rigid way, as specifying a certain type of act without regard to the needs of the particular situation, it becomes nothing more than a rule to be applied mechanically and without study of the situation. But a principle should not be conceived and applied in this wooden, unimaginative fashion. It should be defined in broader and more general terms than a specific rule. For it is meant to tell us the general direction we are to go, not the specific road we are to take. Thus, the command to love our neighbor should always be conceived as a principle rather than a rule. It does not specify a certain kind of act; it requires many different kinds of acts appropriate to the needs of different situations and leaves us free to determine what it requires of us in each situation. Thus, it is not true, as Brunner implies, that we must determine our duty *either* by reference to a principle *or* by considering the needs of our neighbor in the concrete situation; we must bring together *both* factors, general principle and particular needs, in reaching our decision.

In reality, Brunner himself treats as principles the idea that the Christian should perform the duties of his "calling" and the idea that he should accept but improve the "created orders" of society. In a sense, therefore, his repudiation of the guidance of moral decisions by "principles" is only a verbal matter. But it is also more than that. Time and again, he speaks of each situation as if it were essentially different from every other situation and must be approached without any presuppositions. This nominalistic tendency to stress the particular at the expense of the universal aspects of moral situations leads Brunner perilously close to the abyss of irrationalism. For the discernment of one's duty he seems to depend upon the guidance of the Holy Spirit alone, without the aid of rational principles of any kind.

This seems to be due to his profound distrust of reason. As we have said, he is not consistent in the matter. He insists that, in arriving at political decisions, reason should be fully employed. But he seems to imply that in personal relationships the task of reason is over when it has considered the needs of one's neighbor in the situation. The decision itself is made under the guidance of the Holy Spirit without the aid of reason.

Since the time of Aristotle moral philosophers have recognized that there is an intuitive element in moral decision. Each must apprehend by a kind of "knack" or "insight" the act which is suitable to the particular situation and the manner in which it should be performed. But only extreme ethical Intuitionists have believed that intuition could be trusted to function without control by rational principles. Again, Christian moralists have always insisted that the illumination of our minds by the Spirit is necessary for the discernment of duty. But, here again, everything depends upon the way we conceive of that illumination. Does it replace the application of principles by reason to a particular situation, or does it make the work of reason more effective? The danger of the former conception is not only that it may deprive man of responsibility for his own decisions but also that it may emphasize spontaneous activity at the cost of deliberation and lead to the fanaticism which identifies absolutely man's interpretation of his duty with God's will for him.

Apart from the dangers of irrationalism, however, the crucial question that must be addressed to Brunner is, how can one determine one's *duty* without the help of principles? In the presence of conflicting claims from many different persons in a situation one cannot possibly meet all of them. It is not enough to say that one must open oneself to all of these claims and then listen for the command of God. He must also have principles that will help him to determine which claims are primary and how different claims can be reconciled. These principles must be derived from an analysis of the various kinds of human needs and relationships and the best methods of dealing with them. After all, if the command to love one's neighbor means that one is to serve his needs, one must use all the knowledge of his needs that is available from any source.

A similar criticism must also be made of Brunner's attitude towards *values.* He asserts that the development of a "system of values" in detail is the task not of ethics but of the philosophy of values. This is true in the sense that certain technical questions about the nature and status of values are investigated by the philosopher of value. But this does not mean that the Christian moralist should restrict himself to problems of duty and turn over all problems of value to the philosopher of value. After all, there are certain fundamental questions about values which every moralist must answer. He cannot delegate the responsibility for answering them to someone else. That Christian ethics must contain principles of value is shown by the fact that it is impossible to understand the nature of duty without reference to the values of human life. I cannot serve the needs of my neighbor, as duty requires, unless I help him to realize values. For a value fulfills a need, as we shall see, and one can fulfill a need only by producing value at the same time. Therefore, if I am to know how to serve the needs of my neighbor, I must know the values which will fulfill his needs and must be in possession of general principles which will help me to choose between different possibilities of value.

Thus, Brunner's interpretation of Christian ethics, though it contains many penetrating insights, is inadequate. A Christian, like anyone else, must have *principles* to guide him in the determination of his duty and in the realization of value. If he refuses to make use of reason to discover and apply such principles, his obedience to the command of love, however sincere, will be irrational. In his search for these principles, the Christian moralist must get whatever help from moral philosophy he can. *Reason should be the ally, not the rival, of love.*

THE CHRISTIAN'S NEED FOR MORAL PHILOSOPHY

We have attempted to show that the repudiation of "philosophical ethics" by theologians like Brunner is unjustified and that it is necessary for Christian moralists to appropriate valid insights of moral philosophers concerning duty and value if their interpretation of Christian ethics is to be adequate. "But," it may be asked, "are not Christian faith and love sufficient? If we say that they must be supplemented with principles derived from non-Christian moralists, do we not admit that Christian ethics is imperfect?"

While Christian faith and love are an adequate *basis* for all morality, they do not by themselves provide the whole *content* of morality. This does not imply that Christian ethics is imperfect. Christian ethics was never intended to be an "ethical theory" which would solve in a systematic and comprehensive manner all the problems of morality, as it was not intended to be a new code of laws specifying what men should or should not do in every kind of situation. It is part of the Gospel, and the Gospel came into the world as a religion, not a theory. Unlike Judaism and Hinduism, which are religious cultures, the Gospel was concerned almost exclusively with the relation between man and God and between man and his neighbor in the Kingdom of God. Consequently, its ethic was purely religious and had little or nothing to say about the social institutions, civic virtues, and values of culture. As we have seen, this has been the source of many difficulties and disagreements among Christians who have had to concern themselves with problems of society. If they were not to withdraw from the world, they could not avoid these problems, and yet they could find no solutions of them in the Gospel. Therefore, they were forced to look for solutions wherever they could find them. It was no accident that from the second century they went to the best social and political philosophy which was available to them and that they have continued to do so ever since.

In short, since Christian ethics defines the right relationship between man and God and between man and his neighbor, it provides the *adequate foundation* of any morality which is to stand the test of life. To hear Jesus' words and to follow him is to have one's house built upon a rock. But Christians have the *responsibility of building* upon this foundation the best and fullest lives they can, using the materials of human nature and shaping them with the help of reason and experience. In this process of building, moral philosophy, like literature and history, is indispensable to them because it contains the wisdom of serious and thoughtful men during more than two thousand years.

At what specific points can the Christian moralist hope to derive valuable help from moral philosophers? We shall attempt to answer this question in some detail in the following chapters. One of the problems with which moral philosophers have concerned themselves from the beginning has been the problem of the nature and conditions of *happiness*. We shall find that certain moral philosophers have contributed much to man's understanding of this problem. Christians may also derive much help from moral philosophers in defining principles of *value*. The New Testament does not attempt to analyze, differentiate, and rank the major values which enrich life. Since its interest is in the attainment of the Highest Good, the blessedness of the Kingdom of God, it says little about values such as truth and beauty. On the other hand, philosophers since the time of Plato have devoted much attention to the analysis of different types of value and their relations to one another. It would be strange if they should have nothing to tell Christians about the values which contribute most to the good life. Finally, Christians can derive help from moral philosophy in formulating principles for the determination of their *duties* to their neighbors and in defining the *virtues* which constitute character.

THE CHRISTIAN TRANSFORMATION
OF MORAL PHILOSOPHY

While Christians must accept the insights of moral philosophers if they are to build rich and full lives for their neighbors and themselves on the foundation of faith and love, their acceptance should be *critical* and *discriminating*. For example, they should reject Egoistic Hedonism because its conception of the good as pleasure and its view that each should seek the good for himself alone are false. On the other hand, they should accept certain elements of Kant's ethics of duty, particularly his view that the imperative of duty is "categorical" or unconditional. But the crucial question is, in what *form* should the Christian accept these elements of truth? Obviously, he cannot accept them in the form in which they appear in a secular moral philosophy, since the meaning of a true insight is often distorted or obscured by its association with false ideas. Consequently, it is necessary to disentangle it from other ideas and then restate its meaning.

For example, Aristotle contains valuable insights into the nature of moral virtue, but these should be detached from his humanistic and eudemonistic conception of the good and reinterpreted in the light of the Christian conception. Thus, insights derived from moral philosophers must be *revised* and if necessary *transformed* in order to make them consistent with Christian faith and love.

It was St. Augustine who first demonstrated this method of dealing with the insights of moral philosophy. He was able to do so because, on the one hand, he understood clearly what was new and distinctive about Christianity, and, on the other hand, he had read the Greek and Roman moralists and had reflected upon the issues they raised. In the "Confessions," he describes the way he was inspired as a young man with love for the philosophic quest by reading a treatise of Cicero[1] and how the Neo-Platonists brought him to a spiritual view of the world before his conversion.[2] What was his attitude towards the classical philosophers after his conversion? The answer is not simple. On the one hand, he was frequently critical of the conclusions of the philosophers about ethical and religious issues. He believed that reason without the illumination of faith could attain no certainty on ultimate issues and pointed out that the philosophers disagreed about these issues.[3]

On the other hand, he recognized the importance of many of the issues with which they dealt and he had obviously learned much from them. It is significant that he spent some months after his conversion in philosophic discussion with friends and that he wrote several treatises on philosophical questions. Still more important, *The City of God,* which was written during the latter part of his life, is full of discussions of philosophical issues raised by Greek and Roman thinkers. For example, he discusses the primary question of classical moral philosophy: what is the "Highest Good" for man? After criticizing the various answers to the question which had been given, he sets the Christian answer against them.[4] He also examines and rejects the political idealism of classical philosophers from Plato to Cicero with respect to justice.[5] Thus, he takes seriously the prob-

---

[1] Augustine, *Confessions,* III, Ch. IV.
[2] Ibid., VII, Chs. XIX, XX.
[3] Augustine, *The City of God,* XVIII, Ch. XLI.
[4] Ibid., XIX, Chs. I-XI.
[5] Ibid., XIX, Ch. XXI.

lems of moral and political philosophy, even if his Christian solutions differ from the pagan ones.

If the Christian moralist follows the example of St. Augustine, then, he will revise or transform the insights he accepts from the moral philosophers in order to bring them into harmony with Christian faith and love. If he fails to do so, he will produce a synthesis of elements which are really incompatible with one another. This is the fundamental weakness of St. Thomas Aquinas' attempt to make use of the Aristotelian analysis of the "moral virtues" and the Stoic conception of "natural law." In accordance with the principle that "grace does not destroy but fulfills nature," he incorporates these ethical ideas into Christian ethics and supplements them with "theological virtues" given by grace and "divine laws" revealed by God. In working out this synthesis, he displays both intellectual ability and a rare spirit of inclusiveness. Unfortunately, he distorts Christian ethics by trying to harmonize with it these classical ideas without sufficiently modifying them. Thus, his juxtaposition of unmodified Aristotelian ideas with Christian ones tends to obscure the latter.

This confirms our contention that valid insights drawn from moral philosophers must be *transformed* or "converted" before Christians can make use of them. It must be admitted that to accept and transform these insights is not as easy as to accommodate one's thinking to them, on the one hand, or to repudiate them completely, on the other. Uncritical accommodation to secular thought is easy, fatally easy, when Christians have lost their awareness of the radical difference between it and Christianity. Uncompromising repudiation is also easy and makes a strong appeal to intensely religious persons, however impossible it is to put it into practice. But the critical acceptance of ideas derived from one source and the thorough transformation of them to make them compatible with a faith and a way of life derived from a very different source is more difficult. It requires not only a combination of critical with constructive thinking, but also a *creative tension* of Christian faith and love with a generous open-mindedness to truth from every possible source. Consequently, there is always the danger that the Christian thinker, lacking one or more of these qualifications, will be able to produce nothing more than an eclectic synthesis. Despite the difficulty and the danger, however, it is necessary to follow the method of critical acceptance and transformation because it is the only method which can both maintain the principles of Christian ethics in their integrity and do justice to the indispensable insights of moral philosophy.

CHAPTER 18

Happiness

THERE are three major conceptions of happiness in Western thought: 1) that it is identical with pleasure; 2) that it is a state of well-being arising from the harmonious exercise of human functions accompanied by pleasure; and 3) that it is a spiritual state of blessedness. The first of these conceptions has been defended by the ethics of Hedonism; the second by the ethics of Aristotle; and the third by the ethics of Christianity. Moral philosophers have usually held either the first conception or the second. Both of them are products of a fundamentally humanistic view of life. "Pleasure" is regarded by Hedonists and "happiness" by Aristotelians as states which are attainable by man in the normal course of his life by the use of his natural capacities. The main difference between them is that Hedonists regard pleasure alone as the good to be sought by men, while Aristotelians believe that the fulfillment of human potentialities accompanied by pleasure is the good. More succinctly, the former regard pleasure as *the* good, the latter as *a* good or an accompaniment of the good. Christians differ from both in striving for a state of "blessedness" which is attainable only at a high spiritual level of existence and in relation to a transcendent Being and Good.

HEDONISM

The dominant form of Hedonism in modern ethics is *Utilitarianism*. It was developed in the eighteenth century by Jeremy Bentham and was modified in the nineteenth century by John Stuart Mill and Henry Sidgwick. In Utilitarianism, the Egoistic Hedonism of the Greeks was transformed into a Universalistic Hedonism. Utilitarians accept the hedonistic doctrine that pleasure is the only good, but assert that the end to be sought in moral conduct is "the greatest happiness of the greatest number" or "the greatest happiness on the whole."

Jeremy Bentham sought to develop the Utilitarian theory on the basis of an egoistic and hedonistic *theory of motivation*. Though leading moralists of the eighteenth century such as Shaftesbury and Hume had asserted that there are social impulses and sentiments as well as egoistic ones in human nature, Bentham insisted that the only motives of human actions are desire for one's own pleasure and aversion to one's own pain. Pleasure and pain are man's "sovereign masters," he says, and "it is for them alone to point out what we ought to do, as well as to determine what we shall do."[1] In this famous passage he affirms not only "psychological hedonism," the theory that pleasure *is* the motive of all actions, but also "ethical hedonism," the theory that it *ought* to be. It may be well to note at this point that "psychological hedonism" is the most obvious argument for "ethical hedonism." If men *are* always moved by desire for pleasure and aversion to pain, it is meaningless to say that they *ought* to be moved by a desire for something else. On the other hand, it is possible to reject psychological hedonism as contrary to fact and yet to accept ethical hedonism on other grounds.

The other major contribution of Bentham to the Utilitarian theory is his theory of a *hedonistic calculus* or "moral arithmetic." Pleasures differ in quantity, not in quality. If it produces an equal quantity of pleasure, "push-pin is as good as poetry." Now, according to the Utilitarian principle, an act is *right* if it is likely to produce the *maximum quantity of pleasure* and the minimum quantity of pain. The only way to determine whether a particular act is right is to measure the quantity of pleasures and pains likely to be produced by it and compare this with the quantity of pleasures and pains likely to be produced by any alternative act. In order to calculate the amount of pleasure, the amount of pain, and the surplus of pleasure

---

[1] Bentham, Jeremy, *An Introduction to the Principles of Morals and Legislation*, London, 1823, I, p. 2.

over pain resulting from each act, it is necessary to apply the principles of a "hedonistic calculus." For this purpose a number of "dimensions" or aspects of each pleasure and pain must be taken into
account: its "intensity"; its "duration"; the "probability" of its occurrence; its "proximity" or nearness in time; its "fecundity" or
tendency to be followed by other pleasures or pains; its "purity" or
lack of attendant pains if it is a pleasure or lack of pleasures if it is a
pain; and its "extent" or the number of persons affected by it.[2] If
the balance of pleasure over pain obtained by calculating in this
manner all the pleasures and pains likely to follow an act is higher
than the balance any alternative act would be likely to yield, the act
is right; if not, it is wrong.

The greatest of Bentham's disciples was *John Stuart Mill*. In his
"Utilitarianism," Mill defended the theory of his master against criticisms. But in his defense Mill restated the theory and departed at a
number of points from his teacher. He agrees with Bentham in
basing ethical hedonism upon *psychological hedonism*. Since "the
sole evidence it is possible to produce that anything is desirable is
that people do actually desire it" and since happiness is desired by
men as the end, he argues, happiness is desirable.[3]

But Mill stresses the fact that there are *differences in quality* as
well as quantity between pleasures. The criticism of Utilitarianism
as "a doctrine worthy only of swine," he says, wrongly assumes that
the pleasures of a man must be qualitatively the same as those of a
beast. But men have faculties "more elevated" than animal appetites
and the "mental pleasures" derived from these faculties are intrin-
sically superior to pleasures derived from the animal appetites.[4] What
makes one pleasure more valuable than another? Of two pleasures,
the one "to which all or almost all who have experience of both give
a decided preference" and do so "even though knowing it to be
attended with a greater amount of discontent" is superior in quality.[5]
Now, persons who are equally acquainted with and capable of appreciating different kinds of pleasures agree in preferring those which
accompany the higher faculties. Man's "sense of dignity" makes him

[2] Ibid., Ch. IV.

[4] Ibid., p. 7.

[3] Mill, J. S., *Utilitarianism,* New York, Dutton, 1914, pp. 32, 33.

[5] Ibid., p. 8.

choose them despite the fact that they may be accompanied by much suffering. "It is better to be a human being dissatisfied than a pig satisfied," Mill says, "better to be Socrates dissatisfied than a fool satisfied."[6] He even asserts that a pleasure resulting from the exercise of the higher faculties is incommensurable with a pleasure from the exercise of the lower appetites in the sense that men "would not resign it for any quantity of the other pleasure which their nature is capable of." One is not surprised, therefore, to note that he quietly drops all mention of the "hedonistic calculus" of Bentham.

Mill sees more clearly than Bentham the importance of the *inner side* of morality. Thus, he argues that *virtues* are desired in a sense as "parts" of happiness. By this he does not mean that they are intrinsic values, but that as means to happiness they become associated with it and after a time come to be regarded as parts of it. As he puts it, Utilitarians not only regard virtue "as a means to the ultimate end" but "they also recognize as a *psychological* fact the possibility of its being, *to the individual,* a good in itself, without looking to any end beyond it."[7] Thus, virtue can be "desired and cherished, not as a means to happiness, but as a part of happiness."[8] In saying that it has become "a part of happiness," Mill means that it is now accompanied by pleasure so closely that it *seems* to be an ingredient in happiness itself.

As we have seen, Mill rests his case for ethical hedonism on psychological hedonism, i.e., the fact that men actually desire their own happiness. What proof does he offer that we should desire the *general* happiness rather than merely *our own* happiness? "No reason can be given," he answers, "why the general happiness is desirable, except that each person, so far as he believes it to be attainable, desires his own happiness . . . each person's happiness is a good to that person, and the general happiness, therefore, a good to the aggregate of all persons."[9] It should be noted that this proof rests upon the premise of psychological hedonism that each person desires only his own happiness. If that premise is false, the conclusion is false. There is also a logical fallacy, which has often been pointed out, in

[6] Ibid., p. 9.
[7] Ibid., p. 33 (italics mine).
[8] Ibid., p. 34.
[9] Ibid., pp. 32-33.

arguing from the fact that *each* person desires *his own* happiness to the conclusion that the *aggregate* of all persons desires the *general* happiness. For every person might desire his own happiness without any person desiring the general happiness. In that case, the aggregate of all persons would desire the general happiness only in the sense that each person would desire *a part* of the general happiness, i.e., his own.

In making these additions and changes in the Utilitarian theory, Mill enriched and deepened it. Indeed, he almost abandoned Hedonism at times in his honest attempt to meet the objections to it. But we shall give reasons for thinking that he failed.

Psychological Hedonism

Bishop Butler refutes Psychological Hedonism by pointing out the existence, along with desires rooted in "self-love," of "disinterested" desires which are directed towards objects apart from any thought of good for the self. There are, he says, "particular movements towards particular external objects—honour, power, the harm or good of another," and "the very idea of an interested pursuit necessarily presupposes particular passions or appetites, since the very idea of interest or happiness consists in this, that an appetite or affection enjoys its object."[1] As Sidgwick puts it, "we could not pursue pleasure at all, unless we had desires for something else than pleasure; for pleasure consists in the satisfaction of just these 'disinterested' impulses."[2] This is notably true in the case of "pleasures of pursuit" such as games or scientific investigations, in which "the impulse towards pleasure, if too predominant, defeats its own aim."[3] It is also true in the case of other active pleasures. For example, the pleasures of art require an absorbing desire on the part of the artist for the creation of beauty; and "pleasures of benevolence seem to require, in order to be felt in any considerable degree, the pre-existence of a desire to do good to others for their sake and not for our own."[4]

This argument is unanswerable. Men do not always, in fact, desire either their greatest happiness on the whole or their im-

---

[1] Butler, Joseph, *Works,* Oxford, The Clarendon Press, 1896, II, pp. 22, 23.
[2] Sidgwick, H., *The Methods of Ethics,* London, Macmillan, 1884, I, p. 44.
[3] Ibid., p. 47.   [4] Ibid., pp. 47, 48.

mediate happiness. The whole dismal record of human recklessness and folly testifies that they do not always seek their *greatest* happiness but often grasp childishly at lesser pleasures that are near at hand. Nor do men always choose their *immediate* happiness. Poets are not the only men who "scorn delights and live laborious days" for the sake of a future achievement. Insofar as we aim directly at pleasures, we tend to seek them in both ways, sometimes taking those that are easy and within reach, sometimes striving for remote pleasures such as those of success and security. But normally we do not aim at pleasures of either kind. When we are healthy physically and mentally, we aim at the fulfillment of our purposes and the exercise of our powers in play and work. Pleasure is usually present in some measure, but it is subordinate to this aim. We do not set out deliberately to seek pleasure or to avoid pain; we take both of them as they come, sometimes separately, sometimes together. Ordinarily, we do not stop to ask whether what we are about to do will be more pleasant than painful. We simply assume that it is worth while to seek the objects of our various interests, whatever the pleasures and pains associated with them.

The most striking proof that we do not always seek either immediate pleasure or the greatest pleasure on the whole is self-sacrifice, which is as old as humanity itself. Doubtless, it is always possible to say that the mother would not sacrifice pleasure and even life itself for her child, the patriot for his country, or the martyr for truth, unless the act of self-sacrifice were accompanied by an exalted pleasure that seemed incommensurable with every other pleasure, or by the glorious image of future fame, or by the feeling that one could not live with oneself if one betrayed his cause or his friends. But this is an artificial explanation and one that does not really explain. *Why* should the martyr feel an exalted pleasure greater than all the other pleasures of existence? *Why* should the patriot desire the brief pleasure of contemplating his possible future fame above the lasting pleasures of life and love? *Why* should pain at the thought of betraying truth or right outweigh, with Socrates or Joan of Arc, all the pleasures of life? The explanation of conduct by the psychological hedonist turns out in such cases to be no explanation at all. Apart from "disinterested" desires for ends quite different from pleasure, e.g., devotion to truth, love of country, loyalty to duty, and concern for the welfare of others, the possibility of deriving pleasure from self-sacrifice would not exist. For it is only the presence of a "disinterested" desire for a particular end, e.g., the welfare of one's own people, that can explain why the pleasure of *this* act should be chosen, e.g., an heroic deed in battle, rather than that of some *other* act quite different, e.g., an act that insures safety.

We conclude from all of this that psychological hedonism is false. How does it arise? Its source is to be found in the fact that, while pleasure normally accompanies the satisfaction of desires for other things, it can become through reflection upon past satisfactions a secondary object of desire itself. When this occurs, pleasure may be abstracted in thought from the objects and activities which ordinarily give rise to it and may then seem to be the primary object of desire. This is only an appearance, but it may be rendered plausible, like egoism, by reference to an hypothetical unconscious motive of pleasure behind our conscious motives. The causes of this abstraction of pleasure from its normal association with other objects of desire and the substitution of it for these objects are to be found by psychological inquiry. One cause is probably the tendency of men whose interest in ordinary objects of desire has been frustrated by failure to attain them or dulled by self-indulgence to turn away from the active pursuit of them and make the sweet taste of life a substitute for life itself. Another is the theoretical desire for a single, simple explanation of the many kinds of value by means of a monistic theory of value which reduces all values to the pleasure that is the usual accompaniment of them.

Ethical Hedonism

We come now to a consideration of the fundamental principle of *Ethical Hedonism,* that men *should* make pleasure the sole end of their actions whether they actually *do* so or not. Psychological hedonism is not the only argument for ethical hedonism and Sidgwick accepted the latter while rejecting the former. Since one of the main criticisms of Ethical Hedonism from the time of Plato to the present has been that it does not account for the superiority of some activities over others and that it would give rise to a gross life unworthy of human beings, we may ask first whether Mill's qualitative distinction between higher and lower pleasures can be maintained. That Mill was pointing to something important when he made a distinction between the pleasures of a pig and those of a man, those of a fool and those of Socrates, few would deny. Bentham's assertion that, apart from difference in quantity, "push-pin is as good as poetry," is plainly false. Most persons would also agree with Mill that the difference between higher and lower pleasures is related to the difference between the higher faculties of man and the lower appetites he shares with the animals. But the difference is not between qualities of different pleasures; it is between qualities of the experiences of which pleasures are parts. C. D. Broad points out that of two experiences which have exactly the same "hedonic quality" one might be better than the other because of some difference in "non-hedonic quality" or "relational property."[1] This is probably what Mill had in mind when he stressed the fact that the superior pleasures arise through the exercise of the higher faculties of men. His mistake was simply that he attributed the differences of quality to pleasure as such rather than to the "non-hedonic qualities" and "relational properties" of pleasant experiences. If this is the case, it opens the door to the recognition that not only the hedonic quality but also other aspects of an experience have value.

This brings us to a consideration of the main argument for Ethical Hedonism. We have shown that, when it depends upon "psychological hedonism," it leans upon a broken reed. Recognizing this, Sidgwick used the quite different argument that while cognitive and volitional states of consciousness such as knowledge and virtue are actually desired, they are really "neutral in respect of desirability" when we consider them apart from the feelings of pleasure that accompany or result from them.[2] The validity of this argument depends upon the accuracy of Sidgwick's inspection of the facts of consciousness and his abstraction of feeling from the other

---

[1] Broad, C. D., *Five Types of Ethical Theory*, New York, Harpers, 1930, p. 232.
[2] Sidgwick, H., op. cit., pp. 398, 399.

elements with which it is associated. Actually, one never finds pleasure alone, as if it were a thing by itself; it is always a quality that accompanies an experience. Since the value of the experience often seems to disappear when the pleasure is absent, pleasure seems usually to be a necessary condition of it. But it is impossible to show that it is the sufficient condition of value, because there will always be some other element besides pleasure where there is value. This is conclusive against Sidgwick's argument that pleasure is the only intrinsic value. His argument falls because pleasure cannot be *abstracted* from the whole experience and shown to be the only element with value.

Moreover, it is not true, as Sidgwick asserts, that "the ordinary judgments of mankind" support Ethical Hedonism. Common sense takes it for granted that all men *do* seek their own pleasure and that they *should* seek the pleasure of others, but it does not affirm that pleasure is the only intrinsic value. Indeed, it counsels men to subordinate pleasure to wisdom, virtue, and love. It also warns them that pursuit of these higher values is hard and may require the renunciation of many pleasures. According to the prudential side of common sense, wisdom and virtue will be rewarded in the future for the sacrifices which may be necessary for their sake. But on its nobler side common sense also approves of the acceptance of poverty for the sake of truth and beauty, the renunciation of comfort and ease for the sake of love, and the sacrifice of life itself for the sake of goodness. Thus, it is false to say that knowledge, virtue, and love are approved in proportion to their productiveness of pleasure; indeed, pleasure is regarded as secondary to these values, to be sacrificed to them whenever necessary.

If we return now to Mill's qualitative distinction between pleasures, we see that it has a different and a deeper significance than he realized. The fact that a human being would not exchange his nature for that of a pig or Socrates for that of a fool, despite the fact that he is not as satisfied as he would be if he did so, means that his possibilities as a man can be fulfilled only at the cost of dissatisfaction with himself and his achievements. His spiritual nature is such as continually to urge him to transcend himself by the exercise of his higher faculties without regard to whether or not he is satisfied. If he is an artist or a poet, he is impelled to create beauty at whatever cost of struggle and pain. If he is a scientist or philosopher, he is driven to seek truth at whatever sacrifice of comfort and ease. If he is a patriot or reformer, he is ready to endure any suffering. In brief, when man lives at his best, under the control of the spiritual principle in him, he devotes himself to ideal ends in disregard of pleasure and pain. This does not mean, of course, that he is indifferent to the pleasure or impervious to the pain that comes his way. He is not inhuman; he enjoys the one and suffers from the other. But pleasure is not his aim and pain is not the worst evil to him. He is grateful for the sweetness pleasure bestows upon his existence and he suffers from the pain that afflicts him; but he has his gaze fixed upon that which is beyond pleasure and pain.

When we understand this, the "hedonistic paradox" ceases to be a paradox. If his nature as a spiritual being is fulfilled only through the ideal end he serves, he must forget pleasure and give himself to values and persons for their own sakes. It is true, as Sidgwick says, that in the case of "passive" pleasures of the senses such as relaxing after a hard climb or revelling in a warm bath the desire for pleasure does not interfere with the attainment of it, for there is no value being sought besides the pleasure of the moment itself. But in the more "active" pleasures of the mind the "hedonistic paradox" is inescapable. The artist who paints or the poet who sings must do so not to "please himself," but to "be himself" in creating that which will embody his vision and feeling. Otherwise, he becomes a sophisticated poseur with nothing to say. The lover must love not his pleasure in the beloved, but the beloved. Otherwise, he is "in love with love," i.e., with his own pleasure, and not with her. The saint must seek not his own bliss, but obedience to God and the welfare of his fellows. Otherwise, he ceases to be a saint and becomes a pious sentimentalist.

Thus, the true significance of Mill's "qualitative distinction" and Sidgwick's "hedonistic paradox" is understood only when we reject Ethical Hedonism and acknowledge other values besides pleasure. When we do so, we also gain a clearer view of the relation of *pain* to the good life. Hedonism has a purely negative conception of pain. It assumes that pain is simply an evil and that in calculating the consequences of an act the quantity of pain must be subtracted from the quantity of pleasure. But if man's good includes values that cannot be attained or enhanced without pain, we must look at pain in a different way. There is an eloquent passage in Paulsen's *System of Ethics* which states the difference, though perhaps with some exaggeration. "A life absolutely free from pain and fear would, so long as we are what we are, soon become insipid and intolerable. . . . Life would be pure satisfaction without obstacles, success without resistance. We should grow as tired of all this as we do of a game which we know we are going to win."[3] A life of ease and content "would fail to exercise and satisfy the most powerful impulses of our nature. Who would care to live without opposition and struggle? Would men prize truth itself as they do if it were attained without effort and kept alive without battle? To battle and make sacrifices for one's chosen cause constitutes a necessary element of human life."[4] We do not have to accept the ethics of Self-Realization in terms of which Paulsen has stated his point in order to recognize that it is profoundly true. The quest for pleasure alone, regardless of its source, is not in accordance with the nature of man. As a spiritual being, man has possibilities that cannot be realized without strenuous activity, frequent frustration, conflict with evil, and, consequently, pain. The ultimate reason is, not merely that other values besides pleasure are needed "to exercise and satisfy the most powerful impulses of our nature," but that man cannot fulfill the destiny for which he was created as a free spiritual being without striving for ideal ends that transcend pleasure and pain.

The Hedonistic Calculus

We have seen that both Psychological Hedonism and Ethical Hedonism are false. But we have not finished our task of criticism until we have considered the claim of Hedonists like Bentham and Sidgwick that the *calculation* of pleasures and pains is possible and desirable. For one of the great attractions of Ethical Hedonism for the scientific type of mind is that it claims to provide a way of

[3] Paulsen, Friedrich, *A System of Ethics,* New York, Scribners, 1899, p. 260.
[4] Ibid., p. 263.

determining accurately the greatest good attainable by human conduct and thus a way of overcoming men's uncertainty as to what is really right in any situation. Utilitarianism was an inspiration and guide for many social reformers in the Age of Liberalism. Was not the hedonistic calculus of Bentham an ideal instrument in the hands of the social reformer or legislator? Would it not enable him to determine with mathematical precision the probable effect of a social arrangement or law on all those affected by it? Indeed, what better principle was there to guide any public-spirited citizen than "the greatest happiness of the greatest number," especially when there was a way of discovering with accuracy how to bring it about? Even as sober a thinker as Sidgwick felt the appeal of this hope, though he saw the practical difficulties in realizing it. In our day many conscientious statesmen and private citizens still assume that "the greatest happiness of the greatest number" is the only rational basis of social justice, and, though they know that a practicable "hedonistic calculus" has not yet been developed, they sometimes long for one to put an end to their own uncertainties and to banish differences of opinion between men as to what is right.

Though one may sympathize with this hope or longing, one must recognize the futility of it. Uncertainty is an inescapable aspect of the moral life, and moral risks can never be banished by the application of any scientific device. It is not surprising, therefore, that moral philosophers have refused to accept the principles of Bentham's "hedonistic calculus." The first reason is that we cannot measure numerically the *intensity* of a pain or pleasure. "Intensities have degrees," says C. I. Lewis, "but they are not extensive or measurable magnitudes which can be added and subtracted. That is, we can—presumably—determine a serial order of more and less intense pleasures, more and less intense pains, but we cannot assign a measure to the interval between two such."[1] We could arrange them in the order of their pleasantness but we could hardly say that one was exactly twice as pleasant as another.[2] Even if it were possible to do this, there is the further difficulty that "the combina-

---

[1] Lewis, C. I., *An Analysis of Knowledge and Valuation,* La Salle, Ill., Open Court Publishing Co., 1946, p. 490.
[2] Ibid., pp. 490, 491.

tion of two pleasures or two pains in one single experience is not a calculable mathematical function of their intensities when taken separately. . . . The pleasure of good company *and* the concert is not the pleasure of the company *plus* the pleasure of the music but is the pleasure found in the total state of affairs including these constituents."[3]

Second, there are difficulties with respect to the dimension or aspect of *duration*. The duration of a pleasure or pain can be measured, but it is dubious whether the pleasure of playing a game of tennis for two hours is twice as great as the pleasure of playing it for one hour. Moreover, we remember past pleasures and anticipate future ones incorrectly, and we do not appreciate at their just value absent pleasures because they are not presented as vividly as present ones.[4]

When we remember that the "hedonistic calculus" requires us to measure *both* the intensity *and* the duration of *each* of the pleasures and pains which will be likely to result from an act and to do this for every alternative act, the complexity of the calculation begins to be understood. For example, how are we to compare pleasure A which is of great intensity but short duration with pleasure B which is of small intensity but long duration? Even if we could measure the intensities of the two pleasures in terms of a unit of intensity and the duration in terms of a unit of time, a mere multiplication of the number of units of intensity by the number of units of time in each case and a comparison of the two results would convince few persons. For there has always been sharp disagreement between those like Aristippus who prefer intense pleasures, however brief, and those like Epicurus who prefer enduring pleasures, however mild. Three minutes of a pleasure with an intensity of ten will always seem to some superior to ten minutes of a pleasure with an intensity of five, despite the fact that the quantity of the first is only thirty while that of the second is fifty.

Third, the difficulty with respect to *purity*, the freedom of a pleasure from attendant pain or of a pain from attendant pleasure, is also great. Even if we assume that the presence of an accompany-

[3] Ibid., p. 491.
[4] Ibid., 492.

ing pain always decreases the quantity of a pleasure, how are we to determine *how much* it does so? As we have seen, there is no way of measuring the intensity of a pleasure or a pain. Even if there were, it would be necessary to establish a definite relation between the unit of pleasure and the unit of pain employed, in order to determine how much must be subtracted from the quantity of pleasure because of the presence of a certain quantity of pain. Furthermore, some persons are more sensitive to pain than others, so that a greater amount would have to be subtracted from the quantity of pleasure in their cases. Above all, it is not at all certain, as we saw, that the value of an experience is always made smaller by the presence of pain. Some forms of pleasure are necessarily "impure," e.g., the pleasure of witnessing a tragedy, of mountain climbing, or of intensely loving another person. It seems paradoxical, to say the least, that these pleasures should be estimated as smaller in proportion to the pain in them; indeed, they depend for their value in many cases upon overcoming or transforming the pain.

Fourth, the *number* of those affected by an act is of crucial importance in the "hedonistic calculus." In the thinking of the Utilitarians the principle of equality, "each to count for one and only one," is regarded as essential in the distribution of pleasure among different persons. Unfortunately, the application of this principle raises difficulties. Obviously, the general principle that one should seek the good of as many persons as he can is a sound one. But it is well known that the quantity of pleasure conferred upon each of a number of persons often decreases when the number increases beyond a certain point. For example, it can hardly be maintained that a teacher confers twice as much pleasure—or knowledge— when she teaches forty pupils as when she teaches twenty. Therefore, it is misleading to multiply the amount of pleasure supposedly bestowed upon each person by the number of persons. This is true also because the same pleasure is likely to be enjoyed more or less intensely and for a longer or shorter duration by different persons in the group upon whom it is bestowed. Moreover, if each person is to count equally with every other in the distribution, the principle of "the greatest happiness of the greatest number" may result in a wide diffusion of lower pleasures at the cost of a decrease in higher pleasures. For if all that counts is the maximum amount for the maximum number, the quality of pleasures distributed is irrelevant and may be disregarded.

However, the *most fundamental* criticism of the "hedonistic calculus" is that it is based upon the assumption that the good life consists of an aggregate of the values of its various experiences rather than a whole of interrelated values. This assumption is false. Experiences are modified in value by their presence in the whole of experience. Of course, the value of the constituents also conditions the value of the whole. "But we can quite well imagine," says Lewis, "that two such wholes might be made up of constituents separately comparable in their immediate and momentary values, and yet that one might be better than the other."[5]

The conclusion we must draw from all of this is that the value of the "hedonistic calculus" is extremely limited in dealing with fundamental moral issues. The desire of the scientific mind to escape from moral uncertainty by the use of a "moral arithmetic" must be put aside. It is a result of the immense prestige of the scientific method in the modern world and the naive assumption that the method which has proved so fruitful in dealing with nature can solve the problems of man. There are, of course, some situations in which reflection upon the probable duration and intensity of the pleasure following an act may be useful in determining whether the act should be done. They are situations in which the pleasure of those affected is the *only* or the *primary* value to be considered in an act. But the calculation of pleasures and pains can never be made the primary basis of a crucial moral decision such as choosing a vocation, marrying a wife, or devoting oneself to a cause.

Virtue and Duty in Utilitarianism

In our analysis of Utilitarianism we pointed out that for Hedonists *virtues* are simply means to the end of pleasure. Similarly, a right act or *duty* is obligatory only because it is judged to be conducive to the greatest happiness. Thus, both virtues and duties have only instrumental, not intrinsic, value. Because of this definition of

[5] Lewis, op. cit., p. 495.

virtues and duties in terms of their "utility," Utilitarians have always been accused of having an "external" view of the moral life, i.e., of being concerned with acts and their consequences rather than with persons and their goodness. Mill's assertion that virtue has much to do with the worth of persons but not with the rightness of acts has failed to satisfy the critics of "utility." They are convinced that virtue or goodness of character and its expression in duty are good in themselves and good in a higher sense than pleasure.

Critics of the principle of "utility" have also made much of the danger of identifying that principle with mere "expediency." Mill defended the principle of "utility" by pointing out that duty is not to be determined by reference merely to immediate and selfish ends. This is true, but it does not answer the objection that in the practical application of the principle men are likely to consider only such ends, since virtue and duty have been dethroned from the position of primacy in morality. A closely related danger is that Utilitarianism will encourage the natural tendency to make exceptions, in our own favor, in applying the principles that define our duties. For this reason, says Bradley, it is likely "to make possible, to justify and even to encourage, an incessant practical casuistry; and that, it need scarcely be added, is the death of morality."[1] "If in certain South Sea Islands the people have not what we call 'morality,' but are very happy, is it moral or immoral to attempt to turn them from their ways?"[2] Recent developments have shown that the danger of laxity is far from hypothetical. This is illustrated by the breakdown of sexual standards due to the widespread use of contraceptives for the sake of pleasure outside marriage. Of course, a Utilitarian could argue that sexual purity and marital fidelity are required by the greatest happiness principle, since the pleasures that result from sexual abstinence before and fidelity after marriage outweigh those of sexual license when the happiness of all those affected is taken into account. But it is not at all certain that this conclusion can be justified by a calculation of pleasures and pains alone.

Thus, despite the superiority of modern Utilitarianism to the

[1] Bradley, F. H., *Ethical Studies,* Oxford, Oxford University Press, 1927, p. 109.
[2] Ibid., p. 110.

Egoistic Hedonism of the ancient world, it cannot be maintained. We have seen that *psychological hedonism* and *ethical hedonism* alike are contradicted by the facts of experience, that the *calculation of pleasures* necessary to determine "the greatest happiness of the greatest number" is impractical, and that the *subordination of virtue and duty* to pleasure endangers morality itself. Hedonism is essentially a superficial and narrow theory which flies in the face of the most fundamental facts of the moral consciousness.

HAPPINESS AS WELL-BEING

According to Aristotle, "happiness" must be distinguished from "pleasure." Instead of a series of fleeting feelings, "happiness" is a more or less permanent state of "well-being" ("eudaimonia"). Its basis is to be found in healthy activity or the *exercise of natural capacities and energies.* Normally, this brings pleasure with it not because pleasure is the aim of action, but because it is a sign of the successful development and exercise of man's natural functions.

Aristotle insisted that a sufficiency of material possessions and friends was also a necessary condition of happiness, though not its essence. But the main source of happiness is not external but *internal.* Few have been willing to follow the logic of this to the extreme conclusion of Plato, who held that a virtuous man could be happy on the rack, or the Stoics, who believed that the worst vicissitudes of fortune could not affect the tranquility of the virtuous man because he would be in complete mastery of his passions. Indifference to everything external to the soul is, humanly speaking, impossible. It comes only at a higher spiritual level than that which man can attain by the exercise of his natural capacities. However, since happiness is primarily a general state, it is not destroyed by the pains that come and go in the normal life. For the same reason, the criterion of happiness is not a balance of pleasure over pain as measured by a hedonistic calculus. While a happy life would normally be thought to be a life that is on the whole and in some degree pleasant, it is a qualitative state rather than a quantity of pleasures which can be measured and shown to be greater than the quantity of pains.

Aristotle assumes that human nature as a whole is good, although some impulses are evil and must go undeveloped. His main emphasis, however, is upon the fact that man's natural capacities must be developed and exercised *in a rational way*. Man is a being who shares his appetites with other animals but is distinguished from them by the possession of rationality. His natural capacities are to be used for ends or values approved by reason. Only through education and experience are the objects and activities most suitable to them gradually discovered; and in the process of discovering these reason plays a large part.

The natural capacities must be developed and exercised in such a way as to be *harmonious* with one another; they must be integrated into a consistent pattern or whole. This is possible only by restraining and limiting each of them by reason, imposing upon them patterns of habit in order to prevent any one of them from overwhelming the others. Thus, Aristotle's definition of happiness as "activity in accordance with virtue" is equivalent to "harmonious activity of the natural energies of man for the sake of ends and values approved by reason."

It must be added that, according to Aristotle and the modern Self-Realizationists, the ends or values sought in this harmonious and rational activity must be such as not only to realize the potentialities of the self but also to further the common good of society. For man is a *social* or "political" no less than a rational animal. He participates in the common life of his society. The worth of his existence is derived largely, if not wholly, from this fact. Consequently, the happy man is integrated not only in himself but also with his society. The manner and extent of his integration with his society may be conceived in different ways. But his happiness will always depend partially upon the exercise of his social impulses and affections. Since he is a social being, the common good is also his personal good; in serving it he is realizing his own potentialities. Though self-sacrifice may be necessary for the sake of the group, it is thought of as a higher form of self-realization.

In the modern period, under the influence of Renaissance Humanism and other forces, there has been a tendency to think of happiness in more *individualistic* terms. The Renaissance revived the classical ideal of happiness as the development and exercise of natural capacities in a harmonious fashion. But the individuality of man was often stressed at the expense of his social nature. The happiness of the individual was to be found in the development of capacities which were unique in him. Romanticism often carried this individualistic tendency to the extreme of rebellion against society. At the same time, it denied the central importance of reason as the source of happiness. Happiness was sought in the creative *imagination* and in *feeling*. Romanticism was also responsible for the idea, foreign to classical Humanism, that happiness is to be attained not through the harmonious development and exercise of all the natural capacities but through the intensive and one-sided development and exercise of one or a few of them, in accordance with the genius of the individual. It recognized that this would often lead to inner discord and tension, as well as conflict with society, but believed that only at the price of suffering can intense and exalted happiness be won. Thus, the keynote of Romanticism is intensity rather than tranquility, high moments of joy rather than stable and enduring happiness. It is obvious, therefore, that modern Renaissance individualism and Romanticism have led to a conception of happiness that is very different from that of Aristotle. Yet this conception, too, is rooted in the humanistic ideal of developing and exercising the natural capacities of man and for that reason is closer to Aristotle's than it is to either the Hedonistic or the Christian conception.

What are we to think of the idea that happiness is "the harmonious development and exercise of natural capacities and energies in accordance with ends and values approved by reason"? Obviously, it is *superior* to the idea of happiness as pleasure. It recognizes that, while the importance of pleasure in life cannot be minimized, it is not the primary value but an accompaniment of other values. The happiness of man obviously springs primarily from his experience of striving and fulfillment, of living at the highest level of his powers, in devotion to values he regards as more important than personal comfort or pleasure. These values are normally those approved by his society or by its best men, so that his devotion to them is shared with others. Moreover, happiness in this sense has as much stability and permanence as the life of a being in time can possess. For these reasons, this conception of happiness must be preferred to that of hedonism by anyone who wishes to live a distinctively human and civilized life. It is one of the great insights and contributions of Humanism.

However, a closer examination reveals serious *limitations* in it. In the first place, it presupposes a development of *rationality* which is far beyond that of most men. Reason is required both to approve the ends and values to be striven for and to restrain the natural passions by imposing patterns of virtue upon them. Otherwise, the aims of conduct will be irrational and unworthy of a human being. Plato, the noblest defender of classical Humanism, regarded happiness as a consequence of virtue but based virtue upon a knowledge of the good which could be attained only by a minority in the ruling class who are favored by nature and educated far beyond most men. Even the "auxiliaries" of the military class who were closely associated with them were capable only of "right belief" rather than "knowledge" of the good and had to depend upon the ruling class to inculcate this in them. Thus, happiness in the fullest sense was restricted to a small aristocracy of philosopher-rulers. Plato was able to minimize this restriction by insisting that each individual or class in the "Republic" should seek happiness not by and for himself but as part of the happiness of the whole. But this is a tacit admission that the happiness enjoyed by a person of the lower classes, especially the lowest, must be derived from his participation in the social whole rather than from the exercise of all his natural capacities under the guidance of his own reason. Thus, the conception of happiness we are considering is inevitably *aristocratic,* since it presupposes a degree of rationality—and, we may add, educational and other opportunities—which the majority do not possess. It is not surprising, therefore, that it has been suitable in the modern period mainly to the upper and middle classes which have had the economic means for higher education and leisure. This suggests that the development of reason and its control of the irrational in man can never be the primary source of happiness for most men.

In the second place, it must be remembered that, while the primary source of happiness is internal activity, there are also *external conditions.* Happiness in the humanistic sense of the word requires enough material things to provide opportunities for the development of natural capacities, e.g., through education, and the exercise of them in activity, e.g., in the vocation of a scholar, artist, writer, or teacher. Again, a person may be happy with few friends, but hardly with none. If he is forced to live in complete isolation from his fellows, or if he is ostracized and persecuted by them, he cannot give expression to the social impulses and needs that are such an important source of happiness. Also, few persons who have been blessed from childhood with health can possibly realize how large a part it plays in ordinary human happiness. Apart from the general sense of well-being that pervades their lives, usually unconsciously, health enables them to develop and exercise their natural capacities undistracted and unimpeded by annoying bodily disturbances. It bestows upon them a sense of security through their ability to carry out their purposes without serious interruption and they enjoy a steady feeling of fulfillment in the process of doing so. Thus, health makes it possible both to enjoy the present and to look towards the future with hope and confidence rather than fear and anxiety. If one wants to know how a complete loss of health, as distinguished from an occasional illness, may affect well-being, one has only to consider the effect of an incurable disease accompanied by racking pain. The Stoics asserted that, since inner virtue is the source of tranquility, even the worst misfortunes cannot destroy it. But St. Augustine was quick to point out that their justification of suicide as a "way out" belied their professed conviction.

Thus, an adequate measure of material goods, friends, and relatively good health are indispensable conditions of happiness, in Aristotle's sense of the term. But any realistic observer of human life, past and present, knows that all of these conditions together have been and are present in the lives of only a minority of men. Even among a people favored like ourselves by a high standard of living, leisure for friendship, and advanced medical science, most men are lacking one or more of them. And when one reflects upon the poverty, the social evils, and the diseases which afflict less favored peoples, one sees that we are a privileged minority of mankind.

But, in the third place, many men would not be happy even if all the external conditions were present, because of their *lack of spiritual aspiration* which is essential for the development and exercise of the most distinctive natural capacities of man. It is not merely that most men do not have the degree of rationality to seek ends approved by reason and to discipline their animal impulses in the process; it is also that they do not have a sufficiently strong devotion to the values that fulfill the spiritual needs of man, e.g., truth, beauty, goodness and love. The Humanism of Plato is based upon the assumption that man is not only in possession of reason ("nous") which can know truth but also of love ("eros") which aspires to beauty and goodness as well as truth. However, he recognizes that the capacity for spiritual love of this kind ("the heavenly Aphrodite") as distinguished from physical love ("the earthly Aphrodite") is as limited as the capacity for reason.

It follows from this that the conception of happiness as the development and exercise of natural capacities, insofar as the higher spiritual capacities are included and given an important place, is based upon an ideal that is noble but unattainable by most men without the aid of divine grace. For it is *sin* which is and always has been the main enemy of man's happiness. It sets him against his fellows, and, since he is a social being, divides him against himself. It is compatible with the development of high capacities such as reason and imagination and the attainment thereby of values such as truth and beauty. But it often prevents man from using these for ends beyond his own pleasure or aggrandizement. There is no evidence that the improvement of the external conditions of his life will eliminate this basic internal cause of unhappiness, though it may aid him in his struggle against it. It is due primarily to a condition in his own will and until this is removed it will show itself in any Eden or Utopia in which he finds himself.

Finally, we come to the fourth and most fundamental criticism of the humanistic conception of happiness. The main point of all three of the preceding criticisms is that, because of internal weaknesses or the lack of favorable external conditions, most men are unable to attain complete happiness through the development and exercise of their natural capacities. But even if they could, happiness attained in this manner would not be the highest happiness possible for man, for it would be a happiness won without a radical reorientation of the self. It would be a sign of the fulfillment of the natural capacities of man as a rational and social animal, but this might be accompanied by a *failure to transcend himself* by union with and devotion to a meaning and purpose that is more than human. As a spiritual being, man's nature can fulfill itself only through faith in and devotion to a universal purpose which is more inclusive and enduring than any of the values of ordinary human existence. The happiness man *should* seek, as distinguished from that which he *does* seek, must be a happiness arising from his transcendence of himself through such faith and devotion. It is possible only through the reorientation of his will from self-centered concern for his own fulfillment to disinterested concern for the fulfillment of others. As we saw, the conception of Aristotle is that the individual finds his personal good by participation in the common good. Though this is an advance over crude egoism, it does not overcome the subtle egoism that seeks the common good because it is also one's own good. Thus, the basic weakness of the Aristotelian humanistic view of happiness is that it tends to foster *egoism* and is unable to do justice to the paradox that the highest self-fulfillment comes only through self-renunciation and self-sacrifice and that the purest joy is compatible with suffering. This is the insight behind the religious conception of "blessedness."

BLESSEDNESS

Christian *blessedness* is not, like pleasure, a product of natural existence. It does not depend upon good fortune, prosperity, comfort, or success. Consequently, it is not destroyed by the adversity which takes away these things. Nor is it, like happiness, a product of human activity, something a man can win by his own effort. Rather, it is a *gift of God,* bearing little relation to the external conditions of a man's life or the level of his intellectual achievement.

The source of blessedness is *faith in God* and *participation in the new life of the Kingdom.* Twice in the Beatitudes men are called by Jesus "blessed" on the ground that "theirs is the Kingdom of heaven."[1] Life in the Kingdom is the Highest Good; it is a treasure which is greater than all earthly treasures. Even in the present it in-

[1] Mtt. 5:3, 10.

volves fellowship with God and faith that nothing can separate one from the love of God. "We know," says St. Paul, "that in everything God works for good with those who love him, who are called according to his purpose."[2] In the same passage he expresses his assurance that nothing "will be able to separate us from the love of God in Christ Jesus our Lord."[3]

While the joy of the Christian arises from the present experience of new life, it is sustained and elevated by *hope for the future*. The Christian is already enjoying by anticipation the blessings of the Kingdom, but its consummation is still to come. Thus, the Beatitudes are not only descriptions of the members of the Kingdom; they are also promises of its blessings. Those who mourn shall be comforted, the meek shall inherit the earth, the hungry shall be filled, the pure in heart shall see God, and the peacemakers shall be called sons of God.[4] The eschatological emphasis is also strong in St. Paul. To the Philippians he writes, "For his sake I have suffered the loss of all things . . . that if possible I may attain the resurrection from the dead";[5] and he reminds them that "our commonwealth is in heaven, and from it we await a Savior, the Lord Jesus Christ."[6] As we have seen, this hope for the future must take a somewhat different form for modern Christians who do not believe the coming of the Kingdom to be imminent. But they can look forward in hope to the fulfillment of God's purpose in some way which they cannot understand. The life of the Christian is the life of a pilgrim.

However, the Christian's joy in present and future blessings of the Kingdom is in no way incompatible with joy in *earthly blessings*. In the prayer of General Thanksgiving in the *Book of Common Prayer,* Christians bless God for their "creation, preservation and all the blessings of this life" as well as for "the hope of glory." Theologians who speak only of Redemption through Christ and are silent about the innumerable blessings of Creation and Providence are guilty of truncating the Gospel. Faith in our final salvation in the Kingdom should deepen our assurance of God's love for us here and now. He

---

[2] Rom. 8:28.
[3] Ibid., 8:39.
[4] Mtt. 5:4-9.

[5] Phil. 3:8, 11.
[6] Ibid., 3:20.

has given us the good things of life for our use and enjoyment. Of course, we must not become so enamored of them as to seek our highest good in them and become unwilling to part with them. But love of God, instead of making us indifferent to the value of His creatures, should make us love them and rejoice in them. There is more than a hint of this in Jesus' attitude towards the processes of nature and the drama of human life. And St. Francis, one of the greatest of the saints, loved not only God and men but also animals and inanimate things. Thus, the blessedness of the Kingdom does not exclude the simple pleasures of natural and human existence. The value of Hedonism lies in its reminder that life, despite its evils, is good. The Christian should never allow his awareness of the tragic reality of sin and death to make him morbid or gloomy, as if this world were only a vale of tears.

In the Beatitudes, Jesus has described the *qualities* of men who are "blessed." They are sharply opposed to the qualities which are praised most highly by the world and regarded as conditions of success. Poverty of spirit or humility and meekness or lack of aggressiveness are among the most striking of these qualities. They involve the conquest of self-love and pride which are the sources of so much misery to the self and others. However, there is nothing passive about the "blessed." They are merciful like the Samaritan, showing mercy in their deeds as well as feeling it in their hearts, and they are peacemakers who reconcile men with one another. One of the most fundamental qualities is purity of heart. This may refer in part to the lack of wrong desires, but its primary meaning seems to be single-mindedness. Only those who love God with all their heart, mind, and strength, without inner division or duplicity, can be "blessed." Thus, the secret of blessedness is a wholehearted trust in God which leads one to give up all claims for himself and to surrender his life completely to God as an instrument of His love.

The *paradox* of the Christian life and its blessedness is best expressed in Jesus' saying, "whoever loses his life for my sake and the gospel's will save it."[7] The highest joy springs not so much from being loved as from loving. "It is more blessed to give than to receive." For it is through loving and giving that one escapes from the

[7] Mk. 8:35.

prison of self-centeredness, forgets himself and his private cares, and participates in the redemptive work of God in human life.

The joy of the Christian is not destroyed by *pain* and *sorrow*. This is the point at which the contrast between Christian joy and both pleasure and happiness is most striking. "Blessed are they that mourn," says Jesus, "for they shall be comforted." It is not certain what kind of mourning he had in mind. Dr. Buttrick suggests that he may have been thinking of those who identify themselves with the pain and sorrow of others, who "weep with those who weep," as well as of those who mourn for their own sins and the sins of others.[8] The significant thing is that their mourning does not prevent them from being "blessed." In the eighth Beatitude, Jesus seems to go even further. "Blessed are those who are persecuted for righteousness' sake."[9] Next to physical torment and death itself, the complete disapproval and hostility of others is perhaps the most painful experience in the life of normal men. But it is compatible with the blessedness of the Kingdom.

Worldly men scoff at this, as they scoff at Plato's picture of the virtuous man who is happy even on the rack. They cannot see how a person could possibly know joy despite the presence of acute mental or physical pain. For health, as we have seen, is one of the most important conditions of happiness or well-being. Social acceptance is equally important, perhaps more important. Nevertheless, there have been many Christians who have endured great physical torment from incurable disease with an amazing serenity and whose trust in the love of God has brought them blessedness. And the lives of saints and martyrs abound with stories of joy in the presence of persecution and death.

St. Paul describes himself "as sorrowful, yet always rejoicing; as poor, yet making many rich; as having nothing, and yet possessing everything."[10] How is it possible to be "sorrowful" and yet "always rejoicing"? Part of the answer is to be found in the next clause, "as poor, yet making many rich." St. Paul derived great joy as a missionary from thinking about his converts and the new life into which

---

[8] *Interpreter's Bible,* Vol. 7, p. 281.
[9] Mtt. 5:10.
[10] II Cor. 6:10.

he had led them. But the full explanation of his paradox of joy through suffering is found in his description of himself as "having nothing, and yet possessing everything." He who participates in the life of the Kingdom, living in fellowship with God and in love with his neighbors, has the greatest of all treasures. Although he has "nothing" in the eyes of the world, he possesses "everything" that really matters. This seems to have been one of the reasons St. Francis glorified Lady Poverty. Through the renunciation of every earthly "thing" he had come to know that the pure joy of loving God and imitating Christ perfectly was "everything."

Thus, Christian blessedness is an inner spiritual state which is based upon faith in God's love manifested in Christ and upon the conviction that nothing can separate us from that love. As such, it is not, like pleasure and happiness, at the mercy of time and circumstance. Through participation in the new life of the Kingdom, the Christian already knows the highest joy this life affords. At the same time, he looks forward with hope to the completion of his joy. He knows through faith the deepest secret of the spiritual life, that self-fulfillment comes through self-denial and self-surrender, that giving himself to others in love and spending himself in their service is the source of true life. This is why, though he suffers like other men, it is not impossible for him to maintain his joy and peace.

Although this conception is inconsistent with the hedonistic view of happiness as pleasure, it is quite compatible with full enjoyment of the pleasures which come to the religious man in the course of his life. Although it is inconsistent with the humanistic view that happiness through exercise of one's natural capacities is the primary aim of life, it is not opposed to the humanistic ideal of developing one's natural capacities, using them creatively, and enjoying the happiness which normally accompanies this activity. However, it points to a deeper and purer joy which is independent of all natural pleasure and happiness and which can be maintained despite the loss of these because its source is in God. Since it is not bestowed by nature or achieved by man, it cannot be taken away by the indifference of the one or the frailty of the other.

CHAPTER 19

Duty: Its Nature and Problems

THE PREJUDICE AGAINST DUTY

FOR more than a century most moral philosophers have shunned the problem of duty and concentrated upon the problem of values. There have been exceptions, of course. At the end of the last century F. H. Bradley made an eloquent defense of the conservative principle "my station and its duties,"[1] and in our own time W. D. Ross has taken seriously the problem of what it is "right" to do.[2] But most moral philosophers since Kant who have dealt with the nature of duty have thought of it not in terms of an unconditional obligation to do a certain act, but as a means to the ends or values men seek to attain. They have shown little or no appreciation of the intrinsic value of duty or of the good will which manifests itself in the conscientious performance of duties. Thus, the inner side of morality has been subordinated to the outer. Ethics has been concerned with goods or values rather than goodness. What is the reason for this? Is it that duty has been associated with dullness, with the unexciting performance of monotonous and burdensome tasks? Is it that duty seems to many a prosaic and uninspired thing, which goes against the grain of natural inclination and is at best a necessary evil?

There were historical causes for the neglect of the problem of duty by moralists. At the end of the eighteenth century, there

[1] Bradley, F. H., *Ethical Studies,* Oxford, The Clarendon Press, 1927, Ch. V.
[2] Ross, W. D., *The Right and the Good,* Oxford, The Clarendon Press, 1930.

was a vigorous reaction against the idea that men's lives should be dominated by laws or forced into formal patterns of any kind. In art and literature, this manifested itself in the rebellion of Romanticists against classical forms and rules which had been regarded as universally valid. The claims of individuality and spontaneity were strongly asserted. This rebellion also affected the attitude of the Romanticists towards duty. The poet Schiller attacked Kant's ethics of duty and argued that the "beautiful soul" is spontaneously good.

The Romanticists were not all of one mind on this matter. In his "Ode to Duty," Wordsworth seems to have turned away from his earlier emphasis upon natural impulse and feeling to a more sober submission to the restraint of duty, which is exalted as the "Stern Daughter of the Voice of God." Admitting that in his love of freedom he has often refused to heed the mandate of duty, he now supplicates her to control him so that he may no longer be at the mercy of "chance desires" and hopes which "change their name" but may enjoy "a repose that ever is the same." He accepts restraint because it is needed to create in him a wiser and stronger will:

"Denial and restraint I prize
No farther than they breed a second Will more wise."

While duty is a "stern Lawgiver," her laws do not destroy his freedom, and he can speak of her "benignant grace." By creating a stable and wise will, she makes possible a responsible freedom.

But Wordsworth's attitude did not prevail. To the Victorians, duty was everything, but they conceived it unimaginatively as submission to the rules of social morality. These rules were enforced by the powerful sanctions of social approval and disapproval and left little room for spontaneity. As a result, the Romantic revolt against duty in the name of individual freedom and spontaneity continued. Just as science and religion, reason and faith were opposed to one another in the realm of knowledge, so the head and the heart, duty and impulse were set against one another in the realm of practice.

Moral philosophy and Christian ethics alike have suffered from this dualism of duty and spontaneity. Most *moral philosophers* since Kant have subordinated the performance of duties to the realization of values. They have rejected the traditional conception of duty in terms of universal moral laws imposed by revelation or reason upon the individual without regard for human values, but have made little effort to formulate a more adequate conception. On the other hand, most *Christian moralists* have been unable to free themselves from the traditional legalistic view and relate duty to the needs and values of men. Thus, a philosophical ethic of Value without a strong sense of duty behind it has been pitted against a religious ethic of Duty without a deep appreciation of human values.

This raises the question, can a conception of duty be developed which does justice to the element of restraint implied in obligation, but frees it from its traditional association with legalism and shows it to be necessary to the fulfillment of human needs and values? Can the dualism of duty and spontaneity and the association of duty with dull and uninspired conformity be overcome?

THE CATEGORICAL IMPERATIVE: IMMANUEL KANT

Before we propose such a conception of duty, it will be wise to consider the theory of Immanuel Kant, the greatest modern defender of the ethics of Duty. It is well known that, as the ethics of Value originated with the Greek philosophers, the ethics of Duty began with the Hebrew lawgivers. Of course, some of the Greek thinkers manifested a strong sense of duty, as we see in Socrates' obedience to the laws of Athens in the *Crito,* in the appeal to a law above the laws of the state in Sophocles' *Antigone,* and in the Stoics. Nevertheless, it was the Hebrews who taught Western man to think of duty as obedience to the will of God and the name of Moses has always been associated with the interpretation of God's will in terms of laws.

While Kant's ethics of Duty owed much to Jewish and Christian ethical legalism, he fully accepted the assumption of his age that ethical principles must be based upon *reason* rather than revelation.

In his *Metaphysic of Morality,* he begins with the assertion that there is nothing which can be regarded as "good without qualification" except a *good will.* "Talents of the mind" such as intelligence and "gifts of fortune" such as riches and honor are good only on condition of the presence of a good will. On the other hand, the good will is good in itself. Even if it produced no beneficial results, it would still shine, like a jewel, by its own light. A good will is one which acts from duty or does its *duty for duty's sake.* When the good will does an act for the sake of duty rather than from a natural inclination to happiness, it acts on a "maxim" or principle of a purely "formal" kind, i.e., a principle from which every consideration of an end beyond the act itself is excluded. It acts from *respect for the moral law* itself or with "the conformity of its actions to law in general"[1] as its principle.

Since men's natural desires resist the moral law, it appears to them as a *categorical imperative* which commands acts for their own sakes without reference to any ends beyond themselves. If it is to be universally valid, the categorical imperative must have its origin in *practical reason* in independence of experience. The practical reason must consider only the *form* of the act and disregard its concrete purpose, end, or consequences.

The categorical imperative, so conceived, can contain nothing but the general principle that the maxim of every act should conform to universal law. Therefore, Kant holds that there is but one categorical imperative. The *first* formula he offers for it is: "Act only on that maxim whereby thou canst at the same time will that it should become a universal law."[2] All duties can be derived from this one imperative as their principle. For example, forced by necessity to borrow money but knowing that he will be unable to repay it, a man asks himself whether it is consistent with duty for him to promise to repay it. He sees at once that the maxim or principle of this action could not be willed to become a universal law because it would contradict itself. "For supposing it to be a universal law that everyone when he thinks himself in a diffi-

---

[1] *Kant's Theory of Ethics,* tr. by Abbott, London, Longmans, Green, 1909, p. 21. Used by permission of the publishers.
[2] Ibid., p. 18.

culty should be able to promise whatever he pleases, with the purpose of not keeping his promise, the promise itself would become impossible as well as the end that one might have in view in it, since no one would consider that anything was promised to him, but would ridicule all such statements as vain pretenses."[3]

Kant also offers other formulations of the categorical imperative. The *second* formula is: "So act as to treat humanity whether in thine own person or in that of any other, in every case as an end withal, never as means only."[4] The basis of this formula, Kant tells us, is that a "person" differs from a "thing" in that he is a rational being capable of acting from respect for the moral law. As such, he is an "end in himself," and, since he determines his own ends or purposes, he is a "subject of ends." This suggests to Kant a *third* formulation of the categorical imperative, based upon the idea of "the autonomy of the will" of every rational being which is capable of laying down universal moral laws. "Always so act that the will could at the same time regard itself as giving in its maxims universal laws."[5] Finally, Kant suggests that all moral action is based upon legislation which would make possible a "Kingdom of ends," a "union of different rational beings in a system of common laws."[6] This leads to what he calls a "complete characterization," namely, "that all maxims ought by their own legislation to harmonize with a possible kingdom of ends as with a kingdom of nature."[7]

When the first formula is interpreted in the light of the last three, it becomes more significant. If considered by itself, it seems to isolate entirely the *form* of the good will, i.e., the conformity of its maxims to universal law, from the ends and purposes of human life. However, when conformity to law is regarded as an indispensable condition of a community of persons who respect one another and one another's ends, it is more intelligible. However, Kant did not stress the *content* of ends and values in the moral life or make clear the relation of the form of the good will to these ends and values. In his later treatise *Metaphysical Elements*

[3] Ibid., p. 40.
[4] Ibid., p. 47.
[5] Ibid., p. 52.

[6] Ibid., p. 51.
[7] Ibid., p. 55.

of Ethics, he does speak of rational or moral purposes, as distinguished from the purposes that arise out of natural inclinations. He calls these moral purposes "ends which are also duties."[8] They are: "our own perfection" and "the happiness of others." If this conception of purposes or ends which are also duties had been developed further, Kant's ethical theory might have been very different. But it was never developed.

The strength of Kant's ethical theory has seldom been disputed, even by its critics. Few moralists have been as keenly aware as Kant of the *reality of duty* and of our *unconditional obligation* to fulfill it. This awareness is accompanied by a feeling of the sublimity of the moral law which makes him speak of "awe" and "respect" or "reverence" for it. It is the source of his sharp rejection of all ethical theories which confuse morality with expediency and thereby degrade duty and the good will into mere means to values that are not moral. His awareness of the reality of duty also leads to his repudiation of every type of subjectivism in ethics which would reduce duty to a natural feeling, sentiment, or desire. Moreover, there is a genuine *practical value* in the categorical imperative. It demands that we determine our duty with impartiality, respect other persons as ends in themselves, and further their ends as members of a community of persons. Thus, Kant has set forth some of the major aspects of the moral life in a convincing and unforgettable way.

Nevertheless, Kant's theory is inadequate in several respects. (1) The theory that the good will acts from the *motive of duty alone* is false. True, Kant has often been misunderstood on this point. He did not mean that the presence, along with the sense of duty, of a natural inclination or feeling moving us to do an act for an end beyond itself necessarily disqualifies it from being a dutiful act. All that is necessary is that it be done wholly because it is one's duty and not because of the inclination or feeling. But it is simply not true that the only motive for doing one's duty is the sense of duty or duty for duty's sake. All that is essential to the moral worth of an act is that even if there is no natural inclination or feeling moving us to do our duty, we should do it

[8] Abbott, op. cit., p. 295.

just the same. The goal of moral education, indeed, is to develop a will which does its duty as spontaneously as possible without having on every occasion to struggle against a natural inclination. Paton attempts to defend Kant's view by arguing that other motives than duty are undependable and arbitrary, e.g., "good-hearted mothers have spoilt many children through lack of other requisite qualities."[9] This amounts to saying that natural love, compassion, generosity, and other motives cannot always be depended upon by themselves to make one do one's duty. But this proves only that feeling or impulse cannot be depended upon as the *sole* motive, not that it cannot be a motive for duty. Moreover, Kant's criticism of natural feeling or impulse as arbitrary does not apply to Christian love, which is a settled disposition of the will and an imperative itself. One of the greatest weaknesses of his ethics is that he tended to identify love with natural feeling, overlooking the fact that love can be spiritual.

(2) The most common criticism of Kant's ethics is that it is concerned too much with the *form* and too little with the *content* of the moral life. Kant says explicitly that the moral worth of an action lies "in the principle of the will without regard to the ends which can be attained by the action."[10] The fact that there is a *reference* to ends and consequences in the maxim, as Paton points out,[11] does not free Kant from the charge of formalism since he insists upon a *disregard* of these in determining one's duty.

It is simply false to say that the moral quality of an act does not depend in part upon the intended ends or consequences. To speak of its moral value apart from its relation to its consequences is a meaningless abstraction. We do often ask ourselves whether the principle of an act we are contemplating can be universalized, i.e., whether we could will others who were in our situation and were like ourselves in all essential respects to do it. It is something like this test which Jesus seems to have had in mind in the "Golden Rule": "Whatever you wish that men would do to you, do so

---

[9] Paton, H. J., *The Categorical Imperative,* Chicago, University of Chicago Press, 1948, p. 54.
[10] Abbott, op. cit., p. 16.
[11] Paton, ibid., pp. 135, 136.

to them."[12] We need the test of consistency to help us avoid exceptions in our own favor. If we see on other grounds that an act is our duty, the test of consistency can help us to do it instead of avoiding it. But the test alone cannot tell us that it is our duty.

Does Kant mean that we are to conform our will to universal laws which are to be followed under *all* circumstances or only under circumstances *like our own?* He has usually been interpreted in the former sense, as if he meant that specific moral rules are as universal as the one categorical imperative. If this interpretation of his meaning is correct, he is an inflexible *rigorist* in his view of moral rules, holding that certain kinds of acts are always and under all circumstances right and others wrong. The moral life is bound by rigorism as in a strait-jacket, intelligent adaptation of acts to the needs of particular situations is impossible, and creativity in moral conduct is sacrificed. On the other hand, Kant may possibly have meant that a moral rule is to be applied only in situations where similar circumstances exist and that these circumstances are to be specified in the rule itself or in subsidiary rules. In favor of this interpretation is the fact that sometimes circumstances seem to be specified in his statement of a maxim which is to be put to the test of universality. Thus, in the example of the man contemplating suicide it is specified that he has been "reduced to despair by a series of misfortunes" so that he "feels wearied of life," and his maxim is "to shorten my life when its longer duration is likely to bring more evil than satisfaction."[13] This interpretation would escape the charge of rigorism but would make an elaborate system of *casuistry* necessary. For if moral rules hold only under specified circumstances, it is necessary to state fully what the circumstances are. Otherwise, there would be no principle by which a justifiable exception to the rule could be distinguished from an unjustifiable one. But it is impossible to determine fully all the circumstances which would justify an exception to a rule.

We conclude that the consistency of an act with universal law is often useful as a practical test to secure impartiality, but that it is neither the essence nor an adequate criterion of duty. It is

[12] Mtt. 7:12; Lk. 6:31.
[13] Abbott, ibid., p. 39.

not the *essence* of duty because of its *formalism*. It is not an adequate *criterion* of duty because it either leads to *rigorism* with respect to specific rules or involves us in endless *casuistry* in applying them.

However, Kant was not wholly unconcerned with the *content* of ends and purposes aimed at by the good will. Paton has done real service in emphasizing the fact that the good will furthers a systematic harmony of the ends and purposes of all persons. This raises the question whether Kant escapes from the formalism we have criticized by finding the criterion of the good will ultimately in its coherence with the ends and purposes of the "kingdom of ends."

It seems to me that he does not. Like consistency with universal law, *coherence* with the system of ends is a formal principle. It tells us that in all our acts we are to limit our ends in order to harmonize them with the treatment of other persons as ends and with the fulfillment of their ends. But it does not tell us *what* the treatment of persons as ends requires or *what* ends of theirs we are to further. It is true, as we saw, that in his last treatise on ethics Kant speaks of two "ends which are also duties," the perfection of one's self and the happiness of others. But this is far from adequate as a guide in determining our duty either to ourselves or to others. What constitutes the "perfection" of one's self? Is it the fulfillment of *all* or only of *some* of the potentialities of the self? If all, evil as well as good potentialities must be fulfilled. If only some, we must know which ones and in what order. Again, what constitutes the "happiness" of others? Are we to further the happiness of each person by satisfying all his interests? If not, which interests are we to satisfy and which are we not to satisfy? Thus, the fact that the will of a person is coherent with itself and with the wills of other persons is not necessarily a guarantee that it is a good will. It might be if the self and the others had only good purposes, but it would not be if they had bad or trivial purposes. Hence, the principle of coherence with a kingdom of ends is as formalistic as the principle of conformity to universal laws.

(3) We have reserved to the last a criticism of Kant's ethics which has always been felt but has seldom been emphasized by

philosophers. It has to do with his *legalism*. The fact that Kant takes it for granted that duty is to be defined in terms of law is an evidence of the deep influence of Jewish and Christian legalism upon him. He was also influenced by his conception of *political justice* as a system of rights and duties defined by law to preserve the liberty of all persons. Paton points out that the Age of Revolution was one of the great formative forces in Kant's thinking, especially his "passionate insistence upon freedom as the basis of all progress and all morality."[14] Any system of social justice which is to preserve freedom for all must be embodied in laws to limit the natural inclinations of individuals and transform irresponsible into responsible freedom. Kant's use of terms like "universal laws," "legislation" and "kingdom of ends" shows the influence of his conception of political justice upon his ethical theory. This is borne out by his strong emphasis upon justice in his *Lectures on Ethics*. Because men who habitually do their duties from benevolence are not always as sensitive to the rights of others as those who do them from justice, Kant says, the duty of justice is prior to the duty of benevolence. "There is nothing in the world so sacred as the rights of others. Generosity is a superfluity. A man who is never generous but never trespasses on the rights of his fellows is still an honest man, and if everyone were like him there would be no poor in the world. But let a man be kind and generous all his life and commit but one act of injustice to an individual, and all his acts of generosity cannot wipe out that one injustice."[15]

This indicates both the strength and the weakness of Kant's legalistic ethic. Its strength lies in the fact that there can be no stable and unified society where there is no respect for persons and where their rights are not protected by corresponding duties of others defined by law. But the insistence upon conformity with universal laws makes no allowance for the special talents and needs of individuals, and an ethic based upon universal law leaves decisions on many points of personal duty without the guidance

[14] Paton, op. cit., p. 196.
[15] Kant, Immanuel, *Lectures on Ethics*, tr. by Louis Infield, New York, Century, 1930, p. 211.

of any principle. Again, the first aim of this kind of morality is the restraint of egoism, and it depends upon reason alone to realize this aim. But to curb natural inclinations without enlisting the emotional energies of the self in the service of a higher good is a negative method and is sure to fail in the case of men with strong passion and vivid imagination. "Respect" for the moral law and for persons as bearers of it is not adequate to enlist these energies. It inspires men with no vision of a positive ideal to be realized, no enthusiasm for higher values and purposes to which they can devote themselves. Yet, as we have seen, Kant refuses the aid of natural impulses and sentiments such as compassion and generosity, and even spiritual love, as motives for duty.

Ironically, the influence of his ethics has been due in large part to the fact that, despite his legalism and his rejection of every motive but duty, his assertion of the dignity of persons as ends in themselves and of the ideal of a universal kingdom of ends has appealed to deep human feelings and aspirations. The "dignity" of the individual person as an end in himself is a secular expression of the Christian belief in the worth of the individual in the sight of God. The ideal of a "kingdom of ends" is manifestly reminiscent of the Christian hope for "the Kingdom of God." But sympathy, love, and compassion must provide the psychological basis of community between persons without which it is impossible for reason to establish moral laws. Kant will always command the respect of good men because he was filled with awe in the presence of the moral law and refused to compromise its claims. But his conception of morality will never satisfy the hunger and thirst of men for that higher goodness which transcends the demands of every law except the law of love.

DUTY AS FULFILLMENT OF NEEDS

In rejecting the legalism of Kant, we do not mean to imply that moral laws or rules have no place in the moral life. Indeed, we have argued[1] that moral laws, especially those of the Old and New Testaments, have an important, though secondary, role in deter-

[1] Ch. VI.

mining our duties. But moral laws must be regarded by Christians as counsels and aids which are to be held in respect and used in a spirit of liberty. The primary task in determining one's duty is not to find a single moral rule which is applicable to one's situation as a situation of a certain type. It is to analyze one's situation in its own terms to discover how one can best respond to its demands in accordance with God's will. The demands to which one is to respond are always, for the Christian, those of persons. Far from being a mere matter of conformity to an impersonal code or pattern of rules, duty is a matter of personal decision as to the way one can best serve persons. With the aid of this principle, let us now analyze the nature of duty and deal with some of the problems of duty.

A "duty" is an act which one is under *obligation* to do. In the legal sense, an obligation is an act one is bound by law to do or not do, something he *must* do or not do unless he is to suffer a penalty. In the moral sense, however, it is an act he *ought* to do or not do; something due from him though he may refuse to do it. For the Christian, duty also involves *responsibility* to God, the ultimate Ground of all obligation, and is required of him by *obedience* to God. Even good men who are not Christians regard duty as an imperative which is binding upon them, for the sense of duty is not a mere subjective feeling; it is rooted in objective reality.

What constitutes a duty? It is not adequate to say with ethical Intuitionists that a duty is an act we see intuitively to be the right act to do, or to say with Utilitarians that a duty is an act which is likely to produce the greatest good on the whole. The Intuitionist answer is no answer at all, because it does not tell us *why* the act is right to do. The Utilitarian answer is inadequate because it tells us only that the act will bring us something we *want* but does not tell us why we *ought* to do it.

The true answer is so simple that it has often been overlooked. It starts with the obvious fact that in any moral situation there are *persons with claims* upon us. Even when one is quite alone, in the physical sense of the word, one's absent friends, loved ones, and fellow-citizens have various claims upon one. They are "depending upon" one, as we say, to do certain things and refrain from doing others. A particular person or group of persons may not assert a claim upon me as a right or may not even be conscious of having such a claim. Nevertheless, the claim upon me exists, whether I acknowledge it or turn away from it. It arises from the fact that I am in a relationship with him or them and that a *need* arising out of that relationship speaks to me.

We have spoken of *needs* rather than *interests* as the source of claims upon us. For there are many needs which do not appear at a given time as interests. For example, a child may have no present interest in history, but he may have a need for it in view of the fact that he will face social problems as a citizen in the future and that he cannot learn to free himself from provincialism without knowledge of the past. On the other hand, there are many interests which do not correspond to any need. For example, a child may have been taught to steal or take drugs and may have developed an intense interest in doing so, but there is no need corresponding to this interest in human nature. Of course, many interests *do* correspond to needs, and sometimes a lack of interest indicates the absence of a need. Thus, a passionate interest in music indicates a need for it, while the complete indifference to food of a person who has just dined indicates the absence of a need for it. We do not deny, therefore, that interests normally reveal needs or that interests are highly important.

Nevertheless, when we are seeking to understand the claims of a person or group of persons upon us, we are forced to distinguish between interests and needs. Though this is most obvious in the case of a child all of whose needs have not yet manifested themselves in interests, it is also true in the case of adults. Every responsible statesman must decide whether a strong interest among citizens in a certain policy, e.g., an interest among white citizens in the maintenance of racial discrimination against Negroes, corresponds to a need which has a claim to fulfillment or whether it is an expression of a perverse interest which should be eliminated.

Thus, our duty depends upon the *claims* of persons which spring from their *needs*. Our duty is to do the act which will most effectively meet the claims of persons in each situation. A *right* act is a fitting act, one which is suitable to the situation. However, since every situation is complex and the course of events is only partially predictable, we can seldom know with certainty how effectively a particular act will meet the claims of persons in a given situation. Therefore, my *duty* cannot be identified with the objectively "right" act. I must try to decide what is right in this objective sense, but my duty is to do what seems to me to be the right act. I must determine my duty according to my lights.

DUTY AND VALUES

What is the relation of duty to *value?* As we have seen, the attempt of Kant to separate duty from any reference to the ends or values of an act is a failure. The aim of duty is not only to fulfill the needs of persons but also to help them realize *possibilities of value* in their lives. However, this view differs sharply from Utilitarianism with respect to the nature of the relation between duty and value. Utilitarianism regards duty, like virtue, as merely instrumental to the intrinsic values which are its consequences. This view is contrary to the moral consciousness which regards the moral goodness manifested in duty as one of the highest intrinsic values. How can duty be conceived to *promote values* in the lives of persons without being degraded in Utilitarian fashion to a mere means or *instrumental value* itself?

The clue to an answer may be found in the recent criticism by moralists of the conception of morality in terms of "means" and "ends." Moral actions which aim at a certain end form an organic unity with it and cannot be regarded as a mere means to it. Indeed they may be as important as the end itself. In a game of skill, for example, the "end" is not merely victory but the whole series of movements and experiences of the players with the accompanying aesthetic and social values. Similarly, the "end" of a piece of music is not the conclusion but the whole series of notes from the beginning. Is the "end" of a mother in bringing up her children simply to make them healthy and successful adults in the future? It is certainly this, but it is also far more, for every day of the child's and mother's life together has its unique and unrepeatable values in itself and is itself part of the "end." Similarly no moral act is merely a "means" to values or ends beyond itself; it also shares in the values or ends to which it is devoted.

Another implication of the intimate connection of means and ends is that while ends determine means, means also determine ends. A young man sets out to make his fortune in order, as he says, to be able to retire early, enjoy his leisure, and cultivate his mind. But the means he adopts for this end may make him forget the end with which he started and may shape a different end for him. Or a revolutionary leader seizes power in the state in order to abolish the state and establish a classless society. But, finding it easier to gain power than to relinquish it, he succeeds only in increasing the power of the state and creating another dominant class.

All of this signifies that means and ends interpenetrate, and that while a moral act may be regarded as an *instrumental value* in relation to the end or purpose at which it aims, it is also an *intrinsic value* as an expression of spiritual activity. Indeed, it is usually a higher value than any of the non-moral ends or purposes it seeks. While duty is meaningless when separated from the good aimed at by it, the man who seeks to do his duty is aware, when he reflects upon his life, that the moral goodness which is embodied in his acts of duty is not only an intrinsic value but also a higher value than the other values at which these acts are aimed.

Duty aims at the realization of values, not in the abstract, but *in the lives of persons*. The modern ethics of value has often been obsessed with an impersonal conception of values and blind to the fact that values are actual only in and for persons. The primary aim of moral action is to realize not the *greatest quantity* of values, but the values *most appropriate* for the persons whose needs one is seeking to serve. My duty is to aim, not at the *maximum* of value which could conceivably be attained, but at the *optimum* of value which is fitting in the situation.

This way of thinking about the relation of duty to values is required by the fact that duty is primarily concerned with the *fulfillment of persons*. The values which it is one's duty to seek in a given situation will depend upon the needs of the persons in that situation. Of course, there are needs which are common to all men, and there are values corresponding to these needs which are universally valid. For example, the need to know is a common need and the corresponding values of truth and truthfulness are universal. But the form taken by these needs in a particular person depends upon many factors. One of them is his *stage of development.* Obviously, the need for knowledge takes different forms in a three-year-old child and a thirty-year-old man and the kinds of truth necessary to satisfy the need in the two cases will differ accordingly. It must also be remembered that the form taken by the need of a person and the kind of value which will best fulfill it will be largely determined by the *way of life* of his society. The need to know in a pioneer community differs from the need to know in a more settled community, and the need for beauty is fulfilled in different ways among the Navajo Indians and the sophisticated city-dwellers of America.

DUTY AND VOCATION

In addition to the needs of persons and the possibilities of value for them in the situation, a third factor enters into the determination of our duties: the *special capacities of the self.* The full discovery of the individual and his responsibility for the use of his special talents was made by Christianity. St. Paul applied this principle to the life of the Church itself, pointing out that there is a diversity of "gifts" among Christians and that each should exercise his particular gift in such a way as to contribute to the life of the Church.[1] This discovery has given rise to the more general principle that each person has a vocation to serve his fellows in the place and manner best suited to his distinctive gifts.

This principle is indispensable in the determination of one's duty. Some needs of persons and some possibilities of value can be best fulfilled by me because of my special capacities; others can be fulfilled better by others with different capacities. If a person falls ill, I can meet his need for medical treatment only

[1] I Cor. 12.

if I am a doctor. When a war breaks out, I can serve best in one capacity if I am a young man, in another if I am middle-aged. Of course, I should meet as many claims and realize as much value as possible, within the limits of my time and energy. But I cannot do everything that needs to be done and it is usually best for me to do what I am best fitted to do.

It is this principle which justifies a person who has a special talent for science, art, literature, or philosophy in spending years cultivating it, despite the fact that he is able only occasionally during that time to serve the needs of other persons. For it is impossible to make any significant contribution to the discovery of truth or the creation of beauty without long and arduous preparation. But this does not mean that a person with a special talent should forget his fellows. The modern cult of "truth for truth's sake" among intellectuals and "art for art's sake" among painters and poets is often accompanied by a kind of parasitism. It is not surprising, therefore, that Christians like Leo Tolstoy have felt that they must abandon vocations like scholarship and art, in whole or in part, in order to devote themselves to the direct service of basic human needs. One can justify a "cultural" vocation only if he reminds himself constantly that he depends upon others for the fulfillment of his basic needs and that he has a deep responsibility to help fulfill their needs. He must not make an idol of truth or beauty and forget his responsibility to his neighbors.

SPECIAL AND GENERAL CLAIMS

One of the most difficult problems concerning duty is the apparent conflict between the claims of those standing in *special relations* to us and the claims of others. Jesus had to break with his family in order to carry out his mission. Many Christians under the influence of monasticism have believed that it was necessary for them literally to follow his example. Protestants do not accept the monastic ideal. They believe that they are called to live the Christian life in the world as members of families. But how are they to reconcile the special claims of their families and friends with the broader claims of other men upon them?

It seems clear that the *special claims* of persons upon me cannot be set aside for the sake of neutrality between the claims of all. If I am a father, my children have special claims upon me which other children do not. If I am a doctor, the sick of my community have special claims upon me which other sick persons do not. If I am an American, my fellow-Americans have special claims upon me which citizens of other countries do not. It cannot be denied that these special claims, from the point of view of pure reason, seem to be accidental and arbitrary in the sense that they rest upon contingent factors. That these rather than those children are mine, that I practice medicine in this community rather than that, that I was born an American rather than a Frenchman or a Chinese—each of these circumstances seems to be a contingent fact that might have been otherwise. What, then, can justify me in treating the claims of particular persons or groups as special? The Utilitarian answer is that my children and the members of my group have special claims upon me only because each person can best further the greatest good by serving those whose needs he knows best and can most effectively serve. But this answer does not satisfy us, because it is based upon the assumption that there *really* are no special claims at all but that for practical reasons we must act *as if* there were.

The simplest but most convincing answer is that my children or fellow-citizens have special claims upon me because they are bound to me and I to them by natural and social ties which are products of God's work in Creation and Providence. Because of them, my children are dependent upon me as upon no one else, and therefore I am responsible for them. My ties with the other members of my community or country are no less real. For example, we all depend upon the division of labor which makes possible an exchange of services between us. If I am a doctor, I am expected to meet the claims of the sick of the community. In turn, I expect the teacher to meet the claims of my children for education and the policeman to meet the claims of my family for protection. However accidental and contingent it may seem, this network of special relations in which I stand gives rise to special claims upon me and many, if not most, of my duties consist in meeting these claims. For in this network of relations mutual expectations have grown up which must be honored if the life of persons as biological, social, and spiritual beings is to be fulfilled.

But the acknowledgment of special claims must be qualified in several ways. Special claims are by no means the *only* claims upon me. Other children than my own have claims upon me, e.g., the claim to be treated kindly, to be protected from harm when they are near me, to be helped by me as a taxpayer to obtain good schools. Members of the larger community of the nation are also dependent upon me and have claims upon me in all matters concerning the common good. Finally, the citizens of other countries have claims upon me for emergency aid in time of famine or earthquake, for support of a foreign policy which does justice to their needs for prosperity and peace, and for cooperation with them in solving the problems common to all humanity. This emphasizes the fact that there are *general claims* as well as special ones. There is always a danger that emphasis upon special claims will lead to the neglect of these broader claims. It is not necessary that a person should devote all his time and energy to the needs of his own family or local community and should be indifferent to the needs of other families or of the nation. Indeed, special claims and broader claims can often be fulfilled together. For example, a mother can serve the needs of her own children and those of other children at the same time by working for better schools and playgrounds in the community. A citizen can promote the welfare of his own country and that of other countries at the same time by supporting policies that make for peace.

But it cannot be denied that concern for the needs of one's own family or group is likely to lead one to neglect the broader claims of other families or groups. This tendency may be illustrated from the history of Chinese ethics. The ethics of impartial, all-embracing love advocated by Mo-ti was overcome, after a period of struggle, by the ethics of Confucius. To Mencius and other Confucianists, the argument of Mo-ti that a son should love other men's fathers as he loves his own seemed to invite indifference to one's own father. They were also convinced of the educative effect of benevolence towards those in one's own family, maintaining that those who have learned to fulfill their duties to their own fathers and brothers will obey their emperor as a father and treat their fellow-citizens as brothers. Unfortunately, the reasoning of these Confucianists rested upon the optimistic view that man is naturally good and the assumption that social attitudes developed within the family would naturally be extended to relationships outside the family. In fact, nepotism flourished, public spirit was weak, and there was little or no recognition of duty to strangers who stood in no special relation to the individual. As Lin Yu Tang says, there was nothing corresponding to the "Samaritan virtue."[1]

This illustrates the fact that, while special claims cannot be neglected, duty cannot be defined primarily in terms of them. Perhaps the greatest enemy of duty is the egoism of individuals and groups, due to self-love and lack of sympathy for the needs of others. A radical reorientation of the will and an enlargement of the vision of men is necessary if they are to serve the needs of those who do not stand in special relations with them.

DUTY AND COMPETING CLAIMS

In most, if not all, moral situations there are *competing claims* upon us. This is most obvious in situations where two or more persons' needs call for our help. It is also true in situations where only one person seems to have claims upon us because he may have different needs which conflict with one another. Because of the complexity of the situation resulting from these competing claims, it is tempting to say that ethics can give us no help in dealing with them and that the decision as to our duty simply rests with intuition. In the words of C. D. Broad, we seem to be "reduced to something analogous to those perceptual judgments on very complex situations which we have constantly to make in playing games of skill."[1]

It is true that ultimately decisions on duties in particular situations must be made by *intuition*. But the wisdom of such decisions

---

[1] Lin Yu Tang, *My Country and My People,* New York, John Day, 1939, p. 180.
[1] Broad, C. D., *Five Types of Ethical Theory,* New York, Harcourt Brace, 1930, p. 223.

depends in part upon the extent to which we have reflected upon the problem of competing claims. Are there any useful *principles* in the form of "middle axioms" between the very general principle that our duty is to serve the needs of all our neighbors in love and the intuitive judgment as to our duty in a particular situation? If so, they may help to guide our analysis of moral situations, though they do not give us a scientifically precise method of reaching moral decisions.

(1) Obviously, one principle is that in many cases of conflict some of the claims of persons upon us cannot be fulfilled but must be *denied*. Thus, Jesus demanded of the man who wished to follow him but only after burying his father, "Leave the dead to bury their own dead; but as for you, go and proclaim the Kingdom of God."[2] Even in more ordinary cases of conflicting claims, a similar solution is often necessary. Among such cases are those in which one of the claims expresses an *interest* of certain persons but rests upon no real *need*. Thus, a small class of rich landlords may claim that the unconditional property rights they have enjoyed in the past should be left untouched, despite the claims of thousands of peasants for a more just distribution. Or a privileged race or caste, e.g., the white race in America or the Brahman caste in India, may claim that the system of discrimination and segregation from which they have always profited should not be changed despite the claims to justice of millions of those oppressed by them. In cases like these, the principle is that claims which are *not* necessary to the fulfillment of needs should be denied if they conflict with claims which *are*.

In other cases, even claims representing real and important needs cannot be met, e.g., the need of two children to go to college when there is not enough money to send both. In cases of this sort, of course, we may be able to find some relevant difference indicating which need should be fulfilled. Even if we cannot do so, we may be able to avoid arbitrary preferences by fulfilling at a *later* time the needs of those we have not been able to satisfy or by fulfilling *other* needs of theirs which we are able to satisfy.

(2) In most cases of conflicting claims, however, both claims or

[2] Lk. 9:59, 60.

sets of claims can be met in some measure if one or both of them are *limited* or *modified*. If I am free for an hour and each of my two children wants me to play a game of his choice with him, I can partially meet both of their claims by playing half an hour with each of them, or by suggesting another game which they both like equally well. In the one case, both claims are limited; in the other, they are modified. If it is not possible by either of these methods to meet both claims, I may be able to meet one today and postpone the other until a free hour tomorrow. Of course, this is a simple case of conflict. Often, many claims have to be considered and there is not such an easy solution. In addition to the claims of different members of my family, there are the claims of my work, the claims of my friends and neighbors, and the claims of the community at large. The satisfaction of these competing claims is much more difficult, but the same methods will sometimes help in dealing with them, provided I have the desire to fulfill as many needs as possible and will exercise my imagination in finding ways to do so.

The method of *limitation* is of special importance in the process of resolving conflicts between the claims of different classes or other groups of the community. Almost always a class or other group tends to exaggerate its claims, and the full satisfaction of them would put in danger the welfare of other classes or groups. A compromise between its claims and the equally exaggerated claims of another class or group is made possible only by using the method of limitation. It is one of the advantages of democracy that it clearly recognizes this fact. Obviously, the method of *modification* often goes hand in hand with that of limitation, though it may also be employed independently. When two impulses are opposed to one another, Hobhouse points out, one may subdue the other (repression), or one or both impulses may undergo a certain modification whereby they become consistent.[2] "One of the impulses, to take the simplest case, is moderated in intensity or guided towards one class of objects to the exclusion of another, and so remodelled it is found not less satisfying in itself, and fully consistent with the indulgence of its former rival. A leading instance would be sexual feeling which, indiscriminate in its purely animal phase, is by a fusion of psychical

[2] Hobhouse, L. T., *The Rational Good*, London, Allen & Unwin, 1921, p. 99.

influences, concentrated in an impassioned devotion to one person wherein, as long as the fusion endures, its satisfaction is complete."[3] There can be no doubt of the importance of this process of modification for the personal as well as the social fulfillment of needs.

(3) The application of the principles we have just described, however, must be governed by two higher principles: the principle of the gradation of needs and the principle of inclusiveness. With respect to the first of these, the proper subordination of one need to another presupposes a *gradation of higher and lower needs*. For example, the sexual need of married persons is subordinate to the higher needs of the family. Again, when a parent insists that his son should leave his play in time to study his lesson in English or history, he is acting from this principle and asserting that the need for play, however legitimate, is ultimately inferior to the need for knowledge in the life of men. If the principle is not valid, the subordination of any need to any other need is arbitrary.

We have in mind, of course, an *objective* rather than a subjective order of needs. At this point, we must differ from those who hold a subjective theory of value. Professor Perry, for example, speaks of the "preference" of one object of an interest to another, but he uses the term "preference" to refer simply to "the fact that a subject is in some sense more interested."[4] Therefore, if we are to further another person's interest, we must accept his scale of preference. Love must be "indulgent," seeking to promote the other person's "achievement of what he desires or enjoyment of what he likes."[5] This cannot be accepted. Apart from the fact that it rests upon Perry's subjective theory of value as object of interest, it would make it impossible for us to distinguish the needs from the interests of others, as we must when we seek to do our duty. Love is not "indulgent" to all the desires and preferences of the loved one. In actuality, love must often seek the real rather than the apparent, the ultimate rather than the immediate, good of the loved one. If it

[3] Ibid., pp. 99-100.
[4] Perry, R. B., *General Theory of Value,* New York, Longmans, Green, 1926, p. 597.
[5] Ibid., p. 677.

were always "indulgent," it would sometimes have to bestow evil rather than good on the loved one.

(4) The most fundamental principle for the determination of duty, however, is that of *inclusiveness*. This is the principle that each of us should fulfill the needs of *as many persons as possible*. The practical meaning of the principle is simply that everyone has a claim upon us whom it is possible for us to help. We shall not be able to meet the needs of all our neighbors, but we must do our best. Nor may we neglect or be indifferent to those whose needs we cannot personally fulfill. As an isolated individual, I can do little about the plight of millions of homeless refugees on a continent across the sea or about the poverty of hundreds of millions in an undeveloped country. As a citizen, with the help of other citizens who share my concern, I may be able to help.

The principle of inclusiveness is required by the Christian principle of the universality of love. It is more fundamental than the other principles we have been describing and governs the application of them. For example, it does not permit us to *deny* or eliminate the needs of anyone unless it is impossible to satisfy them in some form. Again, it requires us to *limit* or *modify* needs when it is necessary to do so in order to meet higher needs or the needs of other persons. Even the principle of the *gradation* of needs is secondary to the principle of inclusiveness. Despite the contrary view of defenders of an aristocratic society, the general needs of *all* for fundamental values take precedence over the special needs of *some* for higher values.

DUTY AND LOVE

To summarize, duty arises in response to the needs of persons One's duty is to do the act he believes to be the right one in the sense of best fulfilling the needs of persons in the situation. The needs of persons can be fulfilled only by helping them realize the possibilities of value for them in the situation, since values are correlative with needs. The moral act or duty is not only a means to other values but also possesses an intrinsic value itself. Its primary aim is not to realize the greatest quantity of values but the values most appropriate for the persons in the situation. In determining one's duty, one must consider one's vocation and the special claims of those with whom one stands in special relations. But there are many claims with respect to which one's vocation is irrelevant, and special claims must never be allowed to exclude broader claims. Competing claims should be dealt with by a process of elimination, limitation, and modification. There is an objective gradation of needs which is the basis for the subordination of one need to another. The fundamental principle of inclusiveness requires us to fulfill the needs of as many persons as possible, and the other principles for dealing with competing claims are secondary to it. Of course, the final decision as to one's duty must rest with intuition, but it is more likely to be correct if it is made after reflection on the situation guided by the principles we have described.

However, the determination of one's duty depends, not only upon the *analysis* of moral situations with the help of these principles, but also upon *appreciation* of all the needs and values involved. To *recognize* their existence is not enough; it is also necessary to *feel* them, to identify oneself imaginatively with them. That is why the most intellectual men are not always the best men, for intellect is not always accompanied by sensitiveness, sympathetic imagination and the will to respond to the needs of every moral situation in a practical way.

Obviously, we cannot meet these conditions without *love*. As love is the source of virtue, it is the mainspring of duty. As St. Paul says, "love is the fulfilling of the law." It is because men so often attempt to do their duty without love that it seems cold and is even felt to be opposed to love. But duty at its best is simply love in action; and love which does not manifest itself in duty is hardly worthy of the name. Again, because men so often confuse duty with passive conformity to law imposed from outside, they think it stifles spontaneity. But duty at its best is a free response springing from love within. As such, it is a creative act which contributes richly to the art of living.

The dependence of duty on love can be seen in several ways. First, the discovery of our duty requires that we open our minds to the needs of others. As we have said, it is necessary not only to know their needs but also to feel them as if they were our own. But how can we appreciate their needs if we are always preoccupied with ourselves? It is only when we are freed by faith in God's love from anxiety about ourselves that we can turn towards our neighbors and listen to their needs. Second, when we attempt to help them realize possibilities of value in their lives, we are tempted to impose upon them our own limited conceptions of their good. We assume that the kind of truth which best fulfills our need for knowledge will best fulfill theirs, that the kind of beauty or play which satisfies us will satisfy them. We also forget that there is an art of giving and that clumsy giving can be almost worse than no giving at all. By patronizing those we would help, we humiliate them. By doing for them what they should do for themselves, we destroy their independence and initiative. Here, again, it is only love which can enable us to overcome the self-centeredness which prevents us from realizing the kinds of values *they* need and from giving to them in such a way as to help *them* instead of expressing our own superiority. Third, love makes us aware of the needs of those outside the circle of our own families, friends, and fellow-citizens. We pointed out that those who stand in special relations to us within this circle have special claims upon us but that these need not prevent us from responding to the claims of those outside it. In actuality, however, the needs of those who are near and dear to us do tend to absorb all our interest. The needs of others are likely to be overlooked unless we deliberately enlarge our horizon to include them in our concern. The most powerful incentive for doing this is Christian love.

Moreover, the *most important* need is just to love and be loved. We may fulfill many other needs of a person, but, if we neglect this primary need by withholding our love from him, we have failed to do our whole duty to him. His other needs, lower and higher, should be fulfilled if he is to be fulfilled as a person; but his need for love is even more essential, for without it his whole life is empty. Therefore, the beginning of our duty to him is the acceptance of him as a person and the establishment of community with him in love. In this way, our duty to fulfill his needs presupposes something more fundamental than itself. After all, the fulfillment of needs is only a means to the fulfillment of persons and this can take place only in a community of persons who love one another.

Even when we cannot fulfill the *other* needs of our neighbors, we can fulfill in a measure their *primary* need for love. There are many persons whose needs it is impossible for us to fulfill. But if we are willing to give them our love, we give them the best thing we have to offer. In short, our highest duty is just to give our love, as our greatest privilege is to receive the love of others.

CHAPTER 20

Values

As THE ethics of duty gives priority to the concept of *the right,* the ethics of value emphasizes the concept of *the good.* The one concerns itself with the question, What is it right for me to do? The other attempts to answer the question, What values should I seek? However, the ethics of value has taken several different forms in recent philosophy. Some of these have been based upon the "objective" theory of value, some upon the "subjective" theory. We shall examine briefly two representative ethical thinkers of our time as examples of the influence of "objective" and "subjective" theories of value. We shall then deal with certain crucial issues concerning the nature, the absoluteness, and the gradation of values.

THE OBJECTIVE THEORY: NICOLAI HARTMANN

One recent ethical theory which has been based upon an "objective" theory of value as an "indefinable quality" is the "Ideal Utilitarianism" of G. E. Moore[1] and other British moralists. This theory is similar to the older Utilitarianism in holding that the criterion of right acts is their utility for the production of the greatest good on the whole and their impartial distribution of the good between different persons. However, it maintains that the good includes values such as aesthetic enjoyment and personal affection as well as pleasure. Consequently, in calculating the values likely to result from an act, it takes into account not only quantita-

[1] Moore, G. E., *Principia Ethica,* Cambridge, University Press, 1946.

448

tive differences of value but also the qualitative superiority of some values over others.

Despite the great influence of Ideal Utilitarianism early in the century, it has been on the decline during the last generation. The reason is clear: it reduced moral value to the status of a merely instrumental value by making the fulfillment of duty only a means to the attainment of value.

To a considerable extent, this weakness has been overcome in the theory of Nicolai Hartmann. When a value is intuited by the phenomenological method, says Hartmann, it is seen to be wholly independent of existence. It is "objective," not in the sense that it is an object in time and space, but in the sense that it is an *"essence"* in an ideal "realm of essence."[2] When it is intuited, its rank in a *scale of values* is intuited or felt along with it.[3] There is no way of rationally proving that one value is higher in the scale of values than another. However, there is nothing arbitrary or subjective about this, since values are ranked according to an "order of the heart" or "logic of the heart." It is true that values are ranked differently by different persons. But this is not a ground for supposing them to be subjective. It is merely an indication that some men have a penetrating insight into values and their rank while others are "value-blind."

If values belong to a realm of essence entirely independent of the realm of existence to which man belongs, why does man feel impelled to realize them in his acts? Hartmann's answer is that they are characterized by an *"ought-to-be."*[4] In saying that values "ought-to-be," he seems to imply a sort of inherent tendency in them towards manifesting themselves in the realm of existence. But that would mean that they have a relation to existence, a fact which he has denied. Perhaps he means only that they are characterized by a worthiness to exist. In any case, whenever a person intuits a value and, with it, the fact that it "ought-to-be," he intuits at the same time an obligation to act in such a way as to bring it into existence, an *"ought-to-do."*[5]

[2] Hartmann, N., *Ethics*, New York, Macmillan, 1932, I, pp. 183 ff. Used by permission of the publishers.
[3] Ibid., Vol. II, p. 46.
[4] Ibid., Vol. I, Ch. XVIII.
[5] Ibid., I, Ch. XIX.

The *moral life* consists in the effort of persons to realize values according to their rank in the scale of values. A morally good act is one the "intention" of which is to realize the *higher value* in a particular moral situation. "All the concrete situations of life," he says, "are such that several values are involved in them at the same time. . . . It is essential to choose one (or a few) and to pass over the others. Now within such a constellation of values, goodness is always the turning towards the higher values, evil a turning towards the lower."[6] This decision between "situational values" is complicated by the fact that values differ not only in the sense that they are higher or lower in a scale, but also with respect to "strength." The "strength" or appeal of values, Hartmann thinks, varies inversely with their "height."[7] Although the lower is "only the base for the moral life, not a fulfillment of its meaning," it is more fundamental because the fulfillment of the higher depends upon it. For example, "the man who is hungry or suffering in body loses his sense for spiritual enjoyments."[8] Consequently, morality is double-faced like the head of Janus, looking towards the higher values which lie before us waiting for fulfillment but also watchfully protecting the interest of the lower ones when they are in danger.[9]

The *goodness* which is common to all "moral values" is a quality which belongs to the will by virtue of its intention to realize higher values. "Goodness, and with it all moral values," says Hartmann, "are values of the *intention* of the act, not values of the act itself. But the quality of the intention, which is the point at issue, depends on its own content, on the *intended value*."[10] This view attempts to do justice to Kant's view that moral value or goodness belongs to the *will* alone, not its consequences, but also to the view that the good will aims at values *beyond itself*. The "moral values" are simply virtues. They are distinguished from one another as dispositions of the will to prefer higher to lower values in different kinds of situations. Hartmann devotes a large part of his *Ethics*[11] to a careful analysis of the essence of each of the major "moral values" and

[6] Ibid., II, p. 185.
[7] Ibid., II, pp. 52-53.
[8] Ibid., II, pp. 453.

[9] Ibid., II, p. 459.
[10] Ibid., II, p. 182.
[11] Ibid., II.

the relations between them, but with the details of his treatment of them we are not concerned.

Finally, Hartmann's ethics is *humanistic* rather than theistic. Man is endowed with freedom of will and has the full responsibility for determining his own destiny. He stands alone as he faces this responsibility, without support or guidance from any cosmic will or purpose and without responsibility to any Being above himself. He confronts the realm of objective values, on one side, and the realm of existence to which he himself belongs, on the other, and brings them together by free acts of his autonomous will. Hartmann's exaltation of man and his free will is militant. He explicitly rejects belief in a divine Purpose or Providence because he regards it as incompatible with man's autonomy.[12]

There are two main advantages of Hartmann's ethics of value over Ideal Utilitarianism. The first of these is that he emphasizes *higher values* rather than the *maximum of value* as the aim of moral conduct. As a result, he does not involve himself in the hopeless attempt to develop principles for the calculation of values. The second advantage of his theory is that it recognizes *moral values* or virtues to be more than merely instrumental values. While the will is good only in relation to the "intended values" at which it aims, its goodness belongs to itself. Thus, justice is done to the inner side of morality as well as to the consequences at which it aims.

Nevertheless, there are serious weaknesses in Hartmann's theory. The first is that his *objective theory of values* is too abstract. By divorcing values from all relation to the realm of existence, he makes them completely independent of man and his needs. If they are independent of man, it is impossible to understand why they arouse feelings of appreciation or satisfy desire in men. How they can have the characteristic expressed by the term "ought-to-be" is inexplicable. How they can give rise to the experience of obligation, the "ought-to-do," when there is nothing in their nature which relates them to persons is equally strange. Thus, the objective theory of value is as one-sided and extreme as the subjective theory it criticizes.

[12] Ibid., I, Ch's. XXI, XXV.

The second weakness is that moral values or virtues are directed primarily towards the realization of *situational values* rather than the fulfillment of the *needs of persons*. Thus, the emphasis is upon the attainment of value rather than the performance of duty to one's neighbors. As a result, Hartmann does not escape from the temptation which besets every ethic of value: self-centeredness and pride. Virtue is primarily the disposition to realize as many and as high values as possible and to develop one's own personality in the process. It is true that Hartmann scorns Egoism and Hedonism and stresses the fact that the good man directs his attention towards objective values. But there are passages which show that this devotion to values is not as disinterested as it seems, e.g., his defense of pride as a virtue. Because his ethic of value neglects duty to others, it tends to fall, though unintentionally, into a subtle and noble but nonetheless real egoism.

In the third place, moral values are conceived as *distinct* qualities or "essences" rather than as aspects of an organic whole. The "essence" of each type of moral value is distinguished from that of every other by abstracting it from its content in experience. But we do not know what the essence of a value by itself would be; values are always experienced as *related* to other values and to the whole self. The result of Hartmann's atomistic view is that moral conduct is identified with the process of appreciating and producing one value after another. As one flower after another is plucked to make a bouquet, one value after another is to be accumulated to make the richest and fullest personality possible. The moral life would consist, in this view, of the enjoyment in succession of a great number of values—of what Hartmann calls "richness of experience"—rather than an organic unity of distinguishable but inseparable values.

Finally, Hartmann's *militant Humanism* prevents him from recognizing that moral goodness and the moral values or virtues in which it expresses itself need to be strengthened and enlightened by a power above the human will. He has a noble belief in the dignity of man and in the capacity of the individual to shape his own destiny by his freedom of will. But the moral optimism to which this leads him is dangerous. It overlooks completely the limitation of the moral will by its own weakness and egoism. Consequently, it encourages the unrealistic belief that man can attain moral goodness without a radical change in his will. In reality, the freedom of the will to attain virtue is made effective only when the power of sin over it is broken. At this point, Hartmann is blinded by the modern humanistic glorification of man. Without the transformation of the will by divine grace, it is unable either to devote itself to higher "situational values" *for the neighbor* or to attain true moral goodness *in the self.*

THE SUBJECTIVE THEORY: R. B. PERRY

If the objective theory of value as an ideal "essence" is an inadequate basis for ethics, what are we to think of the *subjective* theory? Perhaps the most careful statement and defense of the subjective theory of value during the last generation is that of Professor R. B. Perry.[1] According to Perry, value is to be defined as "any object of any interest." "Interest" is a state or attitude which consists in being "for" some things and "against" others, in viewing things with "favor" or "disfavor."[2] Interest, in this sense, "invests" an object with value, and the object "acquires" value when an interest is taken in it.[3] Interest is "constitutive" of value, "confers" value upon the object.[4] In the definition "value is any object of any interest," the emphasis upon the word "any" is meant to affirm that value is not a "*qualified object* of interest"[5] or an "object of *qualified interest*,"[6] but *any* object of *any* interest. Thus, Perry's theory is hospitable to interests of all kinds in objects of all kinds.

Since there are no values apart from interests and since there is a diversity of interests among persons, the idea of a scale of values according to which values are ranked as higher or lower becomes meaningless. However, this does not mean that he is not interested in "comparative value." Although values cannot be ranked as higher or lower, they can be compared with one another quantitatively by

[1] Perry, R. B., *General Theory of Value*, New York, Longmans, Green, 1926.
[2] Ibid., p. 115.
[3] Ibid., pp. 115, 116.
[4] Ibid., p. 122.
[5] Ibid., Ch. III.
[6] Ibid., Ch. IV.

measuring the amounts of interest involved in them. It is this *comparison of values* which is the basis of Perry's ethical theory. A moral act is one which is conducive to the attainment of the *maximum value* or *fulfillment of interest.*

In determining the acts which are most likely to lead to this goal, three ways of comparing values quantitatively must be taken into account: the *intensity* of interests, the *preference* of one object of an interest over another, and *inclusiveness* of different interests.[7] The "highest good" is the satisfaction or fulfillment of as many interests of as many persons as possible (principle of "inclusiveness") in an harmonious system of interests, each interest of each person being satisfied by the objects preferred by him (principle of "preference") and at the highest degree of intensity possible (principle of "intensity"). In applying these principles, Perry puts first the principle of "inclusiveness" according to which an object of interest is enhanced in value if it is also the object of other interests ("overlapping" of interests).[8] This principle implies that *all interests* have a claim to be fulfilled and that *every person's* interests should be included among the interests to be considered.

The maximum fulfillment of interests or "highest good" requires an "all-benevolent will" from each person. For the harmony of all interests can be attained only through a "universal love,"[9] an "indulgent" love which accepts and supports the interests of every other person. Since this would lead to the greatest happiness, Perry has much in common with the older Utilitarianism.

The main *advantage* of a subjective theory like this over objective theories is that it relates the nature of value more closely to man and his good. Thus, it avoids in a measure the abstractness of the objective theory which reduces moral activity to the realization of values in and for themselves. Moreover, by making the principle of "inclusiveness" the primary standard for the comparison of values, Perry avoids the tendency to self-centeredness in the quest for values. Moral activity is centered upon the fulfillment of the interests of all persons from the motive of "universal love."

[7] Ibid., Ch. XX, sec. 248.
[8] Ibid., Ch. XXI, sec. 259.
[9] Ibid., Ch. XXII, sec. 267.

Unfortunately, these advantages are purchased at too high a cost, for Perry's theory is vitiated by several fatal errors. The first and most fundamental of these is his *subjective definition of value* as "any object of any interest." The view that value exists exclusively in relation to and by virtue of interest is entirely opposed to men's consciousness of value. In valuing something, they do not think of themselves as bestowing a value upon it but as appreciating and responding to a value which in some sense belongs to it. In experience an object is "given" as beautiful, a moral act is "given" as good. Interest in it presupposes something in it which makes it *appropriate* to be an object of interest. For example, why do men have an interest in truth rather than error unless truth has and error lacks something which makes it worthy of interest? Moreover, higher values like truth are experienced as making claims upon us. If we are to possess them, it must be on their own terms. We must acknowledge truth and goodness where we find them and as we find them; we cannot judge them according to our likes and dislikes but only as they are.

Perry holds that many have confused value in the "generic" sense with value in the "comparative" sense. They have not been concerned to describe value in general but to determine what values are uniquely and superlatively valuable. Accordingly they have held that "the desires and affections of living creatures are not to be accepted as they stand, but condemned as partial, blind, apparent or unauthorized as compared with some standard will which is complete, enlightened, real or imperative."[10] But can we really define value in the "generic" sense without distinguishing between what Perry calls "partial" and "complete," "blind" and "enlightened," "apparent" and "real" values? In the case of the value of truth, at least, it is obvious that we cannot. The whole history of science and philosophy consists in the persistent and continuing effort to supplant "partial" with "complete" truth, the "apparent" truth of mere opinion with the "real" truth contained in knowledge. Perry would hardly say that the definition of truth is "any object of any opinion." Men seek to pass from opinion to knowledge, and, although they may value an opinion as a stage in the process of knowing, they do

[10] Ibid., pp. 81, 82.

so only insofar as they think that it contains or leads on to knowledge. Is the case really different with other values, as Perry seems to assume? If not, is it not misleading to speak of an interest as conferring value on "any object" upon which it may momentarily light?

We may illustrate by two examples. In fulfilling their interest in food, men have to learn by experience to discriminate between objects which are right in the sense of healthful and nutritious and those which are not nutritious and may even be harmful. Are we to say that an interest in a certain mushroom or drug is a ground for attributing value to it despite the fact that experience may later prove it to be deadly? Again, the interest in sexual experience often takes forms which, as later experience shows, pervert its true function and even enslave a person. Are they to be regarded as valuable merely because an interest has been taken in them? Both of these examples indicate that a thing or experience may be an object of an interest and yet be without value or even be evil. Perry would doubtless reply that in such cases interest does confer value in the "generic" sense, but that when it is compared with other interests it is found to thwart other and greater values. But a judgment of value is not intended to express merely a tentative, momentary, or unconsidered interest; its purpose is to express the attitude of the self as a whole in the light of its whole experience and reflection. If so, an object of an interest cannot be judged to be valuable unless it fulfills something deeper and more enduring than a present and often fleeting interest. As we cannot say that a passing opinion possesses the value of truth, we cannot say that "any" interest, however casual or superficial, confers value.

The subjective theory of value also inevitably leads to *relativism*. If A is interested in an object but B is not, it is a value for A but not for B. It is impossible to put this view into practice consistently in ethics or politics. For example, if the lack of interest of A, a schoolboy, in knowledge means that it has no value for him, on what ground do his parents and teachers insist that he go to school and study his lessons? Is it not on the ground that truth is a value whether he is interested in it or not? Again, it would seem that, according to Perry's theory, if nation A is interested in justice and liberty for all and B is not, they are values for A but not for B. If so, how can democracy, a form of government which is interested in justice and liberty for all, claim to be the best form of government or even a better form than a tyrannical dictatorship?

Moreover, if values are wholly relative to and dependent upon interest, how can there be any basis of *social unity*? Perry is not disturbed by the danger of social disunity because he believes that if each person in a society has an "all-benevolent will" and is interested in the interests of all the others, the greatest diversity of interests can be permitted without destroying the general harmony. But there is clearly a limit to the diversity of interests which is possible without disrupting a society. For example, it is obvious that the value upon which Perry relies to hold a society together, i.e., benevolence or interest in the interests of others, must be generally if not universally present. But this assumes it to be a value for all, whether they are interested in it or not. Thus, Perry's *relativistic* tolerance of all interests would be possible only in a society in which all accepted the value of benevolence as an *absolute!*

Finally, there is no adequate basis for *obligation* in Perry's theory. Like the Utilitarians, he seems to think that it is necessary only to define the "highest good" as the maximum fulfillment of interests in an harmonious system and that men with an "all-benevolent will" will seek it. But what is the basis of obligation for those who have no interest in the interests of other persons? If one has no interest in others, why ought he to seek their good? The only possible answer is that it is his *duty* to do so whether he has an interest in doing so or not. This implies that whatever may be thought about non-moral values like beauty and truth, moral value cannot be either subjective or relative. Indeed, the ethical idealism of Perry's own theory of the "all-benevolent will" is based upon the tacit assumption that *this* value, at least, is objective and absolute.

THE NATURE OF VALUE

We have rejected both the objective and the subjective theories of value in their extreme forms. Is a theory of value possible which avoids the errors of these theories but does justice to the elements of truth in them?

There are two main elements of truth in the objective theory. First, it preserves the common sense view that when we value something we value *it* and that our subjective feeling about it and interest in it are due to *its* character. If we should become convinced that there is no value in an object except that with which we invest it by our interest, we would cease to value *it* and would value our own *interest* instead. Indeed, this is what is done, in considerable measure, by the hedonist, sensualist, and sentimentalist: they do not value things or persons but their own pleasures, satisfactions, and feelings. But the result is introversion and isolation from all normal relation to reality and value. Second, the objective theory reminds us that values make claims upon us and give rise to *obligations* in us to realize them. Though Hartmann fails to give an adequate account of this fact because of his abstraction of values from relation to man, he does acknowledge that values are the source of imperatives. This is possible only if they are not projections of our own interests but are in some sense objective.

There are also two main elements of truth in the subjective theory. First, it points to the fact that we know nothing of values which stand in no relation to man. Things and persons are known to us as valuable only in and through our response to them. Though our response does not confer value upon them, as we shall see, we could not discover or appreciate them without it. Second, the subjective theory emphasizes the fact that the aim of moral acts is the realization of values not in and for themselves but as a necessary condition of the fulfillment of persons. It reminds us that in realizing values we serve the welfare of persons.

It is the task of the philosophy of value to show how these elements of truth can be harmonized with one another in a general theory of value. It is necessary here only to state the basic principle of such a theory and to indicate some of its implications for ethics. The basic principle is that *value is a unique property which is present in the relationship between a subject and an object*. It is grounded, in quite different ways, in both the object and the subject. If the object did not have the *structure* or character it has, it would not be valued; and if the subject did not have something in his nature which *called for* an object with that kind of structure, he would not value it. Let us look briefly at these objective and subjective factors in turn.

The *structure of the object* valued differs according to the kind of value in it. The structure of a landscape which is valued for its beauty is obviously different from the structure of a proposition which is valued for its truth. Both differ from the structure of a person's character which is valued for its goodness. It is unnecessary for our purposes to analyze these different kinds of structures. But we must emphasize the fact that they are *objective* and that none of them is in any sense created or conferred upon the object by our relation to it. Since we value each of these kinds of structure (including its qualities as well as relations), it is appropriate to say that it *has value*. Since its value is actual only when the subjective factor is in relation to it, however, it would perhaps be better to say that it is *valuable* in the sense that it is suitable to be valued by persons. Though it is valuable even when it is not being valued by a subject, it is so because of its potentiality to be valued, and this potentiality must be actualized by a subject.

However, it is necessary to distinguish carefully between moral values and non-moral values. Where the moral will seeks to realize the potentialities of value in a situation, the values it "intends" or aims at are what Hartmann aptly calls "situational values." It was about these that we were speaking when we said that objects are valuable but that their values have to be actualized. But the moral value of "goodness" in the will is not a "situational" but a "personal" value. This moral value of a person, once it has been attained by him, is in no way dependent for its existence upon recognition by another person or even by the person himself. It is wholly objective, not only in the sense of being valuable but also in the sense of having already been actualized as a value. However, it is also possible to aim at the moral goodness of another person as a "situational value," i.e., a value which is *to be actualized* in a situation through moral influence and education. Thus, the moral value of goodness is a "personal" value insofar as it has been actualized by a person, but it is a "situational" value insofar as it is to be actualized for another person.

What, now, is the nature of the *subjective factor* in value? We have spoken of something in the subject as "calling for" a valuable object of a certain kind. What is it that "calls for" such an object? As we implied in our criticism of Perry's theory, it is clearly something deeper and more enduring than an "interest." Although it may manifest itself as an "interest," it is not a psychical state which may come and go like an interest but is a permanent aspect of man's nature, whether at any given time he is conscious of it or not. In simple terms, it is the *need* of a person which "calls for" valuable objects of a certain kind for its fulfillment. How are we to understand this need?

A person is characterized by the fact that, from birth to death, he is always growing. His potentialities are never fully realized; he is never complete. His nature is not static but ever changing and developing. It is never finished but always in process of fulfillment. His *needs* are aspects of his drive towards fulfillment. If he were an infinite and perfect being, like God, he would have no needs in this sense because his nature would be fulfilled. If he were an inanimate being, needs would also be lacking in him, so far as one can see. But he is a finite living being, and life involves growth and change. He is also a spiritual being, and spirit, as we have seen,[1] involves self-transcendence which seeks to go beyond the limits of the self. Consequently, he has biological and spiritual needs which press for fulfillment. In certain persons and under certain physical and social conditions, one or more of these needs may scarcely rise to the level of consciousness and, if it does, it may have to be fulfilled in a very crude form. For example, a feeble-minded child may be almost unaware of the need for knowledge, and a person brought up from childhood in a military state like Sparta may never be fully aware of the need for romantic love or artistic expression. Nevertheless, there is a structure of biological and spiritual needs which belongs to the nature of man universally.

The fact that under unfavorable conditions one or more of these needs may not be clearly recognized or adequately fulfilled reminds us that, while needs belong to human nature, they must be awakened, stimulated, developed, and directed under the influence of a social environment which provides valuable objects suitable for

[1] Ch. VII.

them. This is most obvious in the case of social needs like the need for friendship or justice. Though these needs belong to him as a person, they arise in him only because he is a social being, a person in a community of persons. Therefore, his relationships with other persons in his family and in the larger community will largely determine the way in which these social needs will be expressed and fulfilled. For example, his need for love may be repressed by the lack of love in others or may be fully satisfied by the unstinted affection of his family. Similarly, though less obviously, the need of a person for truth will be defined and shaped under the influence of a society which prizes one kind of knowledge more than others, e.g., in a primitive society he will learn to prize knowledge of nature and tribal lore while in a society like ours he will be taught to prize technical knowledge or other useful information. Again, his need for beauty will be developed under the influence of the forms and styles of art in his group. Thus, while the needs of persons belong to them by *nature,* the forms they assume and the ways in which they express themselves are largely determined by *society* and its *culture.*

The needs of a person, though distinguishable from one another, must never be thought of as discrete entities. They form a *system of interdependent needs,* each of which affects and is affected by the others. These needs, as we shall see, form an order or scale of needs in which some are lower than and subordinate to others. Both the integration of a person and the unity of a society depend upon the subordination of some needs to others. The fact that needs form a system also corresponds to the fact that the values which fulfill needs are experienced not as atomic qualities or essences but as patterns of interrelated values. This is what makes possible that *interpenetration of values* which is so important for the art of living. It is seldom, if ever, that an act realizes only one value; values come into our lives together. For example, pleasure usually accompanies other values. The value of truth is greatly enhanced by the social values which attend cooperation with others in discovering it. Even a simple social gathering realizes together the values of friendship, play, beauty, and pleasure. In the family, all values are enhanced by the value of love. For this reason, the more fully a person develops all his major needs, the richer in values his life will be. Thus, the interdependence of needs and the corresponding interpenetration of values implies that the *fulfillment of needs* brings *fullness of life.*

One of the main implications of this for ethics is that education in the appreciation of values of different kinds is indispensable for the good life. As Plato has pointed out in the *Republic,*[2] when youths are surrounded by beautiful objects and noble persons, not only in life but also in art and literature, they learn to delight in beauty and goodness and to be repelled by ugliness and baseness. The most effective moral education is not that which is done by precept and exhortation but that which results from continuous association with good men. It must be confessed that education in values is one of the least successful phases of modern education. Another implication is that needs cannot be fulfilled when the opportunity to make use of valuable objects is denied by social injustice. Millions who suffer from economic oppression and racial discrimination are doomed to have many of their needs unfulfilled. For example, the need for truth is frustrated in the case of those to whom an opportunity for education beyond the elementary level is denied and who are discouraged by a sordid home environment from making use of the opportunity they have. Thus, the necessity for a more effective education in values and a more just distribution of opportunities to realize them is clear.

In analyzing the nature of need as the subjective factor in value, we have not meant to imply that need confers or constitutes value. Value is given to us in experience as a value *of the object,* though it is a value *for the subject.* Indeed, it can be a value *for* the subject only if it is a value *of* the object. The act of valuing is directed not towards a state of the subject but towards the structure and properties of the object. Though value is given only in a relationship with the subject, it is not in any way bestowed by the subject upon the object. Indeed, it can fulfill the need of the subject for value just because it is not a product of that need. It is because the object is itself valuable that the need "calls for" it and can find "fulfillment" in it. Thus, to say that there is a subjective factor in value or that a value can be actualized only in the presence of a subject is not to

[2] *The Dialogues of Plato,* New York, Random House, 1937, I, p. 665.

deny that it is actualized *in the object*. "The object is not merely such as to *occasion* a valuable experience in the Mind," says Archbishop Temple; "the Mind in appreciating it appreciates *it* as valuable"[3] *Thus, value is essentially objective, though it is appreciated and actualized only through a subjective response.*

This point is important because it affects our view of the *aim* of realizing values. It might be supposed that, since the realization of values brings about the fulfillment of persons, the aim in realizing them is to "develop the personality." If this were so, the activity of realizing values would be egoistic in its motivation. In reality, it should be precisely the opposite. It should be an activity through which the self transcends itself by devoting itself to values beyond itself, surrendering itself to their claims at whatever cost to itself. It should be a spiritual activity by which the self unites itself with values and the divine Source of values. While it is an activity of the self, it is an activity through which the self can overcome the limitations of its separate existence as an individual and participate in a universal order of value. The needs of the self are fulfilled and happiness is attained in the process, but the aim of the process is not to *satisfy the self* but to enable it to *participate in the Good*.

ABSOLUTISM AND RELATIVISM

What is the implication of this view of values for the perennial question as to whether values are absolute or relative? The "loss of absolutes" is one of the most striking expressions of our cultural crisis. The lives of many are without conviction or purpose, because they have lost their belief that the claims of truth and justice upon them are valid. They have been taught by naturalistic psychologists and philosophers that values are simply objects of desire or interest which are to be used by man as far as they bring satisfaction to him but which impose no absolute demands upon him. They have been told by anthropologists that values are products of a particular culture and have no validity outside that culture. The relativism which has resulted from these and other causes has seriously weakened Western civilization at a time when it is being forced to struggle

[3] Temple, William, *Nature, Man and God*, London, Macmillan, p. 165 (italics mine).

for its very existence against the absolutistic ideology of Communism.

The traditional belief in absolute values was based upon the extreme objective theory of values which we have seen to be untenable. Though *absolutism* in this traditional form lingers on and still has considerable influence, it has been largely abandoned by thinking people. The error of this traditional absolutism was in the way it conceived values, on the one hand, and in its exalted view of reason, on the other. Since values were regarded as objective "Ideas" or "essences" wholly independent of man's response to them, it was thought possible to intuit Truth, Beauty, and Good above their particular and changing manifestations. These absolute values were regarded as eternal and immutable. The disinterested reason of the philosopher, it was supposed, could free itself from false opinions and apprehend these values, undistorted by private interest or arbitrary preference. We now realize that this is not possible. Beauty or Good is not an unchanging Idea or Essence which can be grasped fully and finally in a single act of intuition; and man's finite reason always operates under the influence of irrational forces within and without.

On the other hand, the claims of values like truth, goodness, beauty, and love are experienced as unconditional. As Kant says, the claims of duty upon the will come in the form of categorical, not hypothetical, imperatives. The pursuit of truth by the scientist or philosopher would be meaningless unless he could presuppose the existence of fixed and final truth as the goal of his efforts. Without this, what would be the meaning of scientists' persistent attempts to develop more adequate hypotheses for the explanation of nature, or of philosophers' repeated efforts to construct world views more adequate than those of their predecessors? Thus, the quest for the higher values requires us to *postulate* absolutes. However, to postulate them is not to *possess* them. The error of traditional absolutism lay not in its effort to attain absolute values but in its proud assumption that man could clearly grasp them. Those who accept the Christian view of man as a finite creature and a sinner will not pretend that they can ever do more than strive towards absolute truth and goodness.

What we mean when we postulate absolute values is not that there exists an absolute Idea of each value in a Platonic realm of Being but that there are *absolute principles* which should govern the creation and judgment of all examples of it. There is no ideal or archetype of Beauty which all beautiful things must "imitate" or in which they "participate," but there are principles which should be followed by all artists in creating beautiful things and by all critics in judging them. Similarly, there is no ideal of Justice to which every just state must conform, but there are principles of liberty and equality which must govern any state which is to be called just.

The error of traditional absolutism at this point has been to identify these universal principles with specific rules or standards which have been formulated by the men of a certain culture. The result has been to treat these rules or standards, which are relative to time and place, as if they were absolutes. In the ethical sphere, an example is the attempt of Catholic thinkers to identify the principles of "natural law" with specific rules which do not have universal validity. In the aesthetic sphere, an example is the identification of the canons of classical art and literature in the eighteenth century with universally valid principles. Therefore, it must be strongly insisted that the absolutes of which we have been speaking are *general principles* rather than *specific rules*. Moreover, the formulation of these principles can never be regarded as final but must be revised again and again.

This conception of absolute principles of value enables us to do full justice to the important elements of truth in *relativism*. The main source of modern relativism is the historical diversity of values such as beauty and goodness in different cultures. This diversity has been emphasized by the rapid and radical changes in the West during the last century, changes which have made men more aware of the mutability of values. For example, one school of painting after another has developed since the early nineteenth century, and social institutions have undergone revolutionary changes. In the light of these historical facts, relativists are fully justified in insisting that the *forms* of a value like beauty or justice are many and that the form it assumes in a particular culture is relative to that culture. Their error is in concluding from this that there are no absolute *principles* of beauty or justice which govern all of its forms. The differences between the forms and conventions of Chinese, Renaissance, and Impressionistic painting are very great, but there are fundamental principles to which all of them conform. This is why an aesthetically sensitive and educated person can appreciate the art of different ages or cultures. Essentially the same thing is true of the value of moral goodness. The differences between the forms taken by goodness in different societies have been great, sometimes so great that one may have difficulty at first in understanding them. But there is more agreement between them than is often recognized. In all societies, for example, the good man serves values recognized by his group and limits his own desires by its demands.

The acknowledgment of *absolute principles* of value, as we have described them, is not incompatible, therefore, with the recognition of a large degree of *relativity of the forms* in which a value has been and can be realized. Indeed, it is necessary for Christians not only to recognize but to insist upon this relativity. Because of the absolutism of traditional Catholic and Protestant legalistic ethics, which identified the will of God with moral rules laid down by the Church or discovered in the Bible, many people assume that Christian ethics is absolutistic in a sense which excludes all relativity. But the Christian ethic, we have held, is an ethic of love and liberty and only secondarily an ethic of law. It requires obedience at all times and under all conditions to the command that we love our neighbor. In this sense, it is absolutistic. But the law of love not only permits, it also demands, that we determine our duty in each situation in the light of its unique demands. Therefore, a large element of relativity is required in applying the absolute law of love itself.

The appeal of John Dewey's "moral experimentalism" is largely due to his emphasis upon the relativity of values and ideals to changing situations. According to Dewey, all ideals and values, however old and respected, should be held tentatively. They should be tested by the consequences of acting upon them. If they increase values and further the growth of individuals and society, they are to that extent confirmed. But they are never to be accepted as finally and absolutely valid. They are always to be acted upon in an experimental way, the mind keeping itself open to new possibilities of value. The danger of this view is obvious. It would put all ideals and values in flux and make it impossible to establish any of them as a firm basis for personal and social life. As a result, it would make unity and continuity in the life of the individual or society impossible. Actually, Dewey and his followers themselves accept certain values and ideals as absolutely valid, e.g., those of scientific knowledge, growth, individuality, and freedom. Thus, unlimited experimentalism in morality would be as disastrous as complete relativism.

Nevertheless, moral experimentalism, like moral relativism, points to a truth that is highly important. As we have said, while principles of value are absolute and unchanging, the forms assumed by values in different times and places are relative and changing. There are several reasons for this. The most obvious is that changes in human knowledge and social conditions are continuous, and values and ideals are modified as a result of these changes. Another reason is that there are *indeterminate possibilities* of value in our complex world. At any given time and place, only a fraction of these possibilities is recognized. For example, men's knowledge of nature is still very partial; and there are many different forms of beauty which are still to be created. Thus, the mind should always be open to new forms of value which may be discovered and realized. But the most fundamental reason for change in values, perhaps, is that man is a spiritual being characterized by freedom and by the capacity to transcend himself. He is essentially *creative,* always seeking to produce forms through which he can express new possibilities of value. That is why he cannot be content with one style of art or literature, merely copying the masters of the past and repeating their achievements again and again, for he is always seeing things in fresh ways and experimenting with new methods of expressing what he sees. In the same way, he is always seeking to improve social institutions and relationships or invent new ones. Thus, the boundless possibilities of value in nature and history interact with the creative spirit of man to bring new forms of value into being.

This is particularly characteristic of the modern world in which the scientific method of knowing and the democratic way of life have combined to emphasize rapid change. Although life in such a world is difficult because of the constant necessity of making adjustments to changing situations and demands, Christians should remember that they serve a God who is always active in creating and redeeming His world. Moreover, they should never fall into the temptation of absolutizing the values of the past or the present. Their task is to respond freely and creatively to God's demands in their own time and seek always for more adequate ways of realizing values in the lives of their neighbors here and now.

HIGHER AND LOWER VALUES

One of the main questions with which moral philosophers have concerned themselves is the question of *comparative value*. This question may take the form, What is the "highest good," the "summum bonum," which men should seek above all other goods? Or it may take the form, What is the right "scale of values" or order of "higher" and "lower" values? In either case, the question arises out of the *necessity of choosing* between the various values which can be realized in each situation and of having some standard to guide one in his preference of one value over another.

What should be the attitude of the Christian to the many attempts of moral philosophers to discover the right "scale of values"? On this issue Christian moralists who are Biblicists differ sharply from those who are not. Biblicists tend to regard the issue as irrelevant to Christian ethics. They point out that in the New Testament the commandment to love God and the neighbor is bound up with the Gospel or "good news" that God is going to bestow eternal life upon those who accept His Kingdom. In this sense, Christian ethics itself has a doctrine of the "summum bonum" or highest good of man. But this doctrine of a "highest good" has nothing in common with the theories of moral philosophers about "higher" and "lower" values. For the "highest good" of eternal life in the Kingdom is incommensurable with all the values of natural human existence in the present age. It is the "pearl of great price" which is of such surpassing value that a man should sell all he has in order to possess it. Therefore all human values, "superior" as well as "inferior," are unimportant in comparison with it; in its presence, "higher" values are as insignificant as "lower" ones. How can a point of view like this have anything to do with the point of view of philosophers for whom all that matters is to realize the "higher" values of the present age?

It must be acknowledged that the early Christians, who lived in eager anticipation of the coming of the Kingdom, did not concern themselves with philosophical problems of value. They had their eyes upon a Good beside which all earthly goods were of little consequence. Even in the early fifth century St. Augustine manifested a measure of indifference to earthly values. In *The City of God* he examined in turn the various answers which had been given by classical thinkers to the question, what is the "summum bonum"? He rejected the answers which identified the highest good with intellectual activity, moral virtue, or social life as completely as those which identified it with pleasure or wealth. When measured against the highest good of the Christian, which is "eternal life in peace," "higher" as well as "lower" goods seemed to him imperfect and mixed with evil.[1]

But the Christian must live in this life as well as prepare himself for the next. Even St. Augustine was not so other-worldly as to be wholly indifferent to the values of this world. Christians, he held, may *use* the things of time provided they do not seek their ultimate fulfillment or *fruition* in them. Moreover, he followed this principle in his own life. From his youth, he had been a passionate seeker after truth. After his conversion, he did not desert philosophy, but dealt with many philosophical questions from his new Christian perspective. He had also been a lover of beauty and eloquence. After he became a Christian, he wrote a treatise on music and continued to practice the art of rhetoric in his writing. Thus, he continued to prize the "higher" values of the Greeks although he did not seek in them his "highest good."

Can it really be the will of God, the Source of all truth and good, that modern Christians should have nothing to do with an important aspect of the good life because the New Testament is not explicitly concerned with it? They cannot share the eschatological outlook of the early Christians, for whom the present age and its values were

[1] St. Augustine, *The City of God*, Bk. 19.

soon to pass away. They look forward to the indefinite continuation of history and must consider their responsibilities to their neighbors in the light of that expectation. In short, they must not only prepare themselves for eternal life; they must also live and help others to live the most worthy lives possible in this world. When the question is approached from this point of view, it is evident that the Biblicist answer is wholly inadequate. Modern Christians dare not neglect the insights of moral philosophers and others concerning the order of higher and lower values. For these insights are indispensable to all who are seeking to manifest their love for their neighbors in an intelligent way. We have pointed out that man's needs "call for" appropriate values to fulfill them. If he is to do his duty well, therefore, the Christian must gratefully accept any insight into the rank of different values in the scale of values and must make use of it in serving the needs of his neighbors.

It is a striking fact that so many moral philosophers throughout the history of philosophy have agreed that human values should be ranked in a scale of higher and lower. In Plato's *Apology,* Socrates urges his fellow Athenians, who have just condemned him to death, to teach his children that virtue is of more worth than riches.[2] In the *Philebus,* Plato ranks pure above mixed pleasures and wisdom above both.[3] In the modern period, Mill insists that man is required by his sense of dignity to choose pleasures which are qualitatively superior rather than inferior and that these are the pleasures of the mind.[4] Among recent philosophers, G. E. Moore argues that intrinsic values can be ranked in a scale, with appreciation of beautiful objects and personal affection at the top.[5]

It is true that there has not been complete agreement with respect to the order in which different values should be ranked. Matthew Arnold pointed out that "Hebraism" prized above all else moral earnestness, whereas "Hellenism" cared most for beauty and truth, "sweetness and light."[6] Even among the Greeks there was a striking difference between Athens, which devoted itself at its best to freedom

[2] *The Dialogues of Plato,* New York, Random House, 1937, I, p. 423.
[3] Ibid., II, p. 402.
[4] Mill, J. S., *Utilitarianism,* New York, Dutton, 1931, pp. 7-10.
[5] Moore, G. E., op. cit., p. 188.
[6] Arnold, M., *Culture and Anarchy,* Ch's. I, IV.

and the arts and sciences, and Sparta, which sought military power and glory above all else. In our own time, G. E. Moore does not even include all virtues in his scale of intrinsic values;[7] but W. D. Ross thinks they are the highest values.[8]

Despite this diversity of opinion, the extent of *agreement* has been impressive. First, virtually all moral philosophers, as well as religious thinkers, have agreed that material possessions have only instrumental rather than intrinsic value and that they belong at the bottom of the scale. Second, there is almost complete agreement that bodily or biological values, such as the pleasures of eating and drinking, are inferior to mental values. Despite the modern cult of health and long life and the modern emphasis upon sex, sober thinkers have not usually regarded them as the highest values. Third, there is wide agreement that worship, love, goodness, truth, and beauty are "superior" or "higher" on the scale of values than both economic and bodily values. Although there has been considerable difference of opinion with respect to the relative positions of these "higher" values among themselves, there has been broad agreement that *all* of them are to be placed among the higher rather than the lower values.

Does this scale of values have any *basis in human nature?* In an earlier chapter[9] we pointed out that man is a natural being but that he also possesses the capacity for spiritual activity. Now, spirit is a unique capacity of man, irreducible to the biological level. Moreover, it is man's highest capacity, and it seeks to subordinate other aspects of his nature to its purposes and values. It is clear that this distinction within human nature is correlated with the distinction drawn by moral philosophers between higher and lower values. The higher values of worship, love, goodness, truth, and beauty can have no meaning for creatures which lack man's capacity for spiritual aspiration and activity. It is also obvious that bodily or biological values such as health and sex in its purely physiological aspect are rooted in man's animal nature.

Several things, however, should be pointed out concerning this

---

[7] Moore, G. E., op. cit., pp. 173-180.
[8] Ross, W. D., *The Right and the Good,* Oxford, The Clarendon Press, 1930, p. 152.
[9] Ch. VII.

distinction between higher and lower values. In the first place, because of the unity of man's personality, *the lower values are fundamental to the higher ones*. For example, though economic values are instrumental rather than intrinsic, they provide a necessary basis for spiritual values. A scientist in quest of truth needs a laboratory equipped with suitable apparatus; an artist must have paint and canvas and a musician an instrument; members of a religious community must have a church, books, and other material objects for their corporate worship; and one of the highest moral values, justice, is attained in society only if the material things which are needed by all are fairly distributed. Similarly, though bodily or biological values are inferior to spiritual ones, their presence or absence has a profound effect upon spiritual values. For example, health provides a flow of energy and a feeling of well-being that normally makes easier the creation of beauty and the discovery of truth, and it furthers friendship and love by setting us free from the distractions of pain. And life is obviously the most fundamental of all values, because it is the basic condition of all the rest.

Thus, one must not falsely "spiritualize" human life and its values. While spiritual values are *higher,* bodily values are more *fundamental*. An important inference may be derived from this with respect to the practical application of a scale of values: a community must realize at least a decent minimum of lower values before it can or should make the attainment of higher values its primary concern. Pioneers have to build homes and assure a food supply before they can turn their attention to the building of churches and schools. The importance of this principle in the struggle of Democracy against Communism among the underdeveloped peoples of the Orient we are only beginning to recognize. People without bread have little interest in political liberty.

In the second place, *the presence of spiritual values bestows upon lower values a higher significance* than they would otherwise possess. Since the human self is one, its spiritual activity penetrates and transforms its bodily existence. With man, eating and drinking are occasions not only for the satisfaction of the animal needs of hunger and thirst, but also for the gathering together of friends and loved ones. As such, they are associated with the intellectual, aesthetic, and moral values that are generated on such occasions. Again, sex is more than a physiological function; it is also an expression of love and a symbol of all the higher values shared by husband and wife. Thus, when we distinguish between spiritual and bodily values, we must always remember that they are interwoven in the life of the self. As the lower values are indispensable conditions of the higher, the higher invest the lower with something of their own spiritual significance. Any sharp separation of the two is artificial. Indeed, it destroys the integrity, the wholeness of the self. Ideally, all activities of a truly human person realize spiritual values, and all are carried out with the aid of bodily energies and usually of material means.

In the third place, *differences between individuals and groups profoundly affect the way they realize spiritual and other values.* Man is conditioned in all he does by his individual aptitudes and his social environment. If he has a strong aptitude for intellectual activity, he may become a scholar; for artistic activity, a poet or painter; for technical proficiency, an engineer or a skilled worker. As a result of conditioning factors such as these, as well as of the division of labor required by every society, there is inevitably a differentiation and specialization of individuals, societies, and groups with respect to the values which are realized by each of them. This helps to account for the disagreement we have noted between moral philosophers and even whole societies as to the relative positions of certain values on their scales of values. The effect of the "personal equation" and of "social conditioning" is such that all scales of values are bound to be defective. Consequently, a scale of values can only point to the general superiority of certain values over others, and should be regarded as a *counsel* which is to be followed with discrimination rather than as a *law* which is to be mechanically obeyed.

Finally, it must never be forgotten that *man's pursuit of spiritual values as well as of other values is corrupted by sin.* It is possible to pursue high values from low motives. The self-centered man seeks truth or beauty as a means to his own glory or profit, uses friendship to serve his own ends, and even prays to God to further his own interests. Thus, the apparent pursuit of the "higher" values on a scale of values is no proof that a man is devoted to truth and beauty or that he loves God and his neighbor. On the other hand, the pursuit of what appear to be "lower" values is often ennobled by a spiritual motive. Therefore, we should never judge whether a man is serving spiritual values by looking at his *vocation* or his external *behavior;* rather, we must consider his inner *intention.* Is a farmer who spends his days plowing his fields, repairing his barns, and milking his cows realizing only lower economic and bodily values? He is certainly growing food that will sustain his biological existence and making money that will procure material things. But he may be primarily motivated by a deep love of his family; he may be a loyal friend to his neighbors, sensitive to the beauty of field and sky, an humble servant of God. This in no way invalidates our contention that Christians should, in general, choose spiritual in preference to lower values; but it should prevent us from making the silly and snobbish assumption that a "cultured" person is always spiritually superior to an "uncultured" one or that the spiritual life is only for those who follow one of the traditional professions and not for those who toil with their hands.

TRUTH

We can make clearer the attitude of Christian ethics towards spiritual values if we consider by way of illustration the values of *truth* and *friendship.* It is not easy to find a definition of truth that will satisfy everyone. For our purposes, however, truth may be defined in terms of conformity with reality. Its value lies not in the mere fact of this conformity, but in its capacity to bring man into relation with reality. Since true knowledge replaces opinions that are based upon superficial acquaintance or hearsay, it enables man to get behind the appearances of things to reality.

Modern men tend to identify truth with the sum total of truths about different parts or aspects of reality. Truth, on this view, is nothing but facts, *information* about many things. Consequently, knowledge of a large number of miscellaneous facts is more prized than depth of understanding. The "free elective" system in our universities was in part a product of this way of thinking. It was based upon the assumption that all an educated man needs is a modicum of knowledge about a number of special fields and that integration of his knowledge by means of general principles and beliefs is unnecessary. Moreover, since the time of Francis Bacon, men have valued knowledge as *power* because it has enabled them to master nature and use her resources to serve their own ends. Truth has been regarded, not as an intrinsic value, but as a means to the satisfaction of men's desires. This "technical" or "instrumental" view of knowledge is based on the assumption that we should try to know not in order to love and appreciate things more deeply but in order to use them more efficiently. The restriction of knowledge to specialized information about facts has been encouraged by the growth of "positivism," which asserts that the only real knowledge man can attain is scientific knowledge of phenomena and that he must give up the hope of gaining metaphysical knowledge of the reality behind phenomena. The belief that the aim of knowledge is the power it bestows upon man has been fostered by the attitude of "utilitarianism." It is hardly too much to say that "positivism" and "utilitarianism" together have seriously weakened the ideal of liberal education and all but destroyed the ideal of wisdom.

Christians must begin their thinking about the value of truth, therefore, by *rejecting* this modern conception of truth. The ultimate goal of knowing is that understanding of universal reality and value we call wisdom. Truth is much more than unrelated knowledge of facts. Moreover, the value of truth is not to be found primarily in the power it gives to man over his environment. To think of it in such terms is to foster man's egoism and to treat reality merely as an instrument of his purposes. It is to lose the capacity to appreciate the order, beauty, and wonder of the Creation in itself. Thus, it both impoverishes man's view of reality and makes him narrow and self-centered.

What, then, should be the Christian conception of truth? First, the value of truth lies primarily in the fact that it enables man to transcend himself by *participation in being* beyond himself. The pursuit of truth, for anyone who is a real lover of truth, cannot stop at any point but must press on beyond every limit in the effort to know reality as a whole. Moreover, the lover of truth seeks knowledge of the meaning and value of being as well as of being itself. Truth enables man to embrace the *fullness of good*. Thus, it bestows upon him the power to participate in universal being and value. The individuality of a person would be a defect if it merely separated him from others and confined him within himself; but truth gives him the opportunity to open himself to the universal reality of which he is only a small part.

Second, if the goal of truth is participation in the whole of reality and value, it is obvious that *all of man's faculties* must be enlisted in the quest for it. One of the fallacies of modern thought is that truth is discovered only by reason working on materials provided by sense experience. This may be adequate as an account of the process by which scientific knowledge is attained. But it is completely misleading as a description of the process of attaining truth in morality, religion, the social sciences, and the humanities. In these fields, intuition, imagination, feeling and action are also involved in the discovery of truth. Even the knowledge of nature, as Whitehead has said,[1] requires not only the description of causal relations by the scientist's reason but also the apprehension of quality and value by the intuition of the poet. The truth about human personality in all its complexity can be known only by one who does not look at man from the outside as a spectator but sympathetically listens to him and identifies himself with him in all his joys and sorrows. Moral truth can have meaning only for one who has developed a good character, as Aristotle pointed out. And religious truth can come only to him who is pure in heart, who seeks God with his whole self and surrenders his will to the divine will. Thus, rational analysis and synthesis must be supplemented by intuition, imagination, feeling, and commitment of the will if the whole truth is to be discovered.

Third, the Christian holds that truth must ultimately be understood from the *religious perspective*. The knowledge of natural laws by the scientist, the appreciation of qualities and values by the artist, and the synoptic vision of reality as a whole by the philosopher are all partial expressions of the Truth that is in God. St. Augustine asserts that all truths must be seen in the light of the universal Truth which is the Wisdom of God. How can man know the final

[1] Whitehead, A. N., *Science and the Modern World*, New York, Macmillan, 1925, Ch. 5.

secret of this divine Truth? In the Greek view, man knows truth by reason since it is an impersonal and universal structure or order. In the Christian view, he cannot know ultimate truth by philosophical speculation alone; he must interpret it with the help of God's revelation of His Truth in concrete historical events. God has revealed Truth in *Christ,* not merely in his teachings but also in his person. This is why Christ is called in the Fourth Gospel the "Word," the self-utterance of God. "The Word became flesh and dwelt among us." This means that the fullest and clearest expression of God's nature and of His purpose for man has come through His incarnation in Christ. The words of Christ in the Fourth Gospel reflect the faith of the early Church about him: "I am the Way, the Truth, and the Life."

This is a stupendous assertion, of course, and it can never be demonstrated by scientific or philosophical arguments. It originated through revelation and is accepted by faith. But there is nothing inherently irrational in it. The fact that it seems irrational to the common sense of the natural man or to the reason of the secular scientist and philosopher is not hard to explain. Common sense judges every thing and event in the light of man's experience of ordinary things and events. It is bound, therefore, to be suspicious of that which is unique. The scientist's reason explains every occurrence as but an instance of a class of phenomena which can be described by a law applicable to all instances of the class alike. Obviously, it can do nothing with an event which is unique and falls into no class. The reason of the philosopher explains a thing or event as a part of reality, having its particular place and standing in definite relations with the other parts. Non-Christian philosophy almost inevitably rejects the claim made on behalf of any particular event that it is not merely a part but the clue to the meaning of the whole. In other words, common sense, science, and philosophy alike explain the individual simply as a particular instance of a universal or as a manifestation of the whole.

Now, Christianity does not deny the value of this kind of explanation. It recognizes that man as a rational being must interpret reality by means of universal concepts that delineate its structure. But it insists that the *meaning and purpose* of reality, as distinguished from its *general structure,* can be understood only by referring it to God, who is not a universal but a concrete living Being. If God is personal, is it not reasonable to think that the best clue to His nature and purpose may be found in the human person in whom the whole process of creation and redemption has reached its highest perfection? Is there anything inherently improbable in the conviction that the secret of the meaning and purpose of God as Ultimate Reality may be most adequately understood by looking at Christ?

But, fourth, the Christian conviction that the ultimate Truth about reality has been made known through revelation does not imply a depreciation of the *value of other truths* which can be known by the methods of common sense, science, and philosophy. Indeed, it enhances their value immensely, for it enables us to see these truths in relation to their divine Source and to the Creation as a whole. In this way, our knowledge is endowed with a broader and deeper meaning, every fact pointing beyond itself to its ultimate origin and taking its place in the whole of truth. Perhaps the best proof that the religious perspective enhances the value of every kind of truth is that the loss of it by modern man has led to the degradation of truth and reason. Since truth has become for many a mere instrument of power, it has been distorted or denied again and again to serve the will to power of a state, a party, or a class. Moreover, loss of belief in the very possibility of truth concerning the ultimate issues of religion, ethics, and politics has produced widespread irrationalism. Not since the light of ancient learning was extinguished by the barbarians at the end of the Roman Empire have truth and reason been regarded with such contempt as they have been in the secular totalitarian states of our own time.

Fifth, the value of truth should not be divorced from *other values* in the life of man. There must be an interpenetration of values if there is to be unity in the personality and completeness in the spiritual life. This may be illustrated by the intimate relation between truth and *goodness.* Since the time of Socrates and Plato, there has been a long tradition in Western philosophy linking the love of wisdom with the love of virtue. In modern thought, however, there has been a tendency to assert the "autonomy" or independence of truth and to insist upon "truth for truth's sake." As a result of tendencies like these, there has developed a dualism between theory and practice, truth and goodness. To the Christian, truth is "autonomous" in the sense that it should not be determined by an appeal to authority, and "truth for truth's sake" is justified as an affirmation of the intrinsic value of truth. But the value of truth is not self-sufficient and independent of other values. Since truth enables the self to transcend itself by participating in reality and value beyond itself, it exists not merely for its own sake but for the sake of the enlargement of life. Truth is "in order to goodness," or, since there are other forms of the good than moral goodness, it is "in order to the good." If so, the modern specialization of function which requires some persons to spend virtually all their time and energy in intellectual activity and permits them to neglect their moral and social responsibilities must be condemned.

Christians must also reject the *intellectualism* which overlooks or minimizes the dependence of reason upon the will. It may be that mathematical and scientific thinking is not essentially affected by the goodness or badness of the will. But in the social studies and the humanities, where values are involved, man's interests and character affect his thinking profoundly. Self-interest and class-affiliation always distort man's perspective upon the problems of self and society; and only insofar as goodness has overcome the bias of self-interest can reason attain true objectivity and see things and values in their true light. In the realm of religious and moral thinking, the relation of truth to goodness is still more obvious. Only as a person acts upon the truth he already sees can he make it his own and discover new truth, for only as he lives by truth can he validate it, deepen its meaning, and develop his sensitivity to new truth. If truth is so closely related to moral goodness and if moral goodness at its best is dependent upon love, the capacity for the highest kind of truth requires a liberation of the will from its bondage to self through faith and love.

FRIENDSHIP

Friendship has not received as much attention from Christian moralists as it did from Greek philosophers like Plato and Aristotle.

Perhaps the main reason for this is that Christians have given a higher place than the Greeks to the family and to love between man and woman. In Greek society, the attitude of most men towards the family was very practical and love between man and woman was seldom regarded in romantic fashion. As a result, friendship between men was idealized more than it is among us.[1] Among us, on the other hand, the family is the most fundamental and important form of human association. Love between man and woman is idealized as the source of the highest as well as the most intense happiness. In addition, children are prized as they were not in the ancient world, and parental affection strengthens the bonds between husband and wife.

In *youth,* friendship gives rise to a close comradeship based upon mutual affection and need. At a time when the potentialities of life are rapidly unfolding, it is a powerful stimulus to growth. During a period of inner uncertainty and tension, it bestows a sense of security and worth through mutual affection and approval. On the other hand, friendships in *middle age* are usually formed on the basis of common interests and tasks. Our friends are likely to be our fellow-workers, our partners or colleagues. For this reason, the friendships of middle age are normally less ardent and more impersonal than those of adolescence or early manhood. Spontaneous affection plays a smaller part in attracting one to a friend than his moral qualities, his ability, or his congeniality. As a result, there is a tendency for friendship to become less important for its own sake but more essential for the fulfillment of purposes. There is also less time for friendship in the case of busy men as they become more involved in the responsibilities of a family and the tasks of a vocation.

However, this is not inevitable. It is possible for two fully mature persons to be closely united by common interests and at the same time to be bound by the ties of mutual affection. Their friendship may not be as intense as the friendships of adolescence, but it is likely to be purer and nobler. Though the friendships of adolescence often give rise to loyalty, they spring not only from affection for one's friends but also from one's need for the strength and encour-

[1] Taylor, A. E., *Plato,* New York, Dial Press, 1929, p. 65.

agement they can give. In full maturity, if one has learned to serve values and causes that transcend himself, one is capable of more disinterested friendship. Devotion to a common task one shares with a friend may blend with a quiet but deep affection for him as a person. It must be admitted, however, that a pure friendship like this is a rare attainment, for the spur of ambition which goads men into restless activity leaves little time for the leisurely conversation and comradeship without which friendship soon withers.

What is the *essence* of friendship? Friendship is a more or less enduring relationship between two persons which is based upon mutual affection and acceptance and which expresses itself in the desire of each for companionship with the other. Let us examine this definition more closely. It asserts, first, that friendship is more or less enduring and is not to be confused with a friendly disposition. One may be friendly to many persons without having a single friend. For friendliness requires only that one shall be genial and well-disposed towards people in general, not that one shall desire a close relationship with any of them. It may spring from mere gregariousness and the desire to escape boredom through being with others. On the other hand, friendship means involvement with the life of another person. As such, it tends to be relatively enduring, though not always permanent. Second, friendship is based upon acceptance and affection. We may admire a person without seeking his friendship, as in hero-worship; and we may have a friend with some qualities we do not admire. But we must accept and like him on the whole and we must have confidence in him. Third, friendship expresses itself in the desire for companionship. Friends want to be together, to talk together, to do things together. For friendship involves not only an affirmation of the welfare and worth of one's friend, but a desire to share the experiences of life with him.

What are the *conditions* of friendship? The first is that it shall be *reciprocated*. Of course, one may continue to feel friendly towards a person who no longer returns one's friendship, but friendship requires mutuality. In this respect, it is like erotic love between man and woman. One may long for friendship with another person, but unless he desires it also, one's longing leads to frustration rather than fulfillment. The reason is that, like erotic love, friendship must receive as well as give. Consequently, it is one of the tragic aspects of life that friends often cease to be friends. Despite the intensity of friendship in youth, most of the friends of one's youth cease to be friends in mature life. This is seldom due to conscious disloyalty or renunciation of the friendship on either side; it is usually a result of the development of new interests, separation from one another, the formation of new friendships, and the pressure of work. Of course, there are exceptions. Life-long friendships are possible, especially when friends remain in the same community and when their interests do not undergo any radical change. But the fact that friendship in maturity has a somewhat different basis than friendship in youth makes such friendships rare.

The second condition of friendship is the willingness of each to regard himself as the *equal* of the other. A friendship is possible in spite of actual inequality in many respects, e.g., in ability, character, and success. But it becomes impossible if one makes his superiority in one or more respects a ground for refusing to treat the other as fundamentally equal to himself. The superior one either becomes indifferent to the other or in his pride begins to dominate him. In either case, the spontaneous interplay of giving and receiving ceases. Consequently, friendship requires forbearance. Proud and ambitious persons are not likely to have friends. As Plato says somewhere, tyrants are surrounded by parasites and flatterers rather than friends.

The third condition of friendship is closely connected with this: it is the capacity in some measure to *overcome egoism* and *give oneself* to another. One whose policy is to receive as much and give as little as possible is unlikely to have friends. Friendship requires generosity. Otherwise, one will have no real affection for a friend or concern for his happiness. This is why friendship, like parental and filial feelings, has always been regarded as a training-ground for public spirit and civic virtue. It is also the reason why the highest level of friendship can be attained only by noble and good men.

What is the relation between *friendship* and *Christian love?* The differences between them are obvious. Unlike friendship, Christian love is not selective but inclusive. It gives without expecting a return and continues to give even when there is no return. It is bestowed on those who are unequal as well as those who are equal to the self.

It does not demand enduring and close companionship with a particular person, but treats any person as one's neighbor and serves his needs. One reason for these differences is that even if we had the inclination, we could not share our lives fully with many friends as we can serve the needs of many neighbors. But there is another and less creditable reason. Unlike Christian love, friendship always has some measure of egoism in it. We give to our friends, but we also expect to receive something from them. That is, in part, why friendship dies when it is not returned. For friendship springs not only from affection for others but also from the need for others. The values our friends bestow upon us may not be tangible—they may not make us richer or more successful—but they are nonetheless real: affection, encouragement, sympathy, counsel, and, when necessary, help.

But this is only one side of the matter. Genuine affection is one of the essential elements in friendship and an association based solely on utility or mutual convenience is not friendship. *Willingness to give* and to give without a nice calculation of the probability of an equal return is indispensable to friendship. The fact that giving is accompanied by receiving does not disprove this; it merely shows that disinterestedness and interest are bound up together in friendship. Moreover, the fact that it is given to some but not to others does not destroy its disinterestedness, though it severely limits its scope. The proof of this is the willingness of true friends to undergo hardships and make sacrifices for one another in peace as well as in war. Therefore, the Greeks were not wrong in regarding friendship as the source of some of the highest and purest joys of human life. They saw that friends not only please one another but also stimulate one another to live creative lives. Inspired by his friend, Socrates points out, a man is encouraged to seek truth and virtue; and Plato's devotion to philosophy, originally inspired by his master, is a proof that he was right.

In consequence, Christian love of neighbor transcends but is not opposed to friendship. It is true that one may make an idol out of a friend or be tempted to narrow his interest to a small circle of friends. If this occurs, friendship becomes a rival of Christian love in his life. But if disinterested affection and concern for the happiness of another is characteristic of friendship and if it expresses itself in giving to him, it can become an ally rather than a rival of Christian love. For this to occur, however, Christian love must purify it. Only then does special affection for one's friends become compatible with the more general demands of love for one's neighbors and strengthen the will to serve them.

CHAPTER 21

Moral Virtue and Character

MORAL education is usually concerned above all with inculcating those dispositions which are called *virtues*. This is due in part to the recognition of parents, teachers, and elders in general that the root of moral conduct is *character*. The concern for character is accompanied by instruction in what are regarded as duties. But this instruction is not thought to be fully successful unless it leads to the formation of virtuous habits which make the performance of duties spontaneous and in a sense natural. There is nothing that is prized by thoughtful men more highly than the character which results from this process, both for its own intrinsic worth and for its fruits in right conduct.

Yet no problem has received less attention in the recent moral philosophy of Great Britain and America than that of the virtues and character. How are we to account for this strange fact? One cause is that the rapid social changes of the present century and the profound moral difficulties into which they have plunged us have shattered our confidence in the traditional theories of virtue. Though Aristotle's discussion of the virtues is still widely read and respected by students of ethics, the interest in it is mainly historical. Thomas Aquinas' elaborate analysis of the virtues is less well known among most philosophers and is generally dismissed as little more than a restatement of Aristotle with a few curious theological additions. What is not so understandable is the all but total neglect of the task of working out a modern theory of virtue. Though Nicolai Hartmann's analysis of virtues in terms of objective values might have been expected to arouse new interest in the problem, it has provoked very little serious investigation into the nature of virtue.[1]

There is needed not only a renewed study of classical theories for the light they throw on the notion of virtue and character, but also a fresh attempt to deal with the problem in more modern terms. Philosophers will need the help of modern psychology and anthropology as they make this attempt, but they can make a distinctive contribution of their own to the problem. In dealing with it, they will have to consider the following questions: (1) What is the *nature* of virtue? Is it a habit? If so, what kind of habit is it? (2) What is the *function* of virtue in the moral life? More particularly, what is its relation to the duties which should be done and the values which should be realized? (3) What is the relation of virtue to *society*? Is a virtue relative to a particular society or is it universal in its essence? (4) What is *character*?

ARISTOTLE'S THEORY OF MORAL VIRTUE

Before we attempt to answer these questions, it will be well for us to analyze and evaluate the most important philosophical theory of moral virtue, that of Aristotle in his *Nicomachean Ethics*. According to Aristotle, "happiness" or *well-being* arises from the activity of the highest and most distinctive capacity of man, reason. It consists of rational activity or functioning "in accordance with virtue." But what is "virtue"? We shall confine ourselves to what Aristotle says about "moral" virtue. A moral virtue is a *habit or state* which is attained through the actualization of a potentiality in our nature. The raw materials of our nature, irrational as well as rational, are potentially good. But we must actualize the potentialities in them by action. "We learn (the virtues) by doing them," "we become just by doing just acts, temperate by doing temperate acts, brave by doing brave acts."[1]

This must not be interpreted in terms of the Romantic view that man's natural impulses and feelings are good and that moral evil

---

[1] Hartmann, N., *Ethics,* New York, Macmillan, 1932, II. Used by permission of the publisher.
[1] Aristotle, *Nicomachean Ethics,* 1103a.

is due to the interference of reason or social institutions. On the contrary, the raw materials of our nature are only potentially good and actual goodness is attained by the activity of reason under the influence of society. On the other hand, there is nothing in Aristotle's view corresponding to the Christian conception of a tendency of the will to sin alongside of the natural tendency to good. For this reason, he says nothing about the need for a radical transformation of the self to overcome the tendency to sin and to stimulate the development of potentialities of virtue in the soul. All that is necessary is *moral education*. Aristotle expresses the importance of moral education in the strongest terms: "legislators *make* the citizens good by forming habits in them."[2]

In addition to the potentialities of virtue in human nature and the influence of moral education in actualizing these potentialities in a youth, *moral effort* on the part of the individual is presupposed. He is not mere plastic clay in the hands of a potter; he is an active being who must perform the acts which are necessary to make him virtuous. Moreover, his acts will not be fully virtuous until he does them willingly and with pleasure. While he may perform good acts for a time without being good himself, he must do them from a deliberate moral purpose of his own before he can do them in the right way, at the right time, and with the right motive. Thus, moral education may begin with the imposition of authority from outside but it should lead up to the achievement of a kind of autonomy on the part of the individual.

Moral virtues, then, are not natural "passions" or "faculties"— these are neither good nor bad—but *acquired "states of character" which involve "choice."* But what makes a virtue not merely a state of character but a good or excellent one? The answer of Aristotle to this question constitutes one of the most important doctrines of his Ethics: moral virtue is a *mean*. Assuming that in passions and actions it is proper to speak of excess, defect, and intermediate, he asserts that moral virtue is a "mean" between extremes of excess and defect. "For instance," he says, "both fear and confidence and appetite and anger and pity and, in general, pleasure and pain may be felt both too much and too little, and in both cases not well; but

[2] Ibid., II, Ch. 1, 1103a.

to feel them at the right times, with reference to the right objects, towards the right people, with the right motive, and in the right way, is what is both intermediate and best, and this is characteristic of virtue. Similarly, with regard to actions also there is excess, deficiency, and the intermediate."[3] But we must distinguish between the "intermediate in the object" and the "intermediate relatively to us" which is not the same for all. "If ten pounds are too much for a particular person to eat and two too little, it does not follow that the trainer will order six pounds; for this also is perhaps too much for the person who is to take it, or too little . . . too little for Milo (the famous wrestler), too much for the beginner in athletic exercises."[4] Therefore, the mean must be determined by each individual for himself. Although he is to determine it with "practical wisdom," says Aristotle, "the decision rests with perception."[5]

The assumption behind this doctrine is the Pythagorean principle that "evil belongs to the class of the unlimited," "good to that of the limited." Good, like music and health, has a quantitative basis, and, like them, requires a definite ratio between opposites. But why must the good be found at the "mean" rather than somewhere else? The answer, which is implicit rather than explicit, seems to be that men's passions tend to excess and *moderation* is necessary if all are to be satisfied and an harmonious personality achieved. To the question, Why should *all* be satisfied in a moderate degree instead of giving free rein to *some* of them?, Aristotle gives no answer. He simply assumes, like other Greeks, that all of the potentialities of human nature should be realized but that they must be moderated if they are not to destroy the unity and harmony of the self. However, he recognizes that some passions and actions are by their very nature evil and should be repressed rather than moderated, e.g., envy, spite, theft, and murder.[6]

The *value* of this theory of virtue has always been recognized. It strongly affirms that goodness requires mastery over the irrational elements of human nature. At the same time, it implies that the natural impulses should not be subject to mere repression. More-

---

[3] Ibid., II, Ch. 6, 1106b.
[4] Ibid., II, Ch. 6, 1106b.

[5] Ibid., II, Ch. 9, 1109b.
[6] Ibid., II, Ch. 6, 1107a.

over, it puts full responsibility upon each person for his character. It will not allow a drunk man to plead innocence on the ground that his will was too weak to resist his desire; it might have been stronger if he had not formed the habit of drinking in the past. Again, the whole theory is based upon the assumption that, while man is an animal sharing his appetites with other animals, he is distinguished from them by his reason and can find happiness only by subordinating his animal to his rational nature. Thus, it is an expression of humanism which lays upon man the responsibility of developing his higher nature.

But there are also serious *limitations* in Aristotle's theory. The first of these is the *self-centeredness* of the virtuous man as described by him. Although he does not identify happiness or well-being with pleasure, he asumes that virtuous activity will be accompanied by the enjoyment of pleasure. His treatment of the virtues of "ambitiousness" and "great-mindedness" takes for granted that the desire for honors will be a dominant motive of the virtuous man. The picture of the "great-minded" man is on the whole a repellent one, not because he is unworthy but because he is so conscious that he is worthy. It is true that many of the moral virtues described by Aristotle have a social as well as a personal purpose, e.g., courage and justice. It would be unfair, therefore, to see in his view nothing more than crude egoism. Nevertheless, the lack of any explicitly altruistic element and of any stress upon self-sacrifice suggests that he is thinking primarily of the happiness of the individual. Perhaps this tendency to egoism in Aristotle's theory is connected with the absence of a sense of duty which would subordinate self-realization to the service of one's neighbor or of humanity. The theory of the mean, Stocks points out, defined "the terms on which the power of free self-determination, which we call will, can be attained and maintained. It is a victory over internal disorder. What the theory has failed to define is the conditions of the exercise of that freedom when it has been attained."[7] The self is directed to an end within itself, its own development and perfection, and is not devoted to a wider purpose which requires it to subordinate and even sacrifice itself.

[7] Stocks, J. S., *The Limits of Purpose,* London, Benn, 1932, p. 262.

Again, the theory of virtue as a *mean* is not an adequate definition. It is of some value in describing virtues like courage, temperance, and liberality. For it emphasizes the necessity of controlling
the passion of fear, the desire for pleasure, and contrary impulses to
action like hoarding and spending. But the definition of a virtue
in quantitative terms as a mean between excess and defect is often
misleading and sometimes false. It suggests that a virtue is opposed
to each of the two "extremes" between which it is a "mean" and
therefore that these are both vices. But, as Ross says, "it is unnatural
to oppose courage to rashness as well as to cowardice. The opposite
of courage is cowardice, and the opposite of rashness is discretion.
. . . And generally, we may say, the trinitarian scheme of virtues and
vices is mistaken; each virtue has but one opposite vice; the opposite
of temperance is intemperance, that of liberality meanness, . . . that
of good temper bad temper, that of justice injustice."[8] Rashness
is not a second vice opposed to courage but a failure in the intellectual virtue of discretion; insensibility to pleasure is not a second vice
opposed to temperance but an innate or acquired defect for which
one may not be to blame; and prodigality, while a vice, is really
opposed to the virtue of thrift rather than liberality.[9] Perhaps the
best example of the distorting effect of the doctrine where it is
artificially applied to the facts is to be found in the description of
"justice" as a mean between acting unjustly and being unjustly
treated. "The only person who really chooses between the too much,
the too little, and the right act," says Ross, "is the man who chooses
either to take exactly his own share *or* to take more *or* to take less.
And there is no selfish instinct towards the *third* course; if he adopts
it, he does not behave viciously."[10] In other words, the one vice
opposed to justice is that of taking too much; and taking too little,
even if it were a vice, is a quite different matter from being unjustly
treated.

Again, the doctrine of the mean unduly exalts moderation and
tends to check heroic action. Sometimes a feeling should be "followed to the uttermost" rather than limited to the mean between ex-

[8] Ross, W. D., *Aristotle,* London, Methuen, 1930, pp. 205-6.
[9] Ibid., p. 205-7.
[10] Ross, Ibid., p. 214.

tremes. Certainly, from the Christian point of view we are called upon to give ourselves unstintedly, to be immoderate[11] and uncalculating in our love, to forgive "seventy times seven times." In sexual life, temperance requires continence before and fidelity after marriage, if monogamous marriage and the equal worth of women are to be maintained. This obviously means suppression rather than moderation of the pleasures of sex on many occasions. Again, it is meaningless to speak as if there were an "excess" of courage. Courage should be "followed to the uttermost," though this is quite compatible with discretion and caution. Even liberality at its best flows from a generosity which is opposed to the spirit of calculation, as the Gospel story of the widow who cast in all she had illustrates.

Aristotle's failure to realize this is partly due to his *rationalism*. In his view, reason is the highest and most distinctive faculty of man, and the passions and actions must be brought under "right rule" imposed by "practical wisdom." Now, this is an important part of the truth about man, to be affirmed again and again whenever romanticism or any other form of irrationalism raises its head. Man is a rational being and his virtues are not fully human unless they have the approval of reason. But this is not the full truth about him and his virtues. Aristotle says nothing about the spiritual faculty through which man is able to transcend himself by uniting himself to an ideal Good. As we have pointed out, man is moved by a powerful aspiration after a perfection that lies forever beyond his attainment. At this point, Plato is a surer guide than Aristotle because he realizes that it is not mere natural desire guided by reason that drives man towards his good but a spiritual passion of love for the Good. In contrast, Aristotle has no vision of a universal and eternal Good which transcends the well-being of the individual and his society, and he seems often to reduce the life of virtue to little more than a prudent calculation of the means to personal happiness and social solidarity.

This lack of faith in a transcendent Good which can generate moral passion is perhaps the most fundamental defect in Aristotle's theory. Control over the natural passions and impulses of the self is obviously an indispensable condition, but it is hardly the essence,

[11] Ramsey, Paul, *Basic Christian Ethics,* New York, Scribners, 1950, Ch. VI, sec. III.

of moral virtue. Besides the capacity to avoid extremes, there is needed a positive *devotion to an end* which transcends the well-being of self and society and which provides a worthy goal for the efforts of both, for the true function of moral virtue is to channel all the energies of the self into the service of a worthy end. Without such an end, there will be little moral passion, enthusiasm, and power. Moreover, it will be impossible to avoid one of the greatest temptations of the moral life, self-righteousness. The temptation which arises from moral achievement and superiority to others is one of the most subtle of temptations. There is no escape from it in an humanistic theory of virtue like that of Aristotle. If one has no higher purpose than the attainment of happiness through his own virtue and no sense of obligation to those beyond his own society, he tends to center his attention upon himself (or his group) and to preen himself on his (or its) goodness before the mirror of self-consciousness. Aristotle's acceptance of *pride* as a virtue is sufficient proof that he was not even aware of this danger. How could he be? When a man compares his goodness with the imperfect goodness of men rather than the perfect goodness of God, he cannot know how far short he falls.

THE NATURE AND PURPOSE OF VIRTUE

A moral virtue is a *habit* or *disposition* of the will. Although it is an enduring state which tends to maintain itself, it is not necessarily permanent. As it is acquired, it must be preserved, by free decisions in moral situations. A virtue is a product of freedom, and, like every achievement that depends upon freedom, its permanent existence is not guaranteed. For virtue does not make freedom unnecessary by replacing it with automatism; its function is to make freedom more effective. This becomes more clear when we recognize that, although virtues are habits, they are not fixed and rigid habits characterized by the mere repetition of specific acts in specific kinds of situation. "Repetition," says Dewey, "is in no sense the essence of habit. Tendency to repeat acts is an incident of many habits but not of all. A man with the habit of giving way to anger may show his habit by a murderous attack upon some one who has offended. His act is nonetheless due to habit because it occurs only once in his life. The essence of habit is an acquired predisposition to *ways* or modes of response, not to particular acts except as, under special conditions, these express a way of behaving."[1] For this reason, habits of virtue can be modified by intelligence and thus serve the cause of moral progress. Of course, a habit requires a "mechanism of action" which operates "spontaneously,"[2] but if it is kept under the control of intelligence it may be much more than that. In Dewey's words, "A flexible, sensitive habit grows more varied, more adaptable by practice and use."[3]

This dynamic conception of virtue as a *flexible habit adaptable by intelligence to changing situations* is opposed to the traditional static conception of a virtue as a rigid pattern formed in the past by repeated acts and showing itself always in the same acts. Forgetting the Christian conception of man as a spiritual being having indeterminate possibilities and consequently of society as capable of indefinite progress, men tended to think of virtue as a fixed and unchanging form of the will. In contrast, modern psychology, sociology, and history have developed a dynamic conception of man and society. Personality is now regarded as growing and changing constantly, though there are relatively permanent factors in it. Society is seen as undergoing one challenge after another which makes new demands upon it and forces it to change or perish.

Some thinkers have asked whether any habit of virtue is not necessarily evil from the moral point of view, since it may prevent further growth of personal character and adjustment to the changing needs of society. If moral goodness requires the freedom of the self to realize itself and to adapt itself to the possibilities and responsibilities of the present situation, is not a virtuous habit a contradiction in terms? Does not every habit determine our present and future acts and thus deprive us of our freedom of will? As J. S. Stocks has pointed out, these questions are based on the assumption that will is "a capacity of free adaptation" while habit is merely "a tendency to the repetition of the same manoeuvre."[4] In reality, virtues like courage and temperance are not "habits of

---

[1] Dewey, John, *Human Nature and Conduct,* New York, Holt, 1935, p. 42.
[2] Ibid., p. 70.
[3] Ibid., p. 72.
[4] Stocks, J. S., *Reason and Intuition,* London, Oxford University Press, 1939, p. 252.

routine." They are *habits of control* over emotions and appetites, e.g., courage over fear and temperance over the desire for pleasure.[5] Through them the will acquires a mastery over emotions and appetites which enables it to act freely in response to changing situations. The will is not *determined* by the virtuous habit to respond in a definite way; it is *freed* by the habit from subservience to the passions so that it can determine its response by the needs of the situation. In a dangerous situation, for example, the virtue of courage insures that the emotion of fear will not drive one to a cowardly act but does not determine in advance what kind of act will be done. Courage does not always mean standing fast in one's place in the line of battle; it may mean a counter-attack, a pretended flight followed by a stand, or a retreat to a better position.[6] The circumstances and the possibilities of value in the particular situation, as judged by intelligence, must determine the act. Thus, a moral virtue is not a product of training or conditioning like that to which a dog or horse is subjected. It is not an automatic and unconscious mechanism. It is a habit of mastering passion and impulse in order that the self may serve a higher life. As such, it belongs to the spiritual life which is a life of freedom.

The *purpose* of a moral virtue is to dispose the will to act in such a way that it will always further the higher life of man. Nicolai Hartmann holds that moral values or virtues are dispositions of the will to realize the higher values in every moral situation.[7] This is an inadequate view because men are seldom called upon to choose between distinct values, higher or lower, in a moral situation; usually, they must choose between different groups or patterns of values.

The test of a person's virtue is not whether the values he aims at directly are higher values but whether he intends to contribute, directly or indirectly, to the realization of a higher form of life or pattern of values. For example, some persons may choose vocations in which the values they will realize directly will be "fundamental" rather than "higher" values, e.g., the protection of life and property

[5] Ibid., p. 256.
[6] Cf. Plato's *Laches.*
[7] *Ethics,* II.

in the case of policemen or firemen. But their purpose may be to further, though indirectly, the "higher" values which are possible only if life and property are secure. To take another example, the soldier may intend through his courage directly to defend the life of his fellows but indirectly to preserve also the values of freedom and justice realized by them.

What is the purpose of virtue in relation to *duty?* Virtues are dispositions to perform duties. Courage would be meaningless apart from the duty to cope with dangers that threaten the good. It must not be supposed, however, that there is an exact correspondence between each virtue and *one* specific kind of duty. For example, the virtue of courage is necessary to the fulfillment of *many* duties, e.g., to defend life, to tell the truth when it hurts to do so, to deal justly with others at the cost of loss to ourselves, and to endure hardship and pain. Similarly, justice disposes us to perform many duties, because it requires that we render to everyone that which is due him.

The fact that there is no one-to-one correspondence between virtues and specific duties should warn us against the idea that a virtue is a separate part of the will which is more or less independent of other virtues. Although duties are distinct, the virtuous dispositions from which they spring are interrelated. Indeed, a specific duty may be performed under the influence of several different virtues. Thus, virtues should be regarded not as *independent parts,* but as *distinguishable aspects* of the moral will. This does not imply that it is unimportant to distinguish different virtues from one another or useless to inculcate specific virtues, for the unity of the moral will is a unity of diverse aspects, and men need to be nurtured in these. For example, courage must be inculcated to restrain the passion of fear, temperance to restrain the desire for pleasure. Nevertheless, each virtue is a disposition of the will as a whole, not of a part of it.

SOCIETY AND THE VIRTUES

We have spoken thus far of moral virtue as an enduring but flexible disposition or habit of mastering passion or impulse which enables the self to realize a higher life and fulfill its duty in a dependable way. The self is also a member of a community and its relation to the needs and values of the community determines in large measure the virtues required by it for the fulfillment of its duties. In this sense, virtues have a *social origin and function.* Although a virtue is a habit of personal will, it is developed by the interaction of a person with the society of which he is a part, reflects its demands upon him, and has its value in the social function it serves as well as in its own intrinsic quality as an aspect of personal character.

Since the origin and function of virtue are partly social, it must *change* along with the society that has brought it into being. There are three distinct attitudes towards change in the virtues: "conservative," "radical," and "liberal." Bradley's "my station and its duties" illustrates the "conservative" view. The basis of this view is the necessity of loyalty to the accepted virtues and duties for the sake of the solidarity and continuity of a society. At the opposite extreme is the "radical" view. According to Nietzsche, classical virtues like moderation and Christian virtues like pity and brotherly love are products of human weakness and decadence and have value only for the common "herd." In contrast, the "free spirits" who belong to the "master" group have the right to create new virtues to express and at the same time strengthen their will to power. As the "conservative" seeks to preserve the past and its values, the "radical" aims at the creation of new values suitable to a better future. In contrast, the "liberal" believes that virtues should be so modified under the direction of intelligence that they can at once conserve the achievements of the past and adapt themselves to the demands of the present.

Of these three conceptions, both the "conservative" and "radical" conceptions are inadequate. The "liberal" conception is obviously superior to them because it attempts to do justice both to the need for continuity stressed by the one and the need for change stressed by the other. But it should not be conceived in such a way as to lead to a relativistic view of virtue. Relativism is likely to arise when the conception of a universal human nature which remains the same throughout the changes of history is abandoned. If there is no fixed structure of capacities and needs in human nature, the origin and development of virtue must be attributed to social factors alone. Virtue ceases to be partly a product of voluntary effort on the part of the individual and becomes solely a result of social conditioning.

Now, the form of a virtue is relative to a particular society and to the changing conditions of that society. It is foolish to absolutize the form of a virtue dominant at some period of the past. Moral life through the ages has been narrowed and impoverished by rigid conceptions of virtue as well as by rigid rules of duty. For example, the form of moral virtues has been shaped in large part by the demands of a "closed" tribal or national morality which distorts virtues by forcing them to serve the good of a limited group only. If the demands of an "open" universal morality are to be met, the form of these virtues must be modified. Justice, for example, must be extended in its scope to include concern for the interests of persons of other nations than our own. But while the *form* of a virtue must change, its *essence* is unchanging. For there is a universal human nature, with needs and capacities that are permanent, and there are universal and enduring values which must be realized by any person or society that is to be truly human. Since virtues are dispositions to do our duties and to realize values, their essence is as universal as the duties and values they further. This can be denied only by one who denies that there is anything permanent and universal in human nature. "If man were infinitely malleable," says Eric Fromm, "then, indeed, norms and institutions unfavorable to human welfare would have a chance to mold man forever into their patterns without the possibility that intrinsic forces in man's nature would be mobilized and tend to change these patterns. Man would be only the puppet of social arrangements."[1] Man "can adapt himself to almost any culture patterns, but insofar as these are contradictory to his nature he develops mental and emotional disturbances which force him eventually to change these conditions since he cannot change his nature."[2]

Whenever it is said, for example, that we need a "new" or

---

[1] *Man for Himself,* New York, Rinehart, 1947, p. 21.
[2] Ibid., p. 23.

"different" *sex* ethic in which "purity," "prudery," and "repression" will be replaced by the "acceptance" of sex as something natural and good, we need to be on guard against specious reasoning. We need to remember that sexual "purity" is not arbitrary but is demanded by the spiritual conception of man and his needs, and that monogamous marriage is the best way to fulfill all of man's needs. The modern development of contraceptives has made it possible to separate sex experience from procreation and to make it an expression of love. There can be little doubt that this has bestowed great benefits on men, women, and children. But it has not lessened the need for "purity" and self-restraint; indeed, it has increased their importance because it has put a great temptation to self-indulgence into the hands of unmarried couples and could easily become the cause of a weakening of family life through voluntary childlessness. A similar point might be made about the effect of the new scientific knowledge of sex discovered by physiologists, doctors, and psychoanalysts. This new knowledge has led to a better understanding of the importance of sex, its relation to physical and mental health, and its influence upon the spiritual life. But it has discredited none of the virtues of the sexual life, such as "purity" before and "fidelity" after marriage; it has only made us more aware of the necessity of intelligence in sexual as in other personal relationships and of the preciousness of sex as a natural gift which enriches or degrades life according to its use. It may well lead us to be more "honest" in the sex education of young people in order to prevent the unhealthy secrecy with which the discussion of sex has been surrounded as if it were a necessary evil to be ashamed of; it may show us that it should be accepted as an integral part of the normal adult life and an essential expression of love in the lives of married people. But "honesty" and "acceptance" in this sense support rather than replace "purity" and "fidelity." Thus, new knowledge may bring about some changes in the form, but it will leave unchanged the essence of these virtues.

The development of *courage* furnishes an excellent example of an actual change in the form of a virtue during its history. No society or individual could possibly dispense with the virtue of courage. Fear is biologically and spiritually indispensable and yet the need to control it in the struggle of good against evil is unavoidable. The essence or kernel of courage has always been the same: the conquest of fear for the sake of a resolute facing of any danger that threatens the good. Its form may and must change with the good that is threatened, the danger that threatens it, and men's understanding of the most effective method of defending it against that danger. With Plato and Aristotle physical or martial courage was still primary, though Socrates' more subtle kind of courage at his trial and on the day of his death had deeply moved Plato and though Aristotle was well aware of the existence of such courage. Under the influence of the later Stoicism and Christianity, courage became primarily the fortitude that endures the vicissitudes of fortune cheerfully and suffers persecution with steadfastness. A third form of courage is that which is required to face the loneliness, discouragement, uncertainty, and partial failure that attend the highest human enterprises such as the scientific experiment of the Curies leading to the discovery of radium and the medical work of Schweitzer in Africa. All three of these forms of courage will always be necessary, though one of them will be more needed than another by a particular person or in a particular situation. In the three forms, the dangers and the values threatened differ and the methods of dealing with these dangers differ correspondingly. But the fundamental disposition is the same in all of them.

CHARACTER

Virtues are aspects of *character,* and the level of virtues in any person is largely determined by his character as a whole.

What is the *essence* of character in the moral sense of the term? It is the relatively *permanent structure* which underlies the moral conduct of a person as a whole. How is this "permanent structure" manifesting itself in the acts of a person to be understood? According to Eric Fromm, it is the "form of relatedness" of the self to things and persons, and types of character may be classified according to the different forms of "orientation" manifested by persons towards their environment.[1] In this view, the function of character

[1] Fromm, op. cit., pp. 57-59.

is to enable the self to act consistently and to adjust itself properly. Thus, character is not merely a structure within the person but it also involves an *attitude* towards his environment. It should be added that his environment includes the realm of values as well as the realm of society.

Another important aspect of character has been stressed by Roback. Character is defined by him as "an enduring psychophysical disposition to inhibit instinctive impulses in accordance with a regulative principle."[2] This view stresses the negative element in character and is based upon the distinction between irrational and rational elements of the self. Many persons are motivated by altruistic feelings like sympathy, but are lacking in the firmness based upon principle which is essential to character.[3] Thus, "high character" consists of an *inhibition of instincts* that is based not upon another instinct nor upon a feeling, but upon rational principle. This conception of character is too negative in its emphasis. Inhibition of impulses is an indispensable element but it is hardly the essence of character, as Roback admits when he recognizes the necessity of "devotion to a cause." The other main weakness of the theory is its rationalistic character. This shows itself, for example, in Roback's restriction of the higher levels of character to men of intellect or vision and in his depreciation of social and religious motives.[4] Like Kant, he thinks that any motive except that of rational principle would destroy the autonomy of the man of character. Accordingly, he will not admit that an instinct may be mastered by a man of high character with the aid of an emotion. This is a serious error. Important as rational principles are in the moral life, they do not have the motivating power of an imaginative vision of the good accompanied by strong feeling and enthusiasm.

Our examination of these psychological conceptions of character has made it clear that *character is an enduring structure of the self which relates it in a consistent way to values and to the community,* and that *both readiness to inhibit impulses and devotion to the good are its necessary conditions.*

How does good character *manifest* itself? In the first place, it

---

[2] Roback, A., *The Psychology of Character,* New York, Harcourt, Brace, 1927, p. 430.
[3] Ibid., p. 454.
[4] Ibid., chart facing p. 468.

manifests itself in a consistent choice between values or patterns of value according to a definite order of preference. It can be depended upon to choose those values which belong to a higher form of life for the self and others. Thus, the character of Socrates was most evident in his unswerving allegiance to truth and virtue and in his preference of them to wealth, honor, and life itself. What is essential is not the quantity, but the quality of the values he serves and the steadfastness of his devotion to them. In the second place, character manifests itself in the consistent performance by a person of his duties to other persons and to the community as a whole. It is immanent in the virtues that predispose him to fulfill his duties. Indeed, the virtues may be regarded as simply aspects of character. Since duties differ in certain respects in different societies, there is an element of relativity in the manifestations of character in conduct.

Character manifests itself in each person in an *individual* and *unique* way. Though it always requires the development and exercise of essentially the same virtues, the virtues of each person inevitably bear the imprint of his individuality. Moreover, the nature of his vocation and of his society helps to shape the structure of his character by stressing certain virtues and values rather than others. Hence, the characters of good men are infinitely diverse. Yet good character is always fundamentally similar. It always seeks, under the limitations imposed by a person's individuality, vocation, and society, to fulfill the universal requirements of morality. For example, there were striking differences between the characters of Socrates and Thomas More due to the fact that one was a citizen of ancient Athens, the other of Tudor England; that one was a philosopher, the other a literary man and statesman; that one was a noble pagan, the other a faithful Christian. Yet essentially the character of the two men had much in common, as manifested in their courage, their kindness, their cheerfulness, their patriotism, their ultimate loyalty to truth as they saw it.

ETHICAL IDEALS AND PERSONAL EXAMPLES

What is the *basis* of character? What is the center around which the whole structure is built, the moving principle which animates it? It is an *ethical ideal* or what Fromm calls a "framework of orientation and devotion." The need for such a "framework," he says, is "an intrinsic part of human existence" and "there is no other more powerful source of energy in man."[1] "Man is not free to choose between having or not having 'ideals,' but he is free to choose between different kinds of ideals, between being devoted to the worship of power and destruction and being devoted to reason and love."[2] If we are to discover the secret of character, therefore, we must examine the origin and function of ethical ideals.

What is the *origin* of an ethical ideal? This is primarily a problem for sociology and psychology rather than for ethics, but the neglect of it by moral philosophers has been responsible for much of the abstractness of recent ethics. It has been assumed that an ethical ideal upon which character is to be based should consist of abstract principles and be wholly or mainly a construction of the pure reason of philosophers. In actuality, ethical ideals have sprung from the moral experience of communities and have been shaped by the creative imagination of statesmen, poets, prophets, and sages. The moral experience of a people leads to the acknowledgment of values, duties, and virtues which are passed on from generation to generation by oral tradition, ritual acts, personal example, and in other ways. This material is subjected to a process of selection and idealization by the creative imagination and fused into a living, concrete whole. The ethical ideal that results, e.g., that expressed in the funeral oration of Pericles, in an eighth-century prophet like Isaiah, in the sayings of Confucius, or in the Gettysburg Address of Lincoln, is a composite of many elements, some primary and some secondary, fused together by a dominant principle. The moral philosopher such as Aristotle arises only after there has been a long development of ethical ideals in this manner and he expounds in abstract terms an ethical ideal that is already formed and waiting for him. In the process of rationalizing it, he makes it more precise and consistent but also transforms it from a concrete whole that can be grasped by the imagination into a body of abstract concepts

[1] Fromm, op. cit., p. 49.
[2] Ibid., p. 49.

that can be understood only by the reason. There is both gain and loss in the process, a gain in intellectual clarity, a loss in moral power.

What is the *function* of an ethical ideal? Its most obvious function is to provide a common goal for the members of a community and inspire them with the desire to attain it in their lives. Thus, it furthers the unity of the group. It also gives consistency and continuity to the conduct of the individual. It is one of the strongest forces making for a better integration of the interests of a person. Under its influence secondary interests are gradually subordinated or eliminated for the sake of primary ones. It provides incentive and inspiration for the struggle of the higher with the lower self, arousing the will and kindling the feelings in behalf of the good. It puts the various duties of the self in proper perspective by relating them to an ultimate aim. In ways like these, an ethical ideal becomes the basis both of unity in the community and of moral strength and inner harmony in the individual.

In the development and inculcation of an ethical ideal, the importance of *personal examples* can hardly be exaggerated. Whether they are found in present experience or in past history, they embody the virtues and duties of an ethical ideal in a vivid, concrete manner. Thus, they arouse our admiration, reveal to us moral possibilities hitherto unknown, and quicken our moral wills by planting images and stirring feelings in us.[3] However, imitation of a personal example should never be literal and slavish. It is only imitation of the spirit or attitude manifested in the deeds of another person that is compatible with the moral independence and initiative of the individual. Therefore, the right use of any personal example requires moral discrimination and judgment, if uncritical devotion to him is not to endanger one's moral freedom and creativity.

In view of this danger in the imitation of personal examples, Kant's opposition to their use is understandable. "Nor could anything be more fatal to morality," he says, "than that we should wish to derive it from example. . . . Even the Holy One of the Gospels must first be compared with our ideal of moral perfection

---

[3] MacCunn, John, *The Making of Character,* New York, Macmillan, 1916, Ch. X.

before we can recognize Him as such. . . . *Imitation* finds no place at all in morality, and examples serve only for encouragement."[4] As a protest against slavish imitation, this is justified. But Kant's criticisms of personal examples are not conclusive against a critical and discriminating use of them. It is true that the selection of a personal example requires a moral judgment on his worth. But this does not mean that óne must already have developed fully an ethical ideal before he can make such a moral judgment. The practical reason cannot construct an ethical ideal out of nothing; it must use materials derived from moral experience, and contact with personal examples constitutes an important aspect of that experience. Therefore, one should not deprive oneself of the guidance and inspiration provided by personal examples for the sake of an hypothetical but unreal absolute autonomy.

[4] *Kant's Theory of Ethics,* tr. by Abbott, London, Longmans, Green, 1909, Sec. II, p. 25.

CHAPTER 22

Moral Virtue and Character:
The Christian Ideal

ACCORDING to the Christian ethical ideal, moral virtue is a product of the development of the potentialities in man's nature through a *response to God's love in Christ*. As we have seen, Aristotle assumed that human nature was potentially good and saw no radical evil in it which would frustrate the development of its potentialities of virtue by moral education and action. In contrast, Christians believe that human nature, though created good, has been corrupted by sin and that the will has been turned in upon itself in self-love. Consequently, the will cannot build up the virtues in itself by repeated virtuous acts, as Aristotle thought. The self-centered will cannot do acts that are really virtuous bcause all of its acts are corrupted by its self-interest. Of course, it can acquire habits which are approved and rewarded by society, but these habits will be corrupted by the self-love of the will and cannot be true virtues. In short, the will must be good before it can do genuinely good acts; *being* good is prior to *doing* good.

This is why St. Augustine denies that the virtues of the pagans were true or perfect virtues. Although the Romans performed courageous and public-spirited acts which are worthy of emulation by Christians, he says, these acts were not based upon the right motive, love of God. The Romans showed great courage and self-mastery in conquering and ruling their empire, but it was for the sake of their own power and glory.[1] Moreover, if justice is essential to a commonwealth, as Cicero said, Rome was not a true common-

[1] Augustine, *The City of God*, V.

505

wealth. Without love of God, how could the Romans have attained true justice?[2] Thus, true virtue is impossible without a *transformation of the self* which will subordinate love of self to love of God and love of neighbor. The self must cease to put its trust in its own efforts and turn in faith to God. This faith, which is man's response to God's love and mercy in Christ, awakens in the self a grateful love of God and a desire to do His will. It manifests its love and obedience to Him through love of its neighbor, serving his needs like Christ. Only when faith in God's love has awakened this answering love, does man's will become good and capable of doing good works.[3]

Love is the root of true moral virtues. The virtues are awakened and developed in the self through its response to the love of God in Christ. They are *expressions of love* elicited by the love of God for man. As love fulfills all the law, it generates all the virtues. The virtues are simply ways in which love controls and directs the energies of the self in order that it may serve God and fulfill the needs of persons in a stable and dependable way. The most famous statement of this Christian insight is that of St. Augustine. He defines virtue as "nothing else than perfect love of God" and the four cardinal virtues of Greek moral philosophy as "forms" of this love. Thus, "temperance is love keeping itself entire and incorrupt for God; fortitude is love bearing everything readily for the sake of God; justice is love serving God only, and therefore ruling all else, as subject to man; prudence is love making a right distinction between what helps it towards God and what might hinder it."[4] The value of this definition is that it points to the ground of all the virtues, the *love of God*. Christians hold not only that the love of God is the first commandment but also that it is logically prior to the second commandment, love of neighbor. Unless we love God, we will not love our neighbor as God loves him and wants us to love him, unconditionally and for his own sake. For love of neighbor in the Christian sense of the term is not a natural affection

[2] Ibid., Bk. XIX.
[3] Luther, Martin, *Treatise on Christian Liberty, Works*, Philadelphia, A. J. Holman, 1915, II.
[4] Augustine, *The Morals of the Catholic Church*, Ch. XV.

or even a moral duty that can be attained by effort; it arises from the response of faith to God's antecedent love for us and from our recognition that we cannot love Him without loving our neighbor. St. Augustine's definition, therefore, reminds us that love of God is the ultimate *ground* of all true virtue.

The *essence* of temperance, courage, justice, and prudence is that they are, on the one hand, expressions of love for the neighbor and, on the other hand, products of the self's aspiration for perfect goodness. That they are expressions of *love for the neighbor* needs little argument. The purpose of virtue is service of one's neighbor as a person and of the Kingdom of God as a universal community of persons. The virtues are forms of readiness to fulfill the needs of persons in every situation. There are no purely "self-regarding" virtues, i.e., virtues which serve the good of the self alone. Even temperance in eating, drinking, and sex indirectly affects the good of others. Perhaps the best way to avoid self-centeredness and self-righteousness in one's effort to acquire such virtues is to think of them primarily as preparing one to serve the needs of one's neighbors. Virtues like justice, liberality, and fidelity exist even more obviously than temperance for the sake of our neighbors. Justice renders each neighbor his due, restraining the tendency of the self to aggression against him; liberality bestows benefits upon him; and fidelity keeps faith with him. While it is possible without Christian love of neighbor to develop these virtues in an imperfect form, they can be generated in their perfect form only by love. Only Christian love can overcome the selfishness and indifference in us that prevents us from seeking justice for all equally; from giving ourselves as well as our gifts generously; and from being faithful to others when it costs dearly to do so. In this way, love of neighbor provides the motive that perfects all the virtues.

Thus, the virtues are ultimately grounded in the love of God, and are expressions of love of neighbor. At the same time, they are products of the *self's aspiration for perfect goodness*. "Seek ye first the kingdom of God and his righteousness,"[5] says Jesus. "Be ye therefore perfect even as your Father which is in Heaven is perfect."[6]

[5] Mtt. 6:33 (A.V.).
[6] Mtt. 5:48 (A.V.).

Passages like these clearly imply that the self should seek to attain the righteousness of the Kingdom, based upon the perfection of the Father, and with it the life of the Kingdom which is the highest of all blessings. It is not correct, therefore, to say that the virtues are exclusively expressions of neighbor love; they are also products of aspiration for the righteousness of the Kingdom. For example, temperance enables us to restrain our natural desire, not only for food, drink, and sex, as Aristotle held, but also for comfort, luxury, play, excitement, or anything else that interferes with perfect goodness. It disposes us to discipline these desires not because they are wrong, but because they threaten the integrity and single-mindedness of the self in its devotion to the higher life of the Kingdom. Temperance is often regarded merely as moderation in the satisfaction of physical desires for the sake of some private aim of the self. Christian temperance, in contrast, restrains the natural desires because they fix one's attention upon his own satisfaction and therefore interfere with perfect love of God and neighbor.

Corresponding to this conception of the origin and nature of moral virtue is the Christian view of its *purpose* and *scope*. Since Aristotle has no vision of a transcendent and universal Good, he regards virtue simply as a means to the happiness of the individual and the particular society of which he is a member. In contrast, Christians believe that the primary purpose of a moral virtue is the more effective service of *all* men, whoever and wherever they may be. Obviously, this implies that the virtues should be enlarged. If one believes that God's purpose is to redeem all men everywhere and to bring them into His Kingdom, the scope of one's duties will be extended and the virtues which predispose him to perform his duties will need to be enlarged. At the same time, the demands laid upon him by his duties will be more strenuous and his virtues will have to be stronger. For example, the duty of justice will require of him far more than respect for the rights of his fellow-citizens as defined by the laws of his own society. It will also demand that he champion the rights of underprivileged or persecuted groups and that he concern himself with the interests of other nations. Thus, the virtue of justice must be strengthened and broadened until it becomes a creative force seeking equal justice for all men.

Since Christian virtue is an imitation of God's perfect goodness, it can never be fully *attained,* it can only be *aimed at* as a goal. Though the will of the Christian has been reoriented by faith towards love of God and neighbor, he must continue to struggle with sin. As a result, virtue is never wholly secure. It requires steady, unremitting vigilance and striving. It can be approximated only by holding before ourselves constantly the goal of Christian perfection and surrendering ourselves to the Spirit of Christ. Virtue is no finite end that can be attained and then maintained as a possession of the will; it is a direction of the will towards a goal which is never reached. Of course, moral growth is possible in the Christian life, and some have advanced farther than others. Otherwise, moral striving would be futile and we would fall into despair. Since true virtue rests upon faith and love, however, it can be lost if faith wanes and love grows cold. For faith is not a habit; it is a decision which must be made again and again. If one ceases to make that decision, he loses it and the love that springs from it. Moreover, every rise to a higher level of virtue brings with it the possibility of new and more subtle temptations that did not exist at lower levels. A man may master sexual temptation or drunkenness only to find himself confronted with the temptation to anger, or he may control the latter only to be faced by the temptation of intellectual or moral pride. This is the Achilles heel of virtue: no matter how many victories one may have won over particular vices, sin remains in the will and from it as from a root new vices may grow. For man carries a burden of freedom from which he cannot escape, and at any time he may turn back upon himself in self-love. Thus, Christian virtue can be *progressively approximated* but *never finally won* in this life. The Christian will never reach the point where he will no longer need to repent and pray for forgiveness.

Finally, the development of the virtues depends upon *moral effort.* To this extent, they are acquired by acts, as in Aristotle's theory. Therefore, Aquinas' sharp distinction between virtues "acquired" by human effort and virtues "infused" by divine grace is very misleading, since it implies that the former can be acquired without the aid of divine grace and the latter can be infused without the help of human effort. In truth, all moral virtues are products at once of divine grace and human effort. The coming of faith and love does not automatically produce perfect virtue and enable us to dispense with further moral effort. Faith and love bestow upon us the moral power that enables us to progress toward perfect virtue, but the victory can be actually won only if we exert our own wills. "Work out your own salvation with fear and trembling," says St. Paul, "for God is at work in you, both to will and to work for his good pleasure."[7] It is not that God is to do certain things for us and we are to do other things by ourselves, but that we work with Him and He with us in everything that we do. Every step forward is at once—and primarily—His work and—though secondarily— our own.

Much harm has been done in Protestantism by the idea that, love being the source of virtue, moral effort and struggle are unnecessary. In attacking the tendency to depend upon good works for salvation, Luther sometimes gives the impression that we do not need to exert effort to do good works since they will arise spontaneously in us from faith and love. Nygren is only carrying this way of thinking to its logical conclusion when he speaks of our love for our neighbor as if it were really God's love that pours down into us and through us to our neighbor as if we were pipes. Though Christian love transforms the will and gives us the power to struggle more effectively against love of self, it does not enable us to dispense with the struggle. In this sense, we must acquire the virtues by our own effort, while we also trust God to bestow them upon us as gifts of His grace.

DISTINCTIVE CHRISTIAN VIRTUES

Christianity brought about a *moral revolution* in the Western world, effecting what Nietzsche calls a "transvaluation of values." It dropped or subordinated some of the pagan virtues. It retained but transformed others. It added distinctive virtues of its own. As a result, it developed an ideal of character that was completely new.

First, it *dropped pride* from the list of virtues. Aristotle had taken

[7] Phil. 2:12, 13.

it for granted that pride is a virtue. If it is based upon a true estimate of one's worth, he held, it is appropriate. In contrast, pride is the primary sin in Christian ethics, and, in the broad sense of self-love, it is regarded by Aquinas as the root of all sins. Pride is based on the illusion that man is responsible for his moral achievement by his own effort, while the Christian view is that he must depend upon God's grace for help. Above all, pride is a form of self-love, and makes it impossible to love God and one's neighbor. At the same time, *humility* became one of the roots of true virtue in Christian ethics. Humility reminds one of the great distance between his feeble virtues and the perfect goodness of God; it expresses his dependence upon God for the goodness he possesses; and it is the antithesis of the self-love that separates him from God. However, humility does not mean self-contempt or even self-depreciation. It is quite compatible with a self-acceptance based upon the belief that, however unworthy, one has been accepted by God. It is also consistent with recognition of one's abilities in relation to those of other men. Whether one is superior or inferior to other men is of no ultimate importance; what counts ultimately is how far short one falls of the divine perfection as manifested in Christ. Therefore, one can be humble before God but strong before men. He can confidently affirm the truth he sees, though without dogmatism. He can stoutly resist those who oppress him or others, though without self-righteousness. Christian humility has nothing to do with Buddhist self-negation which leads to quietism.

Second, Christian ethics *added new virtues* of its own. One of the most striking of these is *meekness,* the opposite of self-assertiveness. Meekness is akin to gentleness. It requires a complete conquest of anger. To Aristotle the right sort of attitude with respect to anger is shown when one grows angry on the right occasion and with the right people, and also in the right manner, at the right times and for the right length of time.[1] This is not an ignoble attitude, because it allows an expression of anger only when it seems to be appropriate. In Christian ethics, on the other hand, anger must be kept under restraint. How difficult, if not impossible, this is has always been recognized by Christians. "Be angry but do not sin," says the

---

[1] *Nicomachean Ethics,* IV, Ch. V.

Letter to the Ephesians; "do not let the sun go down on your anger, and give no opportunity to the devil."[2] "Let all bitterness and wrath and anger and clamor and slander be put away from you, with all malice, and be kind to one another, tenderhearted, forgiving one another, as God in Christ forgave you."[3]

Again, *willingness to forgive* is one of the most distinctive Christian virtues. Jesus emphasized again and again that it is a condition of being forgiven by God and that it is to be unlimited. Like meekness, it is an expression of humility, for only those who know their own need to be forgiven are likely to forgive others. But it also springs from the need to be reconciled to one's neighbor and from the impossibility of this without willingness to forgive on both sides. Similarly, *forbearance,* which is the exercise of self-restraint under provocation, is an expression of love's willingness to endure anything for the sake of others. As St. Paul puts it, "Love bears all things" and "endures all things."[4] Finally, *patience,* which combines perseverance with the uncomplaining endurance of wrongs or misfortunes, is closely related to meekness, willingness to forgive, and forbearance. Like them, it requires a degree of self-abnegation which is made possible only by humility and love.

Equally distinctive are the more active virtues of mercy and kindness. *Mercy* towards the sinful and the weak is not identical with the natural feeling of pity; it is the treatment of the guilty, the suffering, or the helpless with compassion. It is based upon sympathy and generosity. As such, it is one of the most characteristic expressions of love. *Kindness* is also a practical disposition, not a mere feeling. It is the disposition which manifests itself in service to others. Service, which is the external expression of mercy and kindness, is love active in relieving the suffering and furthering the good of others.

SELF-DENIAL

As we have said, it is love which is the primary source of all the virtues. But there is also a negative condition of the virtues,

[2] Eph. 4:26.
[3] Ibid., 4:31, 32.
[4] I Cor. 13:7.

especially of virtues such as meekness, forbearance, and patience. It is *self-denial*. The function of self-denial in the Christian life is to negate everything in the self which stands in the way of love. That self-denial is an important aspect of Jesus' teaching requires no proof. He demands that his disciples shall be ready to abandon their possessions, break with their families, pluck out an eye or cut off a hand, and endure persecution for the sake of the Kingdom. He requires that, from loyalty to himself and the Kingdom, they shall be prepared to suffer with him even to the point of death. His insistence upon self-denial and self-sacrifice has always repelled as well as fascinated men. Many are attracted to Christian love and liberty, as they understand those terms, but are perplexed by Christian self-denial. They refuse to face the fact that love and liberty are not Christian if they are not accompanied by self-denial. The *modern reaction* against self-denial is due in part to the fact that self-denial was associated for so long with the world-negating attitude of medieval asceticism and the remnants of this in early Puritanism. But it is due, ultimately, to the natural tendency to long for happiness and to shrink from suffering. This tendency is bound to dominate men's minds when they do not feel strongly the claims of Christian perfection, and do not understand the necessity of renunciation because they do not see what it is for. Since the eighteenth century, under the influence of an optimistic view of man, the power of sin has been minimized and the necessity for religious and moral discipline has not been understood. At the same time, the modern world has sought in every possible way to persuade itself that natural goods such as wealth, health, and comfort are the primary source of man's happiness, and has denied the necessity of renouncing these things for the sake of the spiritual life. In contrast, Christianity has insisted that only through willingness to deny the self and the world can the blessedness of the Kingdom be won.

Thus, the doctrine of self-denial is not morbid and arbitrary. It is not based upon contempt for the self and the world. It arises from the fact that perfect fellowship with God and love of neighbor can be attained only by a *transformation of the will*. This requires discipline and sometimes suffering. It is not merely that our natural impulses are hard to restrain, it is that they have been perverted

by sin. Moreover, the goal of the Christian life is perfection and this
calls for complete rather than partial transformation. For example,
envy is not to be concealed; it is to be eliminated. Malice is to be
stamped out not only in deed, but also in word and thought. Greed
for possessions, Mammon, is not to be served along with God; it
is not to be served at all. The will to power is to be destroyed, not
only in its overt but also in its covert and petty forms. In short, all
the roots of self-centeredness are to be dug out.

Two qualifications are necessary at this point if we are to avoid
misunderstanding. When we speak of denying the self, we do not
mean a negation of the self as such but a negation of the self *as evil*.
Christianity is sharply contrasted with Hinduism and Buddhism at
this point. These great Oriental religions regard as evil the natural
self and its desires for things in the world of space and time. Consequently, they insist upon self-negation and world-negation in a
sense quite different from that of Christianity, i.e., an absolute
renunciation of self and world as a whole. On the other hand, Christianity regards the self and the world as essentially good, since they
constitute the creation of a good God, and condemns only the
perversion of the self by sin and its idolatry of things in the world.
As a result, it calls for negation, not of the self and the world, but of
the egoism of the self and its tendency to find its highest good in
the world. The second qualification is that self-denial is not an end
in itself. It is a means to perfect love of God and neighbor. When
it is divorced from love and sought for its own sake, it becomes a
prolific source of evils. It leads to self-mortification in body and
mind. It emphasizes human effort and techniques of discipline
rather than dependence upon God's grace. As a result, it encourages
the self-righteousness of the professional "holy man" who takes
pride in his control over physical and mental functions and is often
wholly irreligious. Finally, it exalts suffering in a pathological fashion that blinds one to the fact that self-denial should issue in joy.

We have seen that only through self-denial can distinctively
Christian virtues such as meekness and forbearance be attained,
since these virtues are impossible unless the tendency to self-assertiveness has been overcome. We must also point out that the Christian
ideal of greatness rests upon self-denial. "The Son of Man came not

to be ministered unto, but to minister, and to give his life a ransom for many."[1] "The Kings of the Gentiles rule over them, and their authorities take the name of 'Benefactor': not so with you. He who is greatest among you must be like the youngest, and he who is chief like a servant. Which is greater, guest or servant? Is it not the guest? But I am among you as a servant."[2] Such sayings as these, made vivid and concrete by the example of Jesus' life, have stamped indelibly upon the imagination of the Western world the ideal of greatness through service rather than domination. The effect of that ideal upon the conception of leadership has been incalculable, especially in the democracies. But it is often not recognized that, like the distinctive Christian virtues we have mentioned, it is possible only for those who have learned to master the will to power through self-denial.

Moreover, the *willingness to sacrifice* for a cause is strengthened by the practice of self-denial. The Cross most Christians are called upon to bear is neither death nor persecution nor ostracism, but the less dramatic, though often painful, struggle against evil in themselves and their society. But we have learned once more during the last few decades that the Christian must be prepared to suffer unpopularity, persecution, and, if need be, death. There is that in the Christian life which can help him do so: the practice of denying the ego and its selfish desires. As Socrates faced death in prison, he spoke of the constant "rehearsal" or practice of dying through which the true lover of wisdom continually detaches his soul from the senses and appetites of the body and seeks eternal truth and good. Similarly, as Christians spend themselves in the service of their fellows, they can learn to deny themselves until what happens to their bodies comes to matter little. Most of us are not far enough advanced in self-denial to do more than glimpse the full meaning of this from afar; but the principle is clear.

But self-denial is not a gloomy thing. The discipline of self-denial is the source of progress towards *self-fulfillment* and the abiding *joy* it brings. Though Albert Schweitzer has done without things most men take for granted, he is happier than they are, for

[1] Mk. 10:45 (A.V.).
[2] Luke 22:25-7, (Moffatt).

the spirit of man, though dependent upon his body and its natural environment, has a life and a good of its own. It fulfills itself only as it brings the natural impulses of the self into the service of higher ends and purifies itself of selfishness and pride. This is a painful task and none of us ever completes it. But we can escape from the necessity of undertaking it only at the cost of denying our spiritual nature. The true Christian does not evade this task but accepts it willingly and joyfully. He is able to do so because he believes that the task has been laid upon him by a God of love rather than an impersonal fate and that it is the way to true self-fulfillment.

THE COMPLEXITY OF CHRISTIAN CHARACTER

Thus, the Christian ideal of character is that of the person who from love and humility does not assert himself aggressively or insist upon his rights but yields to others and denies himself in order to serve them. Sometimes this ideal has been criticized as weak and effeminate. But it must not be interpreted in a passive and quietistic sense; it is intensely *active* and *creative*. Love is the fundamental principle of the Christian life, and love is the practical disposition to serve the needs of one's neighbors. Though it requires us to master our egoism and self-assertiveness by self-denial, it does so in order that we may serve God and our neighbor more effectively. Therefore, it is a fundamental error to identify love with a weak submissiveness. Indeed, it is an error to identify love with *any* specific type of act alone, even kindness. For love requires us not only to humble and deny ourselves in order to overcome our own egoism, but also actively to further the welfare of our neighbors in every way possible. If so, we must recognize that, in a world in which sin is universal, love may require us to be *stern* as well as *kind*.

This illustrates the fact that Christian character, while simple in its underlying principle, is complex in its structure. It includes *opposite qualities* in balance and tension. In addition to the balance of kindness and sternness, we may notice the combination of grateful *acceptance of the world* and one's fellows with uncompromising *hostility to evil* wherever it shows itself. On the one hand, the Christian is not to judge or condemn others; on the other, he is to oppose any person, however high his reputation and position, who is a source of harm to others. Again, he is to balance *earnestness* in carrying out God's will with *serenity* in accepting whatever may come from his doing so. His earnestness arises from his moral responsibility and freedom; his serenity is the result of his trust in God and consequent lack of anxiety for the ultimate consequences of his actions. Finally, the balance of *gentleness* and *courage* is characteristic of Christian character. It has been pointed out that Plato stresses the necessity of weaving together the same virtues, but that for him "the warp or groundwork is courage, the woof gentleness and temperance" while for Jesus "it is rather love or gentleness that forms the groundwork."[1] But it is well to remember that "early Christianity was a school of bravery and endurance, as well as of those more feminine virtues—gentleness, forbearance, kindness, brotherly love—which we more readily associate with the teaching of Jesus."[2]

The reason for this many-sidedness of Christian character is that love requires a *diversity of qualities* in any person who is to fulfill the claims of many different persons in a wide variety of situations. "I have become all things to all men," says St. Paul, "that I might by all means save some."[3] It is the aim to "save" and serve all kinds of men that necessitates complexity of character in the Christian. He is not an unprincipled opportunist, varying with circumstances because he wants to please everyone. But love demands of him that he adjust his acts and attitudes to the various needs and situations he faces. His character is marked by unity of principle rather than uniformity of behavior. If it were otherwise, love would be the prisoner rather than the master of its own virtues.

THE PRACTICALITY OF THE CHRISTIAN ETHIC

Is the Christian ethic practical? Can its principles become the basis of the actual conduct of men? During the Age of Liberalism,

[1] Barbour, G. F., *A Philosophical Study of Christian Ethics,* Edinburgh, Blackwood, 1911, p. 14.
[2] Ibid., p. 13.
[3] I Cor. 9:22.

Christians usually answered these questions confidently in the affirmative. But their confidence was due in large part to the fact that the optimistic temper of the nineteenth and early twentieth centuries had almost blinded them to the tragic factor in human existence. Optimism was natural during the nineteenth century, which was a period of substantial achievement in Western civilization. Since the First World War, however, the optimism of man about his future possibilities has been shattered by war, revolution, and the threat of annihilation. The idealistic view of man has been sharply attacked. Moreover, careful study of the New Testament has revealed once more the radical and perfectionistic character of Jesus' ethic. As a result, it is no longer possible for Christians to assume that men can put the law of love into practice fully in their conduct. Realistic Christians of today see more clearly than the Christians of the Age of Liberalism how "strait is the gate, and narrow is the way, which leadeth unto life."[1] It is essential, therefore, that the question be once again faced frankly in our time: Is the Christian ethic practical?

There is a striking passage in the Gospel which gives us a clue to the answer. A rich man has just refused to give all of his wealth to the poor and follow Jesus. "How hard it will be for those who have riches to enter the kingdom of God!" says Jesus. "It is easier for a camel to go through the eye of a needle than for a rich man to enter the kingdom of God." Astonished at this, the disciples ask, "Then who can be saved?" Jesus' reply throws a bright light upon the question we are considering. "With men," he says, "it is impossible, but not with God; for all things are possible with God."[2]

This passage illustrates the fact that from the beginning men have raised the question of the practicality of the Christian ethic in personal conduct because of the difficulty of obeying its radical demands. However, the "hard sayings" constitute only the negative side of Jesus' teaching, and should be understood always in relation to the positive side, especially the law of love. Now, the law of love may seem less difficult to fulfill than the negative teachings. But this is only because we tend to think of love in terms of the

[1] Mtt. 7:14 (A.V.).
[2] Mk. 10:23-27.

natural love we know and do not stop to realize how much more costly is the love Jesus demands of us. Is it really less difficult to love God with all one's heart, mind, soul and strength and to love one's neighbor as oneself than to give one's possessions to the poor or to break with one's family? On the contrary, it is much more difficult! A man cannot even *imagine* what it would be like to love God with his *whole self* or his neighbor *as himself*. Man's love is always imperfect, limited and weakened by his self-love. His complacent illusion that he can fulfill the demands of the law of love is dispelled when he realizes that love of neighbor includes any and every neighbor, even his enemy, and that it requires him to serve all his neighbor's needs and to forgive him over and over again.

When we ask whether the Christian ethic is practical, then, we are asking the question with respect to both the negative demand for complete self-denial, and the positive demand for a perfect love like that of God. Once we realize that this is the meaning of the question, we are likely to reply: "Of course it is not practical!" If we know ourselves as we really are, the radical demands of Jesus are bound to seem beyond our moral capacity. Moreover, those who are not Christians have usually maintained that his demands are beyond the moral capacity of men. Indeed, this has always been the source of the most common criticism of Christian ethics. Many Muslims, for example, have pointed out that Mohammed made no such radical ethical demands as Jesus did and they infer that he was a greater teacher because he was more practical. For example, he compromised with the polygamy of the Arabs, requiring only that a man should limit the number of his wives. Similarly, Confucianists have usually felt that there is something irrational and extravagant about an all-embracing love, and they rejected Mo-ti when he advocated it in a less radical form than Jesus demanded.

It must be acknowledged, then, that it is not possible for man by himself to attain the complete self-denial and perfect love demanded by Jesus. This requires an absolute conquest of man's egoism, and experience shows that while man may be able to overcome particular manifestations of egoism in his conduct, he never succeeds in destroying its roots in the will. He may beat down "carnal" forms of self-love, only to succumb to the more subtle "spiritual" forms of it of which he is not even conscious. This is why Reinhold Niebuhr refers to Jesus' ethic of love as an "impossible possibility"[3] and insists again and again that sin persists in the life of the redeemed.[4]

However, there is a danger that, in reaction against the optimism of Liberal Protestantism about man's moral possibilities, we shall fall into a pessimism which is equally unjustified. The image of God has not been destroyed by sin. Even unregenerate men can respond in some measure to the appeal of love. Moreover, redeemed men have often lived saintly lives and performed deeds of love and self-denial which would have seemed impossible to others. Saintliness has not been confined to monks or to those who have been officially designated as saints. As Douglas Steere has pointed out, it has never been reserved for a few religious "geniuses"; it has been achieved by men in various conditions of life who have been willing to make the absolute commitment it requires.[5] When we study the lives of the saints, we are struck by the fact that they were very much like the rest of us before their lives began to be radically changed. Before his conversion, St. Augustine does not seem to have been morally better —in some ways he may have been worse—than many who have not been saints. St. Francis was probably as full of the love of pleasure and fame as other young men of Assisi. Many Americans feel that, while Abraham Lincoln was hardly a Christian saint, he scaled the heights of Christian compassion under the terrible burden of the Presidency and the Civil War. The impact of the moral challenge of slavery transformed "an honest, capable, but essentially self-centered small-town politician of self-developed but largely unsuspected talents into a statesman who will grow to world dimensions."[6] No definite limit can be set beforehand to the moral possibilities of a man who at some point in his life begins to be mastered by faith and love.

Again, it must not be forgotten that the Christian idea of perfection differs from the Greek. As we have indicated,[7] the Christian

[3] Niebuhr, Reinhold, An Interpretation of Christian Ethics, New York, Harpers, 1935, Ch. 2.

[4] Niebuhr, Reinhold, The Nature and Destiny of Man, New York, Scribners, 1941, II, pp. 122-126.

[5] Steere, Douglas, On Beginning from Within, New York, Harpers, 1943, p. 35.

[6] Thomas, Benjamin, Abraham Lincoln, New York, Knopf, 1952, p. 143.

[7] See Ch. IX.

ethic does not expect the attainment of an absolute perfection which admits of no further growth, but conceives the Christian life as a process of development toward perfection. When this is overlooked, the gulf between the Christian ethic of perfect love and the realities of human nature becomes so wide that the effort to bridge it appears hopeless.

For these reasons, the conception of the Christian ethic as an "impossible possibility," unless it is carefully interpreted, can be dangerous and misleading. If it is interpreted to mean that the law of love demands that which it is impossible to attain in perfection but which can be fulfilled in increasing measure in the Christian life, it is valid. But if it is interpreted in such a way that the "impossible" not only qualifies but negates the "possibility," it should be rejected. The "impossible" and the "possibility" should be asserted together and with the meaning which is given to each of them by Jesus. When we are thinking about the perfect love and self-denial demanded by Jesus in relation to the *moral capacity of man,* we must say as he did, "With men it is impossible." The will of the unregenerate man cannot lift itself out of self-love as long as it is itself infected with self-love. But Jesus' teaching is a revelation not only of what God demands of man but also of what he promises to help man to do. Therefore, when we are thinking of Jesus' demands in relation to the *grace of God,* we must also say as he did, "With God all things are possible."

But the question whether the Christian ethic is practical should not be answered merely in general terms; it should also receive a *personal answer* from each individual. For the only way in which a person can be assured of the power of love to transform his life is to repent and turn to God in faith. There is much in his own nature which stands in the way of his obedience to the law of love. But there is nothing which prevents God's grace from helping him except his own refusal to accept it. Thus, while the general answer to the question whether Christian ethics is practical is that "all things are possible for God," the truth of this answer must be tested and confirmed by each for himself through a personal decision of faith.

BIBLIOGRAPHY

I

Christian Ethics

St. *Augustine, Basic Writings of.* Edited by Whitney Oates. 2 vols. New York: Random House, 1948.

Barclay, Robert. *An Apology for the True Christian Divinity.* Philadelphia: Friends Book Store, 1908.

Barth, Karl. *The Knowledge of God and the Service of God.* New York: Charles Scribner's Sons, 1939.

Beach, Waldo and Niebuhr, H. Richard. *Christian Ethics.* New York: The Ronald Press, 1955.

Bennett, John C. *Christian Ethics and Social Policy.* New York: Charles Scribner's Sons, 1946.

————. *Christianity and Communism.* New York: Association Press, 1948.

Berdyaev, N. *The Destiny of Man.* London: The Centenary Press, 1937.

St. Bernard. *On the Love of God.* Translated by T. L. Connolly. New York: Spiritual Book Associates, 1937.

Bertocci, P. *The Human Venture in Sex, Love, and Marriage.* New York: Association Press, 1949.

Branscomb, Harvie. *The Teachings of Jesus.* New York: Abingdon-Cokesbury Press, 1931.

Brunner, E. *The Divine Imperative.* New York: The Macmillan Co., 1937. (Philadelphia: The Westminster Press, 1947.)

————. *Justice and the Social Order.* New York: Harper and Brothers, 1945.

Bultmann, R. *The Theology of the New Testament.* Vol. I. New York: Charles Scribner's Sons, 1951.

523

Butterfield, H. *Christianity and History*. New York: Charles Scribner's Sons, 1950.

Calvin, John. *Institutes of the Christian Religion*. Translated by John Allen. 2 vols. Philadelphia: Presbyterian Board of Christian Education, 1936.

D'Arcy, M. C. *The Mind and Heart of Love*. New York: Henry Holt and Co., 1947.

Dibelius, Martin. *The Sermon on the Mount*. New York: Charles Scribner's Sons, 1940.

———. *Jesus*. Philadelphia: The Westminster Press, 1949.

———. *Paul*. Philadelphia: The Westminster Press, 1953.

Dodd, C. H. *The Epistle of Paul to the Romans*. New York and London: Harper and Bros., 1932.

———. *The Parables of the Kingdom*. New York: Charles Scribner's Sons, 1936.

———. *Gospel and Law*. New York: Columbia University Press, 1951.

Eckhart, Meister, a Modern Translation. Translated by R. B. Blakney. New York: Harper and Bros., 1941.

Edwards, Jonathan, The Works of. 4 vols. New York: Leavitt and Allen, 1856.

Enslin, M. S. *The Ethics of Paul*. New York and London: Harper and Bros., 1930.

Fletcher, J. F., ed. *Christianity and Property*. Philadelphia: The Westminster Press, 1947.

Fosdick, Harry E. *Great Voices of the Reformation, an Anthology*. New York: Random House, 1952.

Graham, G. A. *Morality in American Politics*. New York: Random House, 1952.

Gore, Charles and Others. *Property, Its Rights and Duties*. London: The Macmillan Co., 1913.

von Hildebrand, Dietrich. *Christian Ethics*. New York: David McKay Co., 1953.

Hunter, A. M. *A Pattern for Life*. Philadelphia: The Westminster Press, 1953.

Husslein, Joseph, ed. *Social Wellsprings*. 2 vols. Milwaukee: The Bruce Publishing Co., 1943. (The Papal Encyclicals of Leo XIII and Pius XI.)

Kierkegaard, Soren. *Works of Love*. Princeton: Princeton University Press, 1946.

Knudson, A. C. *The Principles of Christian Ethics*. New York and Nashville: Abingdon-Cokesbury Press, 1943.

Lee, Umphrey. *The Historic Church and Modern Pacifism*. New York: Abingdon-Cokesbury Press, 1943.

Lindsay, A. D. *The Moral Teachings of Jesus*. New York and London: Harper and Bros., 1937.

———. *The Modern Democratic State*. New York and London: Oxford University Press, 1947.

Luther, Martin, Works of. 4 vols. Philadelphia: A. J. Holman, 1931.

Mackinnon, D. M., ed. *Christian Faith and Communist Faith*. New York: St. Martin's Press, 1953.

Major, H. D. A., Manson, T. W., and Wright, C. J. *The Mission and Message of Jesus*. New York: E. P. Dutton and Co., 1933.

Maritain, J. *True Humanism*. New York: Charles Scribner's Sons, 1938.

———. *The Rights of Man and Natural Law*. New York: Charles Scribner's Sons, 1943.

———. *Man and the State*. Chicago: University of Chicago Press, 1951.

Myrdal, G. *An American Dilemma*. New York: Harper and Bros., 1944.

Nichols, James. *Democracy and the Churches*. Philadelphia: The Westminster Press, 1951.

Niebuhr, H. Richard. *The Kingdom of God in America*. Chicago and New York: Willett, Clark and Co., 1937.

———. *Christ and Culture*. New York: Harper and Bros., 1951.

Niebuhr, Reinhold. *Moral Man and Immoral Society*. New York: Charles Scribner's Sons, 1932.

———. *An Interpretation of Christian Ethics*. New York: Harper and Bros., 1935.

———. *The Children of Light and the Children of Darkness*. New York: Charles Scribner's Sons, 1944.

———. *The Nature and Destiny of Man*. New York: Charles Scribner's Sons, 1949 (1 Vol. Edition).

———. *Faith and History*. New York: Charles Scribner's Sons, 1949.

———. *Christian Realism and Political Problems*. New York: Charles Scribner's Sons, 1953.

Nygren, Anders. *Agape and Eros*. London: S.P.C.K., 1932-1939.

Oldham, J. H., ed. *The Oxford Conference: Official Report*. Chicago and New York: Willett, Clark and Co., 1937.

Otto, R. *The Kingdom of God and the Son of Man*. London: Lutterworth, 1943.

Paton, A. *Cry, the Beloved Country*. New York: Charles Scribner's Sons, 1948.

Perry, R. B. *Puritanism and Democracy*. New York: The Vanguard Press, 1944.

Piper, O. *The Christian Interpretation of Sex*. New York: Charles Scribner's Sons, 1941.

Ramsey, Paul. *Basic Christian Ethics*. New York: Charles Scribner's Sons, 1950.

Rauschenbusch, Walter. *A Theology for the Social Gospel*. New York: The Macmillan Co., 1918.

————. *A Gospel for the Social Awakening* (selections), compiled by B. E. Mays. New York: Association Press, 1950.

Scott, C. A. A. *New Testament Ethics*. London: Cambridge University Press, 1930.

Scott, E. F. *The Ethical Teaching of Jesus*. New York: The Macmillan Co., 1924.

Scott, R. B. Y. *The Relevance of the Prophets*. New York: The Macmillan Co., 1944.

Tawney, R. H. *Religion and the Rise of Capitalism*. New York: Harcourt, Brace and Co., 1926.

Temple, William. *Christianity and Social Order*. Harmondsworth: Penguin Books, 1942.

St. Thomas Aquinas, Basic Writings of. 2 vols. New York: Random House, 1945.

Tillich, Paul. *The Protestant Era*. Chicago: University of Chicago Press, 1948.

Tolstoy, Leo. *A Confession and What I Believe*. London: Oxford University Press, 1920.

Troeltsch, Ernst. *The Social Teaching of the Christian Churches*. New York: The Macmillan Co., 1931, Vols. I, II.

Ward, A. D., ed. *Goals of Economic Life*. New York: Harper and Bros., 1953.

Weber, Max. *The Protestant Ethic and the Spirit of Capitalism*. Translated by Talcott Parsons. New York: Charles Scribner's Sons, 1930.

Wesley, John. *Standard Sermons*. Edited by E. H. Sugden. 2 vols. London: Epworth Press, 1921.

Wilder, A. *Eschatology and Ethics in the Teaching of Jesus*. New York: Harper and Bros., 1939.

World Council of Churches: *Report of the Findings and Decisions of the First Assembly of the World Council of Churches*. Geneva and New York: 1948.

World Council of Churches: *Evanston Speaks*. Geneva and New York: 1954.

II

Moral Philosophy

Aristotle. *The Nicomachean Ethics*. Translated by W. D. Ross. London: Oxford University Press, 1925.

Bentham, Jeremy. *Introduction to the Principles of Morals and Legislation*. Oxford: The Clarendon Press, 1879.

Bergson, Henri. *The Two Sources of Morality and Religion*. New York: Henry Holt and Co., 1935.

Bradley, F. H. *Ethical Studies*. Oxford: The Clarendon Press, 1927.

Broad, C. D. *Five Types of Ethical Theory*. New York: Harcourt, Brace and Co., 1930.

Butler, Joseph. *Sermons*. 2 vols. Oxford: The Clarendon Press, 1896.

Dewey, John, and Tufts, James H. *Ethics*. New York: Henry Holt and Co., 1932.

Dewey, John. *Human Nature and Conduct*. New York: Henry Holt and Co., 1935.

Fromm, E. *Man for Himself*. New York: Rinehart, 1947.

Green, T. H. *Prolegomena to Ethics*. Oxford: The Clarendon Press, 1906.

Hartmann, N. *Ethics*. 3 vols. New York: The Macmillan Co., 1932.

Kant's Theory of Ethics. Translated by T. K. Abbott. London: Longmans, Green & Co., 1909.

Kant, Immanuel. *Lectures on Ethics*. London: The Century Co., 1930.

Mill, J. S. *Utilitarianism*. New York: Longmans, Green & Co., 1901.

Moore, G. E. *Principia Ethica*. Cambridge: Cambridge University Press, 1946.

Paton, H. J. *The Good Will*. New York: The Macmillan Co., 1927.

———. *The Categorical Imperative*. Chicago: University of Chicago Press, 1948.

Perry, R. B. *A General Theory of Value*. New York: Longmans, Green & Co., 1926.

Plato: *Dialogues*. New York: Random House, 1937.

Ross, W. D. *The Right and the Good*. Oxford: The Clarendon Press, 1930.

Schlick, Moritz. *Problems of Ethics*. New York: Prentice-Hall, 1939.

Sidgwick, H. *Methods of Ethics*. New York: The Macmillan Co., 1901.

Spencer, H. *The Principles of Ethics*. New York: D. Appleton & Co., 1910.

Tawney, R. H. *Equality*. New York: The Macmillan Co., 1952.

Wheelwright, Philip. *A Critical Introduction to Ethics*. New York: The Odyssey Press, 1949.

INDEX